# Philosophical Perspectives on Communalism and Morality in African Traditions

# Philosophical Perspectives on Communalism and Morality in African Traditions

Polycarp Ikuenobe

LEXINGTON BOOKS

A Division of
ROWMAN & LITTLEFIELD PUBLISHERS, INC.
*Lanham • Boulder • New York • Toronto • Oxford*

LEXINGTON BOOKS

A division of Rowman & Littlefield Publishers, Inc.
A wholly owned subsidiary of The Rowman & Littlefield Publishing Group, Inc.
4501 Forbes Boulevard, Suite 200
Lanham, MD 20706

PO Box 317
Oxford
OX2 9RU, UK

British Library Cataloguing in Publication Information Available

**Library of Congress Cataloging-in-Publication Data**

Ikuenobe, Polycarp, 1959-
  Philosophical perspectives on communalism and morality in African traditions /
Polycarp Ikuenobe.
    p. cm.
  Includes bibliographical references and index.
  ISBN-13: 978-0-7391-1131-4 (cloth : alk. paper)
  ISBN-10: 0-7391-1131-0 (cloth : alk. paper)
  ISBN-13: 978-0-7391-1492-6 (pbk. : alk. paper)
  ISBN-10: 0-7391-1492-1 (pbk. : alk. paper)
  1. Philosophy, African. 2. Philosophy—Africa. 3. Communalism—Africa. 4.
Ethics—Africa. I. Title.
  B5305.I38 2006
  199'.67—dc22                                                    2006007058

Printed in the United States of America

♾™ The paper used in this publication meets the minimum requirements of American
National Standard for Information Sciences—Permanence of Paper for Printed Library
Materials, ANSI/NISO Z39.48–1992.

# *Dedication*

To the memory of my father, Julius Ikuenobe, who died prematurely and did not see us grow up, and to my mother, Lucy Ikuenobe, who, after the death of my father, provided the family anchor and foundation for my life.

# *Contents*

# Acknowledgments

This book and its ideas are, in some respects, a culmination of my life, academic career, and research work in African philosophy. I wish to acknowledge many important people who have played positive roles in my life, education, and career that have brought the ideas in this book to fruition. I will start by acknowledging the strength, sacrifice, and guidance of my mother, Mrs. Lucy Ikuenobe, who, after the premature death of my father, took on the responsibility of raising myself and my eight siblings in the context and with the help of our community. This community did not only help my mother to raise us but it also helped me to internalize and cultivate an understanding and appreciation of the African idea communalism and the value of community. The communal values I internalized have contributed positively to my upbringing, growth, development, education, character, values, career, and have influenced the writing of this book.

I acknowledge the help of my older siblings, Agnes Igodo, Cornelius Ikuenobe, Omoye Imoisili, and Justina Dibua, and my 'brothers' and 'sisters' in my extended family that came together as a small community to ensure our upbringing. I am who I am today to be able to write this book about communalism in African cultures partly because of these people, who showed, taught, and helped me to experience and benefit from the values of community embedded in the idea of communalism.

I acknowledge my professors at the University of Ibadan: Godwin Sogolo, Joseph Asike, Felix Adeigbo, and especially, late Peter Bodunrin, who inspired me and cultivated my interest in philosophy. Professor Bodunrin did not only exemplify the kind of philosophy teacher I wanted to be but he also was the one who advised and encouraged me to go to graduate school and to teach philosophy. I thank Professor Gene Blocker who hired me at the then new Bendel State University (now Ambrose Alli University), Ekpoma, Nigeria, where I taught for four years before coming to the United States to pursue a Ph.D. Professor Blocker did not only help me to start my career as a University teacher, but he also facilitated my coming to the United States. He made my transition into America at Ohio University, Athens, a smooth one by creating a sense of community there that I plugged into. I thank him for having faith in my abilities when others thought I was not good enough to do graduate work or be a teaching assistant in the United States. I thank Professor John Bender who was not only my mentor at Ohio University but also facilitated my going to Wayne State University where I completed my graduate work.

I acknowledge the help, support, and encouragement of some of my professors as Wayne State University, especially, Bob Yanal, my dissertation advisor, Mike McKinsey, Bill Stine, Brad Angell, and the late Barbara Humphries. I also wish to thank those professors at the Department of Philosophy at Wayne State University, who, for reasons best known to them, thought I was not good enough to get a Ph.D. or get a teaching job in philosophy, and then made efforts to frustrate me. Their doubts about my abilities, their lack of encouragement and support, and their efforts to frustrate me and make sure I did not succeed in my graduate work have been part of my motivation to excel or not to fail—at least, so that I can prove them wrong.

Thanks to the professor who told me that nothing good can come from me. It seems to have turned out—if my humble accomplishments are any indication—that something good can indeed come from me. Thanks to the other professor who said he would not waste his time helping me with my job application because it took him fifteen years to get tenure and that I was not good enough to get a job. However, other people who were more perceptive than he thought otherwise and gave me the opportunity by offering me jobs. Thanks to the professors, who, out of pure ignorance and prejudice, said that I got jobs because I was black. I have worked hard to try to show them that being black alone cannot guarantee one a job in academia: being black may give one the opportunity to be considered in order to prove oneself and one's abilities. Being black, in addition to all other things considered, may push one over the edge in landing a job, but being black alone without hard work, the requisite achievements, and publications will neither help one to retain that job nor give one tenure or promotion. My achievements thus far have been the only or perhaps the best payback for these people. It is possible that if they had not doubted my abilities or made efforts to make sure I did not succeed, I would not have been as hardworking and motivated as I have been in my efforts to succeed or not to fail. I acknowledge their negative efforts, which have turned out to be positive for me.

I acknowledge the support of my wife, Roseline Ikuenobe and my children, Oziengbe, Olumhense, and Itua. It is obvious that the time I have spent working on this book has been time I have denied them some deserved attention. They have provided me a nurturing home and an environment to think about ideas and develop them. They have also given me a comfortable place to come back to from school after a long, hard day. I thank them for coping with my absent mindedness when I did not pay attention but was concentrating on my writing and ruminating on the ideas and arguments of my book.

I also acknowledge the help of my friends, Jerry Dibua, Onaiwu Wilson Ogbomo, and Harry Fleddermann. I am grateful to Jeff Wattles, my colleague in the Department of Philosophy at Kent State University, who has supported and encouraged my work. I have occasionally used him as a sounding board for my ideas. He has shown a tremendous interest in this project and has been very forthcoming in giving me positive reinforcement. I acknowledge Terry Corsello for her support and encouragement.

Although drafts of the chapters of this book were written over a long period of time, my sabbatical leave in Fall 2004 gave me the opportunity to concentrate on finishing and doing the final writing and revision of the earlier drafts of the manuscript.

I also wish to acknowledge the encouragement of Professors Ifeanyi Menkiti and Jeffrey Crawford. Menkiti reinforced for me that the idea communalism in African cultures is a very important philosophical issue in African philosophy that African philosophers can contribute to the discipline of philosophy. I am eternally grateful to Professor Gene Blocker for his help and the constructive criticisms of the earlier versions of this manuscript. The final product has indeed benefitted from his suggestions and criticisms. However, I take full responsibility for the problems and shortcomings in the book.

# Introduction

The African saying, 'it takes a village to raise a child', was made popular in the United States of America, in part, by Hilary Clinton, who wrote a book with a similar title. But the idea underlying the title and the book became a contentious issue in the 1996 presidential election when Hilary Clinton made this the theme of her speech at the Democratic party convention. This theme was criticized and ridiculed by Republicans, who snipped at the idea, saying that it does not take a village to raise a child, rather, it takes responsible parents to raise a child. Their idea of 'parents' involved a strong emphasis on a traditional nuclear family, defined to mean a mother and a father. The Republicans also emphasized this issue within the context of their convention's theme of 'family values'. A version of this debate regarding how and who may raise a child reflects a long-standing debate in political philosophy and the social sciences between individualism, liberalism, or libertarianism, on the one hand, and communalism, communitarianism, or holism, on the other. The republicans' idea is predicated on extreme individualism and the idea that it is the responsibility, liberty, autonomy, and prerogative of parents as individuals within a nuclear family to raise a child the way they see fit, without necessarily having the values of the community imposed on them. Hilary Clinton's view reflects a communal or communitarian approach to raising a child: it suggests that a child is raised in the context of a set of communal values, ways of life, and principles, and with support and help from others in the community. The issues as to what precisely, the idea of communalism or communitarianism really means, and in particular, what it involves or entails in African cultures, are debatable. I use the notions of communalism and communitarianism interchangeably throughout this book. Both have their roots in the idea of a community: the idea of people living together as a group in a specific location and sharing some commonalities of history, ideology, belief system, values, lineage, kinship, or political system. Both concepts seem to emphasize, in various degrees, the normative idea that the community has some kind, degree, or level of moral or logical priority over the individual. However, some people may understand and use the notions of 'communalism' and 'communitarianism' differently. Communalism, for some, describes an informal sociological or anthropological phenomenon regarding a group of people living together and sharing common values and lineage or kinship. Such a group may or may not have a formal political or governmental structure that is based on such values or lineage. This idea may be contrasted with communitarianism, which describes for some, a formal political or governmental structure and system in which people live together as a group, in virtue of sharing overriding set of moral, social, and political values or principles. The fundamental idea behind communitarianism, especially in the political sense, involves an affirmation of the logical or moral priority of the community or its interests over those of individuals with respect to issues involving public policies.

The African saying: 'it takes a village to raise a child' reflects the idea of communalism in African cultures, which in my view, is a system of thoughts, values, beliefs or ways of life and a method of inquiry, analysis, and acquiring beliefs that require a philosophical analysis and articulation. What I do in this book is to analyze communalism and the communal nature of moral principles, reasoning, education, ways of life, mode of inquiry, and belief system in traditional African cultures, which have supposedly given rise to the popular saying. I caution that my references to 'traditional' and 'African cultures' are not meant to be descriptive in the sociological or anthropological sense. In other words, my reference to the idea of communalism in traditional African cultures neither (1) indicates something that is necessarily true of all African cultures and traditions nor (2) represents the same set of features or characteristics in those African cultures in which communalism is manifested or practiced. Rather, my references to 'traditional', 'African cultures', and 'communalism' involve an attempt to provide a theoretical or abstract normative (re)construction and to conceptually capture a *dominant* philosophical theme or themes regarding how the modes of thought, values, and practices in traditional African societies ought to be viewed.

My effort involves a logical, systematic, and normative interpretation or analysis of the idea of communalism in African cultures. In other words, my aim as a conceptual and normative analysis is to indicate how one ought to adequately and coherently understand the idea of communalism in African cultures and traditions. So, what I offer is, fundamentally, a defense of a philosophical position regarding how this idea ought to be understood. However, my analysis does rely on some features and facts about African cultural traditions, beliefs, values, proverbs, narratives, and ways of life. One may say that my normative analysis *supervenes* on some descriptive cultural facts about African tradition and practices. In other words, while these descriptive cultural facts are sufficient but not necessary for my analysis to be true or for it to be seen as a proper understanding of communalism in African traditions. Other people may disagree with my philosophical stance or analysis and my reconstruction, by indicating some problems in my analysis and systematization of African beliefs, practices, values, and ways of life within the conceptual ambit of communalism. Here, I presuppose, with some defense and argument, however, a metaphilosophical view about the nature of philosophy, and in particular, African philosophy. This view indicates that philosophy involves efforts to systematize pre-philosophical ideas, commonsense, and intuition into a coherent theory or concept, to present them as a reasonable set of stories or ideas.[1]

My examination of the nature, concept, and idea of communalism and communal moral thought, beliefs, values, and tradition in African cultures, is done within the general context of the metaphilosophical debate regarding the nature and existence of an African philosophical thought. I argue that moral thought in African cultures, as a reflection of communalism, has features of rationalism, naturalism, humanism, and rational authoritarianism, and that these features compare to some features and notions of moral thought in Western philosophy. These features also lend themselves to how people are morally educated in the communal context of African cultures. Moral thought in African cultures does not, as many people have suggested, exhibit the features of pervasive religious supernaturalism and irrational authoritarianism.[2] Moral principles in African cultures function as semantic and epistemic criteria. They are predicated on the attempt to address the fundamental question, 'what ought *we* to do?' as opposed to 'what ought *I* to do?' or 'how ought *we* to behave?' and 'how ought *I* to behave in the context of how ought *we* to behave?'.[3] Such thinking is fundamentally normative and applied in nature, and it is expressed in the form of a means-end scheme. As a result of the communal context in African cultures, moral values, virtues, and principles are encoded in, learned, and taught informally through narratives, folklore, parables, proverbs, mentoring, and the modeling of behaviors by elders. It is taught in an integrated manner, that is, as a broad set of interconnected practical principles of action, and reinforced by every person in the community in words and actions in various aspects of life.

I argue that morality in African cultures is, for the most part, communal because moral principles and moral thought are fundamentally predicated on human well-being in the context of communal needs and interests, within which the needs and interests of the individual make sense. The communal organization of traditional societies also shapes, or in some sense, determines how people are to be morally educated and the contents of moral principles. The communal underpinnings of moral reasoning and moral education in traditional African societies have some advantages that modern Western views can learn from. Moreover, communalism does not, as critics have suggested, vitiate the possibility of rational moral education and autonomous or independent reasoning, or the ability of an tween individuals and the community in African cultures seems to indicate that the notion of a person has a normative import. This relationship provides the basis for moral principles, moral duties, and people's moral reasoning. It defines how people bring moral principles, which are founded on the nature of the community, to bear on their lives and actions. I show how the nature of these principles, responsibilities, and relationships provide the foundation for defining and organizing various aspects of people's lives, identities, interests, beliefs, values, practices, and experiences.

In chapter three, I examine the African conception of moral philosophy as a practice or guide to living and the implication of this conception for the communal view of morality. In this sense, African traditional thought sees morality in terms of both general principles and particular substantive principles of action. However, in some Western philosophical views regarding normative and meta-ethics, morality is seen fundamentally as a formal universal and objective principles that are logically true. Sometimes, these views make no efforts to tease out clearly how these general principles may apply to different particular substantive situations. Morality in African thought is substantive and particularistic in the sense that it is tied to the idea of caring and showing concern for specific relationships that are defined by a community. I indicate that the communal basis for people's lives also provides the basis for the naturalistic and humanistic features, and the 'mixed deontological' character of morality. In this sense, morality involves a combination of justice and utility. In other words, morality is not based solely on justice, which stresses formal relationships among people based on individual rights. Morality is naturalistic and humanistic, in that moral principles are addressed to the social and natural conditions and features of human beings, their needs and interests in the context of their communal existence. Such existence specifies that moral principles are addressed to the question 'how ought *we* to behave' (as individuals in a community) as opposed to 'how ought *I* to behave?' (as an isolated individual) Moral principles are semantic, epistemic, and normative criteria that define various interests, duties, and responsibilities, only in so far as duties seek to bring about utility with respect to meeting certain human needs and interests in the context of community.

In chapter four, I address the communal and informal nature of education, especially, moral education in African cultures. I indicate that African beliefs, values, and principles are encoded in symbols, narratives, proverbs, myths, and folklore, and they are transmitted and learned via oral tradition. The idea of communalism, various communal practices and beliefs, and the relationship between the community and individuals are exemplified in the informal structures, methods, and processes by which people acquire beliefs and learn the requisite values and principles. In other words, the methods and processes of education and the associated principles and values are the means of maintaining social equilibrium and continuity, and as such, they are essential defining features of communalism. I explore how communal context and informal processes and methods make substantive and practicable what people know, learn, and are taught or educated about the values, principles, and interests of the community. I then provide arguments to indicate that the informal communal processes of education are not only rationally justifiable, but are also pragmatically necessary and effective for maintaining and sustaining communalism. Through the informal methods and processes of education, people are able to rationally understand and justifiably believe that the community and its principles and processes exist for certain human well-being and social equilibrium, which are necessary for individuals to lead a meaningful life and achieve their rational life plans. People are able to articulate their rational life plans, act, make choices, and lead their lives on the basis of how they learned and experience the relevant communal principles, in virtue of which the community is preserved, sustained, and perpetuated.

In chapter five, I address the issue of whether the communal structures and informal processes of education in African traditions necessarily lead to authoritarianism. Critics argue that beliefs are accepted in African cultures based on the fact that they are the dictates of elders or supported by tradition. As such, many beliefs lack adequate rational and justifiable foundations. People are not allowed to critically examine or question accepted principles, beliefs, and traditions, which are simply imposed on people. Kwasi Wiredu and Kwame Anthony Appiah argue that the traditional communal principles of African cultures lack the proper rational, critical, and analytic foundations that can engender scientific inquiry and technological development. They suggest that communalism in African cultures is authoritarian and irrational because people are supposedly made to accept beliefs and principles against their will and independent reasoning or judgment. As such, Appiah and Wiredu argue that the communal system in African cultures is not sustained because people rationally accept and justifiably believe that the relevant principles are adequate or that they represent the best means for them to achieve their individual rational life plans. In response, I distinguish between rational and irrational forms of authoritarianism. I argue in favor of a rational form of authoritarianism in African cultures. This rational form is based on *evidentialism*, the principle of epistemic deference, and the social, contextual, and pragmatic nature of knowledge and justification. The context of the community in African cultures requires that social limitations be placed on the scope of evidence, counter-evidence, and relevant alternatives. Rational authoritarianism in African cultures is also founded on the idea that there are limits on individual human rationality and autonomy, and such limits necessitate epistemic deference and dependence. The epistemic basis for the rational form of authoritarianism provides the epistemic foundation for African ways of life with respect to their communal principles of morality. This epistemic basis provides the justificatory and rational foundation for moral education, reasoning and thought in African cultures.

In chapter six, I address specifically the issue of the rationality of moral indoctrination versus moral education. This issue has arisen from the criticism of communalism in African cultures that, the informal methods and processes of moral education and the authoritarian foundation for the relevant principles and values lead to indoctrination as opposed to education. The criticism is that the reliance on the authority of tradition and elders as the repositories of knowledge and the justificatory basis for accepting beliefs or principles implies that such beliefs or principles cannot be questioned or critically examined in order to establish their acceptability on rational grounds. In which case, people do not rationally learn, accept, and reason about their communal beliefs, values, and principles. As a result, they are *indoctrinated* to accept as doctrines or dogmas, ideas for which there are no adequate justifications. Wiredu distinguishes between *indoctrination* and *education*. He argues that education is inherently good because it involves the ability to critically examine beliefs or principles, and to accept them based on rational independent judgment that it is adequately supported by evidence. But indoctrination, he says, is inherently bad because it vitiates rationality and independent critical reasoning. I argue on the contrary that indoctrination is not necessarily bad. Indoctrination is only bad when the process is extreme enough to involve brainwashing. I argue that the informal processes of imparting knowledge in African cultures, as indicated in chapter four, are not extreme. So, if the notion of indoctrination and its processes are properly analyzed and understood, one may find that indoctrination is a necessary part of or a precondition for any meaningful education. It is also necessary and effective as an initial process of education in the context of communalism. Thus, although communalism—based on its rational authoritarian feature of epistemic dependence and deference—involves a moderate sense of indoctrination, it does not necessarily vitiate the ability to rationally accept principles and beliefs. In particular, the communal structures of African cultures do not necessarily vitiate the ability of people to acquire rational beliefs, and to engage in critical and rational moral thinking, and rational moral education.

In chapter seven, I examine the plausibility of some liberal criticisms of communalism in African cultures. One such criticism suggests that there is too much emphasis on the community. Such emphasis places the community over and above the individual to the extent of vitiating individuals' autonomy, will, or their ability to reason and make independent choice. Liberals argue that communalism and the communal ways of life seek to limit individuals' rights and freedoms. I examine these criticisms by questioning their fundamental assumptions, which include the idea that individual autonomy has absolute value, and that the idea of autonomy implies that it cannot be limited or circumscribed under any circumstance. I critically examine another assumption, which indicates that human beings are always—solely and individually—in the best epistemic position to make the best rational moral decisions for themselves. I argue that these liberal assumptions either ignore the limits, or exaggerate the power, of individual rationality and the value of individual autonomy and freedom. It also seems to ignore the limits that the social and natural basis and context for human rights and rational life plans may place on people's ability to meaningfully have rights and freedom. While liberalism may, as an abstract moral principle, be sound, it must also be understood as a cultural artefact of modern Western Europe. The successful application of this principle to an actual context requires sensitivity to the limits and strictures of that context. I then suggest that it is possible to have liberal or moderate form of communalism and that this form of communalism is what we find in traditional African cultures. Finally, I explore the plausible assumptions and advantages of the communal system as a basis for justifying it as a reasonable system.

In the conclusion, I summarize the features of communalism in African cultures and examine some of the principles underlying it. I indicate that there are lessons that could be learned from the assumptions, advantages, dynamics, and implications of communalism in African cultures. In other words, I examine whether there are valuable ideas or lessons that Western liberal individualistic cultures can learn from the African communal ways of life and belief system that are reflected in the saying, 'it takes a village to raise a child'.

## *Notes*

1. For a similar metaphilosophical view, see Nicholas Rescher, *Philosophical Reasoning: A Study in the Methodology of Philosophizing* (Oxford: Blackwell Publishers, Ltd. 2001), especially, chapters 1 through 5, 12, and 13.

2. Although I echo Kwasi Wiredu's sentiments regarding the non-supernatural nature of morality in some African cultures, I do not take his stance that on a comparative basis, morality in the Western philosophy is, for the most part, supernatural. See Kwasi Wiredu, "Custom and Morality: A Comparative Analysis of Some African and Western Conceptions of Morals," in *Cultural Universals and Particulars: An African Perspective* (Indianapolis, IN: Indiana University Press, 1996), 61-77.

3. There is a marked difference in the meaning of the indexical 'we' when used in the African and Western contexts. As a result of the individualism in the West, 'we' refers to individuals as members of a group, whereas 'we' in the African context refers to a fused and collective group. I shall address this subsequently when I analyze the African notions of a person and community.

# Chapter One

# Methodological and Metaphilosophical Issues

My effort is to offer a (re)construction, critical analysis, and defense of the idea of communalism in African cultures and traditions. I do this in order to indicate that the idea of communalism is a philosophical theme in African tradition that provides a foundation for African beliefs, values, social structures, and moral thought. An analysis of communalism may offer some insights for understanding the philosophical thoughts in African cultures, with respect to the system of beliefs and knowledge, the moral principles, methods of moral reasoning, and the nature of moral education. However, such an effort may be seen as raising some methodological or metaphilosophical issues regarding the existence and nature of an African philosophy. My suggestion is that communalism is one plausible theme or subject matter of African philosophy, and that an analysis of this theme will indicate, in part, the existence of an African philosophy.

An analysis of communalism as a common or dominant philosophical or conceptual theme in African thought system, cultures, and tradition is, perhaps, one way to provide an affirmative answer to the contentious metaphilosophical questions of whether there is an African philosophy, the nature of African philosophy, and the plausible themes or subject matter of African philosophy. I indicate that an African philosophy that is indicated by my (re)construction and analysis of communalism is comparable to some of the themes, traditions, and ideas in some historical periods of Western philosophy, especially, the pre-Socratic period of ancient philosophy. In other words, the features that are usually associated with the idea or ideas of philosophy in the Western philosophical tradition can be exemplified in the analysis and critical examination of communalism in African cultures. I say 'ideas' here because there is, plausibly, a general idea of philosophy that

11

incorporates various more specific ideas in terms of approaches, methods, schools, and historical periods.

## Is There an African Philosophy?

Some of the methodological issues raised by my efforts to analyze communalism as a philosophical theme in African traditions are, for the most part, general, theoretical, conceptual, and philosophical or metaphilosophical in nature, while some are particular and specific to Africa and the study of Africa. One such theoretical or metaphilosophical issue is whether there are cultural or ethnic philosophies that qualify as African philosophy. If there are such philosophies, then what is culturally or ethnically unique about them that warrant their specific cultural designation? If they are culturally or ethnically unique, either in content, subject matter or method, then what is philosophical about them? These general questions raise a number of other specific questions. One such specific question is whether we can identify philosophical thoughts or conceptual themes in African cultures and traditions. If we can identify such thoughts or themes, then we have to answer the question: what makes them African or what is African about them? Are such thoughts or themes specific to particular cultures and traditions within Africa, such as Yoruba, Luo, Azande, Igbo, Akan, Kikuyu, etc.? If they are specific to particular traditions, why call it African? Are such thoughts and themes sufficiently similar to the various cultures and traditions to warrant talking about African culture(s) or tradition(s) or philosophy? In other words, does Africa have only one culture; that is, does Africa consist of a monolithic set of ideas, beliefs, cultures, and traditions such that one can find common conceptual elements or themes? Is there any methodological, theoretical, or conceptual basis for grouping together the various traditions, cultures, and thoughts systems in Africa? Is the notion of Africa a geographical, ideological, ethnic, racial, or cultural designation? Given these questions, what is the methodological basis for capturing, at least, conceptually, the nature of the systems of thought, beliefs, and knowledge in Africa as a basis for establishing the existence or plausibility of African philosophy.

Finding a conceptual or methodological basis is essential for capturing and analyzing the nature of communalism as a basis for moral thought, moral beliefs, moral reasoning, and moral education in African traditions. There is a commonplace view that African cultures and traditions are so diverse and different that it would be methodologically and philosophically unreasonable to make a fair generalization about dominant or common philosophical themes in African cultures.[1] Those who take this position argue that each African culture must be treated individually in its own right, which requires analyzing the philosophical and conceptual issues in the thought and belief systems of each culture. These are legitimate issues and concerns that must be addressed. In an effort to avoid treating all African cultures and traditions as a monolith, some African philosophers adopt a particularistic approach, by seeking to examine different thoughts in each different African culture.[2] They have done philosophical analysis, examination, and reconstruction of ideas, thought systems, beliefs, and concepts in specific cultures, ethnic groups, and traditions in Africa. For instance, some have analyzed concepts such as, 'person', 'time', 'chance', 'causation', 'truth', 'destiny', and 'good' in different African cultures and ethnic groups such as, Igbo, Yoruba, Kikuyu, Akan, and so on. Such an approach represents a metaphilosophical stance about the nature of philosophy, which has been characterized as particularism, suggesting that philosophy is particular and unique or relative to some cultural context. In other words, philosophy and philosophical positions or ideas are influenced and shaped by culture and history. In which case, philosophy and philosophical positions or ideas usually reflect, to some significant degree, the ways that people see the world, their experiences and existential conditions.

As such, philosophical ideas have to be understood and interpreted within the context of the culture and traditions from which they emerged. According to some who hold this view, the act of doing philosophy, and in particular, African philosophy, must be seen, fundamentally, as the process of hermeneutics or the interpretation of cultural narratives.[3] This view is a normative stance regarding how the method and subject matter of philosophy ought to be adequately understood and how philosophizing ought to be properly done. It may also reflect a description of what philosophy has been through different historical periods and what, in fact, it is. Although the approach I am going to adopt is different from the stance of particularism, my approach does borrow from, as well as give credence to, some elements of particularism. As such, I do not offer a direct criticism of the particularist stance and its methodology. However, my approach is that philosophy involves theoretical abstraction and a normative or conceptual approach to issues, ideas, and problems. Such abstraction is based partly on data or facts from cultures, experience, and commonsense. Philosophy, in this sense, involves an effort to systematize experience, commonsense, or world-views in a way that is theoretical, conceptual, and abstract.[4] This approach indicates that it is reasonable or plausible to find, by a process of theoretical abstraction, some ideas or concepts that are roughly similar, in significant respects, in most if not all African cultures, ethnic groups, and traditions. These ideas and concepts may be seen as dominant themes in African cultures and African philosophy. It is reasonable to rely on the similarities of these themes as a basis for reconstructing thought systems and philosophical ideas in Africa. Such a reconstruction represents a normative philosophical position —based on theoretical abstraction—regarding how African ideas or thought *ought* to be understood. In other words, it should not be seen as a descriptive account of these ideas or thoughts.

The issue or idea of, or the talk about, African philosophy, or dominant themes in African cultures or philosophy, or the philosophy of African cultures, is legitimate on comparative and other plausible metaphilosophical grounds. The idea of an African philosophy or the idea of communalism as a theme in African philosophy, when understood in terms of a common or dominant conceptual theme in African traditions is, on comparative grounds, as legitimate as the idea of American Philosophy, Continental philosophy, Western philosophy or Analytic philosophy. Surely, these philosophies are not a monolith but they are usually referred to as if they are a monolith. For instance, the idea of pragmatism is usually considered, without question, a legitimate dominant theme in American philosophy. This theme developed out the unique historical situation that the early settlers in America found themselves. Their modes of living and thinking were centered around doing things that will help them to survive in their new environment in America. Their modes of thinking and living were result-oriented, and the result in this case had to do with how they could survive and make their lives pleasant and liveable. According to Barbara MacKinnon,

> The early settlers had to tame nature to their purposes; thus they learned both the meaning and real power of their own action to make a temporal difference. . . . 'Nineteenth-century pragmatism, so often regarded as the typically American philosophical product, is but a pale reflection of an ingrained attitude affirming the supremacy of experience over thought' This attitude emphasized the primacy of experience over reflection. Our reasoning should not dictate in advance how the world or our understanding of it ought to be.[5]

The idea of American pragmatism, which in my view, is an illustration of the metaphilosophical stance of particularism, seems to underscore the role that concrete experience, culture, history, and ways of life can play in the development of a philosophy, system of beliefs, thoughts, values, concepts, ideas, and modes of inquiry. If it makes sense to consider American pragmatism as a philosophical theme that developed out of the early American cultural experience and existential conditions, then it may, at least tentatively, make sense on comparative grounds to talk of an African philosophy in the context of some historical, cultural, and real-life experiences and traditions of Africans. I say tentatively only because, according to the universalist critics, some additional conditions, such as written tradition, systematization, and critical analysis, must be satisfied in order for experiences to engender or constitute a philosophy.

African philosophy or thought systems must be seen in terms of common or dominant themes in African cultures and traditions, which are derived from their commonsense beliefs and real-life experiences by a process of generalization and abstraction. This idea of African philosophy seems to be underscored also, in a parallel fashion, by the idea that American pragmatism is a philosophical theme of American culture or thought system. When we talk about American culture or pragmatism as a philosophical theme in such culture, it does not imply that American culture is monolithic. Although American culture is not monolithic, it is clear that what people refer to when they talk about the philosophy or philosophical theme (e.g., liberalism or pragmatism or empiricism) of a non-monolithic group of people (e.g., America or the West), they are usually referring to a *dominant theme.* According to Barbara MacKinnon, what people refer to as 'American philosophy' represents three items: (i) beliefs, ideas, values, and thoughts—a kind of spirit— that have been molded by certain historical, environmental, and socio-cultural exigencies in America; (ii) some 'foreign' ideas or thoughts that have been transformed by individuals to meet their interests in a socio-cultural setting; (iii) some common themes or common spirit in terms of processes and products that can be found in the writings of philosophers throughout the history of America.[6] In the same spirit of talking about dominant themes, there is a sense in which the idea of communalism is a dominant or common theme or spirit in African cultures that is not just as a set of ideas, belief systems, values, or ways of life but also a methodology by which African people morally, socially, and politically organize their lives and thoughts, acquire and justify beliefs, solve problems, and explain phenomena.

In my view then, the idea and place of communalism as a philosophical theme in African cultures or African philosophy, and the logic and motivation underlying my analysis of communalism in Africa is, in significant respects, similar to the idea or place of pragmatism in American culture or American philosophy. Analogously, the idea of communalism as a methodology may be seen as similar to the way in which logical analysis, phenomenology, existentialism, and hermeneutics are different methodologies that developed out of some cultural contexts, but which philosophers now use universally to address various philosophical problems. In other words, in spite of the unique cultural development and origin of these methods, they have some universal application. So, we must understand the African idea of communalism as a conceptual or philosophical theme or methodology that developed out of the African cultural condition in order to examine the plausibility of universally applying it elsewhere. This traditional African idea of communalism is something that is being gradually lost with modernization and urbanization in Africa, especially in big cities, because people are embracing the Western modern and individualistic ways of life. To understand the idea of communalism in African cultures so that it can be preserved in Africa within the context of modernization and urbanization, we must conceptually analyze and defend it. This conceptual analysis involves a form of conceptual generalization. In spite of Segun Gbadegesin's view that we must not make generalizations about all African cultures and societies, I think such generalization is legitimate regarding communalism and the communal conception and foundation of the moral, social, epistemic, and political structures and principles in African cultures.[7]

It is legitimate partly because it is not a descriptive generalization of what communalism *is* in all African cultures, but a conceptual normative generalization. As a conceptual normative generalization, I am taking and defending a systematic philosophical position regarding how the idea of communalism *ought* to be understood in African cultures. In my analysis, I indicate some of the important features of communalism that can be extrapolated from many African traditional ways of life. I also articulate what these features entail or involve. In this regard, I am also cognizant of Kwame Gyekye's view that: "There is no need to generalize a particular philosophical position for all African peoples in order for that position to be African."[8] However, he also indicates "that in many areas of thought we discern features of the traditional life and thought of African peoples sufficiently common to constitute a legitimate and reasonable basis for the construction (or reconstruction) of a philosophical system that may properly be called African—African not in the sense that every African adheres to it, but in the sense that that philosophical system arises from, and hence is essentially related to African life and thought."[9] The idea of communalism, in its very broad and pervasive sense, is one common or dominant theme or feature in African cultures that emerges from the African way of life.

## Is Africa Culturally Monolithic?

The philosophical approach of abstraction, which is normative because it indicates how ideas ought to be seen or understood, appears to be dominant and common-place in philosophy. The way I employ this method compares to how it has been utilized by various philosophers in the different periods of the history of Western philosophy. The method of theoretical abstraction allows one to talk about conceptual themes in African culture, even though Africa lacks a monolithic tradition and it does not have a monolithic culture. Wiredu addresses a similar issue with respect to traditional cultures in Ghana and Africa. His insight is illuminating with respect to the issue of whether it makes sense of talk about a theme or set of themes as a 'culture', thought or tradition in Africa. In his view,

> I have spoken repeatedly of *our* traditional culture. This not because I wish to pretend that the whole of Ghana (or, even more incredibly, the whole of Africa) has one homogeneous traditional culture. There are in Ghana a variety of ethnic groups with traditional cultures that differ in some respects. Nevertheless, there are deep underlying affinities running through these cultures which justify speaking of a Ghanaian traditional culture. Indeed, for the same reason one might speak of the tradi-

tional culture of Africa, though with a more considerable attenuation of content.[10]

Wiredu argues that if one is able to identify, perhaps by a process of theoretical abstraction, some common trends or dominant views and some underlying affinities among African cultures, this would justify one to speak of an African culture. He then draws from the work of Kofi Antubam and his attempt to provide what he calls "some of the common aspects of African life and culture."[11]

Some of these common affinities, which are of particular relevance to the issue of morality, moral thought, and moral education in African cultures are, (i) African's "'communalistic' custom of holding land and property in general in common with relatives, . . . his tendency to 'clothe all his cherished ideas in verbal and graphic symbols', . . . his tendency to equate age with wisdom."[12] Antubam's list of the common themes in African traditional culture, Wiredu says, "is probably an uncontroversial one."[13] So, although there are many cultures in Africa, it is generally accepted and commonplace in the philosophical literature (and I think it is reasonable to accept) that whenever a 'thought' or 'tradition' or 'culture' is predicated of Africa (and by the way, any group of people, such as the West, British, American, Anglo-American, or Continental), it is not used to denote or describe a homogeneity or unanimism in cultures or thoughts, rather, it is a reference to a dominant theme or common themes or ideal type. The point here is that the use of tradition, culture, or thought is not meant to be factually descriptive. Rather, it is meant to be a conceptually normative abstraction; it is meant to specify how conceptually, certain ideas or views of a group or groups of people *ought* to be understood. This point is underscored by Fred Lee Hord and Jonathan Scott Lee who argue that a reference to African thought involves a set of "common *generative themes* in African cultures."[14]

The idea of using conceptual themes as generalizations or abstractions to refer to and identify different heterogenous groups of people is a commonplace in the literature of various disciplines. In philosophy, for instance, the literature on the debate about the existence and nature of African philosophy is replete with commonplace dichotomies, comparisons, and contrasts between Western (especially contemporary philosophical) tradition, and African tradition(s). These dichotomies, comparisons, and contrasts are based on conceptual generalizations, which are normative rather than descriptive. The fact that such comparisons and contrasts, which are based on generalizations are commonplace, may indicate that there are plausible theoretical or conceptual bases for these generalizations. The criticisms of some traditional African ideas or ethnophilosophy suggest that African ideas, beliefs, and values have the characteristics or common features of being unsystematic, unanalytic, accommodative, collective, unwritten, authoritarian, and dogmatic. Hence, they are seen by critics as not philosophical in a way that is comparable to

Western formal philosophical thought.

Moreover, the literature in comparative studies usually engages in dichotomies, contrasts, and comparisons, based on conceptual generalizations. For instance, there are comparisons and contrasts between East and West, between Africa and Europe, or between Africa and the West. These comparisons and contrasts, which are based on generalizations, do not get embroiled in such considerations as to whether or not Western, Eastern, and African traditions are a monolith. No person raises eyebrows with respect to whether or not there is a monolithic tradition in Western or American or continental philosophy. But any time one makes a generalization about African cultures or traditions, the first objection—mostly from Westerners who claim to be experts about Africa—is that this attempt is wrong headed.[15] Yet, people are quick to compare and contrast the Western tradition with African or Eastern traditions on the basis of this kind of generalization, especially when they want to put the West in a positive light and the others in a negative light. There is a sense in which some Western intellectuals who do not want anything positive to be said about Africa are uncomfortable with someone making a 'constructive' positive generalization about African cultures. Some intellectuals want to continue the negative beliefs and stereotypes that Africa is primitive and uncivilized. These negative features themselves involve a monolithic reference to Africa.

The meaningfulness of this apparent monolithic identification of and reference to Africa, as well talk about ancient, Western, and American philosophies (in spite of the different themes) seems to substantiate my point that whenever one talks about Western or American or African culture, one does so meaningfully only because one is referring to a kind of ideal type, dominant theme(s), or common spirit. The criticisms of the efforts to derive and articulate an African philosophy from African cultural ideas because we cannot get from Africa a single African philosophical system, since Africa is not monolithic, is specious. It is true that African traditions and cultures, are as a matter of descriptive fact, not monolithic. So, the effort to discredit African philosophy or any other positive ideas or features of African thought by raising the question of whether Africa has a monolithic tradition involves a straw man attack. This attack gives the impression that the contents of African philosophy are to be seen as statements that seek to accurately describe facts about African cultures.

One logical way to respond to this criticism is to offer a non-vacuous contrast: if there are negative common themes or features in African traditions and cultures —in virtue of which Africa is criticized and in spite of the fact Africa is not a monolith—then there must also be some positive common themes or features. To say that African cultures have dominant themes or features does not imply that such themes or features may not exist in some specific or particular cultures and traditions of Africa. Similarly, when one says, for instance, that individualism, liberalism, and rationalism are dominant philosophical themes in the modern period of

Western culture(s), one is not implying that there are no pockets of cultures or philosophical traditions in the West or in Western philosophy that are communal or non-individualistic and non-rationalistic, and one is also not implying that all Western cultures and philosophical traditions are monolithic. My view that communalism is a dominant theme in African cultures does not imply that all cultures and traditions in Africa have, in exactly the same way, the features of communalism that I indicate in my analysis. Many African cultures may exhibit communalism in fairly different ways, but they may have some core elements in virtue of which they are characterized as communalistic, according to my analysis.

The criticisms of African cultures are plausible and reasonable only because they presuppose the distinction, comparison, and contrast between the Western and African thought systems. Such distinction, criticisms, comparison, and contrast are reasonable only if there are common features that can be used to characterize and identify the things that are being criticized, compared, and contrasted. The presupposition here indicates that African traditions have some things in common on the basis of which they are jointly criticized and compared or contrasted with Western traditions. The extent to which the commonalities that characterize African or Western traditions are true, or simply a caricature, is a descriptive factual issue. But some of the descriptive facts that sociologists and anthropologists have articulated about these traditions suggest that there are some bases for making generalizations about them. To underscore this point, P. P. Ekeh indicates that, "the British have two sociologies: one was based on individualistic social thought and presumed to be operative in Britain. The other was predicated on Durkheimian collective sociology and was assumed to apply to colonized peoples [of Africa, Asia, and South America]. The two sociological models in Britain never crossed in their paths. . . ."[16] Ekeh goes on to say: "For Durkheim, Mauss, or Levi-Strauss, the collectivistic attributes in non-Western cultures were elementary forms of their more complex representations in advanced Western societies. For the British the collectivistic characteristics they attributed to the non-Western cultures were totally inapplicable to their island civilization."[17]

So, logically or methodologically, I accept at least for the purpose of argument, the plausibility of the characterizations and criticisms of African thought system, which imply that there are some basic features or commonalities that identify African and Western thought systems on the basis of which they are compared and contrasted. The plausibility of the criticisms of African traditions, which for the purpose of such criticisms are seen or characterized as a monolith, also imply that these criticisms raise certain substantive concerns or issues that must be met on the critics' own terms. These terms include the idea that African cultures or traditions have some similarities. One can address these substantive concerns or issues on the critics' own terms only if one assumes that there are some common features that identify Western and African thought systems. These features, which are assumed as a basis for criticism, comparison, and contrast derive, in my view, from what I see as a plausible set of common 'spirit' and themes. We may have substantive disagreement about the nature or contents and legitimacy of these themes, features or commonalities, but we must agree, at least logically, that such common themes could possibly or plausibly exist. Moreover, the idea of articulating, by conceptual abstraction, a set of common themes is consistent with some metaphilosophical approaches or methods of doing philosophy that can be found in the history or different periods of Western philosophy. For instance, when a philosopher argues that reality is material, he is, on the one hand, abstracting the idea of materiality from things in reality, and on the other hand, he is providing the idea of materiality as a normative view of how reality ought to be understood.

## Dominant Themes in African Cultures

The idea of having or specifying a broad set of dominant themes, criteria, or approaches as a philosophical tradition, theory, or school is a commonplace in Western philosophy. One may say that many philosophical theories—in ethics, epistemology, and metaphysics—seek to provide abstract or conceptual normative criteria for capturing or identifying different relevant phenomena. Thus, theoretical abstraction is an essential part of philosophy. For instance, when people talk about analytic philosophy with respect to Anglo-American philosophy, they are talking about a set of themes, traditions, methods or approaches that is manifested differently in ethics, metaphysics, and epistemology. For instance, many of the theories in epistemology regarding the nature of knowledge, or theories in ethics regarding what is good, and theories in metaphysics regarding what is real, attempt to provide answers in the form of abstract normative criteria, which may not adequately apply to all cases and situations regarding what is knowledge, good, and real. Two of the things that analytic philosophers are good at doing are, finding adequate universal, normative, conceptual, theoretical criteria that may be used to capture some phenomena, and finding or using counterexamples in specific cases to indicate that these abstract normative criteria do not generally apply. For instance, Edmund Gettier became famous because he was able to find some counterexamples or articulate specific cases of justified true belief to show that the hitherto accepted criteria for knowledge, i.e., Justified True Belief (JTB), were inadequate and do not generally apply to the efforts to distinguish between knowledge and ignorance.[18]

One of the issues that emerged from Gettier's work was whether or not his counterexamples were unique cases or indications of types of knowledge, i.e., inferential knowledge, to which the accepted criteria (JTB) did not apply. The other issue that arose out of Gettier's work is whether we need different criteria for different types of knowledge—empirical knowledge, *a priori* knowledge, inferential knowledge, and so on. Moreover, the analytic approach as a dominant theme or tradition in contemporary Western Anglo-American philosophy is 'non-exclusionary', in the sense that it does not totally exclude other themes or approaches, and it does not imply that Anglo-American analytic philosophers may not use or employ the historical, constructive, phenomenological, hermeneutical, existential, pragmatic, and postmodernist approaches. Any effort to capture or characterize the analytic approach or the themes, subject matter or issues that characterize what is called analytic philosophy can only represent a kind of 'ideal type' or theoretical framework that is 'abstracted' from the different approaches that are used in metaphysics, ethics, and epistemology, in particular, the use of linguistic, conceptual, and logical analysis. The idea of finding some underlying (necessary or sufficient) features to define a concept or phenomenon appears to be what philosophers, especially analytic philosophers, do in their attempts to provide abstract theories for explaining issues, answering questions, and analyzing philosophical problems. Thus, many philosophical theories are attempts to look for an underlying idea that could provide a basis for apparent commonalities or discrepancies in our beliefs and experiences so that we can make sense of them.

Philosophical theories do this by universalizing or generalizing about some particular and specific experiences and beliefs on the basis of speculation, conceptualization, and abstraction. The philosophical idea of making generalizations about facts based on theoretical abstraction is what Fred Lee Hord and Jonathan Scott Lee calls "the universalizing tendency of philosophical reflection," which they argue, "ideally carries with it a critical tendency."[19] This universalizing tendency of philosophical reflection and abstraction is an essential feature of philosophy and has persisted throughout the history of Western philosophy. This idea of Western philosophy is sometimes used as the sole normative standard for determining what constitutes a philosophy, and whether African philosophy is a philosophy. But what critics of African philosophy seem to ignore is the fact that the nature, contents, methods, and enterprise of philosophy have changed in some subtle and obvious ways from one historical period (ancient, medieval, modern, and contemporary) to another. Some of these changes, both in content and methods, can be understood in terms of how cultural beliefs, history, and people's world-views have influenced the now formalized philosophical ideas that are now done professionally and individually, and studied in universities. These subtle changes must also be taken into consideration when one is trying to articulate a holistic and synthesized view of what philosophy is or what it has been in a way that draws on its historical and cultural developments, and what it ought to be. Any view regarding, what philosophy ought to be, must draw from or be sensitive to these developments that shape our metaphilosophical views of philosophy.

Another issue or criticism that has been raised against the plausibility of an African philosophy has to do with whether such a philosophy is authentic or unique to Africa or whether such a philosophy has been inspired by other civilizations and cultures, especially those of the West, because of the colonial influence. This stance raises another metaphilosophical issue about the requisite nature and features of philosophy and African philosophy, and whether an African philosophy must be a philosophy that is unique, authentic, autochthonous to Africa. Some people have questioned whether there are any ideas or thoughts and belief systems that developed in African cultures and were influenced and shaped by the unique experiences of Africans that also have validity solely for Africans. Moreover, critics also question whether such African philosophy is comparable in some significant respects to what is described as Western philosophy, which is said to be the paradigm of philosophy. Some of the requisite features of Western philosophy that African philosophy seems to lack include having a written tradition and universal rational validity. To address these metaphilosophical and methodological issues that may be raised about my analysis of the idea of communalism as a philosophical theme in African philosophy, as well as the nature of African philosophy, it is pertinent to say that my analysis of communalism is being done in the context of a particular pedigree involving the metaphilosophical debates about the existence and nature of African philosophy. This debate has arisen from at least three fundamental sources or pedigrees.

One such pedigree is the fact that there is, within the discipline of philosophy, a metaphilosophical debate about the nature of philosophy: its features, methods, contents, or subject matter. The relevant issue is, what is it that distinguishes philosophy from other disciplines? As a result of this debate, not all philosophers agree on what the nature of philosophy or 'Western' philosophy is, in terms of its contents and methodology. Any conception, view, or idea about the nature of philosophy is, in itself a philosophical position that needs to be defended: one must provide arguments to indicate why one's view of philosophy is plausible. Because philosophers do not agree on what constitutes philosophy, it is reasonable to question the basis for questioning the nature and existence of African philosophy. Any view that questions the nature and existence of African philosophy must implicitly conceive of philosophy in a particular way. Such a view must show why that view is reasonable in order to indicate that there is nothing in Africa that matches that specified conception. If the metaphilosophical problem about the nature, method, and contents of philosophy did not exist, such that there is a clear idea, criteria, or view of what philosophy is that everyone can agree on, then the issue of whether there is an African philosophy will be an easy one to settle, in that we will have clear criteria of identity. The pertinent issue would, in essence, involve the process of identification, which involves applying clear criteria to a set of subject matter and ideas in order to determine whether the subject matter and contents in question regarding African thoughts or ideas, fit or match the generally accepted or clear criteria or idea of philosophy.

Unfortunately, the fact is that idea or concept of philosophy is contentious and there are no clear criteria regarding what philosophy is. In this regard, Nicholas Rescher argues that the issue of what constitutes philosophy, and "the question of what philosophy's problems in fact are is a philosophical question. What the proper mission of philosophy is constitutes in fact one of the definitive and most significant issues in the field. And this means that metaphilosophy is a part and parcel of philosophy itself."[20] This point about the philosophical nature of metaphilosophy and the metaphilosophical nature of philosophy underscores the need for or the significance of this chapter in this book. So, if my effort to analyze communalism in African cultures is to succeed as a philosophical enterprise, it must be placed within the context of the metaphilosophical issues that such analysis raises. An understanding of the relevant issues and my metaphilosophical stance will substantially illuminate why what I am doing—that is, an analysis of communalism in African cultures—is philosophical, and why the resulting analysis, which is a content or subject matter of African philosophy, also implies that there is, indeed, an African philosophy. It is clear that the enterprise or activity of philosophy requires that the idea or concept of philosophy must be analyzed, and that such analysis must be defended.

One way to address the issue of whether there is an African philosophy involves the following: (1) do a conceptual analysis of philosophy, by indicating its essential features, methods, and contents, (2) provide a defense of such an analysis by showing why it makes sense and why it is reasonable to accept, and then (3) show how these features methods, and contents capture or fail to capture ideas, thought system, beliefs, concepts, and values in African cultures. The defense of such analysis is particularly important to the idea of philosophy, because one of the things that philosophy seeks to do is, according to Rescher, "to bring rational order, system, and intelligibility to the confusing diversity of our cognitive affairs. It strives for orderly arrangements in the cognitive sphere that will enable us to find our way about in the world in an effective and satisfying way. Philosophy is indeed a venture in theorizing, but one whose rationale is eminently practical."[21] In this regard, my analysis of communalism in African cultures, which is a venture in theorizing, abstraction, and conceptualization, seeks to bring rational order to our cognitive affairs as a way of helping us to understand many practical issues, such as moral reasoning, moral education, the role of elders, belief acquisition, political and social structures, and ways of life in African cultures.

Many of those who question whether there is an African philosophy, or whether certain themes, ideas, or concepts in African cultures and traditions are philosophical, also raise legitimate and specific comparative, methodological, and metaphilosophical issues.[22] The first methodological issue, as indicated, has to do with whether Africa has a monolithic culture or tradition and whether African has a single or monolithic philosophy. This issue is related to the metaphilosophical one, which involves the essential features of philosophy or the conditions that must exist in order to have a philosophy, and the idea that African ideas and beliefs do not have these features or satisfy these conditions. The comparative issue has to do with whether African philosophical ideas compare to Western philosophical ideas.

## Trends in African Philosophy

It is on the basis of these specific comparative and metaphilosophical issues raised that Peter Bodunrin, Appiah, and Wiredu have objected to or questioned the idea of an African philosophy. Bodunrin argues that what many people have thus far considered to be the plausible contents and subject matter of African philosophy do not match or compare to what is considered philosophy in the Western tradition. What people have considered to be the subject matter of African philosophy include four sets of ideas. They are: (1) *ethnophilosophy*, which includes myths, folklore, values, and beliefs in African cultures. One may see communalism that I seek to analyze as one such belief, value, or practice. (2) *Philosophic sagacity* represents the ideas of sages, thinkers, and people of wisdom in African cultures —those who were not influenced by the West. (3) *Ideological and political philosophy* represents the ideas of African political leaders and nationalists, such as Kwame Nkrumah, Nnamdi Azikiwe, Kenneth Kaunda, Julius Nyerere, Leopold Senghor, who mobilized their peoples around some political ideologies and values in order to gain independence from colonial powers. Many people who object to the existence of African philosophy offer different sets of arguments to show why the above ideas are not a philosophy or why they cannot in their current states be called philosophy. Moreover, Wiredu argues that a legitimate African philosophy that is comparable to Western philosophy cannot be reconstructed from African cultural ideas and beliefs. Some argue that these ideas may pass as a legitimate philosophy if and when they are clearly written in a systematized manner, reconstructed, subjected to critical analysis, and infused with some rigor. The last set of ideas in African thought, which many accept as a legitimate philosophy is, (4) *professional philosophy.* These ideas represent the views of professional philosophers who have been trained in the Western tradition and the canonical academic disciple of philosophy and are now teaching philosophy in Universities and publishing works that address perennial questions in philosophy.

It would appear that what I seek to do by analyzing and defending the idea of communalism in African traditions is a combination or hybrid of what is called professional philosophy and ethnophilosophy. This may indicate that ethnophilosophy is, in some sense, a legitimate 'ancient' African philosophy and a significant pedigree or precursor for modern and contemporary African professional philosophy. One of the arguments against ethnophilosophy is that it represents ideas that are not systematized, critically analyzed, examined, or well argued for.[23] Ethnophilosophy represents culturally held ideas which do not include systematic arguments regarding why people hold them and why they are reasonable. What is regarded as Western philosophy in the formal sense of philosophy are not the folklore, folkwisdom, myths, and world-views of people in Western cultures. The metaphilosophical stance underlying this view seeks to distinguish between *formal philosophy* and *folk-philosophy* by indicating the different characteristics of each.[24] Appiah argues that these African world-views are only philosophy in the 'folk' and 'debased' sense of philosophy that represents a set of unsystematic ideas, beliefs, dogmas, myths, sayings, and values that people have or share in common as a basis for living.[25] Appiah, among many others, has argued that the question about the existence and nature of African philosophy involves the need to show that an African formal philosophy exists. To reiterate, the question is not whether an African folk or ethnophilosophy exists. As such, critics claim that the contents or subject matter of ethnophilosophy cannot be characterized as a philosophy or set of philosophical themes because they lack certain important features that formal philosophy has. In other words, ethnophilosophy is not comparable to the contemporary *formal* view of Western philosophy, which is not the folk-philosophy or ethnophilosophy of various Western cultures.

These criticisms presuppose a metaphilosophical view, which indicates that philosophy involves the formal process and technical activity that must be learned and practiced only by professionals. The assumed metaphilosophical idea here is that in order for anything to pass as a philosophy, it must be a set of systematic ideas that has been critically examined and argued for, in terms of providing evidence to indicate their truth or reasonableness. This formal conception of philosophy implies that philosophy has certain essential characteristics that distinguish it from its folk African counterpart. If any idea or subject matter that is suggested as a candidate for philosophy is deemed to lack these essential characteristics, then it is not formal philosophy. The view that philosophy must be formal, according to this metaphilosophical view, also raises questions about whether such view is reasonable or whether it is the only plausible conception of philosophy. If this is the only plausible conception, then one can argue that if African philosophy is not formal according the given criteria, then it is not comparable to or does not march the features of formal Western philosophy, and as such, it is not a philosophy. Some of the essential characteristics of formal philosophy indicated by this metaphilosophical stance, as gleaned from the works of Paulin Hountondji, Appiah, Bodunrin, and Wiredu, include the following: (1) it deals with conceptual and abstract questions and issues, (2) it adopts analytic, critical, systematic, and adversarial approach; (3) it uses the rigorous and rational method of science; and (4) it has a written tradition that involves the documentation of individual persons' thoughts as opposed to the thoughts of a group of people. It is questionable whether the features of formal and professional philosophy as indicated by Appiah, Bodunrin, and Wiredu, are necessary conditions for having a philosophy such that not having these features indicate that there is no philosophy or whether they are only a set of sufficient conditions, in that satisfying these conditions may indicate the existence of a philosophy but not satisfying them does not necessarily indicate the lack of a philosophy.

As a metaphilosophical question, it is open to philosophical debate whether these characteristics or criteria ought to be considered necessary or sufficient or both necessary and sufficient to have a philosophy. This formal view about the nature and activity of philosophy, which is the basis for the criticisms of ethnophilosophy by Appiah, Bodunrin, and Wiredu, among others, has a foundation in the following: (i) logical positivism and its view that philosophy can be reduced to either science or logic, or that philosophy must use the scientific method or the method of logical analysis, and (ii) the analytic tradition and its view that the method of philosophy involves conceptual, logical, critical, or ordinary language analysis.[26] The first, second, and third characteristics imply that any philosophical principle or belief or idea, in order to be meaningful, must have universal validity and must be logically or empirically verifiable. The need for such validity and verifiability derives from the view that formal philosophical ideas and statements are conceptual in nature, universally rational, and are subject to logical and rigorous analysis and critical examination. By relying on this feature of philosophy, Appiah argues against the philosophical status of ethnophilosophy as follows: "The urge to give arguments and evidence for what you believe, and make your beliefs consistent with each other so that they form a system, is one of the marks of formal philosophy."[27] The fourth feature is connected to the first two, in that as Appiah and Wiredu claim, ideas, beliefs, and thoughts cannot exhibit the first two characteristics if they are not documented. It is difficult, if not impossible, to use rigorous and critical methods on ideas which are not documented but are transmitted only by oral tradition.

Wiredu and Appiah rely on this formal view of philosophy to show that (a) a discourse or set of ideas, beliefs, or thoughts can be placed into the conceptual category of philosophy if and only if it has their requisite characteristics. So, according to this view or conception of philosophy, any discourse, X, is a philosophy, if and only if, X has the above four characteristics in (1), (2), (3), and (4). Appiah and Wiredu argue that African ethnophilosophy does not have the requisite characteristics, and therefore, it is not a philosophy. According to this conception of philosophy, ethnophilosophy is not a philosophy because it is not universal but culturally specific or relative, and it is cognitively relative and descriptive. In Appiah's view, the suggestion that the contents of ethnophilosophy may be characterized as formal philosophy implies the philosophical thesis of strong cognitive relativism. This thesis indicates that what is true about matters of fact, which philosophy attempts to address in its statements and theories, depends on one's conceptual scheme, of which culture is a part.[28] His argument is that the contents of ethnophilosophy, which include dogmas, values, and beliefs such as witchcraft, cannot be empirically verified. Instead, these dogmas, values, and beliefs seem to have truths that are relative to the cultures and conceptual schemes of Africans. In his view, philosophy involves efforts to critically examine beliefs about matters of fact in order to determine their truth or the methods for verifying or establishing their truths. The idea is that ethnophilosophical beliefs, ideas, and discourses in African cultures are not documented or that they are dogmatic, and as such, they cannot be critically examined by using the rational, analytic, conceptual, critical, and rigorous methodology of science and logic.

This analytic and formal conception of philosophy is inadequate partly because it is circular, parochial, and reductionist. It assumes a narrow analytic view of philosophy and it uses such analytic methods of analysis to reduce the method of philosophy to one methodological tradition—the analytic tradition, which is understood either as a scientific method or the method of logical and linguistic analysis. It ignores, in this reductionist approach, other elements or characteristics and traditions of philosophy. Usually, there is no sound argument regarding why these other elements and traditions—the historical, interpretative, phenomenological, existential, normative, and descriptive—that are ignored are not philosophical. Sometimes, analytic philosophers assume without argument that the formal conception of philosophy or the analytic method is the only legitimate conception or method of philosophy. As such, some analytic philosophers proceed to use the assumption of this conception or method of philosophy to eliminate other methods or conceptions of philosophy as illegitimate. They seem to ignore other plausible views of philosophy that indicate other elements, features, or methods. Some of the other conceptions, methods, views, or elements of philosophy that can be found in other traditions in the different historical periods of Western philosophy, include the idea of philosophy as a constructive process or as a normative, historical, speculative, reflective, synthesizing, experiential, or interpretative process. Usually, the analytic conception of philosophy does not consider or take seriously how social, cultural, and historical conditions and experiences of a people may have influenced the constructive and reflective elements, various views, traditions, approaches, and development of the methods and sub-disciplines of philosophy.

In my view, ethnophilosophy is, in a relevant sense, a legitimate philosophy. Ethnophilosophy involves and raises legitimate epistemic and metaphilosophical issues about (a) the appropriateness, rigor, and universality of some philosophical methodologies and the legitimacy of oral tradition, (b) the meaningfulness, logical verifiability, and rationality of statements and beliefs in African cultures, and (c) the relevance of the relative social and cultural context of evidence for the reasonableness of a belief. In Rescher's account of philosophy, which in my view, is reasonable, ethnophilosophy is a philosophy in the sense that it offers pertinent data, contents, subject matter for African philosophy and raises some interesting questions for which a coherent and systematic story in the form of an answer is being sought.[29] Wiredu seems to suggest that African ethnophilosophy may be a precursor for a legitimate African philosophy. He argues that "the closeness of the relation between traditional philosophy [ethnophilosophy] and practical life makes a thorough examination of traditional philosophical ideas an imperative."[30] Two important points stand out from Wiredu's comments: (1) There is a close connection between traditional African philosophy or ethnophilosophy and practical life. Thus, philosophy in African cultures is, indeed, a practice or concerned about practical issues and principles. (2) He indicates that it is imperative to critically and thoroughly examine the traditional philosophical ideas of Africans. If such an examination is imperative for philosophy, then ethnophilosophy, which is the content of such examination must be a philosophy or its precursor. Yet, this second point has been used as a basis for criticizing ethnophilosophy and for indicating that it does not consist of or constitutes a philosophy. The idea is that African ethnophilosophy has not been critically examined and argued for; hence, it is not a philosophy. Wiredu suggests that it is the critical process not content that constitutes a philosophy.

In the view of Appiah, Bodunrin, and Wiredu, an essential feature of philosophy requires that ideas must be held on the basis of scrupulously analyzed evidence. Any philosophical idea must be critically examined, and when it cannot withstand criticism, it must be changed in favor of other ideas for which better evidence can be found. This critical view of philosophy suggests that philosophical ideas cannot be dogmatic or be a product of indoctrination, and they cannot be accepted or imposed solely by reliance on elders or authority of tradition. Hence, African beliefs, ideas or ethnophilosophy cannot be characterized as legitimate African philosophy. In order for a people to have philosophy, they must exhibit an attitude of rational autonomy and independence in relevant contexts in accepting beliefs, ideas, and principles. People cannot have a philosophical attitude or engage in the critical enterprise of philosophy if they hold their beliefs simply and solely because such beliefs have been imposed by some authoritarian figure. Such beliefs or ideas must be examined in a liberal or non-authoritarian context where ideas can be freely exchanged and critically examined. In Wiredu's view, beliefs in African cultures are not held on the basis of adequate and critically examined evidence; they are held as the imposed dictates of elders who are seen as the repositories of knowledge or they are dogmatically accepted by relying on the authority of tradition. Legitimate philosophical ideas are not transmitted on the basis of oral tradition but on the basis of carefully documented and systematized written arguments. Hence, having a written tradition or being formally trained to write philosophy is seen as an essential element of formal philosophy.

One may respond to this point about the idea that a written tradition is necessary to have a philosophy and African philosophy by indicating that Socrates who is considered one of the foremost philosophers of the ancient period did not have any philosophical training as such, did not write, and he was interested in addressing practical problems and issues regarding how, in general, people ought to lead their lives. Pierre Hadot argues that the ancient philosophers have a metaphilosophical view, which saw philosophy as a practice and a way of life. In his view, ancient philosophers did not see theory and practice as separate, but conceptually linked.[31] Wiredu also indicates this point in African cultures by saying that: "A fact about philosophy in a traditional society, particularly worthy of emphasis, is that it is alive in day-to-day existence. When philosophy becomes academic and highly technical it can easily lose this quality."[32] The interesting point is that Wiredu among others appears to be using this academic and highly technical view of philosophy to criticize African ethnophilosophy which is more of a practice than theory. In this sense, philosophy is more than the kind of theoretical thinking that contemporary professional philosophers engage in within academia.

Professional philosophers in academia are now engaging in what is now called applied philosophy except that it is different from how it was practiced in ancient times both in the West and Africa. This formal, academic, and professional view of philosophy is historically recent: it is the legacy of the medieval and modern periods of Western philosophy. This point about the subtle changes in the nature, method, and activities of philosophy is underscored by the following comments made by MacKinnon:

> As philosophy became more analytic and language oriented, it turned to analyzing theoretical issues that had little direct bearing on practical or moral issues. . . . As philosophy retreated to academia and to an analysis of its own problems, the problems of men that it had formerly dealt with were left to the social scientists, politicians, and humanists, who suffered from lack of 'training necessary for dealing in a clear and critical way with vague but important issue that are basically of great interest to large numbers of people'[33]

These comments indicate that the idea of philosophy as a technical discipline or activity that is engaged in by trained professional university professors is a contemporary phenomenon and is a departure from the ancient view of philosophy. It is unreasonable to use this contemporary prism or framework for conceiving of the proper nature of philosophy, in terms of what it is, what it has been, and what it ought to be. A reasonable metaphilosophical view of philosophy must consider what it has been throughout history, and such a holistic and synthesized view will be a more reasonable picture regarding what African philosophy ought to be and how it ought to be viewed. The contemporary formal view of philosophy that has now been used to question the existence of African philosophy seems to present only a part of the picture, and not the whole picture with respect to the nature of 'philosophy' and 'African philosophy'.

## Plausible Views of the Nature of Philosophy

A normative metaphilosophical view regarding the nature of philosophy must involve a synthesized view that captures the subtle changes and historical developments of philosophy; otherwise, any view that one comes up with will be parochial. The features that some analytic philosophers now see in what is regarded as formal Western philosophy, thought, intellectual culture and tradition—being analytic, scientific, rigorous, critical and individualistic—do not actually or totally represent the whole reality of what philosophy is and how it is viewed, in terms of the different periods and numerous traditions in Western philosophy. These features could be said to represent a dominant approach, ideas, themes or 'ideal types' of the nature or tradition of philosophy. For instance, the analytic tradition represents different school or ideas which include logical atomism, logical positivism, ordinary language philosophy, and meta-ethics. This formal idea of philosophy represents a philosophical position that needs to be defended, since it may be evaluated and criticized as representing an unsatisfactory view. Perhaps, we need to provide an alternative construal of philosophy or the Western philosophical tradition that is broader than the formal, professional, technical, academic, individualistic, and analytic view. In the history of Western philosophy, the idea of philosophy has not been seen solely as an academic or a written activity that is done by trained professional university professors. The contemporary identification of Western philosophical tradition with the individualistic, analytic, scientific, and critical mode of rationality seems to ignore the fact that there are some pockets of communitarian mode of thinking in different historical periods of Western philosophy. In fact, many of the ancient moral, social, and political thinkers, including Plato and Aristotle, were communitarian. Some people argue that a modern political philosopher like Rousseau sought to combine the communitarian elements or features of the ancients and the individualistic and voluntaristic elements or features of the modern period.[34] In other words, Rousseau saw many advantages of the communitarian tradition.

But the universalists who criticized the idea of culling African philosophy from cultural beliefs argue that, the ideas that are characterized as a philosophy, do not belong to groups. One does not have to accept or share any formal philosophical ideas in order to belong to a cultural group. It is not necessary to have a group who shares ideas in order for such ideas to be philosophical. In most cases, philosophical ideas are the ideas of individuals that have been well argued, systematized, and documented. This is underscored by the underlying argument that philosophy is a rational activity involving rational autonomy and doxastic voluntarism, and that rationality can be ascribed only to individuals and not groups. The idea of seeing group ideas or beliefs as a philosophy seems to imply that we can ascribe a mind or rationality to a group.[35] One of the features that characterizes formal philosophy in the West is that it involves or is a compendium of the ideas and thoughts of individual persons. These ideas are not the culturally shared ideas that people are raised with or world-views and values that ordinary people commonly and socially share and display in their everyday lives. In fact, without formal education, many ordinary people may not be aware of the ideas of an individual philosopher even though the philosopher was raised in that culture and in spite of the fact that the ideas may have been influenced by his culture. For instance, Bodunrin argues that the average Briton may neither be aware of nor hold the ideas in Wittgenstein's *Tractatus*.

For Bodunrin, philosophy is the set of ideas of people who are experts or trained philosophers. These people may hold and systematically articulate ideas that ordinary people in a culture and society may not hold. Moreover, these ideas are claimed to be rationally held and universally and objectively valid—by virtue of their rational basis. In contrast, ethnophilosophy and the ideas in African cultures that people want to call African philosophy are world-views that are commonly held only by a group of people—by virtue of their culture. They are not universally valid by virtue having an objective rational basis. Hence, Appiah argues that the idea of ethno- or folk-philosophy, that is, a philosophy that is based on cultural world-views, folklore, and myths, imply cognitive relativism: the view that ideas and beliefs are relative to cultures, group, and conceptual scheme. It should be clear that this universalist, analytic, formal, and individualistic view of philosophy that has dominated contemporary Anglo-American philosophical literature, which has been used as a basis for criticizing ethnophilosophy, is parochial. The issue of its parochialism involves, whether this view can adequately capture the historical nature of philosophy from the ancient period through the medieval and modern to the contemporary period. The argument against African philosophy is based on the idea that ethnophilosophy represents the ideas of groups and not individuals. Therefore, this argument involves a questionable metaphilosophical assumption, namely, that in order to have a philosophy in the universal, Western, and formal sense, there must be some renowned individual philosophers with a remarkable body of written work that one can formally study.

Another way to raise the question about the existence of an African philosophy is to ask whether there are, for instance, African equivalents of Plato, St. Thomas Aquinas, Descartes, and Wittgenstein, with a substantial body or amount of written works that can be studied. Hence, it is asked whether the unwritten ideas, beliefs, and thoughts in African cultures have comparable systematic, analytic, critical features that characterize the works of these Western philosophers. On the one hand, these questions raise once more the metaphilosophical questions about the nature of philosophy and the necessary or sufficient conditions or features that must exist in order to have a philosophy or identify any thought system as philosophy. The question about the existence and nature of African philosophy is another way of indicating that African cultures and traditions have no individual philosophers, no written tradition, and no written body of work to be studied. The implication is that communalism cannot be a philosophical theme if it is not articulated as a written theory that is systematic and well argued for as universally valid ideas.

The history of Western philosophy does indicate that there is some connection between different cultures or history and the development of different philosophical trends, schools, methods, and ideas in the different periods of Western philosophy.[36] For instance, the thoughts in the medieval period were shaped by Catholic beliefs and doctrines, and ideas in the modern period were shaped by science, liberal individualism, and the revolt against conformism that was dictated by Catholic doctrines. These facts in the history of Western philosophy, which are exemplified in American pragmatism, indicate that ideas must keep in touch with practice, and that thoughts are shaped by the cultures in which they occur or emerge. The history of Western philosophy is the history of diverse themes, different schools of thought, methodologies, and various people's ideas and views, issues, and problems in various Western cultures. The history of Western philosophy is a history of distinctive systems of thought that have been influenced and shaped by people's history, culture, and life experiences, which are the data of philosophy. According to Rescher, the data of philosophy include:

> Common-sense beliefs, common knowledge, and what have been 'the ordinary convictions of the plain' since time immemorial. . . . The lessons we derive from our dealings with the world in every-day life; The received opinions that constitute the worldview of the day; views that accord with the 'spirit of the times' and the ambient convictions of one's cultural contexts; Traditions, inherited lore, and ancestral wisdom (including religious tradition); The 'teachings of history' as best as we can discern them.[37]

This point is insightful because philosophical theories, ideas, justifications, and explanations must not only be sensitive to, but also must draw from, commonsense and one's everyday life experiences.

As a result of the acknowledged connection between theory and commonsense or experiences or existential condition, if a philosophical theory is inconsistent with practical experience or commonsense intuition, it is deemed counterintuitive and is considered a bad theory. The enterprise of philosophy is worthwhile as a theoretical activity, partly because it has practical implications and applications. This point is underscored by the importance and current popularity of what is called applied philosophy. It is my view that African philosophy must be seen as ideas that are sensitive to and shaped by the commonsense beliefs of Africans, in that these beliefs have practical implications and applications for people's real-life experiences. So, the pertinent challenge to the idea of communalism as a dominant philosophical theme, has to do with how this idea can be adequately articulated as a systematized idea or generalization that can reasonably capture the various or distinct communal practices in many African cultures. Hence, critics of this idea may ask, for instance, whether the idea of communalism can be shown to be similar in many African cultures, given that African cultures are so diverse and different. They may suggest that the efforts to articulate communalism rely on a caricature of the different practices in African traditions. Supposing it is plausible to articulate a systematized idea of communalism, how accurately will this idea describe what actually exists in many African cultures?

In order to illuminate my response to these issues, we must recollect and bear in mind that I am not trying to provide a factually accurate anthropological or sociological descriptive analysis of communalism in African cultures. Rather, I am doing a conceptual normative analysis of how communalism ought to be understood based on theoretical generalization and abstraction. Based on this kind of theoretical abstraction and generalizations about African cultures, Wiredu argues that, one feature that characterizes thoughts systems in most African cultures, is communalism and the various dimensions of the communalistic ethos. This ethos includes the idea that beliefs are held not on the basis of adequate evidence but on the basis of the authority and dictates of communal traditions and the elders, who are seen in a community as the repositories of knowledge and values.[38] Another feature is that people are morally educated informally, and they accept moral principles and act on them simply because they are dictated by the authority of tradition. Another feature is that there is overwhelming emphasis on the community and individuals' responsibilities to the community such that the will or autonomy of the individual is overridden by the dictates and interests of the community. Wiredu argues that African cultures and thought systems are characterized and plagued by three essential features: anachronism, supernaturalism, and authoritarianism.[39] These have led to the dearth of modernization in Africa.

In Wiredu's view, authoritarianism in African cultures involves the imposition of tradition and the unquestioning obedience of these traditions and the dictates of elders. This kind of authoritarianism, he argues, is pervasive in African cultures, saying: "The very atmosphere we breathe in many areas of life in our society seems to be suffused with an authoritarian odour. . . ."[40] The implication is that there is no rational independent thinking in traditional African culture. Moreover, people were not formally and 'rationally educated' to think and act rationally with respect to their beliefs or principles. Such structures, he argues, are not conducive to and cannot engender the kind of scientific, rational, analytic, systematic, and rigorous thinking and processes that are necessary to have and develop a philosophy. Wiredu suggests that because the authoritarianism in African cultures and the informal nature of their structure of training and imparting knowledge is devoid of rational and critical thinking, it tended more toward indoctrination. However, he also agrees that authoritarianism in African cultures derives in large part from the communal way of life, which is not only pervasive but is also a strong point in African cultures. For Wiredu, communalism is an important feature of African cultures and way of life.

However, the problem with the criticisms and characterizations of African traditions is that, as indicated, the relevant features that people have identified are only negative. In spite of the fact that these features or generalizations are negative, we must bear in mind that they are also understood as meaningfully or reasonable, in that they are seen as not being oblivious of the heterogenous cultures and traditions in Africa and the West. These features do not characterize each and every Western tradition as the same, and not all African traditions lack them in exactly the same way.[41] These features and generalizations are seen as having some relative merits, and they seem to make conceptual sense when understood as common or dominant themes. The problem is that many of these negative features, which have been used as the basis for comparing and contrasting African and Western traditions, have involved or emerged out of stereotypes, simple-minded abstractions, and unfair and unbalanced generalizations. Some positive features of African cultures such as communalism are criticized as having the negative implications of authoritarianism and indoctrination because they have not been properly analyzed, defended, and understood. Some of the features that people generalize about Africa, in virtue of which it is criticized, compared, and contrasted with the West, are that Africa is uncivilized, primitive, and without any thought systems. Or, if it has any thought system, it lacks systematization, rigor, rationality, critical analysis, and a written tradition. While scholars have focused on these negative features in African cultures and traditions, and have ignored positive features, they have also focused solely on the positive features in Western traditions, and they have, for the most part, ignored the negative features. In the standard comparison and contrast between African and Western philosophical traditions, the Western traditions are characterized positively as rational, scientific, rigorous, literate, analytic, systematic, and critical, while the African traditions are characterized as lacking these features.[42]

As a basis and motivation for my stance, I assume with some arguments, the relative theoretical or logical merits of the spirit of such generalizations, dichotomies, contrasts, and comparisons that are usually assumed by those who criticize or question the nature and existence of African philosophy. However, I wish to make these usual generalizations and comparison more balanced by indicating that one can use the idea of communalism as a positive feature or basis for making generalizations about Africa and for making comparisons and contrasts with the West. It is controversial whether the negative generalizations about Africa are true, and whether those that are true of some cultures and traditions in African are necessarily true of all. Lacinay Keita argues, for instance that, the cultures of ancient Egypt, North Africa, and many empires of Sub-Saharan Africa, such as Mali, Ghana, and Songhai, had sophisticated thought systems and some of the positive features that are used to identify Western thoughts.[43] In other words, these sophisticated cultures and traditions may not have had the negative features that are used to characterize Africa. Some have argued that these cultures, at various stages in history, may have exerted some influenced on Greek thought, which is, in part, the foundation of Western civilization, and Modern Europe and its development of science, industrial revolution, and technology.[44] It is reasonable to believe that this influence is true or plausible based on their interactions and the similarities in beliefs, ideas, and concepts. In some sense, the questioning of the existence and plausibility of a legitimate African philosophy by some Western and African scholars, seems to ignore these facts of history. Some argue that such questioning and denial of thought systems in Africa may be motivated by a number of different factors or reasons beyond those already discussed.

## Denying the Existence of African Philosophy

Some of these reasons are underpinned by factors or attitudes such as imperialism, cultural hegemony, and racism. These illegitimate reasons include the efforts to find some intellectual basis to justify racism with respect to the inferiority of people of African descent (Blacks or Negroes), which culminated in slavery, colonization, and christianization.[45] Examples or indications of such racist attitudes and prejudice abound. Consider the following comments by Hegel:

> At this point we leave Africa, not to mention it again. For it is no historical part of the world; it has no movement or development to exhibit. Historical movements in it—that is in its northern part—belong to the Asiatic or European World. . . . What we properly understand by Africa, is the Unhistorical, Undeveloped Spirit, still involved in the conditions of mere nature, and which has to be presented here only as on the threshold of the World's History.[46]

The racist beliefs that Africa does not have any philosophical tradition or set of ideas or that they are simply intellectually incapable of having a thought system, and have therefore, not contributed anything to civilization are still pervasive.

There is a need to respond to the racist attitudes that Africans do not have the rational ability to engage in any intellectual activities that can engender civilization.

So, some Western philosophers and scholars who raise the metaphilosophical issue of whether there is an African philosophy, or whether Africans have a Western-style of philosophy that is unique, or a comparable brand of philosophy in Africa, seem to do so for reasons other than the view that, African cultures cannot be methodologically treated as a monolith. One illegitimate reason for raising questions about the existence of African philosophy, as Hegel's comments among others indicate, is the pervasive idea underlying Western literature and movies that are replete with stereotypical views about Africa.[47] They indicate that Africa, which is ambiguously described as the 'Dark Continent' and its people are backward, irrational, uncivilized, primitive, and that they lack or are incapable of having a thought system or engaging in intellectual activities.[48] In other words, Africa does not have anything to contribute to World history and human civilization, and they did not, and cannot contribute anything to history and civilization. Even if they have a thought system, because it is characterized as lacking in rigor and it is not analytic, systematic, or rational, it is too inferior to be considered a meaningful contribution. This motivation for questioning African philosophy by some Western scholars is rooted in racist beliefs: that Africans lack intellect and rationality. As such, they do not have any rational thought system and cannot engage in the kind of systematic and critical examination of conceptual and abstract ideas that may be required in philosophy—that is, using the Western philosophical model as the paradigm. For instance, Levy-Bruhl characterized traditional Africans as primitive people with a pre-logical mentality.[49] He indicated that Africans are not capable of logical thinking because they seem to hold contradictory beliefs.

This effort to deny the existence of African philosophy sometimes involves the propagation of negative stereotypes about Africans in the literature.[50] A close look at some of the intellectual efforts that are used to propagate negative stereotypes about Africa, its people, cultures, beliefs, and values will reveal that they are illegitimate, in that they involve false and simple-minded generalizations. The efforts to offer an affirmative answer to the question of whether there is an African philosophy and to defend a positive view about its nature and existence via an analysis of communalism have arisen for me, in part, as a response to Hegel and other racist and stereotypical denigration of Africans and their thoughts or ideas. Although racism and stereotypical denigration of Africa and Africans are a motivation for my response and analysis of communalism as a philosophical theme in African philosophy, such motivation does not necessarily provide the justification for the stance I take and my arguments. My arguments are independent of my motivation. In other words, as I have indicated, my motivation may reflect nationalism and activism, but the rational effort to identify falsehoods and problems in these ideas and concepts, based on reasonable arguments, does not necessarily indicate nationalism and activism. The idea of establishing the theoretical, abstract, or logical reasonableness (or lack thereof) of ideas, concepts, beliefs, principles, and values, is precisely what philosophy is about or tries to do, irrespective of what these ideas and concepts refer to in reality.

But there is a metaphilosophical basis, reason, and justification for my stance that there is an African philosophy, which is based on a conception of philosophy that is given credence by the Western view of philosophy. In this sense, one may emphasize distinction between the *motivation* and *justification* for my stance. The response to racism may be a motivation in this case, but it is not the justification. The justification is rooted in a philosophical argument involving a metaphilosophical stance. This effort to respond to the negative and racist view of Africa, and the philosophical stance underlying it, which some have criticized as an activist and a nationalist approach to doing African philosophy is, in my view, a legitimate motivation. On the one hand, this kind of activism or nationalism is not irrational or inconsistent with philosophy, if it is based on rational arguments. On the other hand, it is consistent with the practical implication and dimension of philosophy. The idea of confronting racism in intellectual history involves an attempt to show that Africans are capable of the intellectual activity of philosophizing; and that Africa has some ancient intellectual traditions. These ancient traditions may not, in themselves, match the rigor, sophistication, and systematization of modern or contemporary thinkers or philosophy. But they need not match contemporary views in order for them to be characterized as philosophy. For instance, some of the ideas of the pre-Socratic philosophers, such as, Thales, Anaximander, and Anaximenes, do match the rigor of modern or contemporary philosophers. But they are considered philosophy.

The ideas of many of these pre-Socratic philosophers have provided some rudimentary data, issues, ideas or basis for some contemporary Western philosophical scholarship, in that many current philosophers are trying to make meaningful, interpret, systematize, and critically analyze these ancient ideas or issues. Usually, when contemporary philosophers infuse rigor and systematization into these ideas that are not in themselves rigorous and systematic, the result is considered legitimate philosophy. One might say that the efforts by philosophers to reconstruct and interpret these ancient ideas, by infusing rigor and systematization that did not exist in these ideas, involves some elements of activism; that is, these philosophers are motivated by some kind of activism. Also, the efforts by St Thomas Aquinas and St Augustine to rationally defend the ideas, doctrines, dogmas, and teachings of the Catholic Church are motivated by a philosophically healthy kind of activism and some attenuated sense of nationalism. They were motivated by their faith, hence, they were not critical. To be critical at that time would have been heresy. But their arguments were not based on and were independent of faith, and the adequacy of their defense and justifications can be evaluated independently of their motivation or faith.

The attitudes of activism and nationalism, as motivations, are therefore, not irrational or necessarily inconsistent with the idea of philosophy. Moreover, these attitudes are not alien to Western philosophical traditions. These activist attitudes are also manifested in the American philosophical tradition of pragmatism. Consider the following statements by MacKinnon:

> There are three dominant or focal beliefs through which our philosophical spirit [American pragmatism] can be articulated. First, the belief that thinking is primarily an *activity* in response to a concrete situation and that this activity is aimed at solving problems. Second, the belief that ideas and theories must have a 'cutting-edge' or *make a difference* in the conduct of people who hold them and in situations in which they live. Third, the belief that the earth can be *civilized* and obstacles to progress overcome by the application of knowledge.[51]

It is reasonable to argue that the three dominant beliefs indicated above from which American philosophy developed, which MacKinnon suggests has an activist orientation, may also provide a comparative justificatory basis for an activist and nationalist orientation in African philosophy. In this case, an activist view or a nationalistic defense of African philosophy must involve, firstly, responding to the concrete situation of racism and racial prejudice. This response must involve the efforts to solve this problem of racism and racial prejudice by trying to erase or disprove false racial beliefs and stereotypes. Secondly, such nationalistic view must also seek to make a difference, in terms of how African people live their lives, by drawing attention to and highlighting the merits of traditional African values such as communalism, and also using such values to make a difference in people's lives. Thirdly, the effort to articulate communalism as an African philosophical theme is rooted in the belief that even a racist can be 'civilized', educated, and intellectually, or perhaps, morally redeemed.

If racists and those who accept false and stereotypical beliefs about Africa and Africans are rational, then one can intellectually engage them and rationally change their minds by making them see the plausibility of the analysis of the idea of communalism in African cultures as a subject matter of African philosophy that indicates a positive feature and 'superior' aspect of African cultures and thought systems. It represents something that the West can learn from, which may also be considered to be an African contribution to universal philosophical thought. To the extent that the different manifestations of racism, imperialism, and cultural hegemony have led to some relative lack of progress in Africa, it can be overcome by the application of knowledge about African traditions to the African situation in order to change the hegemonic relationship between Africa and the Western economic and political powers. This effort reflects an attitude of activism and the practical aspect of philosophy, i.e., philosophy as praxis. Wiredu underscores this point with respect to this attitude of activism and nationalism by indicating that Africa must utilize philosophy to solve Africa's problems, such as lack of modernization, by trying to give philosophy an African practical orientation.[52] If one is to follow this practical spirit and the attitudes of activism and nationalism, then the relevant issue is, whether the racist, false, and stereotypical beliefs about Africa and Africans should be left unquestioned and whether the efforts to disprove them necessarily suggest philosophical activism and nationalism? Even if so, what is the problem with it—is such activism or nationalism necessarily bad?

Bodunrin argues that the kind of activism and nationalism motivating the efforts by African scholars to confront this implicit or explicit racism has prevented them from taking a rational, critical, and objective look at the African ideas and beliefs that they seek to defend.[53] As such, the defense of African philosophy by these 'activist and nationalist scholars' has led to a romanticization of African past, beliefs, cultures, and traditions, which Bodunrin has argued were not very glorious. This attempt, he indicates, is underscored, in part, by the honorific connotation of philosophy as representing the rational or intellectual basis for a people's civilization. This honorific connotation of philosophy cuts two ways: it provides the motivation for some racists to deny Africans of a philosophy or anything that is intellectually honorific, but it also provides a motivation for nationalistic African scholars to provide questionable ideas as philosophical ideas that represent Africa's intellectual tradition. The argument against some African scholars' response to this kind of racism is that their activist and nationalist motivation show that Africans have a stake in proving that there is an African philosophy as a way to establish that they are intelligent or rational. This motivation beclouds their critical and philosophical sensibilities, objectivity, and the kind of 'distancing' that is necessary to do philosophy and have a philosophy. As such, they are prone to accepting unwarranted ideas as philosophical, ideas that they would otherwise not accept if they had no stake in the matter.

This argument against the nationalistic African scholars has elements of the genetic and the *ad hominem* circumstantial fallacies because it conflates the notions of motivation and justification. It seeks to conflate the source or origin of an idea with the justification for that idea, and it concludes erroneously that the source or origin of a view is, essentially, its justification. The adequacy of the stances of the so-called nationalist scholars depends on the adequacy of their arguments and not the legitimacy of their motivation. So, the illegitimacy of their motivation or circumstance has nothing to do with the adequacy of their arguments. Bodunrin argues that some Africans consider the idea of questioning or denying the existence of an African philosophy as a way of casting aspersions on the intellectual abilities of Africans and the status of their intellectual traditions. As a response, Africans have sought to establish African philosophy to indicate that Africans have intellect.

In the process, some African intellectuals are quick to let any thing pass as an African philosophy, at least, to have something to showcase. They seem desperate to find something that they can designate as belonging to African intellectual tradition or African philosophy that is comparable to those of Western traditions. As such, some people have been less critical of African past, cultures, myths, dogmas, folklore, and belief systems. Many of the attempts to establish African philosophy on the basis of African ideas and traditions have not been rigorous and critical in their examination of these ideas and tradition.[54] Instead, they present mythologies, folklore, platitudes, dogmas, oral traditions that have not been critically examined, analyzed, or systematized as elements of African philosophy.

Bodunrin argues that we cannot answer the metaphilosophical questions about the nature and existence of African philosophy by uncritically reconstructing African past and its unsystematized ideas, beliefs, and values. He argues that the traditional African's answers to these questions may be based on error and ignorance that are usually not questioned by people. According to Bodunrin, "Rarely do men turn around to criticize themselves without some (usually external) impetus, rarely do men feel the necessity to provide justifications for their beliefs without some challenge."[55] He indicates that the only challenge to traditional African views has come from outside as a result of Africa's colonial contacts with Europeans. The fact that traditional Africans never sought to critically examine and justify their beliefs indicate that such beliefs had no justification or rational basis. In his view, philosophy must be founded on some rational basis; the idea of philosophy involves finding rational foundations, justifications, and arguments for beliefs. Along the same lines, Odera Oruka cautions that "the greatest disservice to Africa is to deny it reason and dress it in magic and extra-rational traditionalism."[56] The suggestion is that Africans who want to defend and affirm the existence of an African philosophy must be on their guard and must be critical so as to present the best and the most reasonable ideas in African cultures and traditions that can be showcased as representative of the best rational and intellectual activities in Africa. While there is an element of reasonableness to this admonishment, one must also be careful not to throw away the baby with the bath water, in one's effort to be overly critical—in a desperate effort to be an apologist for the West. Nkiru Nzegwu, Odia Ofiemu, and Olufemi Taiwo indicate that trying to be an apologist for a Western audience is a methodological problem or pitfall that is represented by the 'new Africanist' ideology and agenda.[57]

It is necessary to be circumspect in one's criticism so that one can be balanced in identifying problems while appreciating merits. It is wrong to argue, as I shall indicate, that African beliefs had no rational basis simply because people did not explicitly, consistently, and formally engage in the constant process of questioning, criticizing, and providing scrupulous justification. Because of an extreme critical stance, some people tend not to give enough credit to many African cultural and traditional values and beliefs such as communalism. It is easy for someone with an extreme critical stance to dismiss the idea of providing a coherent analysis of communalism as an effort to engage in a romanticization about African past. Moreover, Africans who adopt a nationalist and activist orientation are more likely to engage in such romanticization and less likely to be critical. Critics such as Bodunrin argue that communalism in African cultures is not as glorious as some may want to present. However, before criticizing the efforts to analyze and defend communalism in terms of some kind of nationalism and activism, one must understand its basis, rationale, context, processes, and goal, and more importantly, the arguments for the specific position I take with respect communalism, since activism or nationalism *per se* may not in itself be bad. Besides the efforts to respond to racism and the racist denigration of Africa and its culture, beliefs, and traditions, the kind of activism or nationalism that is exhibited by the efforts to prove the existence of African philosophy has also been necessitated by the troubling presumptuous imperialistic stance of some Western intellectuals about the presumed honorific view of the Western culture and its hegemony, as setting the standard used for judging other cultures.

Sandra Harding argues that, based on cultural hegemony and the efforts to denigrate other cultures and peoples, Europe has made conscious efforts to appropriate all forms of knowledge and intellectual traditions, often claiming as their own, ideas that Europe got from other lands during their voyages of discovery.[58] Such appropriation is one basis for some Westerner's denial of the existence of rational African thought or an African philosophy. If people know that Africans have a philosophy and what the nature of that philosophy is, then they will know that they are not as subhuman, primitive as the Western literature has painted them to be. The idea of an African philosophy will destroy the negative myths and stereotypes about Africans that some people want to perpetuate. It may also indicate or make clear that Africans do have intelligence to the extent that they actually contributed and can further contribute something to human and world civilization. All these factors may also help to undercut the intellectual basis for racism and slavery, and Western cultural hegemony, in that one of the implicit intellectual arguments for racism—that is usually not well or explicitly articulated—is that Africans are inferior, uncivilized, irrational, primitive, and subhuman. As pagans, they are also spiritually inferior and are in need of salvation. Many in Europe insisted, based on this racist attitude, that Africans need to be civilized, humanized, and christianized in order to contribute to their well-being and to save their souls.

The denigration of Africans and Africa was used as an intellectual basis for justifying colonialism and christianization. It was also implicitly argued that the subhuman nature of Africans justified their inhuman(e) treatments as slaves. So, another intellectual way to support this stance, stereotype, and negative generalization about Africans is to ignore their thought systems or to discredit them as irrational, illogical, uncritical, unsystematic, and dogmatic. All civilized thought systems and philosophies are claimed to have the honorific features that African thought systems are claimed to lack. Thus, there is the widespread denigration of African cultures and traditions as backward, undeveloped, and primitive. These features presuppose that there are some common themes or commonalities of African cultures, albeit negative. So, the debate about the existence of an African philosophy and the efforts or response to establish or prove its existence are based on a fundamental premise, namely, that there is something common to many African cultures —except that such commonalities are mostly negative: undeveloped, irrational, uncivilized, and uncritical. There are some Western intellectuals who want the intellectual themes in African cultures and traditions to remain negative, and they have sought to use every intellectual tool to ensure Western cultural hegemony and to deny to Africans any philosophical thought.

This point is troubling, on the one hand, according to Kwame Gyekye, because: "To deny to African people philosophical thought is to imply that they are unable to make philosophical sense of, or to conceptualize, their experiences; it is in fact to deny them humanity. For philosophy of some kind is behind the thought and action of every people. It constitutes the intellectual sheet-anchor of their life in its totality."[59] Gyekye argues that the philosophical ideas of African people are embedded and expressed in their everyday lives: their "real and vital attitudes."[60] Assuming Western philosophy as the standard and paradigm of philosophy, and denying Africans of a philosophy, based solely on the presumptuous assumption that Western philosophy is the standard, are troubling. On the other hand, in light of the controversial views of Martin Bernal and George James that the classical roots of Western civilization have Afro-Asiatic roots or were stolen from Africa, it is not clear how much we should attribute to the West what is now regarded as Western thought or philosophy.[61] George James argues that the efforts to deny and prevent people from knowing that there is an African pedigree for Western civilization is motivated in part by racism and the need to perpetuate the pervasive racist attitudes, as well as Western cultural hegemony. The interesting point about these controversial books is how little attention they have received in academia. It appears that Western intellectuals do not want to acknowledge the issues they raise. This is because to affirm the existence of an African philosophy is, in Gyekye's sense, to affirm their humanity, their ability to conceptualize, and provide a conceptual basis for their lives, beliefs, values, and experiences. The nationalist affirmation of African philosophy therefore involves a denial of Western assumptions of the inferiority of Africans in terms of their rationality and ability to engage in intellectual activities.

# African Philosophy and the 'New Africanist' Agenda

So, my attempt to examine communalism as a philosophical theme in the moral thought of African cultures in order to establish the existence of African philosophy is not going to treat various African cultures separately. Nor do I attempt to suggest a unity among all African cultures, any more than a unity among all Western cultures. In other words, I do not suggest that African or Western thought systems are monolithic. But, I insist that there is a legitimate conceptual basis to discuss communalism as an idea that is common to many or most African cultures and traditions. In trying to reconstruct, conceptualize, defend, and analyze the African idea of communalism from an African point of view, I see myself as an 'Africanist' in two senses: (1) I see myself as a research scholar in the area or subject matter of Africa; (2) I see myself as a defender of an African perspective, that is, someone who takes pride in the beliefs, views, thoughts of Africa. In this second sense, I am motivated partly by a kind of nationalism (Africanism) and I have an activist attitude in my efforts to defend African ideas. But such pride has nothing to do with the justifications I offer for the views or ideas being defended. So, as an African (a person with an African heritage), and as an Africanist who is trained in Western philosophy, and who in various ways, have imbibed Western culture, I have to make a concerted effort not to fall into some of the methodological pitfalls that Nkiru Nzegwu, Odia Ofiemu, and Olufemi Taiwo refer to as the 'new Africanist' ideology and agenda.[62]

The 'new Africanist', in Nzegwu's view, is usually "at home in the social and economic structures of dominance of the Western cultural and intellectual traditions."[63] Not only is the 'new Africanist', in their view, familiar with the literature of the leading intellectual traditions of the West, he must also be willing to engage in the difficult task of making Africa look intelligible to people in the West who are interested in Africa. In some sense, the 'new Africanist' appears to be an apologist to the West, in that he is trying to defend an African position to a Western audience. Yes, there is a sense in which I am at home in the Western traditions and familiar with the literature on the leading intellectual traditions of the West having been trained in the analytic tradition of Western philosophy. Moreover, what I am doing in this work is an attempt to show how the idea of communalism in African cultures and its role in moral reasoning and moral thought can be made intelligible to a Western audience that is interested in Africa. However, I do not think that I am defending the idea of communalism solely to a Western audience, as Nzegwu claims the new Africanist is trying to do. I am also speaking to African intellectuals who argue against or doubt the existence of African philosophy, that is, a philosophy that is culled out of African ethnophilosophy. I speak to Africans whose understanding and views of communalism can be illuminated, sharpened, and deepened. I also speak to African city dwellers who have internalized the Western individualistic way of life that is created by modernization and urbanization, and have ignored their own traditions and the Africa traditional communal ways of life. Thus, there are many Africans who can learn from my conceptual analysis and defense and have a better understanding of the communal system, beyond their ordinary view of it as a lived experience.

Moreover, there are some Africans who also see the idea of communalism solely from a negative and stereotypical Western view that is pervasive in the literature. Usually, these people use these half-baked stereotypical views that have not been examined and analyzed to criticize the idea of communalism in Africa. Although I project my analysis in "the familiar voice the West understands"[64] in terms of the method, concepts, or language of analysis, I do not do so with respect to the subject matter of my analysis, which, in this case, involves communalism, moral thought, moral reasoning, and moral education in the context of African cultures. In fact, the contents of my analysis seek to criticize and object to "the familiar voice the West understands." I also do not think that I am assuring the West of my political or theoretical allegiance as the 'new Africanist' wants to do in Nzegwu's view. In fact, the attempt here with respect to my analysis of communalism in African cultures is to affirm its philosophical legitimacy as an African idea as well as my 'allegiance' to such an African idea. Hence, I see myself as an Africanist with a nationalistic attitude. My defense of communalism involves a critique of the dominant liberal individualistic theoretical and political view in the West. In fact, my critique of the universalist conception of philosophy as parochial involves an internal 'methodological revolt' against analytic philosophy—the tradition in which I am trained—as opposed to affirming my unqualified allegiance to it. Perhaps, I also indicate some allegiance to this tradition because I use its own tools and methods to undercut it and to show its shortcomings.

According to Nzegwu, assuring the West of one's theoretical allegiance involves the new Africanist in another methodological pitfall. The 'new Africanist' "must provide a sweeping overview of continental events [and issues in Africa] which awes, by virtue of its analytic brilliance, but which rests on old stereotypical assumptions about Africa, its social relations, and traditions."[65] This is instructive because there is a sense in which my treatment of communalism in African cultures may be viewed by some critics as a sweeping overview or generalization that is based on a stereotype about African cultures. However, my attempt—without being unduly modest—is to show some 'analytical brilliance' by providing a *positive* view of the theme of communalism in African cultures, in order to rescue it from the claws or jaws of the pervasive negative stereotype that it engenders in the West. So, my efforts go beyond simply trying to turn a negative stereotype into a positive one by giving credence to the philosophical idea of communalism as a reasonable basis for explaining social relations and traditions in Africa. In other words, I do not think that I am analyzing and defending African communalism by trying to "simulate the form and manner of the West and the West's imagined idea of Africa and its culture."[66] I seek to provide a view of communalism that is sensitive to the African lived experiences and ways of life. In this sense, communalism is of interest to Africa and Africans, in that it provides a plausible conceptual and rational bases for explaining the reality and experiences in African cultures and perhaps, their own identity in the midst of Western culture.

Although I am doing something akin to a translation, interpretation, or reconstruction, in terms of an analysis of an African philosophical theme or concept, I am not necessarily doing this, solely, on the basis of Western categories of thought and its modes of explaining reality. I avoid the following pitfall indicated by Nzegwu. According to her, because a

> desired translation of the conceptual . . . and philosophical issues of Africa into Western imagination is conducted on the basis of the latter's categories of thought and its privileged philosophical explanation of reality, the new Africanist, in most cases, has to forgo the meaningful issues that are of interest to Africa. She or he must necessarily ignore what is believed to be a 'trifling' problem of distortions and erasures of Africa's conception of world-being that underpin family life, structures, and relationships.[67]

Perhaps, the aim of this project is to address the problem of distortions, errors, and erasures in Africa's mode of organizing and explaining their experience. I also seek to criticize the conceptual categories of the West and the requirement that an explanation of an African concept must be done from a Western perspective. I obviously do not consider the issue of distortions or errors in African views, which have led to the negative views of Africa, a trifle. This is because many Africans tend to ignore and do not fully appreciate, at least in comparative terms, some of the values and ideas underlying their own cultures. Many are not able to understand and appreciate the intricacies of their own culture, in order to use it as a basis for critically examining the Western alternative. They uncritically accept Western ideas and then use them as the basis for denigrating their own African cultures. In my view, a proper understanding of communalism may provide Africans a plausible basis for evaluating the Western alternative ways of life in order to determine what in general one may accept or reject. By doing this, they are more likely to see from a proper perspective, what to reject about their own culture and what to accept from Western cultures in order to modernize.

Many Africans do not or cannot take pride in their cultures and values because they do not fully appreciate their merits. They do not appreciate them because they do not understand their philosophical underpinnings as the basis for their own set of values. The result is that there has been a drift toward what people might call a kind of 'colonial mentality' and the rejection of their own cultural values in favor of the uncritical acceptance of Western values. In other words, many Africans see their own cultural values in pejorative terms, in terms of how they have been presented in and by the West. They see many values of the West in honorific terms because proper and coherent articulations of African values are not available for them to use as the critical basis for Western alternatives. An analysis of these fundamental African values is pertinent and relevant to Africans and others. To the extent that what I do here is diametrically opposed to what the so-called new Africanist does, I do not see myself as falling into the methodological and attitudinal pitfalls of the new Africanist. In fact, the attempt here is to undercut "the new Africanist firm conviction that salient aspects of Africa's traditional values [such as communalism] can be discarded or modified to blend with salient aspects of Euro-Americanized cultural values."[68] What I argue is that communalism, as a fundamental basis for African values, has some advantages which Africans should retain. I criticize the current or 'new' condition for imperialism, which involves a mode of thinking that dictates that Africans must accept and imbibe everything that is Western, especially, its individualistic, liberal, and autonomy-based values and epistemology. I indicate that the West have some lessons to learn from understanding and appreciating African idea of communalism.

# Notes

1. See Segun Gbadegesin, "*Eniyan*: The Yoruba Concept of A Person." in *The African Philosophy Reader*, eds., P. H. Coetzee and A. P. J. Roux (London: Routledge, 1998), 175. Gbadegesin argues against the idea of generalizing about all African societies or cultures. On the other hand, Kwame Gyekye. *An Essay On African Philosophical Thought: The Akan Conceptual Scheme*, rev. ed. (Philadelphia: Temple University Press, 1995), 129-138, argues that it is plausible to generalize about all African cultures on some issues or ideas because they are shared in common.

2. J. A. A. Ayoade, "Time in Yoruba Thought;" Richard C. Onwuanibe. "The Human Person and Immortality in IBO Metaphysics," both in *African Philosophy: An Introduction*, ed. Richard A. Wright (New York: University Press of America, 1984). Also, see Kwame Gyekye, "The Akan Concept of a Person," *International Philosophical Quarterly* 18 (1978): 277-287. Reprinted in, *African Philosophy: An Introduction*, ed. Richard A. Wright (New York: University Press of America, 1984). And J. O. Sodipo, "Notes on the Concept of Cause and Change in Yoruba Traditional Thought," *Second Order* 2, no 2, (1973): 12-20.

3. Kolawole A. Owolabi, "The Quest for Method in African Philosophy: A Defense of the Hermeneutic-Narrative Approach," *The Philosophical Forum* 32, no. 2 ( 2001): 147-163.

4. These points about the task and data of philosophy are made by Nicholas Rescher, *Philosophical Reasoning: A Study in the Methodology of Philosophizing*, 15-17.

5. Barbara Mackinnon, "Epilogue–Is There An American Philosophy?" in *American Philosophy: A Historical Anthology*, ed. Barbara MacKinnon (Albany, NY: State University of New York Press, 1985), 675.

6. Mackinnon, "Epilogue—Is There An American Philosophy?" 667-679.

7. Segun Gbadegesin, "*Eniyan*: The Yoruba Concept of A Person," 175.

8. Gyekye, *An Essay on African Philosophical Thought: The Akan Conceptual Scheme*, 191.

9. Gyekye, *An Essay on African Philosophical Thought*, 191.

10. Kwasi Wiredu, *Philosophy and An African Culture* (London: Cambridge University Press, 1980), 6-7.

11. Kofi Antubam, *Ghana's Heritage of Culture* (Leipzig: Koehler and Amelang, 1963). Cited in Wiredu. *Philosophy and An African Culture*, p. 7.

12. Wiredu, *Philosophy and An African Culture*, p. 7. (I shall explore fully the relevance of these themes to the issue of morality, moral thinking, and moral education in the course of this project.)

13. Wiredu, *Philosophy and An African Culture*, p. 7.

14. Fred Lee Hord (Mzee Lasana Okpara) and Jonathan Scott Lee, eds., *I Am Because We Are: Readings in Black Philosophy* (Amherst, MA: University of Massachusetts Press, 1995), 7.

15. This kind of objection to the idea of African culture or thought is very commonplace in print. Moreover, in spite of the successful numerous attempt to justify the idea in print, people have been either impervious to the reasonableness of the idea or have been simply oblivious of it. I know this for a fact because of my personal experience. I have attended numerous conferences, and have received numerous reviews from journal reviewers raising this problem as a fundamental methodological problem in all the numerous papers where I have attempted to rationally defend a theme or themes or set of themes, mode of thinking, and beliefs in African cultures.

16. Peter P. Ekeh, *Social Exchange Theory: The Two Traditions* (Cambridge, MA: Harvard University Press, 1974), 3.

17. Ekeh, *Social Exchange Theory: The Two Traditions*, 9.

18. Edmund Gettier, "Is Justified True Belief Knowledge?" *Analysis* 23 (1963):121-123.

19. Hord and Lee, *I Am Because We Are: Readings in Black Philosophy*, 6.

20. Rescher, *Philosophical Reasoning: A Study in the Methodology of Philosophizing*, 39.

21. Rescher, *Philosophical Reasoning: A Study in the Methodology of Philosophizing*, 8.

22. This stance can be found in the following works among others: P. O. Bodunrin, "The Question of African Philosophy," *Philosophy* 56 (1981). Reprinted in African Philosophy: An Introduction, ed., Richard A. Wright (New York: University Press of America, 1984), 1-23. Wiredu, *Philosophy and An African Culture*, Kwasi Wiredu, *Cultural*

*Universals and Particulars: An African Perspective* (Indianapolis, IN: Indiana University Press, 1996), Paulin Hountondji, *African Philosophy: Myth and Reality* (Bloomington: Indiana University Press, 1983). And Kwame Anthony Appiah, *Necessary Questions: An Introduction to Philosophy* (Englewood Cliffs, NJ: Prentice Hall, 1989).

23. See Bodunrin, "The Question of African Philosophy." Appiah, *Necessary Questions: An Introduction to Philosophy.* Kwame Anthony Appiah, *In My Father's House: Africa in the Philosophy of Culture* (New York: Oxford University Press, 1992).

24. Appiah, *Necessary Questions: An Introduction to Philosophy*, 201-207.

25. Appiah, *Necessary Questions: An Introduction to Philosophy*, 201-214.

26. Polycarp Ikuenobe, "Analytic Method, Logical Positivism, and the Criticism of Ethnophilosophy," *Metaphilosophy* 35, no. 4, (July 2004): 479-503.

27. Appiah, *Necessary Questions: An Introduction to Philosophy*, 203.

28. Appiah, *Necessary Questions: An Introduction to Philosophy*, 201-207.

29. Rescher, *Philosophical Reasoning: A Study in the Methodology of Philosophizing,* Chapter one.

30. Wiredu, *Philosophy and An African Culture*, 16.

31. Pierre Hadot, *What is Ancient Philosophy?* Trans. by Michael Chase (Harvard University Press, 2002).

32. Wiredu, *Philosophy and An African Culture*, 16.

33. MacKinnon, *American Philosophy: A Historical Anthology*, 675.

34. Patrick Riley, "A Possible Explanation of Rousseau's General Will," in *The Social Contract Theorists: Critical Essays on Hobbes, Locke, and Rousseau*, ed. Christopher W. Morris (Lanham, MD: Rowman & Littlefield Publishers Inc., 1999), 167-89.

35. See Bodunrin, "The Question of African Philosophy," for this kind of argument and why ethnophilosophy is not a philosophy and why African ethnophilosophy cannot pass as an African philosophy.

36. See Bertrand Russell, *A History of Western Philosophy* (London: George Allen and Unwin, 1975).

37. Rescher, *Philosophical Reasoning: A Study in the Methodology of Philosophizing*, 15-16.

38. Wiredu, *Philosophy and An African Culture*, chapters 1 & 2.

39. Wiredu, *Philosophy and An African Culture*, 1.

40. Wiredu, *Philosophy and An African Culture*, 3.

41. See Lacinay Keita, "The African Philosophical Tradition," In *African Philosophy: An Introduction,* ed. Richard A. Wright, 57-76. Keita argues that some African traditions have many of the positive features that are identified in Western philosophical traditions.

42. See Bodunrin, "The Question of African Philosophy," Appiah, *Necessary Questions: An Introduction to Philosophy,* and Wiredu, *Philosophy and An African Culture.*

43. Keita, "The African Philosophical Tradition."

44. See Sandra Harding, *Is Science Multicultural?: Postcolonialism, Feminisms, and Epistemologies* (Bloomington, IN: Indiana University Press, 1998), especially chap. 3, Martin Bernal, *Black Athena: The Afroasiatic Roots of Classical Civilization Vols. I and II* (New Brunswick, NJ: Rutgers University Press, 1988), George James, *Stolen Legacy*

(Newport News, VA: United Brothers Communications Systems, 1989). Keita. "The African Philosophical Tradition," 57-76. C. A. Diop, *The African Origin of Civilization* (New York: Lawrence and Company, 1974).

45. A similar point is made by James, *Stolen Legacy*. He argues that Western scholars have denied or ignored *the* or *an* African source, pedigree, or influence of Greek philosophy and Western civilization as a result of racism. Also see Emmanuel Eze, *Race and Enlightenment* (London: Blackwell Publishers, Ltd., 1997). Eze analyzes a numbers of intellectuals and a body of works, including philosophers such as Hume, Kant, and Hegel who purported to provide the rational basis for racism and imperialism. These intellectuals argued that Africans were too inferior and lacked the kind of intelligence to produce any intellectual work.

46. Georg Hegel, *The Philosophy of History,* trans. by J. Sibree (New York: Dover, 1956), 99.

47. See Emmanuel Eze, *Race and Enlightenment.*

48. Predicating Africa of 'dark' is ambiguous because it could mean a continent with people that have dark skin color or it has a negative and pejorative connotation of being primitive, uninformed, and uncivilized.

49. L. Levy-Bruhl, *How Natives Think* (London: Allen & Unwin, 1926).

50. See Richard J. Hernstein and Charles Murray, *The Bell Curve: Intelligence and Class Structure in American Life* (New York: The Free Press, 1994), Parker English, "Nigerian Ethnophilosophy, Unitary Experience, and Economic Development," *Journal of Social Philosophy* 22, no.1 (1991): 102-124. English argues that what he observed in Nigeria provides proof for the view that African thought systems or modes of thinking lack validity, formal logical consistency, and clarity.

51. John E. Smith, *Spirit of American philosophy* (Albany, NY: SUNY Press, 1983), 188, quoted in Barbara MacKinnon, *American Philosophy: A Historical Anthology,* 673.

52. Wiredu, *Philosophy and An African Culture,* 26-36

53. Bodunrin, "The Question of African Philosophy," 3.

54. Bodunrin, "The Question of African Philosophy," 3-4.

55. Bodunrin, "The Question of African Philosophy," 4.

56. Odera Oruka "African Philosophy" in *Contemporary Philosophy: A New Survey, Vol. 5: African Philosophy,* ed. Guttorm Floistad (Dordrecht: Martinus Nijhorff, 1987), 66.

57. See Nkiru Nzegwu, "Questions of Identity and Inheritance: A Critical Review of Kwame Anthony Appiah's *In My Father's House,*" *Hypatia* 11, no. 1 (Winter 1996): 175-201; Odia Ofiemu, "Africa's Many Mansions," *West Africa* (July 20-26, 1992):1231-32. Olufemi Taiwo, "Appropriating Africa: An Essay on new African Schools," *Issue: A Journal of Opinion* 23, no. 1 (1995): 39-45.

58. Handing, *Is Science Multicultural?: Postcolonialism, Feminisms, and Epistemologies,* especially, chap. 3.

59. Gyekye, "The Akan Concept of a Person," 200.

60. Gyekye, "The Akan Concept of a Person," 200.

61. Bernal, *Black Athena: The Afroasiatic Roots of Classical Civilization,* and James, *Stolen Legacy.*

62. See Nzegwu, "Questions of Identity and Inheritance," Odia Ofiemu,"Africa's Many Mansions,"and Taiwo, "Appropriating Africa: An Essay on new African Schools."

63. Nzegwu, "Questions of Identity and Inheritance." 175.

64. Nzegwu, "Questions of Identity and Inheritance." 175.

65. Nzegwu, "Questions of Identity and Inheritance." 175.

66. Nzegwu, "Questions of Identity and Inheritance." 175-6.

67. Nzegwu, "Questions of Identity and Inheritance." 176.

68. Nzegwu, "Questions of Identity and Inheritance." 177.

# Chapter Two

# African Conceptions of Personhood and Community

In order to understand and fully appreciate the nature of communalism in African cultures as a way of life and as a philosophical or normative theory and practice, one must understand the conceptions of a person, community, and the relationship between a community and a person. These conceptions must also be seen in relation to the African ideas and practice of morality, moral thought, moral reasoning, and moral education. The relationship between an individual and her community and the responsibility that is dictated by this relationship indicate the foundation for moral reasoning, moral principles, and moral education in African cultures. There are two plausible conceptions of personhood: metaphysical (descriptive) and normative. In the African view, the idea of a person has descriptive and normative dimensions.[1] Gail Presbey indicates this point about the African concept of personhood by indicating that the normative conception of personhood is based on an intragroup moral and social recognition. According to her, "the Massai (and some other African groups') concepts of 'personhood' are not to be understood primarily as metaphysical stances on the nature of the self, but rather as descriptions of intragroup recognition."[2] The recognition of a person implies that there are normative standards of recognition. The standards that are normatively used to describe a recognized person indicate a moral view of personhood. Thus, the moral view of a person, which is based on the social and moral identity that a person has or acquires comes from social recognition.

For Presbey, "Recognition of a person comes at different levels, both when one achieves the benchmarks of success (as outlined by the society in a conformist sense), and for some, when they excel in an individualist way, for example as heroes or healers, in what Honneth describes as the transition from 'person' to 'whole person'."[3] By contrast, a descriptive or metaphysical conception of person-hood seeks to analyze the ontological make-up of a person. It examines whether a person is material or immaterial, or whether a person is made up of one or two essential natures. For instance, the metaphysical analysis of the nature of the mind and body and the relationship between them is a descriptive account of person-hood.[4] As a matter of emphasis, it is the normative conception of a person that is relevant to the idea of communalism in African traditions. So, the conception of a person that I am concerned about is not a purely metaphysical conception, but a normative (social and moral) conception of a person. However, such a normative conception or dimension of a person does illuminate, and in some sense, depend on the metaphysical conception or descriptive dimension of a person. One cannot be described as a person if one has not satisfied the normative dimension and one cannot satisfy the normative criteria if one does not have the descriptive features of a person. You cannot evaluate an 'object' as failing to satisfy the criteria of moral personhood if such 'object' does not satisfy the descriptive and metaphysical features of being a person or human being. An object, X, must satisfy the meta-physical criteria of personhood before X is can be evaluated, recognized, and said to have satisfied the communal criteria of personhood.

Moreover, the normative conceptions of personhood and community provide the foundation for an understanding of African ontology, which indicates the con-crete reality and circumstances that help to account for the personal and social life of people. A community, in a normative sense, is a group of normative persons, principles, processes, and structures that defines social norms or moral expectations and responsibilities, on the basis of which a person is recognized and the commu-nity is sustained. The moral or social recognition of a person depends, in part, on the metaphysical view that a person is not a deterministic or 'determined' physical object that is governed solely by physical laws over which a person has no control. The normative view of personhood also depends on the idea that a person has a mind, is metaphysically free, is capable of rational, voluntary, and moral agency, and hence can be ascribed moral responsibility.[5] Without this assumption about a person, one cannot contribute to a community and there will be no basis for evalu-ating one for communal recognition. Verhoef and Michel indicate that "an individ-ual is obligated to contribute to the community not because it is expected of him or her, but because *it [the community] is* him or her."[6] So, personhood is norma-tively and descriptively tied to the community such that one's moral obligations and rights derive from such a normative and descriptive connection. A person is described in terms of his community, his responsibility, and social status in the community. According to Gyekye, "The individual is by nature a social (commu-nal) being, yes; but she is, also by nature, other things as well; that is, she possesses other attributes that may also be said to constitute her nature."[7] So, the idea of communalism in African traditions as analyzed here represents a normative theory about what a moral person, community, and their connection ought to be according to African thought systems. I draw from a few African traditions to illustrate this normative view about community and personhood.

One important element of communalism in African cultures involves this normative conception of personhood, community, and the connection between them. However, this is not to suggest that all African cultures, such as, Igbo, Luo, Akan, Azande, Bokis, or Kikuyu have exactly the same normative conception of personhood or that each and every culture in Africa hold or subscribe to a normative conception of personhood. It is important to understand the idea of communalism as a common element or dominant feature in African cultural traditions, at least, on the level of theoretical abstraction. We must bear in mind that my analysis of communalism as a common feature of African cultures is not a factual description of a feature of each and every African culture. The normative conception of personhood is plausible because of the conception of community and its place in African people's normative conceptual scheme. In other words, the idea of community is a conceptual foundation on which most African ideas, beliefs, values, ontology, cosmology, and ways of life are grounded. Anything that exists or is believed to exist must have some connection with the community. In Menkiti's view, the community has metaphysical, conceptual, and normative dimensions. For him the "community, which embraces both the living and the dead [ancestors], not surprisingly, is bound by considerations of mutual concern— paternal care on the part of the ancestors and filial piety on the part of the living."[8] The idea of community is also the logical and epistemic foundation of the normative conception of a person and the basis for a person's own view of self-identity and ways of doing things.

For instance, Verhoef and Michel argue that "the concept of person in the African world-view is first and most importantly that of community . . . this means not that the individual is selfless, but that the self is the community."[9] The self is ontologically, cosmologically, spiritually, and normatively connected to the community. This sense of communalism provides the foundation for African ways of life, logic, and mode of reasoning. To some extent, one cannot understand the rationality of the beliefs and thoughts among Africans if such thoughts and beliefs are not placed in the context of this communalistic logic and conceptual scheme. Just as people communally hold land and property in common with relatives and kinsfolk, they also hold ideas, beliefs, values, conceptual scheme, and attitudes in common with the people in the community in which they live as part of their tradition. Traditional African people lived in closely-knit communities: traditional African societies were founded on this idea of communalism and sustained as a community of shared beliefs and values that transcended the individual person. So, the community is at the center of every activity, practice, belief, and value. One's community helps to shape one's ways of life, values, attitudes, ways of seeing things, and methods of doing things. A community also shapes the moral and social identity of an individual that indicates his or her moral personhood.

This African communalistic ethos, on the basis of which personhood is conceived normatively, can be illuminated when contrasted with the liberal individualistic ethos on the basis of which personhood is conceived in Western thought. Ifeanyi A. Menkiti alludes to this contrast as follows:

> Whereas most Western views of man abstract this or that feature of the lone individual and then proceed to make it the defining or essential characteristic which entities aspiring to the description 'man' must have, the African view of man denies that persons can be defined by focusing on this or that physical or psychological characteristic of the lone individual. Rather, man is defined by reference to the environing community. As John Mbiti notes, the African view of the person can be summed up in this statement: 'I am because we are, and since we are, therefore I am'.[10]

The conclusion that Menkiti draws from this African conception of a person is that the needs, reality, and existence of the community is *logically prior* to those of the individual. In fact the interests and needs of the individual derive from those of the community. The attitudes, sentiments, motives, intentions, mental, and moral dispositions of an individual are formed by virtue of her belonging to a community. So, "the sense of self-identity which the individual comes to possess cannot be made sense of except by reference to these collective facts."[11] In the African view of a person, just as the community helps to normatively define the individual as a person rather than as "some isolated static quality or rationality, will, or memory,"[12] so also is the moral person defined by the moral principles and expectations of the community.

In other words, the moral self is not the Western liberal, rational, autonomous, solipsistic, atomistic, and individualistic self that is exemplified, for instance, in Kantian ethics and metaphysics. So, the moral person is not just the rational and autonomous individual who is capable of reasoning independently about universal and objective principles. Rather, the moral person in the African view is a rational, emotional, and autonomous person who has been sufficiently equipped by the normative attitudes, structures, and principles of his community. It is not enough for a person to have the requisite descriptive features and the rational or cognitive categories of understanding, conceptual scheme, and metaphysical freedom, in terms of being able to make free choices. A moral person in the African view must, in addition to these categories and freedom, also have the requisite attitudes, emotions, principles, values, and norms that give credence to caring, sympathy, and relationships. A moral person must also have or exhibit some requisite facts or features about people, relationships, and the community to which the rational categories of understanding and conceptual scheme can be applied. These principles and values circumscribe the range of things to which freedom, autonomy, rational or cognitive abilities, and conceptual scheme are applied. In this regard, the human moral person is fundamentally, according to Onwuanibe, a subject in whom values are imparted; he is not simply an object that can be analyzed in terms of physical and metaphysical characteristics.[13]

## Western and African Views of Personhood

Lee and Hord give credence to the communalist idea of realizing personhood in a community by arguing that the communalism that defines traditional African culture, which is the basis for black philosophical tradition, "is the idea that the identity of the individual is never separable from the sociocultural environment. Identity is not some Cartesian abstraction grounded in a solipsistic self-consciousness; rather, it is constructed in and at least partially by a set of shared beliefs, patterns of behaviour, and expectations."[14] So, instead of defining the individual self in terms of Descartes' 'thinking I' (*cogito*) and using it as the basis for individual identity, we find in the African culture, an affirmation of the existing community ('we are') as a basis for defining the identity of the existent and thinking self ('I am'). It appears, therefore, that in African cultures, the moral or social account of a person is logically or conceptually prior to the metaphysical account of a person, as opposed to the modern Western philosophical tradition where the metaphysical account of a person as the thinking, rational, autonomous, free individual is logically prior to the moral account as someone who may be shaped by a community. In the Western liberal moral account of a person, credence is not given to the influence of the community because the individual is seen as an autonomous rational individual who has the freedom to decide whether or not to accept the norms of a community and how he uses them to guide his conduct. The individual has a choice whether or not to belong to a particular community.

The Western liberal individualistic perspective indicates that the community is nothing but the aggregate of all the individuals who choose to belong to the group. So, moral personhood, on the Western view, is not dependent on social recognition and social responsibility. A human being is a moral person or agent just in case he or she is capable of acting rationally and autonomously. However, both the African and Western views appreciate the coextensive nature of the metaphysical and moral views of a person. It is pertinent to use these points to further underscore the comparison and contrast between the Western individualistic and African communalistic conceptions of personhood. In contrasting the African view with the Western view, Menkiti argues, the indexical 'we' in African thought systems—as a reference to the group or community—is not simply the aggregated sum of individuals comprising a community. Instead, the 'we' as used here in African cultures refers to "a thoroughly fused collective 'we'."[15] In other words, the 'we' in African cultures is a transcendental or organic 'we' and cannot be reduced to its component parts. It is in this regard that the self is indeed the community.[16] The individual self is, by various organic processes, *constituted* by the community and the community is an *organically fused collectivity* of the individual selves. The 'we' is a reference to some enduring traditions, structures, interests, values, beliefs, and transcendental selves, which cannot be pinned down or reduced to the set of individuals and institutions that make up the community.

In African thought, the community that the 'we' refers to includes traditions, values, and 'spiritual selves' that are metaphysically connected to living people, dead, ancestors, and posterity. The dead are thus a part of the community. Onwuanibe underscores this point by indicating that: "The Ibos do not bury their dead abroad . . . the dead are buried in graves around the home, even in the courtyard of the home; for the deceased members of the family, especially fathers, are said to be present [as part of the community], and are invoked on occasions especially in time of crisis."[17] So, the 'we' in African cultures—a metaphysically and morally fused 'we'—refers to a transcendental community that is based on a moral and concrete tradition, and a social and spiritual reality. The metaphysical and moral connections between a community of values, tradition, and ancestors, and the individuals, which are expressed in terms of social responsibilities and recognition, seem to define moral personhood or self. Myers underscores this point by indicating that the "Self in this instance includes all the ancestors, the yet unborn . . . and the entire community."[18] The tradition, ancestral spirits, and the existential concrete and social reality are a part of the elements in the African view of ontology that fuse the group together into a human community. From the above accounts, it is clear that there is a difference between the Western rational, liberal, and individualistic view of a person, and the African collective, communalistic, and normative view of a person. These differences with respect to the dynamics of a community and its culture will have implications in terms of how people see and identify themselves as individuals.

For the individualist, people see and identify themselves descriptively as metaphysically isolated individuals who have personhood outside and irrespective of the normative and cultural structures of a community and the human relationships that define and sustain a community. For the communalist, people see and identify themselves in terms of how their community trains, shapes, and morally educates them to acquire personhood, and how their moral thinking is shaped by the context of the community with respect to their actions and behavior. Thus, a person is not just a physical or metaphysical object, but a social, communal, or moral subject or self. Onwuanibe insists that we cannot adequately capture the full essence of personhood on the basis of metaphysics alone because a person's aspirations, emotions, values, responsibilities, and relative achievements do not make full sense when viewed from the perspective of materialism and immaterialism. Hence, in his view, "True personhood, as pure subject, is not something that can be analyzed into anything. . . . Personhood is a manifestation or presence even through a body, but never identifiable with it."[19] The notion of a human person makes sense only if it is construed in terms of its physical and transcendental social and moral characteristics. The transcendental aspect of the person, in virtue of which it is fully integrated into the community, includes the material body, the mental, affective, spiritual, and the social values and responsibilities, which provide the normative basis for one's fully integrated identity as a person. Segun Gbadegesin alludes to this point by indicating that the Yoruba concept of a person "has a normative dimension as well as an ordinary meaning,"[20] where we may understand the 'ordinary meaning' to indicate the physical or metaphysical dimension. You need the two meanings to make a robust sense of a person that is a fully integrated moral self. Thus, the moral self in African cultures is a robust, holistic, normative, communal and fully integrated self. Such self or something akin to it, Clifford Geertz has described as "a bounded, unique, more or less integrated, motivational and cognitive universe, a dynamic centre of awareness, emotion, judgment and action, organised into a distinctive whole and set contrastively against other such wholes, and against a social and natural background."[21]

So, in Menkiti's view, the notion of an individual who is not normatively shaped by the community, but is seen as an abstract dangling personality, does not make sense in African cultures. For him, the idea of 'personhood' which is defined by the community is fundamentally a moral notion that includes a set of rights that is acquired developmentally by a process of participation is communal life. As a moral notion, it presupposes some descriptive features about the community that provide the norms that are applied to and internalized by the individual as guide for conduct. According to this developmental normative process, the idea of personhood is a spectrum consisting of different shades or levels of personhood. A person can progress developmentally from the status of an 'it' as a child to full personhood as an adult, to perhaps, 'elderhood', and subsequently, 'ancestorhood'. The developmental stages toward the acquisition of personhood may vary from culture to culture. These stages may represent age groups, where each group is defined not necessarily in terms of chronological age but in terms of responsibility, achievements, and recognition. If you have not satisfied the requisite responsibilities associated with an age group, you cannot be elevated and initiated into a higher age group. For instance, only men who belong to certain age groups can marry because they have proven that they are responsible enough to take care of a wife and children. So, one achieves moral personhood if one is able to act responsibly to meet the requisite communal expectations or standards specifying the relevant duties and responsibilities of an adult.

In African communal tradition, 'personhood' does not just describe a human being with body and mind but also an individual who indicates by his actions that he can accept and meet certain standards of social responsibility to achieve recognition. Being able to act in order to satisfy the requisite social standards of responsibility usually engenders social and moral recognition as a person in the community. Such recognition leads to full initiation and integration into the community as an elder who has recognizable moral and epistemic authority that others can depend on or defer to. This status may be conferred in some cases by a formal ceremonial process of initiation or recognition. However, the process of communal integration, as Wiredu argues, may also be very subtle. According to him, "The integration of individuality into community in African traditional society is so thoroughgoing that, as is too rarely noted, the very concept of a person has a normative layer of meaning."[22] If an elder is able to maintain his full personhood by continuing to act responsibly, then he subsequently makes a transition at death from elderhood to the status of an ancestor. As Menkiti indicates, "ancestorhood . . . is part of the continuing process of elderhood, with those who have achieved its status still tied to the living, still invoked as members of an ongoing moral community."[23]

It is pertinent to note that in Menkiti's account, personhood ought to be understood primarily as a normative and not a metaphysical notion.[24] His view of personhood seems to assume in some sense a metaphysical idea or dimension of personhood. However, it appears that Menkiti is always not clear about the precise nature of personhood—whether it is ontological or moral—and the relationship between the two. This lack of clarity has engendered some of the criticisms of his view. He sometimes suggests that the normative sense of personhood is an indication of an ontological status. He indicates that the earlier stages of life where a child is referred to as an 'it' is not just a distinction in language but "a distinction laden with ontological significance."[25] This significance is manifested in the relative absence of grief when a child dies. But when an old person dies, there is elaborate grief and the funeral is ritualized, which indicates "a significant difference in the conferral of ontological status."[26] This manner of speaking has led people to think that Menkiti is providing a purely metaphysical account of personhood. In my view, it is more reasonable to understand Menkiti's view of personhood as a normative account that presupposes an ontology of personhood or descriptive metaphysical features.

This is an important point to make considering Kwame Gyekye's criticism of Menkiti's account of a person. Gyekye argues that the metaphysical idea of a person acquiring full personhood or becoming more of a person is bizarre and incoherent. Such view, he argues, cannot but be riddled with confusions, unclarities, and incoherencies.[27] Based on the idea that personhood must be viewed metaphysically, Gyekye argues:

> A human person is a person whatever his age or social status. Person-hood may reach its full realization in community, but it is not acquired or yet to be achieved as one goes along in society. What a person acquires are status, habits, and personality or character traits; he, *qua* person, thus becomes the subject of the acquisition, and being thus prior to the acquisition process, he cannot be defined by what he acquires. One is a person because of what he is, not because of what he has acquired.[28]

This criticism may be seen as reflecting the 'new Africanist' agenda of adopting the Western view of the metaphysical account of the isolated or atomic self or personhood and imposing it on the African idea that is communalistic and normative. It is clear that efforts to try to impose Western ideas or concepts on African ideas have culminated in egregious misunderstanding. We see an example of this in the work of Levy-Bruhl whose view suggests that when the Nuers believe that twins are birds (not that they are like birds), they are simply exhibiting illogical or pre-logical mentality that allows them to believe such implicit contradiction that a person is both a person and a non-person, i.e., a bird.[29]

However, Gyekye accepts that if Menkiti's account of personhood is understood as a moral account, then it is interesting and relevant for understanding the communal structures of African societies. Thus, he says: "With all these said, however, this aspect of his account adumbrates a moral conception of personhood and is, on that score, interesting and relevant to the notion of personhood important for the communitarian framework."[30] In Gyekye's view, this moral account of personhood is fundamentally correct because:

> The judgment that a human being is 'not a person', made on the basis of that individual's consistently morally reprehensible conduct implies that the pursuit or practice of moral virtue is intrinsic to the conception of a person held in African thought. The position here is, thus, that: for any p, if p is a person, then p ought display in his conduct the norms and ideals of personhood. For this reason, when a human being fails to conform his behavior to the acceptable moral principles or to exhibit the expected moral virtues in his conduct, he is said to be 'not a person'. The evaluative statement opposite this is, 'he is a person' means, 'he has good character', he is peaceful—not troublesome', 'he is kind', 'he has respect for others', 'he is humble'. The statement 'he is a person', then, is a clearly moral statement. It is a profound appreciation of the high standards of the morality of an individual's conduct that would draw the judgment 'he is truly a person'.[31]

Wiredu underscores this point by indicating that "the very concept of a person has a normative layer of meaning. A person is not just an individual of human parentage, but also one evincing in his or her projects and achievements an adequate sense of social responsibility."[32] In other words, one's actions and choices, which are manifestations of one's duties and responsibilities, constitute the factors that determine whether or not one has acquired personhood.

The idea of social responsibility or duty in African thought, which implies correlative rights, seems to suggest that there are two kinds of moral rights that people have. The first involves the rights that we have in virtue of being part of a community, and as a result, there are duties and social responsibilities that we owe other people by virtue of their moral capacities, potential for personhood, or having acquired personhood. These are communal human rights that people have by virtue of being meaningful members of a community. This correlative sense of communal rights and communal duty or social responsibility is essential to Africans and how they view relationships and social interactions. According to Wiredu, "Bereft of the traditional underpinnings of this sense of responsibility, city dwellers are left with nothing but their basic sense of human sympathy in their moral dealings with the great number of strangers encountered in and out of the work environment."[33] It is pertinent to note that the city dweller that is referenced here is one who has acquired the Western individualistic and atomistic ethos that is engendered by urbanization and modernization. Moreover, having been removed from his community, the city dweller tends to lose or shed his communalistic values, ideas, sense of self, and responsibility. The central point is for city dwellers to appreciate the advantages of the traditional African communal values in order to create the right environment in cities that would engender a sense of responsibility.

The second involves rights that we have naturally and descriptively in virtue of being a particular species of biological organisms and as isolated human beings with a metaphysical selfhood. These rights may engender some moral obligation and provide the basis for extending moral obligation to other things like animals and environment. This latter kind of rights may be classified as natural human rights, which we have by virtue of our nature: they may be classified as specific types of natural moral rights that confer moral dignity on all humans. However, from the African perspective, as I shall indicate, the emphasis in moral discourse is on duty, responsibility, and obligation. The responsibilities or duties that people have toward others do not necessarily derive from the fact that one has a right which correlatively gives rise to the duty to respect one's right. The African moral outlook does not necessarily accept the Western concept of rights as the logical jural correlatives of duties. There are communal and personal obligations that people owe to people and things that do not necessarily derive from rights. We have certain responsibilities to the community or environment not necessarily because they have rights but because these responsibilities are categorical or prudential. One may suggest based on Wiredu's point that the duty to recognize and respect natural human rights, in the absence of communal sense of duty, is motivated by human sympathy. It is in virtue of such rights and sympathy that we have or feel a sense of moral duty to protect and defend infants who have not yet *acquired* personhood because they are not capable of responsible action. In Menkiti's view, the former kinds of rights and duties, which derive from a community that are usually associated with moral personhood, are the basis for justice. In this sense, we may understand justice as a moral notion that is derived from the normative views of community, personhood, and their relationship.

Menkiti indicates that John Rawls is one Western philosopher who comes closest to fully recognizing and appreciating the importance of the African normative and communalistic conception of personhood. According to Rawls, "Equal justice is owed to those who have *the capacity* to take part in and to act in accordance with the public understanding of the initial situation. One should observe that moral personality is here defined as a potentiality that is ordinarily realized in due course."[34] Rawls indicates, in Menkiti's view, that the ethical requirement of respect for persons, implies that only those who are capable of a sense of justice are owed the duties of justice. The idea of 'capability' in the phrase 'who is capable of a sense of justice' is construed in terms of a potentiality that one may or may not realize. In the African view, one needs a community to realize the normative human potential of personhood. In addition to the formal structures indicated by the potential, the community provides the material contents and facilities regarding the relevant moral principles or values for one to actualize one's potential. Some critics may argue that this African view implies that children, who are seen solely in terms of having the potential of personhood, have no rights. But such a criticism may be based on a misunderstanding of the African normative structures and language. The issue for the African is not whether children have rights but the obligations that adults have toward children. Instead of framing the issue in terms of rights, Africans frame the issue in terms of obligation. In this sense, Africans do not believe that obligations or duties are owed solely to people based on their rights. There are other bases for moral obligation that do not involve rights.

Some of the other bases of moral obligation, which may be fundamentally communal, may also be pragmatic and prudential. For instance, we have moral obligations toward children partly because we want them to grow up to be good moral people who can sustain the community and contribute to human welfare as well as sustain the elders when they are older and cannot provide for themselves. In this sense, children have unique moral status and are owed moral obligation and consideration because they display a higher potential of acquiring personhood than animals or trees.[35] It appears that adults have more 'categorical obligations' toward children than other adults. Many of the obligations that adults have toward other adults are hypothetical and contingent on the moral status of a person and the community. If we assume the Western moral idea of correlativity of rights and obligations, one may argue that children have more rights than adults because they are owed more obligations than adults. In some sense, one may argue that the normative idea of a community—what ideally, a community ought to be—in African thought is a normative analogue of Rawls' idea of a well-ordered society that is based on an imaginary social contract where people accept moral principles that specify mutual responsibilities to sustain a community based on respect, concern, and care for each other. As a descriptive fact, all communities in African traditions may not meet this standard of community; some communities may meet it to a certain degree that may be different from other communities. However, the *idea* or *ideal* is pervasive in African thought and how they reason about moral issues, engage in inquiry, and educate people.

## Community and the Moral Basis for Personhood

In order to fully appreciate the nature of moral reasoning in African cultures, we must understand its foundation, in terms of the communal context of upbringing, moral education, and socialization. The context and processes of upbringing, which indicate the foundation for the development of moral personhood, also suggest that we must see the individual moral person as a social and moral organism. As a social organism, a moral person is trained, shaped, and molded by his society or community to use certain principles as the basis for reasoning and determining the proper action that is acceptable in a particular context. Such a person is able to imitate other people's actions or use them as models or as an analogical basis for determining how they should act. By reasoning this way, a person sees or identifies herself or her interests in relation to her community, and acts as an organic part of the community. A moral person is also seen as a social organism in the sense that she is ritualistically initiated into various roles that specify her social rights and responsibilities, and she is thus formally recognized as an active participating moral member of the community. Menkiti underscores this point about the organismic and developmental nature of a moral person by indicating that: "We must also conceive of this organism [i.e., a person] as going through a long process of social and ritual transformation until it attains the full complement of excellencies seen as truly definitive of man. And during this long process of attainment, the community plays a vital role as a catalyst and as prescriber of norms."[36] As an organism, a moral person uses community's norms that specify moral regards, concern, and care for others as the bases for developing moral sensitivity and the general moral point of view that he brings to bear on his actions and decisions. Based on this organismic view, it is believed that anyone who loses moral or social touch or connection with his communal base—the basis for his identity—is lost, or in some sense, dead. This is illustrated by the proverb that, if anyone does not know where he is coming from (his community and the basis for his identity), then he cannot know where he is going in life. In essence, such a person cannot have a reasonable and meaningful life plan and he cannot achieve any life plan. Such a person is bereft of morality, social identity, reality, meaningful life, and personhood.

This transcendental idea of moral personhood in the context of community can be illuminated and underpinned by some African views of ontology, which may also be seen in direct contrast with the modern Western view of ontology. The modern Western view dichotomizes between things, inanimate and animate objects by specifying features by which different things or objects are categorized into types. But the traditional African view sees things or objects as metaphysically interrelated. Thus, Senghor argues: "As far as African ontology is concerned, too, there is no such thing as dead matter: every being, every thing—be it only a grain of sand—radiates a life force, a sort of wave-particle; and sages, priests, kings, doctors, and artists all use it to help bring the universe to its fulfillment."[37] This idea is also captured by Innocent Onyewuenyi's description of African ontology and the African conception of the nature of 'reality' or 'being' as a dynamic force. He argues that "The concept of force or dynamism cancels out the idea of separate beings or substances which exist side by side independent of one another. . . ."[38] The idea of substances or objects that are independent in reality, he argues, is a feature of the modern Western view of ontology.

This point is also captured by Tempels when he argues that the African thought system, as instantiated with respect to the Bantus, holds that things in reality are forces that help to preserve the bond that one has with others, and that reality involves some intimate ontological relationships and interactions among beings. In his view, "It is because all being is force and exists only in that it is force, that the category 'force' includes of necessity all 'beings': God, men living and departed, animals, plants, mineral."[39] Forces may differ in their essences; thus we have divine, celestial, terrestrial, human, animal, vegetative, and material or mineral forces. These forces exist and interact in harmony. The proper or harmonious interaction among forces and lack thereof, provide the basis for explaining causal phenomena with respect to various events or occurrences. Harmony in interaction among forces brings about good events and lack of harmony in interaction among forces bring about bad events such as death or disease. Human actions in relation to community and nature are central to the ability to create harmony.

In the traditional African view, reality or nature is a continuum and a harmonious composite of various elements and forces. Human beings are a harmonious part of this composite reality, which is fundamentally, a set of mobile life forces. Natural objects and reality are interlocking forces. Reality always seeks to maintain an equilibrium among the networks of elements and life forces. According to Dixon, nature, universe, or reality and the human place in it can be understood in terms of a goal or aim, which is,

> to maintain balance and harmony among the various aspects of the
> universe. Disequilibrium may result in trouble such as human illness,
> drought, or social disruption. . . . According to this orientation, magic,
> voodoo, mysticism are not efforts to overcome a separation of man and
> nature, but rather the use of forces in nature to restore a more harmoni-
> ous relationship between man and the universe. The universe is not
> static, inanimate or 'dead'; it is a dynamic, animate, living and powerful
> universe.[40]

Because reality or nature is a continuum, there is no conceptual or interactive gap between the human self, community, the dead, spiritual or metaphysical entities, and the phenomenal world; they are interrelated, they interact, and in some sense, one is an extension of the other. Hence, the developmental process of acquiring personhood in the community usually progresses from the status of an 'it' as a child through full personhood or elderhood to the status of an ancestor in the spiritual world. In this sense, the ancestor, who may be said to have a spiritual self is still part of the community. On its face, this account may be seen as involving or imply-ing a logical or metaphysical 'mind-body' problem of interactionism, which raises the question of how it is possible for spiritual ancestors to interact with or be part of a material community? This problem is resolved if we understand that the com-munity is transcendental and that the African ontology of the community, persons, and nature involves a continuum and harmony between the material and immate-rial. This ontology does not make any logical separation between the material and immaterial or between the natural and supernatural. The supernatural is part of the robust continuum of the natural.

As such, African people see themselves, their actions, ancestors, deities, and the spiritual world in terms of a community, which is not only a part of, but is also in harmony with nature. When a person acts by pouring libation and calling on ancestors, spirits, or gods to partake in a communion with the living, we do not have a case of an interaction between two ontologically different entities of the supernatural (ancestors or spirits) and the natural (the living human person). In-stead, we have in the community, a harmonious interaction between different constituents of nature in the community.[41] In Onwuanibe's account, "Man is part of nature, but also transcends it."[42] A person is physically or metaphysically part of nature but it also transcend physical nature by virtue of its spiritual and moral self. And it is on the basis of the spiritual and moral natures that people, ancestors, and deities in the community are connected in a moral and metaphysical manner that transcends their physical selves. If we properly understand this idea of tran-scendence, then we can appreciate how a moral person and the African community are harmoniously connected by an enduring spirit and moral traditions to their ancestors, forefathers, and posterity. Hence, the communal 'we' is not limited to the immediate here and now, nor is it simply a temporary group or an aggregation of people that happen to exist and live in a particular historical time frame. Rather, the community is an enduring 'fused' group that is connected to a past historical time and the future; it transcends time. This idea of harmony or the goal of maintaining harmony for the human good and well-being is the foundation for communalism, which implies the need to impose social responsibilities on people in order to rationally perpetuate the relevant traditions and maintain harmony. So maintaining harmony with the aid of the community is an essential human interest. The idea of pursuing and maintaining human welfare and interests is at the moral center of communalism and the moral conception of personhood in African traditions. According to Hord and Lee, the African tradition is seen in "the flowering of a humanism that places the community rather than the individual at the center. . . ."[43] As such, communalism prescribes that people should act in a way that would enhance their own interest within the framework of pursuing the goal of human well-being and welfare in the context of natural harmony in their communities.

The logical and moral connection between humanism and communalism in African traditions indicates that the interests of the community and those of individuals cannot be conceived in a way that creates a conflict. To couch communalism in terms of what is beneficial to the community does not necessarily imply that the interest of the community is antithetical to the long term rational life plan of the individual. Rather, such communal interest provides the basis for the individual to pursue her rational life plan in a social and safe context. According to Okot p 'Bitek, the society and community is created and organized to provide means by which individuals can achieve certain ends which they seek in questions, such as "What or who am I?" "What is the purpose of life?" "What is happiness?"[44] He goes on to argue that the individual or his interests cannot and must not be completely removed from the community and its interest. Moreover, the logical separation of individuals and their interests from the community and its interest is not necessary for one to be an autonomous and free individual. The idea that such separation, which does not make sense in the African world-view, is necessary for one to be a person in a Cartesian individualistic sense, underscores why this Cartesian sense of a person does not make sense in the African world-view. One can appreciate, therefore, why communities in Africa, according to Ekeh, which was "the dominant form of social organization consisted of tribal societies . . . in which people found their total existence."[45] These 'tribes' or communities did not only have clearly defined boundaries, but they also had their autonomy of existence in the realm of values and morality.[46] As such, they prescribed certain amount of responsibility, which kept the 'tribes' or communities in some equilibrium.

We can appreciate the sense in which, in African cultures and tradition, people's reasoning and motivations for actions are tied to their interest in the context of human well-being and harmony in the community and also harmony in nature.

So, the idea of a community is essential to an African's way of life and conceptual scheme, in that it is a thoroughgoing practical principle of moral action and thinking, and a method of inquiry and acquiring beliefs. Morality in the traditional African cultures, which is predicated on human well-being and the existence or survival of the community, is not just a set of abstract justificatory principles. Instead, it is a practical communal principle, method, or guide for action that is manifested in every facet of people's lives. Thus, this communalistic ethos is the main social criterion for determining and making sense of personhood, individual identity, beliefs, inquiry, and actions. Again, one's identity is characterized by one's actions, recognition, achievements, and responsibilities that are anchored in a specific moral outlook or expression that is egalitarian and care-oriented. In other words, the African community is egalitarian in that it is based on the equal distribution of communal goods, the equality of communal opportunity and caring to achieve personhood, and the equal application of communal standards of recognition. The community is care-oriented because people have the responsibility to care about others and to provide the goods and environment that will help individuals to achieve personhood. As Onwuanibe remarks about the Ibo culture, the moral outlook and expression involves the ability to be an egalitarian according to the communal ethos. The egalitarian outlook in a communal ethos is founded on the moral recognition of the individual beyond the descriptive physical features or material attributes or status. He indicates that personhood involves transcendence, that is, the ability to morally transcend the ego and its material or physical characteristics. A person is not defined morally solely by his physical abilities and material wealth, but by what one does with such abilities and wealth, in terms of caring for others. Hence, in Onwuanibe's view, "the transcendence or subjectivity of the human person finds expression in the egalitarian spirit."[47] This egalitarian spirit is seen and expressed in the actions and behavior of the individual: the ability to act in a way that reflects the caring values and mutual interests of all in the community. Such actions are beneficial to the community and, they are in turn, beneficial to the individual.

Julius Nyerere uses the idea of *Ujaama* to articulate this egalitarian spirit, which, he argues, provides a foundation for an African conception of communalism that he sees as a version of socialism.[48] He argues that: "In traditional African society we were individuals within a community. We took care of the community, and the community took care of us. . . . Nobody starved, either of food or of human dignity, because he lacked personal wealth; he could depend on the wealth possessed by the community of which he was a member."[49] He indicates that the essential moral feature of socialism or its African version of communalism can be couched in terms of egalitarianism: the equal and fair production and distribution of goods and services in a community. The moral idea of egalitarianism or equality cannot be understood in terms of quantitative or mathematical equality. The equality here is purely qualitative. This qualitative sense of equality is reflected in the idea that a community or communalism is defined in terms of mutuality and fairness in social responsibilities. This point is underscored by Nyerere's indication that "the organization of traditional African society—its distribution of the wealth it produced—was such that there was hardly any room for parasitism."[50] He indicates that there was also no room for exploitation and improper accumulation of wealth. This is because, in his view, when the society is organized on the basis of communal and egalitarian ethos, there is an equal and mutual social responsibility for everyone to work in order to contribute to the community, and to make sure that every person was taken care of. So, the social responsibility of working in order to contribute to the overall wealth of the community is, in his view, part and parcel of, and indeed the foundation and justification of, African communalistic ethos, on the basis of which traditional societies were organized.

Perhaps, the most significant and essential point that is made by Nyerere is the fact that the African moral idea of communalism and its egalitarian spirit involves a state of mind or an attitude that defines who you are—as having personhood. Communalism and its egalitarian ethos is a moral outlook or perspective. In other words, the egalitarian spirit is part of one's conceptual scheme, methodology, and logic, in terms of how one sees, understands, and does things. It is the ability to have and display such logic and moral outlook in one's reasoning that defines one as a moral person. From an internalist point of view, communalism or its egalitarian spirit is not for an African, a simple reference to an external moral, social, or political set of justifications. Communalism and its egalitarian outlook are internalized principles that both justify and motivate people to act; they are not simply principles that are external to a person that he may use to justify his conduct. The egalitarian outlook associated with communalism is an internalized value, a frame of reference, a system of logic, a conceptual category, and a rational basis for action, for conceptualizing and analyzing issues and problems, and solving them. As a part of one's conceptual scheme, Okot p 'Bitek argues that communalism in African cultures also manifests itself linguistically, in that it provides the semantic basis for our meaningful use of language whenever we describe or evaluate things, objects, and actions. Many of the words or concepts that we use to describe or refer to people, such as husband, wife, brother, son, mother, father, uncle, chief among others, are indications of, or references to, complex communal relationships and responsibilities. These concepts cannot be properly understood outside of these relationships or context. Thus, concepts and their meanings also indicate the necessity of such complex relationships and responsibilities that are instantiated in a community. These complex relationships in a community provide the context for determining individual rights, duties, and communal expectations.

For instance, being a son, father, or husband in the African communal context has unique meanings, which may be different in another social cultural context because of the responsibilities and duties that are associated with them. An adult male cannot properly be called a 'father' or 'husband' if he fails to meet the requisite responsibilities to his wife and children. By the failure to meet the requisite responsibilities, such a person may fail to achieve full personhood, in that such moral personhood is defined in part by the requisite responsibilities. Nkiru Nzegwu argues along this line by illustrating how *abusua*, the matrilineal kin, that is, the basis of the community or clan in the Asante culture in Ghana, plays a central role in determining the social formal and informal matrilineal-centered processes of acquiring personal identity in the context of culture.[51] As such, communalism also provides a semantic context or basis for understanding the meaning of relationships and the duties they impose. In this culture, the blood of a person, *mogya*, which is regarded as the basis of lineage and identity, derives its origin from the mother. The matrilineal kin is then the foundation of the community or clan among the Akan people. In other words, the meanings of the concepts of 'mother', 'father' and 'uncle', and the idea of community among the Akans, which is matrilineal, are slightly different from their meanings in the patrilineal Igbo culture. Their meanings are tied to their social responsibilities and the roles they play in the different communities. The structure and dynamics of a community that are embedded in a culture as a way of making meaning will indicate the nature of the responsibilities that individuals have. The Igbo culture which is patrilineal and Asante culture which is matrilineal, manifest different communal structures and arrangements. However, these different cultures reflect a similar African idea of communalism and social responsibilities that are specifically defined by the unique communal structures.

According Nkiru Nzegwu, "the protection of a matriclan [the basis of the community in Asante culture] to which one owes allegiance and which forms one's identity is the ultimate responsibility of every member of the kin-group, both male and female."[52] In her description of the nature of rights and social responsibilities in the matrilineal community and the communal ethos of the Akan people, she argues that: "It is the maternal marker that assigns kinship and status in the Akan network of rights and obligations."[53] As such, the rights of a father with respect to his child in this matrilineal society are different from his rights in a patrilineal society. Moreover, the father's contribution to the identity and social well-being of the child is not as important as the mother's contribution. The maternal uncle of the child now takes over the role that would otherwise be played by the father—that is, in a patrilineal system. So, according to Nzegwu, "how fatherhood is understood [in terms of his role, rights, and obligations] depends on the prevailing kinship system in a given society."[54] In either case, however, one can say that in African cultures, the meanings, duties, and roles of a father, mother, grandfather, uncle, grandmother, or aunt are assigned by the community and its complex relationships. Such roles prescribe the relevant social responsibility, in terms of "providing a spatiotemporal nexus of identification, and extended network of relatives and relations [in the context of an extended family, community, and clan] within which the lineage-diffused character of a self-othered identity is formed."[55] The community or clan functions socially on the basis of the entrenched communal epistemic and moral principles, which are conceptually and practically tied to human welfare, interests, and needs in the context of a community or clan. In other words, the community, its interests, needs, and social structures are the source of beliefs, morality, and what are deemed acceptable behaviors.

The interests of the community provide the moral basis for the various social institutions, such as marriage as well as its underlying relationships and responsibilities, including sex and parenting. We may appreciate this point if we understand, for instance, that some concepts, which describe complex communal relationships and roles in African cultures, have different meanings in the West. For instance, the idea or relationship of a father in the Western sense may connote a filial-biological relationship or a parenting relationship in the case of step or adopted father/child. In the West, one does not need any social recognition or initiation to perform the role or have the relationship of a father. Nzegwu indicates that the roles or responsibilities that are specified by certain relationships, such as being a father, are, in the different African cultural and communal arrangements, exercised only by those who have been formally and publicly declared, ritualistically initiated into adulthood, or socially recognized as adults in the context of the community, based on their readiness to perform the relevant duties. The readiness is determined by social achievements and recognition as an adult in the community; such readiness is not based solely on chronological age. The idea of an elder in African thought has a normative connotation involving high achievement and recognition.

So, Menkiti's idea of the moral status of elders in the context of communalism and moral personhood does not necessarily imply that to be old is to be morally virtuous or recognized for one's social and moral deeds or achievements. This is supported by the proverb "it is one's deeds that are counted, not one's years."[56] It appears that Gyekye does not quite appreciate the distinction between age (one's years) and achievements (one's deeds), which is assumed by Menkiti's moral account of personhood as developmental and as an acquired moral status. He misunderstands Menkiti as saying that all elderly or old people are necessarily moral. As a result, he argues: "For, surely there are many elderly people who are known to be wicked, ungenerous, unsympathetic: whose lives, in short, generally do not reflect any moral maturity or excellence. In terms of a moral conception of personhood, such elderly people may not qualify as persons."[57] This point further indicates that Gyekye does not fully appreciate that Menkiti's account of personhood in the context of communalism is normative, and being an elder is a moral status that confers requisite authority. It is pertinent to stress that the moral and epistemic status of an elder as an authority is acquired; it is an *earned-status*. It is not a status that one automatically gets with old age. Because being an elder does not necessarily mean 'being old' as indication of years in age, it follows that one acquires and earns the status of an elder, in part, by the amount of practical life experiences that one has and how one is able to bring this wealth of knowledge to inform one's actions, moral sensitivity, and judgement.

Being an elder is earned or acquired by demonstrating one's ability to be consistently morally upright in one's actions by meeting one's responsibilities. The corollary of the earned-status is the social and communal recognition of a person based on his consistent responsible moral actions. This distinction between 'being old' as an indication of chronological age and of being 'an elder' as an earned moral status in African cultures can be illuminated by an interesting distinction that I saw once on a car sticker: it says, *growing old* (chronologically) is mandatory but *growing up* (as an earned moral status) is a choice. Not all 'old people' are 'grown ups'. By earning the status of an elder, that is, a 'grown-up', one is then justifiably seen as the repository of justifiable beliefs, wisdom, and good judgment that can be brought to bear on moral reasoning—from which others can draw. Hence, not all old people are elders, in that not all old people acquire the relevant moral status of personhood. Various adult roles and relationships in African communal systems, including that of an elder, father, mother, and uncle, ascribe social and hence moral responsibilities, which are dictated by the interests of human well-being and the community or clan. In other words, these relationships are ties that we have with other people, and they bind us to others as co-members of a community. Such understanding or appreciation engenders an egalitarian or caring spirit.

The relationships that words, such as, father, mother, son, uncle, neighbor, or friend refer to or describe have normative components that are grounded in some foundational principles of egalitarianism, humanism, and communalism. Hence, such relationships, do in fact, prescribe communal norms, certain social responsibilities, and modes of behavior, which are learned in the context of the society and community in which the words have meaning. For instance, polygamy is criticized from a Western perspective—based on the Judeo-Christian tradition and the romantic view of love—as immoral. However, the practice of polygamy in traditional African patrilineal cultures and its moral and pragmatic underpinnings must be understood in the communal, traditional, and historical contexts of the high mortality rate of children and the fact that fathers want many children to help him tend his farm in order to provide for his family. Moreover, the community wants many people who can contribute to its needs and take care of elders when they are old. Having many children in a community will guarantee elders' 'social security earnings' when they are old and cannot provide for themselves. People in community or children have social responsibilities to give food to elders who cannot farm. Traditional Africa cultures did not have government or company run pensions, social security, and welfare systems. While polygamy was allowed and practiced, people did not willy nilly marry many wives. If one cannot meet the responsibilities of taking care of one's wives and children, it is socially expected that one does not do it. It is considered morally reprehensible to marry many wives if one cannot provide for them and their children. This point about the normative basis for the meaning of concepts and the need to define one's character and personhood on the basis of achievements and social responsibilities, is illustrated in Chinua Achebe's, *Things Fall Apart.*[58]

The novel begins with a description of Unoka, the father of the protagonist, Okonkwo. Unoka is presented as a 'failure', in that he was not able to acquire any title or recognition, which is required in the community for achieving elderhood or full personhood. Unoka did not work hard, he did not meet his moral and social responsibilities of caring for his wife and children, and did not do anything to achieve any social status in the community to warrant any social recognition. Not only did he fail to acquire 'personhood', but he also was not a 'father' or 'husband' in the normative sense of the words in the context of African communalism. According to Achebe, "Unoka, the grown-up, was a failure. He was poor and his wife and children had barely enough to eat. People laughed at him because he was a loafer."[59] It is interesting for Achebe to indicate that Unoka was a failure as a grown-up, which means he never *grew up* and did not become *an elder*, even though, he *grew old*. This indicates, in my view, that growing old, in terms of chronological age and years, does not imply the normative status of an elder, which may be described as growing up. Unoka represents a person who was not considered a 'person' or a grown-up in the moral sense because he did not meet the requisite social responsibilities to his wife, children, and community. As such, he did not get any social recognition. Okonkwo was motivated by Unoka's failure. He made efforts not to follow the part of his father. Okonkwo understood the communal ethos and expectations, and unlike his father, he was motivated by the communal ethos to develop morally into elderhood. As indicated by Achebe, "When Unoka died he has taken no title at all and he was heavily in debt. Any wonder then that his son Okonkwo was ashamed of him? Fortunately, among these people a man was judged according to his worth and not according to the worth of his father."[60] This further indicates the egalitarian idea of giving equal opportunity to people and the equal use of fair standards. The worth of a person that Achebe is referring to here, which is the basis for determining whether or not one has achieved personhood, is not metaphysical but normative. Such worth is based on whether you are able to take a title or achieve social status and recognition, and able to perform the social duties of a father and husband. Unoka failed in his duty and social responsibilities in these regards. Okonkwo tried too hard in his actions and efforts to achieve personhood.

In the end, Okonkwo was also a failure because he was overzealous and went overboard in his efforts to achieve elderhood. He did not allow his character, identity, and personhood to develop according to the communal principles. The actions and character traits that created rough edges in his personality, which finally led to his downfall, were not motivated by and were inconsistent with the communal principles, expectations, and responsibilities. In the end, he could not make the transition to ancestorhood because he committed suicide, which is an abomination.[61] That act by itself prevented him from achieving ancestorhood. By contrast, his friend, Obierika, indicates a balanced moral character who achieved elderhood and full personhood. The setting of this novel, though fictional, illustrates in a literary form, at least partially, the communalistic ethos and how such ethos also provides the motivations for people's actions and the semantic basis for understanding relevant concepts, relationships, rights, and duties. The human person is one who obtains an identity or moral character that is molded or shaped by his community's expectations and responsibilities, which require complex relationships with others. Many concepts in African languages describe and prescribe the normative basis for relationships and modes of behavior that have some unique communal implications, meanings and significance in traditional African cultures. Such meanings are taught and learned by the unique informal and communal processes of socializing or morally educating children, and forming their moral and social personhood, and their personal identities as individuals. These unique processes also determine how concepts and underlying beliefs are taught, learned, and acquired. Sometimes, you teach or learn a concept such as fatherhood by living it, experiencing it, seeing it modeled by many people, seeing models in people who have failed, and thereby understanding the rights and responsibilities it engenders.

## Personhood, Autonomy, and Moral Education

In this sense, it is important to appreciate how the integrative idea of moral personhood is a status that is attained or acquired by the complex processes of education: upbringing, indoctrination, imitation, socialization, acculturation, recognition, initiation, learning, acquiring beliefs, living, and experiencing. It is important to indicate that the formal educational system of the West and its view of education may also include all the above processes especially, acculturation, indoctrination, recognition, and initiation. The community as a normative structure involves various kinds of formal and informal processes of education by virtue of which the individuals in the community are, in part, organically fused together as a collective entity—a community. The community in African cultures is a community of learning and learners. In addition to the features of moral personhood, humanism, egalitarianism, another defining feature of communalism in African cultures is its informal processes of education. I shall address this in another chapter. The community is defined by its ability to guide people to achieve moral personhood. Hence, a community is judged by the nature of the people you find in it. The community as a whole and each adult member have the responsibility of morally educating a person. The idea of education involves the broad processes of learning, upbringing, socialization, initiation, acculturation, and teaching people the communal ways of life, tradition, beliefs, values, a broad range of prescribed conduct, and the general and moral principles that determine the acceptable actions and behavior. Such principles are the foundation, on the basis of which the community is able to practically ensure its own social, political, moral equilibrium, and organic wholeness.

Based on this communal principle of education, a child in the community 'belongs to' and is raised and educated (informally) about different aspects of life by the community. A person is always seen both as 'a representative of himself' and an integral part of the community from which he hails. He is judged by how much he has internalized the virtues, beliefs, values, and attitudes that the community has taught him in terms of how he displays them in his everyday actions and decisions. This is part of the moral constraint on the actions and behavior of people —a person always has, as a responsibility to his community, an indirect moral constraint, even in his personal actions. People always want to take pride in being good ambassadors of their kin, families, and communities, and as such, one is considered as a *role model* by his action because he is indirectly teaching young children—by his actions—how to behave. In this case, one is teaching even when one does not intend or consciously aim to teach because one's action is a model for children. An appreciation of this responsibility and the ability to act accordingly are what defines a person in the African communal thought system. This is in contrast with the modern Western view, where a moral person represents himself *qua* his rational, autonomous, and individual self, and his actions represent solely, his own rational thinking and autonomous actions. A person is judged on his own and he does not have the moral constraint of being seen and judged as a moral ambassador of his community, and whether or not he is meeting the responsibilities that are imposed by such ambassadorship. This is one of the bases for the view in traditional African cultures that, it takes a whole community or village to raise a morally good child; the morally good child is the pride and proper representative of the community.

The educational element of communalism in African cultures implies that there is a concerted effort on the part of every person in the community to help others learn how to behave or act properly. This is done by constant and consistent prodding, ribbing, poking, and chiding by neighbors, friends, relatives, or elders. Everyone in the community wants to raise a child that they, as a community, can be proud of. In this sense, parenting is also a communal responsibility. There is a sense of communal activism in the organismic process of educating a person. Parenting is taken as a serious responsibility for the community, which individual parents cannot do alone. The idea underlying the African view that, it takes a community or village to raise a child, is not only an indication of the responsibility of the community, but also an indication of the responsibility of each member to properly represent himself and the community or village by exhibiting good moral character. This idea of communal upbringing or education indicates why, for the African, you cannot meaningfully talk of the human person as having a role or relationship of being a son, father, mother, uncle, chief, friend, enemy or stranger outside of a particular value system and communal context, because it is the context that specifies the responsibilities that are associated with these roles or relationships. For instance, how one deals with a stranger or an enemy will depend on the responsibilities that are specified by the values of the community. The simple fact that a stranger is not treated well in a community is not an indication that the community lack morality.

This idea of education is in consonance with the communal mode of thinking, which emphasizes traditions and customs as the semantic basis for making meaning in people's social interactions, existence, and experiences. In other words, without such traditions of communities as the basis for acquiring language, beliefs, and making meaning of social interactions, human beings would not be able to make sense of anything in the world. In this regard, the idea of communalism is an essential part of one's conceptual scheme, and it has logical and epistemic components and implications. As such, if African people are removed and abstracted from the background of their communalistic conceptual scheme (which indicates the acceptable conduct, way of doing and seeing things, and the methods for acquiring and justifying beliefs), they cannot be seen as rational or moral persons. This may explain why some anthropologists who could not understand the proper conceptual frameworks of traditional people concluded they lacked rationality and the ability to reason morally.[62] The following observation by Charles Taylor underscores an essential point that some of these anthropologists did not understand about human beings and cultures in general when they tried to study African cultures. He observes that, "human life is fundamentally dialogic. . . . We become full human agents, capable of understanding ourselves, and hence defining an identity, through our acquisition of rich human languages of expression."[63] More importantly, human beings can only develop into full human agents and acquire language in the context of a culture that determines the rules of a language game. Human beings live and develop by having various human and social relationships, and by engaging in interactions with their environment and cultures.

The language and concepts that we acquire in our environments and cultures are the basis for our social interactions, and thus the basis for our reasoning and hence our actions. So, our actions are a reflection of our social interactions, the concepts and language that we have acquired, and the context in which those interactions are meaningful. As such, our actions are a reflection of our community, whose traditions and cultures we have to imbibe or internalize in order to be the human beings or persons that we are. This idea makes sense only because a community and its culture and traditions are defined and sustained by their broad processes of education, in virtue of which the community and its traditions are perpetuated as a legacy. Onwuanibe observes that the greatness of a culture is manifested or reflected in its ability, via education, to commit the human person and her development or aspiration to what the culture stands for—its values and beliefs. Conversely, the decline in the values of a person is a symptom of a decline in the culture that the person is a part of. The above point also reflects the earlier observation that African thought systems consider the logical or conceptual priority of the social and moral view of a person over the metaphysical view, but at the same time, it is cognizant of the coextensive nature of these views. Because of the ability of the community to influence or impart its values and beliefs on a person, the community is an essential part of the normative and existential idea of a person. It is by virtue of this existential sphere that the individual can develop his spiritual, mental, metaphysical, or descriptive sphere, and by virtue of which he is also defined as belonging to a community or having personhood.

Let us recall that the notion of community, according to the African view, is not merely a metaphysical entity or a theoretical social construct or a description of some structures, processes, or institutions that exist apart from the individuals. Moreover, a community is not completely reducible to the individuals because, in Menkiti's view, the community is not additive; that is, it is not simply the addition of all the individuals, institutions, and structures in the community.[64] Menkiti contrasts the African idea of community as an organically fused collectivity of individuals with the Western ideas of non-organic *random* and *constituted* community of atomic and loose individuals.[65] In other words, the African view does not see the community as an entity in its own right, independent of the individuals and their organic fusion. As an organic entity, the community is the source of a wide variety of influences and benefits that are not reducible to the isolated contributions of each particular individual; rather, the community is, practically, the organic blend of individuals' contributions. The African normative view of a community is that it is a dimension of shared personal and social responsibilities. The community involves particular kinds of responsibilities that we have toward those with whom we have a special relationship by virtue of our shared interests, beliefs, values, kinship, and lineage. The community is thus conceived and identified in terms of the values, individuals, ancestors, and other facts about the social practices that human beings develop in order to live a meaningful life. This view of community or communalism does not, in my view, imply that it is, primarily, an entity that has a moral and ontological primacy over the individuals such that the individuals are subsumed in the community without any due consideration for the individuals.

However, Gyekye suggests that the commonplace view of communalism in African cultures that is suggested by many accounts is that the community dominates the individual, and each individual is subservient to the community, its needs, and interest. He characterizes this view as a radical form of communitarianism. He criticizes this radical view and argues for a more moderate view of communitarianism in African cultures.[66] In Gyekye's view, radical communitarianism seeks to reduce "a person to intellectual or rational inactivity, servility, and docility."[67] He argues that, a person according the communitarian self or personhood in African cultures, is "held as a cramped or shackled self, responding robotically to the ways and demands of the communal structure."[68] In his view, a moderate view of communalism or community recognizes the claims of the community and individuality, and attempts to integrate individuals' desires or interests with the social demands, duties, values and ideals. He argues that the individual and community have equal moral standing, and their interests are mutually reinforcing. As such, he argues that "no society is absolutely communal or absolutely individualistic, and that it is a matter of emphasis or of priority or of basic concern or perhaps obsession with one or the other. There is some truth in the view that communalism or individualism as applied to a social arrangement is a matter of degree."[69] So, what we should expect to find in any specific society is the extent to which it is more individualistic than communalistic or vice versa. In other words, every society has to consider the relative importance of the communal interests and individual rights.[70] He argues that no individual can live outside the community, and as such, communal life is not optional for people, in that they cannot autonomously and voluntarily decide not to live in a community. Moreover, the welfare and interests of the community cannot dispense of or do without the talents, creativity, initiatives, and works of individuals.

Gyekye argues that individuality is of primary interest and importance among the Akan in spite of the fact that the individual is also partly defined by the community. He analyzes some proverbs and concepts in Akan to illustrate this point. He argues that the proverb "the clan is like the cluster of trees which, when seen from afar, appear huddled together, but which would be seen to stand individually when closely approached" suggests that a person is not only separate from the community but also has a unique individuality that cannot be diminished by the community.[71] He argues that the individuality cannot be seen as a derivative concept from the idea of community. He criticizes Menkiti's view by claiming that it implies that the emphasis that is placed on the community and the normative idea of personhood diminishes the intrinsic value of the individual. The normative ideas of personhood and community or communalism in African thought do not make direct substantive claims about the metaphysical nature of an isolated individual, whose moral or metaphysical autonomy is seen as valuable in itself. Gyekye emphasizes the metaphysical claims about the free-willing and autonomous nature of isolated persons, which Menkiti's view does not make. Instead, Menkiti *assumes* some elements of such metaphysical claims as the basis for a normative claim about an individual who, though metaphysically free and autonomous, is nonetheless morally structured by the communal normative structures that circumscribe the substantive contents or objects of his autonomy. Because Menkiti does not *explicitly* account for a moral person as one who is metaphysically isolated, free-willing, and autonomous, he is understood by Gyekye as implying that the community vitiates the autonomy and freewill of the individual. In other words, Gyekye concludes that Menkiti's accounts of the African views of personhood and community, and the relationship between community and individuals involve radical communitarianism.

In a broad sense, Gyekye is correct that the practical and moral relationships between individuals and community in African thought are mutual, and that they are placed on an equal moral standing. This point is underscored by Helen Haste's view that the idea of communalism, in general, must be founded on the basic idea of mutuality, which implies that "Social order rests on people's interdependence, and society only functions if people recognise and act upon their community's responsibilities."[72] The relationship between an individual and the community is not a one-way street or direction: individuals have to cooperate and socially interact with one another in order for the community to function, and the community has to function properly and in an orderly manner in order for the individual to thrive, survive, and achieve his long term rational life plans, identity, and personhood. It is pertinent to stress along this line that not only does the community and its culture and principles shape people's values and actions, but the community and its culture and values are also shaped individuals' rational creativity, imaginations, and ingenuity. If a culture or community cannot be shaped by individuals, then there would be no cultural changes in the community, and the community and its culture cannot be perpetuated and sustained. If people do not engage in the creative, rational, and imaginative adaptation or modification of cultural principles, many such principles would be outdated, and they would not be able to keep pace with the developments in people's lives. Such developments may come from individuals' own imagination and creativity or from external cultural influences and rationally discovered new ways of doing things.

Although, theoretically, a problem may arise if there is a conflict between the interest of the community and that of the individual, practically, such a problem is rare because the way communal principles are framed and the way people are socialized, it is difficult to find a conflict. To some extent, the resolution of such conflict is already built into the communal principles, in virtue of which one rationally and autonomously articulates one's interests and rational life plans. Theoretically, one may resolve such conflict between the rights or interests of individuals and the interests or demands of the community by trying to balance the different demands or interests in a way that is mutually beneficial. The community must not succumb mindlessly to all the imaginative ideas of every individual, but at the same time, the community cannot totally repress or absolutely vitiate the creativity, imagination, and ability of individuals to come up with new ideas with which the beliefs, values, principles, and ways of life may be modified. The pertinent issue that Gyekye has not sufficiently addressed in his moderate view of communalism, involves the basis on which an individual may develop a normative sense of identity, interests, and rights, and the role that such identity or interest may play in one's own rational choices and moral autonomy. The African communalistic approach to these issues is that an individual's interest and identity, or the rights that individuals have, are claims that make sense only in the context of a given community. In some sense, one's idea of rational options is circumscribed by the community and the options it makes available. In this regard, the community is analytically or logically prior to the individual's normative identity, moral autonomy, rational options, social rights, goals, and aspirations. It appears that in Gyekye defense of moderate communalism and criticism of Menkiti's view, he conceives of the individual and individual's autonomy and rationality, purely and solely, in some isolated, abstract, metaphysical terms. In Gyekye's view, the individual as a metaphysical or abstract entity with metaphysical autonomy, is logically and morally prior to and independent of the community. Thus, a person is an autonomous or a free-willing individual, who has choices and rights or interests prior to, outside of, or irrespective of the community.

For Gyekye, "autonomy must be a fundamental feature of personhood, insofar as the realization of oneself—one's life plans, goals, and aspirations—greatly hinges on it, that is, on its exercise. Autonomy is, thus, valuable in itself."[73] In which case, an individual's rights, choices, and autonomy are absolute, categorically valid, and intrinsically valuable in themselves. Hence, the rights and autonomous choices of the individual, given its categorical validity, must either take precedence over or be balanced with the interest of the community. This idea of autonomy involves the metaphysical freedom of the individual to choose his goals and life plans in order to achieve self-realization. Gyekye argues that a person's actions and choices of goals derive from his rational and moral will. Because he sees autonomy as a fundamental metaphysical feature of a person that is valuable in itself, he disagrees with Raz's view, which seems to capture the African view that is articulated by Menkiti's account of a person, community, and the relationship between them. Gyekye indicates: "I do not think, as does Joseph Raz, that autonomy is valuable only when it is used in pursuit of the good."[74] Raz's view is that autonomy is a moral notion, which is distinct from the metaphysical notion of a free-willing, isolated, and abstract rational individual, who is free to make any choices, irrespective of the moral status or value of those choices. As a moral notion, autonomy is contingent on the pursuit of the good and the normative structure of the community, which indicates the valuable, acceptable or allowable good that one ought to pursue.

## Personhood and the Communal Context of Autonomy

So, the problem with Gyekye's view of a person and autonomy is that he does not see that one's life plans, goals, aspirations, and their realization must hinge on the normative structure of a community, which circumscribes one's choices and makes options available and valuable. In other words, the options that one has in terms of one's life plans, goals, and aspirations are shaped, circumscribed, and made available and valuable to a person by the community. Hence, one cannot have or try to realize a life plan, goal, or aspiration that is not offered, valuable, or conceivable as an option in a community. Although Gyekye accepts the logical necessity of a community, in that an individual has no choice but to live in a community, he fails to appreciate the normative necessity of the community with respect to the moral contents and strictures of autonomy. If I have a life plan to be a serial rapist or a polygamist or a king in a community where these are not available, acceptable, valuable, or conceivable options for me, then it does not make sense in the context of such a community to say that I have metaphysical or moral autonomy to pursue them as goals. Hence for Raz, "Autonomy is only possible if various collective goods are available. The opportunity to form a family of one kind or another, to forge friendships, to pursue many of the skills, professions and occupations, to enjoy fiction, poetry, and the arts, to engage in many of the common leisure activities: these and others require an appropriate common culture to make them possible and valuable."[75] Thus, one's moral autonomy is relative or relationally connected to the various moral and non-moral goods that are made available and valuable by a community, as well as the various material options of personhood that can be acquired by being a member of a community.

Gyekye disagrees with this relational view of autonomy, which in my considered judgment, best captures the African view that autonomy is contingent on the pursuit of good, that is, an individual's good must be place in the context of communal good. In this regard, he has the following reaction to Raz's view: "I find it difficult to understand why the concept of autonomy should be given an entirely moral garb."[76] Gyekye argues that autonomy implies that one is the author of one's life and that one's life is not all moral. It appears that Gyekye fails to see that the goods that Raz is talking about may include both moral and non-moral goods. Although one's life is not all moral, one must conceive of one's robust life plans in the moral and normative context of the rational options that are conceivable, available, valuable, acceptable, and allowable in a society. Gyekye fails to see the fundamental moral nature of a community and personhood in African cultures and how different non-moral goods are circumscribed by the moral values. The non-moral goods that we pursue autonomously must be valuable and meaningful to us according to some normative structures, which cannot be solely private, subjective, or individualistic. The emphasis by the African view of communalism on the moral structures of a community, as the basis or context for autonomy and personhood, speaks to the essential and fundamental role of morality in the life of people. This idea of morality is couched in humanism: pursuing and maintaining human interests, well-being, and welfare.

Gyekye himself indicates that "The concern for human welfare constitutes the hub of the Akan axiological wheel."[77] By axiology, I understand Gyekye to be talking about a broad value system, which includes politics, law, epistemology, economics, religion, aesthetics, and morality. If this is true, then the autonomy to pursue the life of a musician as a non-moral (aesthetic) good must be done in the context of human welfare and the general moral context of what is morally acceptable. I cannot pursue music to the neglect and detriment of my moral responsibilities to my children. Moreover, I may have the metaphysical freedom or autonomy to be the author of my life and to pursue my irrational and immoral passions or to yield to my irrational or immoral appetites. But this cannot be characterized as a meaningful sense of autonomy, according to the African relational view. Hence, in the African view, autonomy must wear a moral garb. By rejecting the idea of giving autonomy an entirely moral garb, Gyekye is suggesting that a person who pursues his irrational and immoral passion is indeed autonomous. I would rather say that such a person is a slave to those passions. It is true that such a person is metaphysically autonomous, having the kind of autonomy which constitutes an essential metaphysical property of a person. But such autonomy is not a moral or normative property of a person. To make a distinction between moral and metaphysical autonomy, and to indicate that moral autonomy requires a communal moral structure, is not to suggest that one must dress autonomy *per se* in an entirely moral garb. The idea is that the descriptive metaphysical concept of autonomy may not entirely have a moral garb, but the meaningful sense in which it is used in African communal thought system indicates, in my view, that it must have a moral garb.

Moreover, the requirement that autonomy must have a moral garb also indicates that the African communalistic view of personhood is fundamentally a normative, existential, and practical stance. The fact that a person's autonomy is viewed in a moral sense does not suggest that Africans lack a theoretical metaphysical view of personhood and autonomy. Such a view does not make sense in the practical and existential scheme of things. Philosophy, for Africans, is, for the most part, a practice. Onwuanibe indicates that, traditional African philosophy of the human person, which is more existential and practical than being theoretical and metaphysical, is also "based in part on the conviction that the metaphysical sphere is not abstractly divorced from concrete experience; for the physical and metaphysical are aspects of the reality, and the transition from the one to other is natural."[78]

One can give a normative account of personhood without expressly offering a metaphysical account. One may simply presuppose the theoretical view that an individual is, metaphysically, a distinct, isolated, atomic, free-willing, and autonomous entity. But one may also contextualize such metaphysical view of personhood within a communal environment as a normative basis for conceiving of a community and moral personhood the way Menkiti and others do. So, Gyekye's critique of Menkiti assumes a purely metaphysical view of personhood and autonomy. And to the extent that Menkiti may, in my view, be seen as not providing a purely metaphysical view, it appears that Gyekye is attacking a strawman.

However, it is also my view that the metaphysical view of a person is not inconsistent with the communal moral view of a person. This apparent lack of inconsistency is clear from the following point made by Gyekye: "Even though the communitarian self is not detached from its communal features and the individual is fully embedded or implicated in the life of her community, the self nevertheless, by virtue of, or by exploiting, what I have referred to as 'its mental feature' can from time to time take a distanced view of its communal value and practices and reassess or revise them."[79] Gyekye's point is that, normatively, the communal self or moral personhood (as conceived by Menkiti) is not morally detached from communal moral structures and features, in that a moral person is fully embedded in the moral life of her community. However, the communal self, conceived of metaphysically as a distinct, isolated, rational individual could be intellectually detached from the community. Hence, the individual can metaphysically, ontologically, conceptually, and rationally distance herself from her own community's values in order to reassess and revise them. This statement by Gyekye not only underscores Menkiti's point but also undercuts his own critique of Menkiti. In other words, this statement by Gyekye illustrates that the normative conception of personhood does not imply radical communitarianism or a denial of metaphysical autonomy. As such, I can imagine that Menkiti and others who hold similar views will not disagree with Gyekye's metaphysical view and the distinction between the metaphysical and moral views of personhood.

The significance of this distinction between metaphysical and moral views of personhood and autonomy is what, in my view, Gyekye tried to make by indicating that the Akan view of personhood does give primacy to the metaphysical or ontological individuality of the person. He illustrates this point in the proverb: "the clan is like a cluster of trees which, when seen from afar, appear huddled together, but which could be seen to stand individually when closely approached."[80] It is important to underscore how the African normative view of a person is not inconsistent with a metaphysical view, and how the normative view presupposes the metaphysical view of a person. The presupposition of a metaphysical view of a personal autonomy comes into play in the moral and practical realms, that is, in the explanation of human agency and in the ascription of moral responsibility.[81] The communally circumscribed moral autonomy makes certain moral options and goods available for one to freely and willingly choose from, but one may exercise metaphysical autonomy to either choose or not choose from these moral options, hence, blame and responsibility are ascribed. So, it appears that Gyekye's critique does not fully appreciate the relevant distinction and connection between moral and metaphysical senses of personhood and autonomy that he himself seems to implicitly accept. In some cases, he actually confuses and conflates the idea of moral autonomy that is acquired in a community with the idea of metaphysical autonomy of an isolated individual, irrespective of a community or a normative structure. The conflation of the different ideas of autonomy is obvious in the following statement: "By autonomy, I do not mean self-completeness but the having of a will, a rational will of one's own, that enables one to determine at least some of one's own goals and to pursue them, and to control one's destiny."[82] Here, Gyekye sees an individual's rational free will, destiny, goals, and his pursuit in an abstract metaphysical sense, in that they are not bound up in one's moral or normative ideas of personhood and identity, which are shaped by and dependent on the community and its cultural values.

Moreover, Gyekye thinks that the metaphysical view of personhood as an autonomous and free-willing individual, which is conceived of as an isolated individual, is a necessary precondition for communally circumscribed moral autonomy, in that such metaphysical autonomy is necessary to have community. Hence, he finds it difficult to make sense of the idea that one can, as a part of one's identity or personhood, acquire in a community one's moral autonomy, as opposed to metaphysical autonomy. In Diop's view, we can understand such moral autonomy as a property or attribute of the individual that is subordinated to the normative structures of the community. It is in this sense that Diop argues that "The individual is subordinated to the collectivity . . . it is on the public welfare that the individual welfare depends: thus private right is subordinated to public right."[83] This idea of the moral subordination of the moral individual to the moral community or collective, he calls, a social collectivism. He argues that such collectivism or moral community exhibits the ideal of peace, of justice, goodness, and an optimism that enhances one's ability to be a moral person. In order to understand the full import of such moral subordination with respect to the dependence of the individual on the collective, we must understand that the moral individual does not exist and cannot be conceived of morally independent of the moral collectivity. This is underscored by Gyekye's own point that "the communitarian self [individual] is not detached from its communal features and the individual is fully embedded or implicated in the life of her community,"[84] and also Raz's view that "Autonomy is only possible if various collective goods are available."[85]

The community and individual are normatively, mutually reinforcing, in that the individual is expected to contribute to the collectivity in order for both to maintain moral equilibrium. Hence, both the interests of the individual and the community require balancing in order to achieve moral equilibrium. However, in the case of a difficult conflict of interest that cannot be balanced, the collectivity takes precedence because, on the one hand, it is in the interest of the individual for the interest of the collectivity to take precedence. On the other hand, it is on the basis of the collectivity that the individual can meaningfully conceive of himself and his own interest. In other words, the individual does not have any absolute interests that are independent of the community. So, when this idea of subordination of the individual to the collectivity is understood in a metaphysical sense, it may be viewed by Gyekye as implying radical communitarianism and the loss of individuality or autonomy. However, if it is understood in a moral sense, then it implies the idea of moral autonomy—the idea of using an individual's will to pursue a required good. The good that is pursued by the individual is defined in terms of the communal range of goods available to the individual—a good that does not make sense if it is isolated from the community. If we appreciate that autonomy in the African conception of a person is a moral property, as opposed to a metaphysical property, then we can appreciate why an individual cannot have moral autonomy outside of the communal moral structures that morally define the person. Such moral autonomy as an element of moral personhood is an acquired property that one cannot have outside the community, although, such a person may have metaphysical autonomy as an isolated or abstract individual outside of a community, but such metaphysical autonomy is not acquired or earned, it is inherent in a person.

From the above discussions, one may argue that Gyekye's critique of Menkiti's account of personhood in the African communalistic thought system, which he sees as having the element of radical communitarianism, derives from the fact that Gyekye does not give enough credence to the normative view of a person or autonomy. He also does not give enough credence to the idea that this normative view is dependent on the normative structures of a community, and how such normative structures may shape the metaphysical, mental, and psychological features of a person. His criticism suggests that because a moral person is fundamentally a rational and metaphysically autonomous individual, one can be morally autonomous in the pursuit of certain goods that a community and its normative structures cannot provide or make available. Because of the absolute value that he places on the metaphysical idea of personhood as a logical, necessary, and ontologically precondition for the moral view of a person that is not dependent on the normative structures of a community, he indicates that a moral individual is necessarily self-governing and self-directing in a way that is not circumscribed by the normative structures of the community in which he lives. Thus, it appears that Gyekye does not quite appreciate that moral autonomy is contingent or dependent on a communal context of choices and the options that the community makes available.

Will Kymlicka seems to appreciate the essential element or spirit of the moral or normative (as opposed to the metaphysical) idea of autonomy. He indicates that "societal cultures are profoundly important to liberalism . . . because liberal values of freedom and equality must be defined and understood in relation to such societal cultures. Liberalism rests on the value of individual autonomy . . . but what enables this sort of autonomy is the fact that our societal culture make variable options available to us."[86] So, Kymlicka's idea suggests that one's moral autonomy will be meaningless if one does not have a community that will make options available in order to teach people or educate them regarding how to navigate their way around the different options so that they can achieve their desired goals of achieving full personhood. It is doubtful whether a metaphysical sense of autonomy that is removed from the context of a rational normative system and moral community is, as Gyekye suggests, valuable in itself. Such autonomy will imply that one can articulate an unreasonable or immoral life plan that is not informed by any normative structure, and that one must actually seek to pursue such a life plan. According to the African view, it is difficult to imagine a person's goal that is not tied to the acquisition of personhood, which is also not placed in the context of a normative community. In my view, Menkiti's account of African views of personhood, community, and the relationship between individuals and community in African thought does not imply Gyekye's idea of radical or extreme communitarianism.

The African view of communalism is not extreme or radical because it does give credence to individual rationality, creativity, imagination, and inventiveness that allow them to adapt to various situations. What the community does as a normative structure, epistemic context, and conceptual scheme is to circumscribe the context of relevant alternatives and counter-evidence, and to provide some basis for one's rationality, imagination, and creativity. I shall offer epistemic and cognitive arguments to support this stance. The idea of radical communalism in traditional African cultures is criticized as implying a kind of authoritarianism, which some argue vitiates the commonplace Western requirements of what it takes for a person to be autonomous, morally responsible, logical, and rational in the acquisition or justification of beliefs, decision-making, and moral reasoning. The commonplace view of moral reasoning in Western philosophy is based on the view that "the core of rationality consists in preserving and adhering to one's own independent judgment."[87] Wiredu suggests that the communal situation in African cultures contradict this view, and as such, people's rationality, autonomy, and freedom of the will in such context, are vitiated. To the extent that communalism in African cultures is seen as implying authoritarianism, it is criticized as epistemically and morally bad.[88] In Wiredu's view, the communal organization of African societies also involves, among others things, the heavy reliance on tradition and the authority of elders.

Elders are seen as the sole repositories of the communal knowledge about the relevant traditions, beliefs, values, practices, and moral principles. It appears that Wiredu does not fully appreciate that the status or authority of elders is a normative one. The normative status or authority of elders provides the basis for their epistemic and political authority. Because Wiredu does not fully appreciate this view, he argues that the authority of elders in the communal system in African cultures involves the imposition of communal principles and values on people in a way that does not allow them to use their free will and rationality. In a similar criticism of communalism in African cultures, Kaphagawami argues that it involves a kind of tyranny by elders.[89] In spite of these criticisms, Wiredu agrees that communalism is one of the strongest points of African cultures, in that it is the basis for the stability and cohesion in many African societies.[90] I agree with Wiredu that communalism is an important and strong element of African cultures. But I disagree that communalism involves the bad authoritarianism that he characterizes —I shall argue this point in a subsequent chapter. These criticisms are based on the idea that an individual's will and autonomy are absolutely valuable, because they indicate one's ability to determine and decide solely for oneself whether or not one's independent or subjective judgment is reasonable and valid. This individualistic and metaphysical account of personhood, autonomy or freedom of the will presupposes that one is in the best position to judge and choose what is reasonable or morally good. This view of autonomy and moral reasoning is unacceptable according to African communalistic view because morality and moral autonomy, and their rational basis indicate that they have a social foundation, which involves communal normative structures that shape choices and judgment.

The conceptions of a person, community, and their connection have implications for how one may conceive of the idea of autonomy, rationality, and moral reasoning. These conceptions indicate a contrast between the communalistic African traditions and the liberal individualistic Western tradition with respect to the ideas of moral reasoning and rationality. According to Menkiti, the Western conceptions of a person, autonomy, rationality, and moral reasoning are couched solely in terms of a person's metaphysical and psychological characteristics, which include her cognitive abilities, will, and memory. Very often, no reference is made to the social environment that contributes to or shapes one's rationality, autonomy, will, and memory. Menkiti argues that the African ideas of rationality, autonomy, and moral reasoning seek to emphasize the moral primacy of the communal world, which forms the reality of a person. These African ideas, he argues, are "rooted in an ongoing human community that the individual comes to see himself as man, and it is by first knowing this community as a stubborn perduring fact of the psychophysical world that the individual also comes to know himself as a durable, more or less permanent, fact of this world."[91] The idea of moral reasoning in African traditions is based on the view that the autonomy and ability to make reasonable choices among available alternatives must be educated, informed, shaped, cultivated, and nurtured by the community which makes the alternatives available and valuable. This idea requires that one must draw from one's experiences based on the examples and behaviors of elders or other peoples whose actions are considered models of good actions.

The Western ideas of moral reasoning and rationality seem to ignore the social context of individual's moral and cognitive development. Rather, moral reasoning is understood solely in the context of individual's will, metaphysical autonomy, and rationality. Rationality is usually understood in the modern Western liberal philosophical tradition to involve the ability of an individual to consciously, freely, and autonomously think for herself in making requisite judgments about alternatives and the choice to accept a belief or value, and to act in a way that is best supported by evidence. This idea is illuminated by Kant's idea of rational individualism, human autonomy, or freedom of the will. He indicates that the maxim of rationality, which is the basis for avoiding errors in reasoning, requires one to "think for oneself."[92] This idea of independent reasoning or 'thinking for oneself,' which is seen as the basis for moral reasoning, requires autonomy, cognitive abilities, and the ability and freedom to develop such abilities on one's own. This idea also requires that one must be able to use one's own reason to make one's own moral decisions and choices. This is the basis for the Kantian view of morality and moral agency. He argues that the ability to use one's own individual rationality to illuminate the goodwill is all that is necessary to engage in moral reasoning and make moral choices. For him, the moral person is one who autonomously performs his moral duty that is shaped solely by his own independent rationality and goodwill, irrespective of the context and the consequences of his actions. Thus, Kant does not think that one's social context or the consequences of one's actions are relevant to one's moral reasoning and goodwill. This Kantian view, which represents a Western liberal idea of moral reasoning is different from the African view.

According to the African communal view of moral reasoning, everyone has some innate natural ability to use their reason or rationality to make moral decisions. However, an individual cannot adequately do it alone. No individual can make good moral choices as an isolated or independent individual who is not guided by others in a normative social context. In other words, one's innate natural ability to use reason must be educated, nurtured, and guided in order to understand the proper context and basis for one's action. The community and morally mature people must take an active part in helping to educate the reasoning faculty of the morally immature. It is assumed that moral maturity or moral personhood, which is a mark of rationality and moral autonomy, cannot be attained in vacuum or by oneself alone. According to the African view, it is necessary for one to be educated, integrated, socialized, acculturated, or assimilated into a moral community in order to develop one's moral reasoning abilities. The Western individualistic and metaphysical view of autonomy and rationality that is adopted by Gyekye as a basis for his criticism of Menkiti seems to think otherwise. It appears that Gyekye fails to appreciate that the African normative views of personhood and community make some essential ontological and metaphysical claims about the interconnectedness personhood and community, and how in reality, both are in harmony with nature. As Onwuanibe indicates, traditional African philosophy of the human person is "based in part on the conviction that the metaphysical sphere is not abstractly divorced from concrete experience; for the physical and metaphysical are aspects of the reality, and the transition from the one to other is natural."[93]

The community of moral persons may be seen in terms of their interconnectedness in nature, shared reality, and the commonly shared social practices, attitudes, values, interests, and responsibilities that individual persons commonly exhibit, on the basis of which they live together as moral persons. The values, practices, attitudes, interests, and responsibilities that individuals exhibit in their actions have to be understood in order to understand the community and also to identify it. Such values and practices are learned by the informal methods or processes for shaping and circumscribing social interactions, which provide the basis for educating, initiating, acculturating, and socializing people into a community. Such practices involve moral deference to elders and the accepted basis for moral reasoning. These practices also indicate some of the shared interests and responsibilities, which indicate the conception of the good life on the basis of which people articulate and pursue their rational life plans. It is pertinent to note that there could be various individual's practices, interests, and values, which may not fall within the domain of the normative conception of the community and to which a community may not have any jurisdiction. The relative moral primacy of the community only comes into effect in case of a conflict, when such practices, interests, and values threaten the interest and hence the existence of the community, on which individuals' existence and survival depend. A community may have broad principles, which allow each different individual to act autonomously in different ways that may be mutually consistent, as well as consistent with the broad communal principles.

# Notes

1. This is a commonplace view that the African conception of a person has two related components. See Segun Gbadegesin, "*Eniyan*: The Yoruba Concept of a Person," 175, and Wiredu, *Cultural Universals and Particulars*, 125-129.

2. Gail M. Presbey, "Maasai Concepts of Personhood: The Roles of Recognition, Community, and Individuality," *International Studies in Philosophy* 34, no. 2 (2002): 257.

3. Presbey, "Maasai Concepts of Personhood," 257.

4. See Lee M. Brown, ed., *African Philosophy: New and Traditional Perspectives* (New York: Oxford University Press, 2004) for a compilation of essays, which provide various metaphysical accounts of personhood in African cultures. Also see Kwame Gyekye, "Akan Concept of a Person," 199-212.

5. See the following essays in Lee M. Brown, ed., *African Philosophy: New and Traditional Perspectives* (New York: Oxford University Press, 2004), Segun Gbadegesin "An Outline of a Theory of Destiny," 51-68. D. A. Masolo, "The Concept of the Person in Lou Modes of Thought," 84-106. Ifeanyi Menkiti, "Physical and Metaphysical Understanding: Nature, Agency, and Causation in African Traditional Thought," 107-135.

6. Heidi Verhoef and Claudin Michel, "Studying Morality Within the African Context: A Model of Moral Analysis and Construction," *Journal of Moral Education* 26, no. 4 (1997): 389-407. They quote L. J. Myer, "Transpersonal Psychology: The Role of the Afrocentric Paradigm," *Journal of Black Psychology.* 12, no. 1 (1986): 31-42, quoted from p. 35.

7. Kwame Gyekye, *Tradition and Modernity: Philosophical Reflections on the African Experience* (New York: Oxford University Press, 1997), 47.

8. Menkiti, "Physical and Metaphysical Understanding: Nature, Agency, and Causation in African Traditional Thought," 130.

9. Verhoef and Michel,"Studying Morality Within the African Context: A Model of Moral Analysis and Construction," 396.

10. Ifeanyi A. Menkiti, "Person and Community in African Traditional Thought," in *African Philosophy: An Introduction*, ed., Richard A. Wright (New York: University Press of America, 1984), 171. This view and the contrast between African sociocentric and Western egocentric conception of personhood have been criticized by Michael Jackson and Ivan Karp, eds., *Personhood and Agency: The Experience of Self and Others in African Cultures* (Washington, D.C., Smithsonian Institution Press, 19990), Didier Kaphagawani, "Some African Concepts of Person: A Critique," in *African Philosophy as Cultural Inquiry,* eds., Ivan Karp and D. A. Masolo (Bloomington, IN: Indiana University Press, 2000), 66-82, and D. A. Masolo, *African Philosophy in Search of Identity* (Bloomington, IN: Indiana University Press, 1994).

11. Menkiti, "Person and Community in African Traditional Thought," 172.

12. Menkiti, "Person and Community in African Traditional Thought," 172.

13. Richard Onwuanibe, "The Human Person and Immortality in Ibo (African) Metaphysics," in *African Philosophy: An Introduction*, ed., Richard A Wright, 186.

14. Hord and Lee, *I Am Because We Are*, 7-8.

15. Menkiti, "Person and Community in African Traditional Thought," 179.

16. Verhoef and Michel, "Studying Morality Within the African Context: A Model of Moral Analysis and Construction," 396.

17. Onwuanibe, "The Human Person and Immortality in IBO Metaphysics," 189.

18. Myer, "Transpersonal Psychology: The Role of the Afrocentric Paradigm, 35.

19. Onwuanibe, "The Human Person and Immortality in IBO Metaphysics," 186.

20. Gbadegesin, *"Eniyan*: The Yoruba Concept of a Person," 175.

21. Clifford Geertz, "On the Nature of Anthropological Understanding," *American Scientist* 63 (1975), 47-53, cited in Helen Haste, "Communitarianism and the Social Construction of Morality," *Journal of Moral Education*, 25, no, 1 (1996): 49.

22. Wiredu, *Cultural Universal and Particulars: An African Perspective*, 71.

23. Menkiti, "Physical and Metaphysical Understanding: Nature, Agency, and Causation in African Traditional Thought," 130

24. Gyekye suggests that Menkiti's account is metaphysical. See Gyekye, Tradition and Modernity: Philosophical Reflections on the African Experience,. 37.

25. Menkiti, "Person and Community in African Traditional Thought," 174.

26. Menkiti, "Person and Community in African Traditional Thought," 174.

27. Gyekye, *Tradition and Modernity*, 49.

28. Kwame Gyekye, "Person and Community in Akan Thought," in *Person and Community: Ghanaian Philosophical Studies 1*, eds., Kwame Gyekye and Kwasi Wiredu (Washington D.C.: Council for Research in Values and Philosophy, 1992), 108.

29. See E. E. Evans-Pritchard, *Theories of Primitive Religion* (Oxford: Clarendon Press, 1965), especially, chap. 5, with respect to his efforts to refute Levy-Bruhl's thesis about the pre-logical nature of the minds of people in the primitive cultures of Africa.

30. Gyekye, *Tradition and Modernity*, 49.

31. Gyekye, *Tradition and Modernity*, 50.

32. Wiredu, *Cultural Universal and Particulars*, 71-2.

33. Wiredu, *Cultural Universal and Particulars*, 71.

34. John Rawls, *A Theory of Justice* (Cambridge, MA: Harvard University Press, 1971), 505-506.

35. I cannot address the issue of whether animals or trees and the environment have rights and the nature of obligations that Africans have toward animals and the environment. I plan to address this issue in an article that is currently in preparation.

36. Menkiti, "Person and Community in African Traditional Thought," 172.

37. Leopold Sedar Senghor, "Negritude: A Humanism of the Twentieth Century," in *I Am Because We Are: Readings in Black Philosophy*, eds., Fred Lee Hord and Jonathan Scott Lee (Amherst, MA: University of Massachusetts Press, 1995), 49.

38. Innocent C. Onyewuenyi, "Traditional African Aesthetics: A Philosophical Perspective," in *African Philosophy: Selected Readings*, ed., Albert Mosley (Englewood Cliffs, NJ: Prentice Hall, 1995), 424.

39. Placid Tempels, "Bantu Philosophy," in *African Philosophy: Selected Readings*, ed., Albert Mosley (Englewood Cliffs, NJ: Prentice Hall, 1995), 67.

40. Vernon Dixon, "World-views and Research Methodology," in *African Philosophy: Assumptions and Paradigms for Research on Black Persons*, eds., L. M. King, Vernon Dixon, W. W. Nobles (Los Angeles: Fanon Center Publication, 1976), 62-63. Also see Gerald G. Jackson, "The African Genesis of the Black Perspective in Helping," in *Black Psychology 2nd Ed.*, ed., R. L Jones (New York: Harper & Row, 1980), 314-331.

41. See A. Okechuckwu Ogbonnaya, "Person as Community: An African Understanding of the Person as an Intrapsychic Community," *Journal of Black Psychology* 20, no. 1 (February 1994): 74-87.

42. Onwuanibe, "The Human Person and Immortality in IBO Metaphysics," 192.

43. Hord and Lee, eds.,*I Am Because We Are: Readings in Black Philosophy,* 9.

44. Okot p 'Bitek, "On Culture, Man, and Freedom," in *Philosophy and Culture*, eds., H. Odera Oruka and D. A. Masolo (Nairobi: Bookwise Limited, 1983), 108-110.

45. Peter Ekeh, "Colonialism and Social Structure," *An Inaugural Lecture* (University of Ibadan, 1983), 20.

46. Ekeh, "Colonialism and Social Structure," 21.

47. Onwuanibe, "The Human Person and Immortality in IBO Metaphysics," 187.

48. Julius K. Nyerere, *"Ujaama*-The Basis of African Socialism," in *Freedom and Unity* (New York: Oxford University Press, 1968), 162-171.

49. Nyerere, *"Ujaama*-The Basis of African Socialism," 165-166.

50. Nyerere, *"Ujaama*-The Basis of African Socialism," 163.

51. Nzegwu, "Question of Identity and Inheritance."

52. Nzegwu, "Question of Identity and Inheritance," 182.

53. Nzegwu, "Question of Identity and Inheritance," 184.

54. Nzegwu, "Question of Identity and Inheritance," 186.

55. Nzegwu, "Question of Identity and Inheritance," 187.

56. N. K.Dzobo, "African Symbols and Proverbs as Source of Knowledge and Truth," in *Person and Community:Ghanaian Philosophical Studies I*, eds., Kwasi Wiredu and Kwame Gyekye (Washington, D.C., : Council for Research in Values and Philosophy, 1992), 97.

57. Gyekye, *Tradition and Modernity: Philosophical Reflections on the African Experience*, 49.

58. Chinua Achebe, *Things Fall Apart* (New York: Fawcett Crest, 1993).

59. Achebe, *Things Fall Apart*, 9.

60. Achebe, *Things Fall Apart*, 11 (emphases are mine).

61. Achebe, *Things Fall Apart*, 190-191.

62. See for instance, R. S. Fortunes, *The Sorcerers of Dobu* (London: Routledge & Kegan Paul, 1963), Colin Turnbull, *The Mountain People* (New York: Simon & Schuster, 1972), and the collection of essays in Bryan R. Wilson, ed., *Rationality* (London: Basil Blackwell, 1970), which examines the nature of rationality and the rational status of some African cultural beliefs.

63. Charles Taylor, *The Ethics of Authenticity* (Cambridge, MA: Harvard University Press, 1991). 32.

64. Menkiti, "Person and Community in African Traditional Thought," 179.

65. Menkiti, "Person and Community in African Traditional Thought," 179-180.

66. For a similar moderate view, see Ananyo Busa, "Communitarianism and Individualism in African Thought," *International Studies in Philosophy* 30, no. 4 (1998): 1-10.

67. Gyekye, *Tradition and Modernity*, 56.

68. Gyekye, *Tradition and Modernity*, 55-6.

69. Gyekye, *Tradition and Modernity*, 41.

70. Gyekye, *Tradition and Modernity*, 36-70.

71. Gyekye, *An Essay on African Philosophical Thought*, 158-162.

72. Haste, "Communitarianism and the Social Construction of Morality," 50.

73. Gyekye, *Tradition and Modernity*, 54.

74. Gyekye, *Tradition and Modernity*, 54.

75. Joseph Raz, *The Morality of Freedom* (Oxford University Press, 1986), 247.

76. Gyekye, *Tradition and Modernity*, 54-55.

77. Gyekye, *An Essay on African Philosophical Thought*, 143.

78. Onwuanibe, "The Human Person and Immortality in IBO Metaphysics," 184.

79. Gyekye, *Tradition and Modernity*, 56.

80. Gyekye, *Tradition and Modernity*, 40.

81. See the following essays: Gbadegesin,"An Outline of a Theory of Destiny," Masolo, "The Concept of the Person in Lou Modes of Thought," and Menkiti,"Physical and Metaphysical Understanding: Nature, Agency, and Causation in African Traditional Thought."

82. Gyekye, *Tradition and Modernity*, 54.

83. Cheikh Anta Diop, *The Cultural Unity of Black Africa: The Domains of Patriarchy and of Matriarchy in Classical Antiquity*, introduction by John Henrik Clarke, afterword by James G. Spady (Chicago: Third World Press, 1978), 144.

84. Gyekye, *Tradition and Modernity*, 56.

85. Raz, *The Morality of Freedom*, 274.

86. Will Kymlicka, *Politics in the Vernacular* (Oxford: Oxford University Press, 2001), 53-54.

87. John Hardwig, "Epistemic Dependence," *Journal of Philosophy* 82, no. 7 (1985): 340.

88. Wiredu, *Philosophy and an African Culture*, 2-4.

89. Didier Kaphagawami, "On African Communalism: A Philosophic Perspective," A paper presented at the First International Regional Conference in Philosophy, May 23-27, 1988, Mombassa, Kenya.

90. Wiredu, *Philosophy and an African Culture*, p. 4.

91. Menkiti, "Person and Community in African Traditional Thought," 172.

92. Immanuel Kant, *Critique of Judgment*, trans. by J. H. Bernard (New York: Hafner, 1951), 136.

93. Onwuanibe, "The Human Person and Immortality in IBO Metaphysics," 184.

# Chapter Three

# Moral Philosophy, Communalism, and Morality

I have indicated that the idea of communalism in African cultures may be understood in terms of the moral ideas of personhood, community, and their connection. This idea of communalism also provides the basis for understanding the nature of moral principles or values, moral reasoning, and moral thought or philosophy in African traditions. In other words, the idea of communalism is essential for understanding moral philosophy in African traditions. Moral philosophy or ethics is one major subject area of Western philosophy that deals with the nature of morality, moral values, principles, and their justification. It also examines the nature of substantive and theoretical rational thinking about morality, moral judgments, and moral problems. Moral philosophy is, fundamentally, about the nature of moral reasoning, in that it seeks to address the philosophical problems of how to articulate and justify moral principles of actions and how to apply such principles in our daily lives. Related to this problem is the issue of how to teach people to practically engage in moral reasoning so that they are able to apply moral principles to their everyday lives and actions. Moral philosophy in Western philosophy is said to be universal, rational, abstract, and systematic enterprise. It is also said be an 'individualistic' enterprise in two different senses.

First, it addresses the question, 'how ought *I* to behave?' or 'what ought *I* to do?'—as an individual. Moral philosophy is seen as the activity of providing some rational basis on which an individual can rationally and autonomously think for himself in order to decide or choose how he should act. In this sense, moral philosophy is not a description of some social norms, group or communal values, or cultural principles of action that are imposed on people against their will. Second, moral philosophy represents the moral thoughts and systematized written ideas and

93

views of individual professional philosophers; these ideas are their reflective accounts of the nature of moral principles and values. The point here is that the contents of moral philosophy are not the beliefs and ideas of groups of people or cultures, but the ideas of individual philosophers. So, moral principles are articulated by individual philosophers as answers to the question, 'how ought *I* to behave?' Thinkers in Western philosophical traditions since Plato have also been concerned about how we may morally educate or teach people about moral values, virtues, or principles, and the very important activity of making moral decisions in our lives. Being able to teach these will offer people the facilities and basis for thinking about how, in a broad sense, they should act, behave, or lead their lives. This issue of moral education is essential to communalism because it is the basis for acquiring moral personhood and for integrating individuals into the communal ethos, practices, and ways of life. Such integration and acquisition of personhood are necessary for the sustenance of the community; thus, they are defining features of communalism.

## Moral Philosophy and African Cultures

The central themes in moral philosophy are, the nature of moral principles, and how people can learn, internalize, and use moral principles to guide their conduct. According to Gene Blocker, "ethics is a branch of philosophy which seeks to establish and rationally defend a universally valid theory of what is right and wrong, good and bad in general, which can be used as a set of moral principles for guiding human actions."[1] This view of moral philosophy, which is pervasive in Western philosophy, is interesting because of its emphasis on the universal rational validity of theories of right and wrong. This view seeks to eliminate particularist and contextualist ethics and other forms of ethics, such as ethics of caring and applied ethics, which in some cases may not involve universally valid principles. This universal rational view of ethics is consistent with the universalist metaphilosophical view of philosophy, with respect to ethics as a sub-discipline of philosophy. The universalists argue that the subject matter of ethics as an aspect of philosophy must be universal in nature and scope, in that moral principles and judgments are universally applicable to everyone no matter the situation. Thus, ethics is seen as a rational, theoretical, and technical discipline in terms of its subject matter and methodology.[2] The particularists argue, on the other hand, that the subject matter of ethics may involve the rational moral thought systems or the moral beliefs, values, and principles of a particular group of people and the cultural ways in which individuals in a culture justify and explain their actions, obligations, interactions, and moral judgments.

The particularists argue that people's moral thought, reasoning, values, and stances are peculiar and unique to their conceptual scheme, culture, and experiences. Hence, moral philosophy cannot be completely universal; it must have some particular and contextual elements of cultures.[3] What the universalists have characterized as moral philosophy (i.e., the technical discipline, which involves efforts by professional philosophers to articulate theoretical, universal, and abstract principles of morality and the justificatory foundations for such principles) is very limited and narrow in scope. As such, universalists limit philosophical moral reasoning or thought to the abstract, theoretical, analytic, critical, and systematic ideas of individuals. In this sense, moral principles, which provide universally valid answers to these questions are thus distinguished from etiquette, cultural norms, customs, social rules, religious rules, and legal rules.[4] The moral idea of communalism in African tradition suggests that moral philosophy and moral principles are contextual, practical, particularistic, and communal. In my view, communalism is, fundamentally, a moral concept that has epistemic, social, and political implications. Communalism thus represents a theme in African moral philosophy, which is an essential part of African philosophy. The pertinent issue then is, whether we can reasonably conceive of ethics or moral thought as a philosophical discipline and a subject matter of philosophy, based on a particularist metaphilosophical stance, or whether we must rely solely on the universalist stance. Thus, we need to examine whether a particularist metaphilosophical view about the nature of philosophy may also have implications regarding how one conceives of the nature of moral philosophy, morality, and moral principles.

Appiah disagrees with this particularist view. Based on his universalist view of philosophy, he distinguishes between philosophy as formal enterprise and philosophy as cultural, folk, or informal style or pattern of thinking, i.e., folk or ethnophilosophy, which is a debased sense of philosophy.[5] He argues that:

> In many a village around the world, in cultures traditional and industrialized, people gather in the evenings to talk. In pubs and bars, under trees in the open air in the tropics, and around fires in the far North and South of our globe, people exchange tales; tell jokes, discuss issues of the day; argue about matters important and trivial. Listening to such conversations in cultures other than your own, you learn much about the concepts and theories people use to understand their experience, and you learn what values they hold most dear.[6]

Appiah argues that in spite of the concepts and values that you learn about other cultures from oral tradition and ordinary conversations, these concepts and values do not and cannot constitute a philosophy in his formal universalist sense. He argues that one cannot reconstruct a philosophy or philosophical theme from such ideas. Such conversations may unearth the folk-philosophy (moral or otherwise) of a group of people, but folk-philosophy is not a philosophy because those involved in conversations are not trained philosophers or experts. This suggests that the idea of communalism in African traditions cannot pass as an African philosophical theme that is comparable to various traditions in Western philosophy, especially, the analytic tradition. We may use the idea underlying the above distinction to illuminate the distinction between ethics or moral philosophy as a technical and formal sub-discipline of philosophy that involves critical reflection and theorizing by 'experts', and ethics as a cultural (folk) pattern of thinking or informal decision making or reasoning that ordinary people are involved with in their daily lives.

The distinction between ordinary people's moral thought and the formal technical moral thought called formal moral philosophy or ethics raises familiar metaphilosophical and comparative issues. The comparative issue has to do with whether ordinary peoples' moral thoughts are, in any way, comparable to the formal moral system of thought, which is seen as the abstract, critical, analytic, and individual's written philosophical moral theories in Western tradition that are said to have universal validity. Based on these features, those who hold a universalist formal technical view of philosophy argue that philosophical moral thinking does not exist in African cultures. As such, the moral idea of communalism in African cultures cannot represent a legitimate philosophical moral thought that is comparable to Western moral philosophy. For some, moral thought or philosophy does not exist in African cultures because moral principles and their ultimate justifications are often tied to supernatural phenomena such as gods, spirits, deities, and ancestors.[7] So, critics question whether a universally adequate moral principle or system of morality can be rationally tied to supernatural phenomena that people accept dogmatically without question or justification. If communalistic moral principles are tied to such supernatural phenomena, then it is doubtful whether they can be justified on rational grounds that are universally valid.

The issue raised by the universalist view of philosophy and the distinction between formal and folk-philosophy is, whether African moral thoughts can be characterized as moral philosophy. In other words, whether Africans have universally valid modes of thinking about morality, moral principles, and values or how to deal with various issues regarding morality that are uniquely African. They may also ask whether Africans have a set of systematic moral thoughts that are comparable to individuals' abstract and universal philosophical theories in the Western tradition. According to Kai Nielsen, many philosophers think that the task of moral philosophy or moral philosophers "primarily consists in setting forth systematically the first principle of morality and in showing how it is possible to justify these principles."[8] According to this view, moral philosophy and moral philosophers are supposed to provide *the ultimate rationale* for moral knowledge as well as *the objective justification* for moral claims and principles. Based on the formal universalist conceptions of philosophy and moral philosophy, critics of African ethnophilosophy and those who question, on comparative grounds, the existence of African philosophy, ask whether traditional African people sought to establish, theoretically and conceptually, 'universally valid' principles of inquiry, knowing, human conduct, or good society.

Moreover, it is not clear, the universalists argue, whether traditional Africans engaged in rational and critical thoughts about their moral beliefs as a basis for providing ultimate rationale or objective justifications for their values, ways of life, moral principles, moral judgments, and solutions for moral problems.[9] If they did, does that imply that they have a system of philosophy in general, especially, moral philosophy? If not, does that imply that they do not have a system of philosophy, and in particular, of moral philosophy? If they did, in general, engage in rational conceptual thinking, and, in particular, moral thinking, and they have a system or systems of philosophy or moral philosophy, then what is African about these systems of thought? If we assume that there are moral thoughts that are uniquely African in subject matter, method, and origin, then the question is, what is philosophical about them? In other words, how are these African systems of thought different from other philosophies, and in particular, Western philosophy and Western modes of reasoning? Do such thought systems have 'universal' features, which make them comparable in any respect to philosophical and moral thought in Western philosophy? Critics of African philosophy doubt whether exponents of African philosophy can answer many of these questions about moral thought in African cultures in the affirmative. In my view, it is important to be able to answer these questions in the affirmative in order to fully understand the idea of communalism in African traditions as a philosophical theme or a fundamental principle of living, value, and method of inquiry.

Critics doubt the existence of an African philosophy partly because, in their view, traditional African cultures had neither the facilities nor made concerted efforts to engage in the formal processes of educating people to think rationally about the validity of their moral principles or other principles that they apply in their everyday actions. Appiah argues that Africans have no written tradition or formal educational system, which for him, is necessary to establish and have a philosophy.[10] Wiredu also argues that being a philosopher in the formal sense requires formal education, which involves mastering the philosophical academic canon, the body of works in philosophy, and learning the methodologies of doing philosophy.[11] Appiah and Wiredu argue that African traditions do not have literacy or written tradition that is usually associated with formal educational systems. As such, African traditions did not have knowledge of formal systems of thought and they could not facilitate the kind of theorizing, rigor, and analysis that philosophy requires. They argue that African traditions have only informal communal processes of socialization, acculturation, and of imparting knowledge. Furthermore, they hold that these informal processes were more or less processes of indoctrination as opposed to legitimate processes of education. Hence, traditional Africans could not have engaged in the kind of conceptualization, theorizing, rigor, justification, and analysis that are necessary for philosophy, and in particular, moral philosophy, in terms of establishing the ultimate, universal, objective foundation and justification for moral knowledge or principles.

Along these lines of argument (i.e., that morality and moral philosophy must be conceptual, theoretical, and abstract) some sociologists and anthropologists have also argued that African cultures do not have a moral system or moral language for evaluating and analyzing moral issues. For instance, R. S. Fortunes argues that the Dobus do not have the concepts of 'good' and 'bad' that are used in purely moral and abstract terms; that is, they do not have a moral language that is not tied to some concrete natural facts or experience, or perhaps, supernatural phenomena.[12] Thus, the concepts of 'good' and 'bad' among the Dobus have meanings that are relative, contextual, and contingent on natural or supernatural facts. In other words, the specific use or meanings of 'good' and 'bad' depend of the concrete natural facts being described. Colin Turnbull also argues that the Iks do not have a system of morality in their culture.[13] It is not clear whether we may understand Turnbull to be saying that the Iks do not have any sense of morality or that their idea of morality is not comparable to the Western view. It is very unlikely that the Iks do not have any sense of morality, in that they do not have principles for regulating and evaluating conduct. Perhaps, what Turnbull is saying is that the Iks do not have morality that is comparable to the Western idea of morality, which is seen as the paradigm or ideal. As such, if any culture or society, such as the Iks, does not have a moral system that is comparable to the Western paradigm, then such a culture does not have a moral system. On the one hand, it is not clear what it means to say that a culture does not have morality. Is it that they have no sense of right and wrong, good and bad? Is it that their sense of right and wrong is not universally valid? Is it that they have no language or concepts to express their sense of right and wrong, good and bad? Is it that they do not engage in the conceptual analysis of moral concepts? Is it that they have no way or standards of criticizing or adjudicating among conflicts regarding good and bad? It is unreasonable to argue that Africans do not have morality in any of these senses. On the other hand, the distinction between specific cultural ideas of morality and the abstract universal idea of morality is specious, because ordinary people who use their cultural context to engage in moral thinking in their everyday decisions do some critical reflection similar to what the technical philosophers do.

This distinction does not appreciate that 'philosophy' is, in general, a process of finding a rational and systematic argument as the basis for a held view or belief. An ordinary person may be doing philosophy in this broad sense. This broad sense of philosophy is the commonsense view that the work of a technical philosopher, who is seen as an expert, must draw from and be sensitive to. It is pertinent to note that what 'expert' philosophers do is actually a reflection based on how ordinary rational people think, what they think about, and do in their everyday lives. Hence, if a philosophical theory is inconsistent with or not sensitive to the ordinary people's understanding of and intuitions about the relevant issues, then there is a *prima facie* reason to think that such a theory is philosophically wanting. This process cannot be seen solely and narrowly as *an activity* in the technical professional sense of what modern university trained philosophers do, which is to teach, research, raise questions about, analyze conceptual issues that confront human beings, and document them in publications to make them public. So, to accept this distinction is to use a specious metaphilosophical assumption about the nature of philosophy or moral philosophy to argue that if a group of people does not have identifiable 'experts' with a body of written work to be studied, then the people do not have or engage in moral thinking or philosophy.[14] In other words, if Africans do not have such identifiable experts, then they do not have a philosophy, and in particular, moral philosophy or moral thought.

The pertinent issue raised by a plausible idea of African moral philosophy, which is worth focusing on, should not be whether traditional Africans engaged in the *formal activity* that is now called ethics in the modern or contemporary day parlance, with its nuances. Rather, the issue should be whether Africans did reflectively seek or provide explicit and latent rational fundamental bases for their moral principles. If they did, whatever ideas or beliefs they came up with, constitute a philosophy. The relevant point is that if it can be shown that they did any of these, then there is a reasonable basis to argue that they engaged in some moral philosophical thinking. However, the other issue to be considered is whether the fact that they did not have professional experts—trained philosophers—who engaged in this kind of moral philosophical thinking, who can profusely and meticulously document their process of thinking, is a sufficient ground to say that they did not have or engage in moral thinking. Is the attempt to analyze the sayings, folklore, beliefs, proverbs, and symbols that depict African ways of life and values a legitimate way to capture their moral thinking? Can such efforts recapture or reconstruct the kinds of reasoning and thoughts, which existed among ordinary Africans that have been passed down by oral tradition to various generations?

A close look at the history of Western philosophy will indicate that the process of critically and systematically reconstructing and reinterpreting the ideas of the past or past thinkers is an essential aspect of contemporary analytic philosophy. Some of the ideas of the past that are reconstructed do not in themselves display the so-called essential critical, systematic, and rigorous features of philosophy. However, the process of reconstruction may infuse rigor and systematization. Usually, the final product is considered a legitimate philosophy. For instance, contemporary analytic philosophers have attempted to use the contemporary concepts of 'functionalism' and 'supervenience' to analyze Aristotle's theory of the soul.[15] Aristotle did not have or use these concepts, but they are currently used by analytic philosophers to make understandable an ancient idea regarding the soul that may appear arcane to a contemporary mind. To do a similar reconstruction and analysis of African traditional ideas such as communalism will pass as contemporary analytic African philosophy. In my view, this kind of analysis, which is what I am doing with respect to the traditional African concept and moral idea of communalism will constitutes a contemporary African moral philosophy. The intent here is to use contemporary analytical concepts and methods to interpret and explain the relevant traditional African beliefs, values, and ways of life that characterize communalism. This philosophical analysis of communalism must draw from ordinary people's understanding of the idea and the practical way in which it makes sense in their daily lives.

Therefore, the pertinent issue for me is, what kind of thinking, and in particular, moral thinking, if any, did traditional Africans engage in? This issue is essential for understanding and appreciating the idea of communalism as a moral philosophy in African traditions. My effort is to illuminate this issue about the plausibility of moral philosophy in African tradition by analyzing the idea of communalism as a basis for understanding the idea of moral personhood, moral education, and moral reasoning. Critics may, from the perspective of the metaphilosophical view underlying meta-ethics, question the plausibility of culling an African moral philosophy from an ethnophilosophical moral idea such as communalism. This metaphilosophical view sees ethics as a philosophical enterprise involving the abstract linguistic and conceptual analysis of moral principles and concepts such as 'goodness', 'ought', and 'obligation', and also finding the logical and epistemological basis for various moral principles and concepts. This view also seems to assume a universalist metaphilosophical stance, which indicates that philosophy and moral philosophy must be formal, conceptual, and analytic. Meta-ethics may be seen as representing this analytic and formal view of philosophy, which has now become the predominant enterprise in the contemporary analytic tradition of Western philosophy.[16] Thus, many contemporary analytic philosophers see ethics solely in terms of meta-ethics.

William Frankena has argued against the attempt by recent moral philosophers to restrict moral thinking or reduce moral philosophy to meta-ethics, that is, the abstract, logical, conceptual, and linguistic analysis of moral notions or principles.[17] He distinguished between three kinds of thinking with respect to morality. The first involves the kind of descriptive empirical inquiry that sociologists, anthropologists, psychologists, and historians engage in. The second involves normative thinking, the type engaged in whenever someone tries to find standards for what is morally good, bad, or obligatory. The second kind of thinking may be done as a practical or theoretical activity or both. The third involves analytical or meta-ethical thinking, which involves the efforts to find and articulate logical, epistemological, or semantical answers to moral questions and to logically analyze moral concepts.[18]

According to Frankena, "Many recent moral philosophers limit ethics or moral philosophy to thinking of the third kind, excluding from it all questions of psychology and empirical science and also all normative questions about what is good or right."[19] However, to limit philosophizing (moral or otherwise) to this kind of inquiry or discourse, which is consistent with the formal contemporary conception of philosophy, involves a parochial metaphilosophical stance about the nature of philosophy, and in particular, ethics.[20]

We cannot ignore the relevance of the works of anthropologists, psychologists, sociologists, and historians for the work of philosophers. This does not imply that the works of the people in these other disciplines are necessarily philosophical, but there are obvious philosophical precursors or pedigrees in them that philosophers must use to inform their work. For instance, anthropologists and sociologists describe the commonsense, cultural, and intuitive moral views of people that philosophical theories must draw from and be sensitive to. In recognizing the connection among the three kinds of moral thinking, Frankena adopts the inclusive approach, which combines the three above kinds of moral thinking. Similarly, moral thinking or moral philosophy in African cultures cannot be limited to the third kind, metaethics, which is purely formal and analytic. Rather, moral thinking in African cultures, primarily, involves the first two kinds. Since the first two are legitimate approaches, it is not legitimate to use only the third as a basis for determining whether traditional Africans have moral thought or a moral philosophy. Kai Nielsen argues that: "Traditionally, moral philosophy has a practical purpose; moral knowledge was not conceived as purely theoretical knowledge of a moral phenomenon but as practical knowledge about how we ought to live. The goal was not that we should simply know what goodness is but that we should become good."[21] The idea underlying the analytic approach is that analyzing moral notions will help people to understand the nature of moral goodness so that they can rationally and autonomously decide how to act based on such understanding. This idea seeks to reject normative ethics, which involves specifying some norms or principles regarding how people ought to act.

## Communalism and the Contextual Basis of Morality

One of the concerns that motivates the meta-ethical or analytic approach to moral philosophy is relevant to the criticism of ethnophilosophy and the idea of getting African moral philosophy from cultural values, beliefs, and principles. The concern is that the normative approach may lead people to internalize or accept normative principles as dogmas and they may act on such principles that they have not critically examined, rationally understood, or justified for themselves. In spite of these concerns, the limitation or restriction of philosophy (moral or otherwise) to analysis or the effort to define philosophy solely in terms of the analytic tradition or method is, from a metaphilosophical stance, inadequate.[22] It seeks to deny that other kinds of moral inquiry that are descriptive, normative, practical and applied in nature, may be characterized as a legitimate philosophical moral enterprise. For instance, Africans do not deem it fit to engage in abstract linguistic analysis of moral notions partly because most African languages are precise, simple, and easy to understand when used in moral discourse. As such, there was no practical or theoretical need to engage in the analysis and clarification of concepts in order to understand moral principles or engage in a moral discourse. Moreover, what these moral notions mean, and how they should be understood, are clearly indicated in experience by their practical implications. Because philosophy or moral philosophy in African traditions involves practice not abstract theory, people typically do not engage in the activity of mere abstract theorizing or linguistic and conceptual analysis of moral notions for its own sake.

Thinkers or people in African traditions do not engage in the kind of abstract linguistic analysis that is devoid of human circumstances and human applications. It is not part of African philosophical practice to examine how moral notions *ideally* ought to be used in terms of its logic. This is usually the kind of abstract linguistic and conceptual analysis that critics of analytic philosophy have bemoaned as lacking relevance to how people actually lead their lives. It is pertinent to emphasize that the fact that abstract linguistic analysis of moral notions is not typically done in African cultures does not necessarily imply that they are not capable of engaging in such abstract linguistic analysis. It is simply that such logical analysis of concept was not seen as a fruitful enterprise given the general outlook or metaphilosophical stance about philosophy as a practice. Moreover, the ability to use language properly and beautifully in conversation to explain a point and convince people was considered a virtue. The ability to use language plainly and figuratively (such as proverbs) is an art. Chinua Achebe alludes to this in his novel, *Things Fall Apart*: "Having spoken plainly so far, Okoye said the next half a dozen sentences in proverbs. Among the Ibo the art of conversation is regarded very highly, and proverbs are the palm-oil with which words are eaten. Okoye was a great talker and he spoke for a long time, skirting round the subject and then hitting it finally."[23] The important point here is the importance of ordinary conversation, narratives, and discourse as context for understanding the meanings of concepts. Hence, there was no need to engage in the logical analysis of concepts.

For the most part, concepts in African thought had meaning only in the discursive context of their use. The meanings of moral notions were learned from conversations and narratives, and moral ideas and principles, which have a bearing on how to become a morally good person, were learned from experience, oral tradition, and by imitation. Moral thought or moral philosophy is an everyday practical enterprise that ordinary people engage in during their daily living when they examine how they should lead their lives and in their efforts to apply moral principles to their daily lives, hence, it is not an activity that only professional experts in philosophy can engage in. So, in the African communal context, to think or reason morally, is to think or reason about how, practically, one ought to behave morally. Such thinking or reasoning also involves, in some sense, thinking or reasoning about the substantive meaning of the moral notions or concepts that describe one's moral actions, in virtue of which those actions are evaluated and understood. However, it is not necessary to rationally think about each and every action in order to find ultimate justification. People may accept principles and act on them even though they have not rationally thought about their ultimate justification. Yet, based on their upbringing, whenever they are pressed to justify such actions or principles, they can usually do so by appealing to their experiences, which are underpinned by some broad ultimate principles such as communalism and humanism.

For instance, a person may act based on the fact that he trusts the judgment of an elder, such that the trust and the moral authority of the elder, provide an indirect rational justification for his action. In which case, this person does not rely on his own individual rational justification alone as a direct basis for his action, independent of his moral deference and dependence on an elder who is trusted and considered as having moral and epistemic authority and the repository of knowledge and wisdom. Moral thought in African traditions was seen, primarily, as an activity that should be 'fruitful' with direct practical relevance. There is a sense in which traditional African traditions subscribe to the idea that philosophical theories, especially with respect to ethics, should be able to illuminate practical problems and substantive issues in a way that people can use to deal with real life situations. So, in the parlance of Western contemporary philosophy, moral thinking among Africans can be described as contextual, particularistic, practically normative, and applied. Moral principles in African cultures are articulated, applied, and evaluated on the basis of the communal human experiences and the context in which people act and live.

A moral rule is therefore morally justified and prescribed as a duty and as an acceptable form of conduct not on the basis of its abstract and logical validity, but on the basis of the practical implications of obeying the rule and the probable utility for the community and individuals. It is in this regard, for instance, that the idea of becoming a good person in African traditions is founded on the ideas of communalism and humanism, in that these ideas provide the basis for understanding moral personhood or the morally good person. Moral personhood is understood in terms of the practical moral virtues that one has acquired, and the ability to, in fact, act in ways that meet the responsibilities that are specified by a community, and the rights or social recognition that flow from acting morally. The ideas of morality, moral principles, and of becoming a morally good person are couched in particularistic, humanistic, naturalistic, and contextual terms. However, they also have universal implications, application, and validity, in so far as they involve the welfare of humans generally. So, moral philosophy in African traditions cannot be seen, simply or solely, as a theoretical enterprise; moral philosophy is a practice.

For instance, Onwuanibe indicates that: "The traditional African philosophy of the human person is more existential and practical than theoretical that is, metaphysical. It is based in part on the conviction that the metaphysical sphere is not abstractly divorced from concrete experience; for the physical and metaphysical are aspects of the reality, and the transition from the one to other is natural."[24] These points about the practical nature of morality and moral philosophy seem to underscore my metaphilosophical view that, in general, African philosophy, and in particular, moral philosophy, must be seen from the perspective of the communalistic normative conceptions of a person, rights, and duties. This view is consistent with Kant's and Henry Sidgwick's thought that "moral philosophy . . . should give a systematic account of the knowledge man already possesses; it should try to unify and show the ultimate rationale of the moral knowledge and practices man already has."[25] The traditional African practical approach to moral philosophy and its communalistic and humanistic view of morality seek to fulfil this task of moral philosophy, which is to use the ideas of communalism and humanism to unify and provide the ultimate justification for the moral practices, beliefs, principles, values, and knowledge. This view of moral philosophy further underscores the metaphilosophical stance that philosophy in African traditions does not simply seek to theorize or develop philosophical or moral theories about abstract and conceptual issues, but instead, to provide as a practice and a practical way of living.

Although meta-ethics dominated Anglo-American analytic philosophy for much of the twentieth century, normative and applied ethics has begun to reassert itself with analytic philosophy. But I also recognize that some philosophers do applied ethics from the perspective of analytic philosophy. These philosophers see ethics as involving humanistic values, which have practical implications or applications for how people should interact and lead their lives socially. In this regard, philosophy, in general, and moral philosophy, in particular, tend to have practical and activist elements, which the formal and universal conceptions of philosophy and ethics lack. The efforts by analytic philosophers to logically analyze concepts and to provide universal or objective principles or justifications, or the emphasis on articulating theories that are logically consistent, seek to remove activism and practical human elements from philosophy. These efforts and their consequences have lead to the commonplace criticism that analytic philosophy is too theoretical and abstract. As such, it removes philosophy from the practical and contextual realm of human existence. This criticism does inform my project because I want the idea of communalism in African cultures to be understood, primarily, as a practical and moral notion, and as a specific moral theory in African moral philosophy. In a broader sense, communalism is also, secondarily, an epistemic, logical or semantic, political, and a social notion. This analysis of African communalism also ties into the efforts by contemporary moral philosophers to go back to its ancient and traditional roots of seeing ethics as a normative, practical, and an applied discipline.

As such, the idea of communalism in African traditions has substantive practical relevance in people's lives, social and political structures, in the context of moral epistemology, moral reasoning, and moral education in African thought. So, my metaphilosophical stances about the nature of philosophy, moral philosophy, and my view and analysis of communalism as a moral and practical philosophical theme, imply that if communalism is to be the foundation for ethics, then the nature of philosophy must have relevance for how ethics as a sub-discipline of philosophy is conceived in African cultures. My plausible views of philosophy, African philosophy, and African moral philosophy involve attempts to provide an alternative to the formal, theoretical, 'individualistic', and universalistic view of philosophy and moral philosophy. This alternative seeks to draw on the non-individualistic, informal, communal, religious, existential, practical, and discursive traditions of the ancient and medieval periods of Western philosophy, and the non-analytic continental traditions of hermeneutics, phenomenology, and existentialism.[26] This point is underscored by Pierre Hadot's view, which indicates that the ancient Western philosophers had a metaphilosophical view that saw philosophy as a practice and way of life. In his view, ancient Western philosophers did not see theory and practice as separate, instead, they saw them as conceptually linked.[27] The idea of being cognizant of the different traditions and approaches of philosophy have a heuristic value regarding how moral philosophy, morality, and communalism in African cultures are understood.

Perhaps, what this African view of moral philosophy suggests is that linguistic analysis may not be necessary for critical reasoning, argumentation, or philosophy, and perhaps, linguistic analysis is not the only legitimate mode of doing philosophy.[28] In a broader historical perspective, linguistic analytic philosophy and meta-ethics are a mere blip on the philosophical screen, at most, half a century out of two millennia of philosophical activities. The principles, values, or duties that moral notions or concepts specify in African cultures are easily understood and appreciated because of their practical import, the relevant context, and the modes of learning them. These moral ideas can easily be grasped because of the way they are instantiated by people's consistent set of actions, experiences, and ways of life. As such, people are able to understand moral principles and notions by understanding people's actions, which are seen as models for making sense of these principles and notions. The actions of elders or those who are regarded as moral authorities, and the way the community is organized, also practically demonstrate the relevant principles as a way of providing models for the youth about the acceptable behaviors. Elders, i.e., those who have acquired moral personhood and the community have to make conscious efforts to educate people informally within the general context of using language in discourse, oral traditions, and narratives by providing actual or conceived models of acceptable actions in stories that indicate the relevant meanings of moral notions and principles, and how to use and understand them.

We must, therefore, understand African moral thought or moral philosophy fundamentally as a process or enterprise in the broad sense that includes a synthesis of the three types of moral thinking that Frankena identified above: (1) descriptive empirical inquiry, (2) normative inquiry, and (3) analytical or meta-ethical inquiry. Nonetheless, this broad sense of moral thought is still studied technically in the formal and strict sense of philosophy as a body of knowledge and as an activity that is engaged in by professional philosophers. Philosophy, in general, and moral philosophy, in particular, must be captured in this broad sense because such thinking existed among ordinary people like the pre-Socratic philosophers, whose ideas among others are now being studied by experts and formally taught in schools as the technical discipline of philosophy. In other words, the theories that constitute the contents of philosophy or moral philosophy as a technical discipline or body of knowledge involve, and draw from, the thoughts and ideas of some ordinary people such as the pre-Socratic philosophers. For instance, many of the ideas of Socrates that are credited to Plato were the ideas of either Socrates' interlocutors who were ordinary people or the ideas of Socrates that emerged primarily from the process of his dialogue with ordinary people. One might even say that Socrates was an ordinary person who thought about and conceptualized various moral ideas from his everyday experiences and people's actions. For instance, he examined the action of Euthyphro in order to attempt a conceptualization of the idea or principle of piety.

Many of the universalists who criticize African ethnophilosophy or doubt the existence of African philosophy may question whether ordinary people in traditional African societies engaged in the kind of philosophical and moral thinking, critical examination, and conceptualization that Socrates engaged in. But the particularists who defend African ethnophilosophy argue that traditional Africans do engage in the kind of thinking that is similar to Socrates', in terms of finding rational, conceptual, and fundamental basis for justifying their every moral knowledge, beliefs, and actions. (I shall fully discuss this form of moral thinking that relies on stories and proverbs in the following chapter.) The argument by the particularist is that the rational foundations for moral principles still exist in the form of narratives, proverbs, folklore, fables, and stories, except that they are not very obvious or clearly articulated. They argue that such latent justification or foundations can be analyzed and reconstructed from their pedigrees, and critically examined by technically trained professional philosophers. Such analysis and reconstruction may constitute a legitimate formal African moral philosophy. If the African idea of communalism in ethnophilosophy could provide the raw materials or pedigree for a formal African moral philosophy, one may say that African ethnophilosophy is a legitimate philosophy, and that there is, indeed, an African philosophy or moral philosophy, at least, in the rudimentary, ancient, Socratic, and pre-Socratic senses of philosophy.[29] When a contemporary analytic philosopher is analyzing what one may call the rudimentary ethnophilosophy of the pre-Socratics and ancient periods, he is in fact doing philosophy.

In a similar manner, when a contemporary philosopher is reconstructing communalism from African ethnophilosophy, he is doing African philosophy. It is pertinent to stress that traditional African moral thoughts are still pervasive today in people's social lives, beliefs, values, and sayings, and these thoughts have been passed on to people by oral tradition.[30] One does not have to dig too hard or go too far to find these traditional African philosophical pedigrees. By drawing from these everyday beliefs, values, and principles, moral theories must seek to answer practical and social questions regarding how people should relate to each other in society and the substantive goals or goods that people should pursue. Thus, Blocker argues that, "In addition to the question what we ought to do, then, moral philosophers are also concerned with the question which goods we ought to pursue."[31] This question involves finding not only theoretical answers, but also commonsense practical or intuitively plausible answers to the issue regarding why certain actions are acceptable in a society and why others are not. The activity of moral philosophy involves the examination of how the moral sensitivity or point of view that is needed to engage in moral thinking and use moral principles are taught and passed on to the youth of society. This is an essential element of what I see in African cultures as the communalistic conception of morality, moral personhood, community, and the moral relations among people in a community.

The idea of communalism, like many moral theories, must draw from and be sensitive to people's intuitions that are shaped by everyday living, social conditions, and experiences. Thus, morality is a social phenomenon and moral philosophy is a social enterprise. Frankena underscores this point by arguing that:

> Morality . . . is a social enterprise, [it is] not just a discovery or invention of the individual for his own guidance. Like one's language, state, or church, it exists before the individual, who is inducted into it and becomes more or less of a participant in it, and it goes on existing after him. Moreover, it is not social merely in the sense of being a system governing the relations of one individual to others; such a system might still be entirely the individual's own construction, as some parts of one's code of action with respect to others almost inevitably are, for example 'My rule is to smile first.' Morality, of course, is social in this sense to a large extent; however, it is also social in its origin, sanctions, and functions. It is an instrument of society as a whole for the guidance

of individuals and smaller groups. It makes demands on individuals
which are, initially at least, external to them.[32]

Because morality is a social activity, phenomenon, and enterprise with cultural
underpinnings, conceptual and theoretical moral thought and its practical applications must, in some sense, be informed by the social or cultural context.[33] Thinking
socially about morality requires that people who are engaged in this kind of thinking must use their everyday experiences to reflect on their moral principles in terms
of its practical implications. Such thinking should not be limited to the abstract,
critical, and linguistic analytic model that is adopted by analytic philosophers,
which has been criticized as sterile and fruitless.

This criticism has, in part, engendered an alternative view, in terms of a new
trend in philosophy and ethics: applied philosophy and ethics. This criticism may
also be seen as a way of giving credence to the African communalistic ethics,
which is humanistic, contextual, particularistic, and care-based. So, the African
communalistic view of morality may be seen as an alternative view, which is a
contribution to moral philosophy world-wide. The communalistic idea of morality,
moral thought, and moral reasoning in African thought may be seen as having a
foundation in the fundamental communal question: 'what ought *we* to do?' (as a
community) as opposed to 'what ought *I* to do' (as an individual). But 'what ought
*we* to do?' and 'what ought *I* to do' are mutually dependent, in the sense that the
community is and depends on the individual and the individual is and depends on
the community. In order to understand this traditional African view of morality,
and dependence of moral personhood on community and vice versa, we must
appreciate how the community socializes individuals and shapes their moral outlook based on the normative conceptions of personhood and community, which
involve the integration of the person into the community. Hence, 'what ought *we*
to do?' as a duty in the community is logically prior to and usually shapes or
informs 'what ought *I* do to?' as an individual, in order to acquire moral personhood. But acquiring moral personhood makes the community better in order to help
the individual lead a happy life. According to Lee and Hord, "If the individual
identity is grounded in social interaction, in the life of the community, then that
individual's good life is inseparable from the successful functioning of his or her
society."[34]

The moral question regarding 'we' is, for the most part, the basis for the later
regarding 'I'. In terms of logical priority, thinking morally about the 'we' (the
communal self) comes before the 'I' (individual self), because it is in virtue of 'we'
that one morally identifies an 'I'. The logical priority of the 'we' does not necessarily imply the normative judgment that the 'we' is more valuable or has moral
priority, in terms of how to resolve possible conflict of interests between the community and the individual. Although for the most part, the interests of the commu-

nity and individuals are coextensive, they are not mutually exclusive. The African idea of the community and individual personhood avoids a reasonable conflict between them. But where there is a difference or conflict, which may be rare, the resolution of such moral conflicts involves the balancing or harmonizing these interests in order to achieve equilibrium regarding the good of both the community and individuals. This reflection assumes the theory that communal interest is fundamental as a basis for an individual's interest and this theory is matched with the individual's interest or immediate intuition regarding what is good in order to achieve equilibrium. This is similar to Rawls' idea of 'reflective equilibrium'.[35] The plausibility of this view would help to justify and explain why morality, moral education, and moral thought tend to focus more on how an individual's moral choices may sustain the structures of the community that make the life of individuals fulfilling. In this regard, morality or moral reasoning is not focused, primarily, on the logical validity of an individual's decision-making process or how that process is brought to bear on her actions. Instead, the logic of an individual's moral thinking is rooted in the ability to articulate principles that would enhance the community and in turn enhance the well-being of the individual and others.

Because the well-being, rights, and interests of the individual are coextensive with the well-being and interests of the community, individuals' rights and communal duties (as specified by the community) are mutually reinforcing. In this regard, the rights and interests of individuals are correlative with the duties and responsibilities to others, which provide the moral basis for the community and communal life. So, the validity of one's practical moral reasoning is based on how one is able to apply or translate general principles, which are anchored in the interest of the community, to one's own principle regarding one's actions. According to the communalistic ethos, one must justify one's actions in terms of placing one's interest in the context of the community's interests. As Wiredu indicates: "The word 'communalistic' might be used to characterize the bent of that ethic. This alludes to the fact that in that outlook the norms of morality are defined in terms of the adjustment of the interests of the individual to the interests of society, rather than the adjustment of the interests of society to those of the individual."[36] Wiredu's point here is a reference to the logical of moral reasoning as opposed to the contents of the relevant interests which are morally dependent and coextensive. In general, the fundamental substantive moral contents of people's interests, according to the African communal view, involve the ability to acquire moral personhood and lead a good life. Such contents indicate a set of principles that people can use to guide conduct, in order to maintain social cohesion in a community, so that individuals can achieve self-realization and acquire full personhood. Being a moral person involves one's ability to act in various ways that are consistent with the broad moral principles of a community that make peaceful and happy life possible for all.

## Moral Reasoning and Communalism

The logic of moral reasoning and the nature of morality in African cultures is based on the mutual and coextensive relationships among all the individuals in the community and between the community and individuals. This underlying logic of moral reasoning in the African communalistic ethos and its normative conception of personhood is, as alluded to by Menkiti, partially evident in Rawls' view of equal justice. Rawls argues that "Equal justice is owed to those who have the capacity to take part in and to act in accordance with the public understanding of the initial situation."[37] In other words, the moral principle of equal justice presupposes that people have the rational or metaphysical capacity to be active participants in a community and to act in accordance with its material principles, which are understood as the acceptable public principles of action. Rawls also suggests that the capacity to take part and act in accordance with those principles is contingent on having a moral personality, which involves internalizing and acting on the acceptable principles of a community. Thus, Rawls indicate, "the sufficient condition for equal justice [is] the capacity for moral personality."[38] Having such moral personality involves having a moral worth that must be treated in a particular moral manner. This moral worth, in the African view, does not derive solely from having biological, psychological, or metaphysical characteristics but also from the moral characteristics of personhood. The corollary of this view is that one of the characteristics of a person who has a moral personality involves having the ability to see others as having moral worth or the potentiality for moral worth or personhood in order to treat them morally. In this regard, being a moral person involves a mutual appreciation of the moral worth of other persons or their potential. This is a plausible reason why Rawls sees moral personality as a kind of potentiality, which human beings have to realize in due course as people continue to live their lives in the proper community. This is consistent with the African view that the community has an important role to play in the process of living one's life as a moral person and acquiring moral personality.

The relevant point in Rawls' account of morality, moral personhood, and moral development that is pertinent to an understanding of the African communal context for moral reasoning is that one's moral potentiality is not realized by the individual alone as a rational, metaphysical, isolated, or abstract individual. Moral personhood must be realized within the context of and with the help of the community and society in which the substantive principles of justice and morality operate. According to Rawls' account of moral choice and reasoning, individuals under the veil of ignorance "do not know how the various alternatives will affect their own particular case and they are obliged to evaluate principles solely on the basis of general considerations."[39] This idea is similar to the moral reasoning in African communalism, in the sense that because individuals do not know how communal principles will affect them or their own interest in each and every situation, they are therefore socially obliged not to be egoistic, but to act as if they are under the veil of ignorance. As such, they must evaluate the relevant communal principles on the basis of some general humanistic and communal considerations, such as how such principles will affect the general human welfare in the community of which they are part. In this case, evaluating principles on the basis of general considerations may suggest, from an African perspective, that people must consider moral principles and actions in terms of how they affect the community, which makes human welfare, individuals' rational life plans, and interests possible or achievable. So, Rawls indicates that the substantive contents and application of the principles of justice, by virtue of which people achieve moral personality, must reflect the context of a community.

To summarize, we may say that the idea of communalism or communalistic morality involves a set of social and public principles, which operate among people who have either acquired moral personhood or seek to acquire moral personhood. People seek and are able to acquire personhood only within a community of people who have developed a normative structure or process for educating and training people to attain moral personhood or personality. The relevant principles require that moral persons do not act in ways that may either threaten moral and social equilibrium, the existence of the community or vitiate the welfare of anyone including themselves. For instance, it is considered to be morally reprehensible for someone not to be hardworking or for someone to commit suicide or to refuse to seek help for problems or treatment for illness because such acts threaten or vitiate the person's own welfare, bearing in mind that the welfare of one person necessarily contributes to the welfare of the community. So, if someone is not hardworking, it means that the person cannot provide for himself and that will require other people to pick up the slack. Doing something that is morally unacceptable in the community—even harming oneself or not pursuing one's own interest or welfare —is regarded as an affront to the community. An affront to the community is also an affront to one's own long-term interest and rational life plan, as well as the interest of others in the community. Since such action is morally reprehensible, an individual who is in tune with his communal moral self, who is making efforts to acquire personhood, ought to feel a sense of shame, guilt, remorse, and disappointment. That person will get some ribbing, chiding, poking, and prodding from others

The rules of a society have a rational, psychological, moral impact on an individual only because an individual must use those rules to rationally and emotionally guide her conduct or behavior in order to acquire personhood, achieve her life plans and conception of the good. For a rationally and emotionally wholesome person, according to the African communal view of personhood and morality,

> the transgression of accepted moral rules gives rise not just to a feeling
> of guilt but to a feeling of shame—the point being that once morality
> is conceived as a fundamental part of what it means to be a person, then
> an agent is bound to feel himself incomplete in violating its rule, thus
> provoking in himself the feeling properly describable as shame, with its
> usual intimation of deformity and unwholeness.[40]

There is a sense in which it is accepted in African cultures that the abilities to understand and feel shame and guilt, are psychological tendencies that must be learned, and developed in the context of a community. Moreover, one must rationally understand why one feels a sense of guilt and shame, and one must be taught what one should feel guilt and shame about. This is where the community plays an important role in teaching people the unacceptable modes of behavior they should avoid. What one should avoid will be what is not acceptable by the community, that is, the requisite factors that may fail to create an environment that will lead to the moral growth of a person or the achievement of personhood, since the idea of a morally grown person depends on the community.

It is expected that a person has been taught by the community to know the accepted ways of acting and what is expected of him. So, what defines a person as having moral personhood is the ability to consider the needs of others and one's own needs in the context the community, and to feel a sense of shame, guilt, remorse, and show moral sensitivity. Having a moral conscience and being morally sensitive to the needs of others in relation to one's own are some of the virtues, values or attitudes that the community instills and cultivates in an individual. The ability to also learn and display such virtues and moral sensitivity is what defines the individual in a wholesome sense as a moral person. Perhaps, knowing the principles that should govern behavior and being able to feel shame or guilt when one violates the principles are essential elements of what it takes to be an adult or a morally educated person in African cultures. It appears reasonable, as Menkiti argues in the context of African communal cultures, that morality (attaining moral personhood) ought to be considered as essential to our conception of what constitutes a person. The ability to feel shame or guilt because of one's improper conduct is a psychological part of what it means for one to be a moral person. One acquires such ability by being able to associate certain improper acts with certain feeling or by understanding the proper feelings that certain acts should generate. Such association or understanding is something that one learns in the community.

What an individual does autonomously and rationally usually depends on the principles and values of his community and how such principles or values have shaped his psychological make-up and moral point of view. In this regard, Menkiti argues that, in Rawls' view, a Kantian ethics is reasonable only because the relationship between a person and rules (in a social or communal context) is possible, in that an autonomous, free, and independent individual must see herself in relation to the moral rules of a community. Without a community of people and rules, where a person can learn about the universal interests and needs of people, one will not be able to reason rationally about the universal application and objective nature of moral principles. In other words, a person would not understand, learn, or know anything about other people in order to reason and accept that they ought to treat them the way they themselves and their loved ones ought to be treated. The adequacy of a moral principle depends, in part, on the normative processes and structures of a community that may be manifested in a member's ability to mold his life and character, and to act in a way that reflects moral sensitivity. A moral character is manifested in one's ability to consistently adhere to and participate broadly— morally and emotionally—in the communal life, which seeks to address the issue of 'what ought *we* to do?'. Addressing this issue requires carrying out what is dictated by the moral principles of the community and the obligations or duties that are associated with these principles. Carrying out such duties is one way of engaging in fellowship with the community.

Fellowship with others in a community of shared values involves explicit communication, which is manifested in active participation in the communal life and the acceptance of one's social responsibilities. The moral relationship among individuals in the community with respect to their responsibilities to each other and the community seems to create a moral problem of asymmetry of responsibility and blame. For instance, when someone turns out to be a good person, the community takes pride in the person and the credit; he becomes the child of everyone in the community. However, when someone turns out to be a bad person, he is chastised, and responsibility or blameworthiness rests solely on the individual because he is seen as a rational autonomous moral adult who is responsible for his own actions. The moral asymmetry arises from the fact that the community does not take responsibility for the possibility that it may not have done a good job training and morally educating the person. The reason for this asymmetry has to do with the fact that the community provides the facilities to help one turn out to be a good person, but it is left to the person to use them; hence, if the person fails to utilize the facilities, he is to be blamed. This problem of moral asymmetry has an interesting implication. It implies that the community does not consider itself to be a factor that strongly determines the actions and choices of individuals. Each person still has to engage in moral reasoning in order to use her discretion and autonomy to determine a particular line of action for herself. Moreover, the community does not consider itself to be brainwashing a person such that one is not able to reason on one's own. The moral conceptions of personhood, community, and relationship between the individual and a community seem to provide the underlying logic behind morality, blame, moral reasoning and judgment in African cultures.

It is pertinent to indicate that, in spite of the fact that Rawls' view seems to appreciate the role of the community in shaping moral personality and character, his view is not entirely consistent with the African communalistic view of morality and moral reasoning. There is an indication that Rawls wants to divorce moral reasoning, morality, and the realization of moral personality from the context of the community and its communal principles. He wants to remove the bias, concern, caring, and partiality that may be created by one's community and social relationships from the realm of morality in order to make it objective and impartial. For instance, he sees the principles of justice as universal and objective principles that rational individuals would accept from an original position—under the veil of ignorance. This means that the principles of justice are not particularistic or contextual or sensitive to some existential human conditions and relationships. Such conditions and relationships are necessary for one to develop a moral point view and the attitude of caring. Without this point of view and attitude of caring for others, one cannot make sense of the formal, universal, and objective strictures on morality. The veil of ignorance is, in my mind, supposed to remove the community and the contextual and substantive contents of the principles of justice, so that they can be fair, universal, rational, and objective. In other words, by being under the veil of ignorance, people do not know their own situation in the context of their community and the available relevant alternatives. As such, they are not prejudiced by their knowledge of their own situation in the community. Rawls uses the idea of 'original position' as a theoretical construct to capture his idea of fairness, which involves being impartial. A moral person for him is one who is fair.

So, the Rawlsian account of a person in the original position as a fair, rational, autonomous, and individualistic subject presupposes that the explanation for an individual's action and choices should be based solely on his reasoning and judgment outside of his social and natural context. A person's deliberation and choices in the original position is free of his social process and influence. As such, a 'complete' moral person—one who is fair—is one who is able to reason competently in order to make universal and impartial judgments, and autonomous moral choices that are fair and objectively valid. As such, the Rawlsian view of ethics has been criticized by proponents of care, feminine, communalistic, and particularistic views of ethics. The communalistic and care views of ethics indicate that morality, as opposed to being impartial, universal, and objective, is indeed, contextual, partial, particularistic, and sympathetic because of the primacy of care and concern for the particular relationships we have with others.[41] Thus, Sandra Harding has argued that Rawls' abstract idea of a moral person who is universally fair, impartial, and just is inconsistent with the African view of morality or personhood and the ethics of caring.[42] Such view of morality and moral personhood that is devoid of particular relationship is implausible in the African communalistic cultures and traditions. It is reasonable to argue that the ethics of care is more consistent or in tune with the African view because it involves a concern for personal and human relationships within a particular community. The universalistic idea of the ethics of justice and fairness seeks to capture in a non-contextualized manner, the abstract relationships that universally exist among individuals who are abstracted from their particular human and communal relationships.

Critics also indicate that this abstract view of a just person is the philosophical basis for Lawrence Kohlberg's view of a moral person and a person's moral development. This is the view that has dominated the literature regarding the basis and nature of human moral education and development.[43] According to Kohlberg, the sequence of moral development of a person—with respect to how the person is conceived—involves, the "universal ontogenic trends towards the development of morality as it is conceived by Western moral philosophers."[44] The conception he refers to here is obviously that seen in the modern Western liberal tradition and in the works of Western moral philosophers such as Locke, Mill, Kant, and Rawls among others. This Western liberal tradition conceives of a moral person as an individualistic, autonomous, and rational subject who is capable of logical reasoning. This underlying view of morality, moral education, moral development, moral reasoning, and moral personhood, ignores the relevant communal contexts in which moral principles are learned, applied, and made meaningful. Such a view also ignores the important role that one's social context or community may play in one's moral reasoning and moral development. This point is illustrated by the idea that people who approach moral principles and reasoning from the perspective of care have learned or are socialized to approach ethics from the context or perspective of personal and human relationships and with the attitude of caring, based on their communal or social relationships and responsibilities. Such relationships, socialization, and responsibilities, which are a significant part of one's moral personality, cannot be ignored by a plausible conception of morality, moral personality, moral development, and moral reasoning.

However, it appears that Kohlberg, in his later work, agrees with the views underlying ethics of caring. He indicates that "central to the ethic of particularistic relationships are effectively-tinged ideas and attitudes of caring, love, loyalty, and responsibility."[45] However, he rejects the view that seeks to draw a sharp distinction between the particularistic ethics of caring and the universalistic ethics of justice. He also rejects the view that seeks to suggest that these two ethical perspectives are inconsistent. He rejects the view that justice and caring are "two different tracks of moral development which are either independent or in polar opposition to one another."[46] He insists that the ethics of caring, which is focused on particular relationships and is characterized by the attitude of responsibility, may be seen as supplementing and deepening the universal sense of obligation that is demanded by justice. Thus, the obligations of justice and the responsibilities that are demanded by our personal and communal relationships need not conflict. Kohlberg's point about the complementary nature of the ethics of justice and caring is instructive for the African communal view of morality. It indicates that the African communalistic view of ethics, which at its core, is concerned about communal and personal relationships, responsibilities, and caring about others in the community, as the basis of meeting one's own person needs and interests, may not necessarily be opposed to a universal sense of justice. According to Aristotle, the idea justice is at the heart of all moral principles; it is the moral ideal that all moral principles aim at. But in his view, justice is also rooted in a community whose primary bond is a shared understanding of what is good for individual human beings as well as what is in the interest of the community, the context in which people achieve their individual life plans, self-realization, and happiness.

It is reasonable to argue from an African perspective that a plausible account of the nature of moral personhood and morality or its rational foundation must consider contexts and practical utility. Thus, the essence of morality and moral principles involves how they impact people in particular social contexts in which people use them, and also, their effectiveness in helping people to achieve moral character for the purpose of preserving communal and personal relationships. This idea is consistent with J. S. Mill's view about the connection between justice and utility, in that people are interested in being just only because just acts and a sense of justice have the utility of preserving social order, which is necessary for individuals to achieve their interests.[47] The African communalistic view of morality, broadly construed, is a blend of the two ethical perspectives of justice and caring, in so far as the idea of caring may be couched in terms of utility, with respect to the preservation of human relationships and welfare. A moral person is one who manifests a sense of caring, utility, and justice. Thus, one may characterize morality in African thought in terms of what William Frankena calls 'mixed deontology'. He defined this as a theory that

> recognizes the principle of utility as a valid one, but insists that another principle is required as well. This theory instructs us to determine what is right or wrong in particular situations, normally at least, by consulting rules such as we usually associate with morality; but it goes on to say that the way to tell what rules we should live by is to see which rules best fulfill the joint requirements of utility and justice.[48]

The moral outlook, justification, reasoning in African thought is, therefore, complex. Morality in African thought has complex universal and particularist elements or features of deontology, consequentialism, and the ethics of caring. For instance, the adequacy of a moral principle is determined in part by the practical adequacy of the consequences and utility of the set of actions that can be captured by or subsumed under such a principle. However, this does not suggest that moral principles and the justification of actions are based solely and necessarily on pragmatic and consequentialist grounds.

In African moral thought, there are emphases on justice, rights, duties, motive, utility, and caring. But the emphases on justice, duty, and motive do not suggest that morality is solely deontological in outlook, because these moral elements are seen as secondary and instrumental values. Thus, justice and rights are not the primary concerns of ethics. Gyekye alludes to this point, in part, by indicating that, "in the communitarian moral universe caring or compassion or generosity, not justice—which is related essentially to a strictly right-based morality—may be a fundamental moral category. In a moral framework where love, compassion, caring, friendship, and genuine concern for others characterize social relationships, justice—which is about relations of claims and counterclaims—may not be the primary moral virtue."[49] Although there is indeed emphasis on care and concern for others—based on personal and communal relationships and responsibilities—this does not mean that the ethical perspective in African moral thought is based solely on caring. Morality in African thought does consider the inherent goodness of an action in itself and the duty it imposes. However, such consideration is not done to the exclusion of caring for others in the community or the goodness of the consequences of the action and its significance or relevance to the care for others and the communal interest of which one's interest is a part. Perhaps, one might say that caring and utility are constituent parts of the notion of 'inherent goodness'. The idea of 'inherent goodness' is a complex notion.

Moral reasoning or judgment about moral goodness involves a process of reflective equilibrium, based on balancing the complex considerations and judgments regarding the inherent goodness of an action as the basis of one's motive, caring for others, and the calculation of its probable consequences based on one's knowledge and experience. In making the contrast between the Western and African conception of morality, Menkiti argues that

> it becomes quite clear why African societies tend to be organized around the requirements of duty while Western societies tend to be organized around the postulation of individual rights. In the African understanding, priority is given to the duties which individuals owe to the collectivity, and their rights, whatever these may be, are seen as secondary to their exercise of their duties.[50]

The African rationale for emphasizing duties as opposed to rights is that the emphasis on rights will suggest to individuals that they have right-claims to make of the community without any corresponding duties. However, the emphasis on duties and obligations implies that an individual's right is contingent on the ability of everyone to contribute to the community as a pool of rights from which individuals can draw. The Western individualistic idea of rational autonomy, which says that an individual can mold her moral character inductively by learning solely from her own choices and realizing her mistakes, Menkiti argues, "cannot but encourage eccentricity and individualism—traits which run counter to African ideal of what the human person is all about."[51] In other words, the point about the nature of morality in African cultures is, that the notion of morality, moral thought, moral education, and moral reasoning are underlined by a strong emphasis on the duty and obligation of the individual to the community, on the basis of which an individual constructs her identity, life-plans, goals, and reason about her actions and moral decisions.

The African communalistic ideas of morality, moral reasoning, and moral judgment indicate that there is a concern for the moral adequacy of the motive and intent of one's action. But such motive and intent must be tied to practical results and acceptable beliefs, principles, and practices. People realize that one's good moral motive and intent may be misguided and uninformed, in that one may not apply the proper humanistic principles and knowledge of one's reality and communal context. Hence, there is strong emphasis on teaching and learning one's social reality, and one's social obligations and moral duties to the community and other people, based on one's relationships. While we may analyze one's communal moral perspective in terms of duties, we also must see the moral reasons for actions from internalist and externalist perspectives. A person may see his action and justify it accordingly in an 'internalist sense' as a duty or the right thing to do, and he may be properly motivated by such justification. He is also able to justify the performance of such duty in an 'externalist sense' by some appeal to the probable utility for him and the community, in that performing or not performing those duties has mutually related consequences for the individual and community. In African thought, some communal moral duties and obligations are 'categorical' in some sense. These obligations must be carried out in the community in order for a person to attain personhood and live a meaningful life—with respect to his rational life plans—in the community. According to Menkiti, "It is the carrying out of these obligations that transforms one from the it-status of early childhood, marked by an absence of moral function, into the person-status of later years, marked by a widened maturity of ethical sense—an ethical maturity without which personhood is conceived as eluding one."[52] Some moral duties must be carried out in order for the community to exist, flourish, and provide the proper environment in which individuals can achieve personhood and their life plans. It is in this sense that, moral personhood is conceptually connected to acquiring moral virtues, performing one's duties, and being able to contextually apply the right principles to one's actions. From this conception of duty, it is obvious that an individual cannot be a moral person by developing her moral character or learning how to reason adequately, based solely on her own individual rational will.

## Communalism and the Justification of Moral Principles

With this said, we can appreciate that morality, moral thought, and moral reasoning in traditional African traditions are more of a pragmatic and humanistic enterprise. This pragmatic enterprise of ethics involves the attempts to find a set of principles as *ends* and *means* in the relevant communal and human contexts, which may vary in different African cultures and traditions. Thus, for Wiredu, African moral thought seeks to "postulate the harmonization of interests as the *means*, and the securing of human well-being as the *end* of all moral endeavor."[53] The emphasis is on understanding the right *end* which is tied to the interest of the community and human well-being , on which the interests of the individual depend. Such understanding calls for the efforts to find the proper means, within the communal context of caring, for achieving the goal of human welfare. As a basis for the pragmatic element of communalistic ethics, an individual's duty in African traditions is informed by the relevant communal epistemic conditions in terms of what, in general, people justifiably believe and accept as the principles for conduct and action. Such beliefs and principles include the idea of communalism, the goal of human well-being in a community, the relationship between the individual and the community, and the duties that such relationship imposes as the basis for moral personhood. As indicated, the complex idea of communalism and its identifying features in each culture provide the basis for peoples' moral conceptual scheme, the rational foundation for moral beliefs, values and principles, and the general moral outlook on the basis of which people reason about moral principles and actions.[54] The relevant epistemic conditions also include the available evidence based on the experiences that people have acquired inductively over time about the adequacy or efficacy of certain actions in terms of their actual results and implications.

The communal beliefs, knowledge, and evidence that people have as the basis for their actions, also seem to provide the corroboratory or confirmatory basis for adhering to certain moral principles, which specify and validate a set of prescribed duties or obligations. In this sense, a moral duty is seen as rational only because, on the basis of some evidence, it is considered to have a high probability of leading to good consequences, such as, preserving human welfare, peace, cohesion, and survival of the community—and by implication, the welfare and happiness of individuals. As a result of the emphasis on duty and the utility of moral principles for humans, in the context of natural human and social conditions, interests, and needs, it is reasonable to say that morality and moral reasoning in traditional African thought is naturalistic and humanistic. In other words, morality is founded on the natural properties and social conditions of human beings in relation to their welfare, long-term interests of happiness and survival, and the natural need or inclination to live together in a social community. So, contrary to the commonplace

Western anthropological and sociological views of African cultures, morality is not as supernatural, spiritual or religious as many people think. For instance, Wiredu and Gyekye deny that the traditional Akan (an ethnic group in Ghana) notion of morality can be substantially characterized as supernatural or having a supernatural foundation.[55] They argue that in Akan culture, which is similar to many other African cultures that emphasize communal kinship and duties, moral principles are not anchored solely in the dictates of gods, deities, supernatural entities, and spirits that human beings are not supposed to question.

According to Wiredu, "Akan ethics is a humanistic ethics in the precise sense that it is founded exclusively on considerations having to do with human well-being and, contrary to widespread reports, has nothing to do, except extrinsically, with religion."[56] He indicates that Akan moral outlook involves the efforts to preserve communal interests as a *means* for securing the *end* of human and individual well-being .[57] To the extent that morality in African traditions involves a means-scheme that is geared toward the *end* of preserving the welfare of human beings as members of a community, it is therefore humanistic. Gyekye underscores this point by arguing that the main preoccupation of Akan moral thought is with human welfare; thus, morality is founded on the idea of humanism. According to him, "The concern for human welfare constitutes the hub of the Akan axiological wheel. This orientation of Akan morality takes its impulse undoubtedly from the humanistic outlook that characterizes Akan traditional life and thought. Humanism, the doctrine that sees human needs, interests, and dignity as fundamental, thus, constitutes the foundation of Akan morality."[58] It is lack of proper understanding of the humanistic foundation for morality and moral thought in African traditions that has led people to argue that moral thought in African cultures in fundamentally religious, spiritual, and supernatural.

In this regard, O. T. Oladipo has argued against what he calls "certain widespread misconceptions about African thought and culture, for example, the widespread, but mistaken, belief that Africans are religious in all things."[59] He argues that this widespread, but mistaken view about morality in African cultures, is based on an inadequate view of religion, and the fact that people have not properly understood African beliefs, in order to make distinctions and systematic connections among the various beliefs and views held by people in African cultures. He argues that a close look at the idea of 'divinity' among the Yorubas will indicate that 'divinities' are not religious and that people do not relate to them as if they were religious or supernatural. The idea of divinity provides the basis on which the Yorubas account for nature, reality, communal living, as well as the naturalistic moral principles that derive from them. The foundation, source, and justification of moral principles in African culture cannot necessarily be couched or seen in terms of the authority of spirits, ancestors, gods or deities, or other supernatural or religious phenomena, which may be seen as specifying authoritarian moral dictates that people cannot question or rationally justify. In other words, moral principles are not necessarily seen as deriving from the gods in the form of absolute, unquestionable, and authoritative dictates that bind categorically. So, contrary to the popular view, Wiredu, Gyekye, and Oladipo have indicated that moral thought in Akan and Yoruba thought systems, which are similar to other African cultures, are humanistic and naturalistic. These views suggest that morality in African thought may indeed be antithetical to the Western sense of supernaturalism. This Western sense of supernaturalism, which is seen as antithetical to humanism, holds the view that supernatural entities, such as spirits and gods, have a metaphysical existence that is logically distinct from and not related to human nature or 'existentially connected' to human existence. Yet, these entities supposedly have absolute and authoritative moral dictates that necessarily guide human actions and behaviors.

This Western sense of supernaturalism involves irrational authoritarianism, in a way that the rational ideas of humanism and naturalism that characterize African morality or moral thoughts are not.[60] The Western sense of supernaturalism is irrationally authoritarian because it implies that people must dogmatically accept the authority of the supernatural basis for certain principles that cannot be instantiated or demonstrated in human and natural terms. The implication is that people do not question the rational basis for such authority or their moral dictates, and they will refuse to modify their views or beliefs even in the face of countervailing evidence. A naturalistic view of morality represents the philosophical view that people see, justify, analyze and understand moral views, principles, and judgment in terms of their connection to or dependence on some natural human and social phenomena or facts.[61] So, morality in traditional African thought is naturalistic to the extent that the principles of morality, judgment, and actions are materially justifiable and connected to some natural human characteristics, social conditions, and the existential reality in which people live. We should recall that according to the African view of ontology, what is sometimes characterized in the West as the supernatural —spirits, gods, and ancestors—is indeed materially and existentially connected and related to the natural world, community, everyday human living. The belief in many African cultures is that supernatural entities do not have existence that is logically or metaphysically independent of the human natural world, reality, and existence. Usually, the so-called supernatural entities are perceived and understood in purely naturalistic and substantial terms.

For instance, people generally see gods and deities in African cultures as entities that are exemplified and perceived through natural objects such as trees, animals, shrines, and their manifestation in priests and priestesses or their practical effects on people's actions. Some people are believed to be reincarnated dead people. Ancestors, the dead, gods, and spirits live among and in the midst of people. They are called upon on a daily basis for help and intervention. Hence, on most occasions, libations are poured to ancestral spirits and they are invited or conjured to join in celebrations and to provide guidance. People have communion with, offer sacrifices to, and feed them on a daily basis. They have material influence of people's lives and existence. They are experienced as part of the natural scheme of human existence. So, what may be characterized or categorized in the West as belonging to the supernatural realm is, according to African ontology, part of the natural. Thus, contrary to the Western view that humanism is antithetical to supernaturalism, Gyekye argues that the humanistic foundation for morality in African cultures is not anti-supernaturalistic. Instead, he argues that humanism in African cultures maintains a supernaturalistic metaphysics, in so far as such supernaturalistic metaphysics does not prevent or divert people's attention away from human welfare.[62] He argues that a Western humanist may object to supernaturalism because their view of supernaturalism prevents or diverts people's attention away from human welfare. In this regard, I agree that the African supernaturalistic metaphysics is not antithetical to the humanistic and naturalistic orientation of morality and moral thought. This is because there is no logical or metaphysical distinction between the natural and supernatural. Instead, the realms of the natural and supernatural are seen as parts of a natural continuum.

In my view, the humanistic and communal foundations of morality indicate that moral thought is naturalistic. And because morality in African thought is not supernaturalistic in the Western sense, it is not irrationally authoritarian. As such, moral principles do allow for creativity, autonomy, freedom of the will, and rational deliberation. A Western supernaturalistic view of morality is authoritarian because it implies that moral principles are the dictates of an infallible and absolute supernatural entity or being. As such, such principles are necessarily correct, absolute, infallible, and immutable, hence, they cannot or must not be rationally questioned. These moral principles are supernaturally imposed on humans against their will or humans irrationally accept them out of fear. Thus, if moral principles in African thought are seen as supernatural, then this means that they impede or vitiate individual will, rationality, and autonomy. And I have indicated that moral and moral principles in African thought are not grounded in some supernatural phenomenon. As such, these moral principles do not impose absolute obligations that bind in such a way as to unjustifiably go against or totally hinder or vitiate someone's rational will and autonomy. As alluded to earlier, moral principles in African thought usually allow individuals to use their rationality and creative imaginations to apply them to specific contexts. Moreover, such rationality and creative imagination may and usually lead to changes in moral practices or principles, or modifications in the duties that moral principles impose in certain contexts. The communal, humanistic, and natural foundations for moral principles in African traditions require rational deliberation by individuals and their ability to make rational decisions in the different natural and existential circumstances in which they may find themselves.

This idea of rationality, autonomy, and discretion is captured by the following proverb: 'you do not have to literally tell a rational or sensible child to get out of smoke'. In other words, reasonable people have to be able to figure out a line of action for themselves depending on the circumstances in which they find themselves. This idea is also indicated by the following proverb: 'The person who refuses to lick his lips or rob oil on them cannot blame the harmattan for drying and cracking them'. These proverbs among others are significant because they allude to the general outlook regarding how African people see rationality and discretion in reasoning, in relation to a person's responsibility. Because communalism and its humanistic and naturalistic foundations of morality do not preclude the use of rationality in certain situations where a moral decision is to be made, it is able to ascribe blame or responsibility and impose sanctions. Such rationality (intellectual and practical) is considered to be a natural feature whose use and development are, in fact, required by the naturalistic and humanistic elements of communalism and its conception of morality.[63] To claim that communalism in African cultures vitiates the intellectual or practical rationality of individuals, is to imply that African people cannot rationally identify problems, conceptualize them, reason about their solutions, and then determine how to practically solve them. This is clearly not true. In African moral thought, there is a hierarchy of moral rules that is applied in moral reasoning as the basis for conceiving, analyzing, and solving moral problems.

In this hierarchy of moral rules, there is a foundational or fundamental or meta-moral rule that any moral principle should have the nature of being predicated on communal human interest, in terms of 'what ought *we* to do (as a community)?' as opposed to 'what ought *I* to do (as an individual)?'. This fundamental moral rule, which is tied to the interests of the community from which individuals derive their interests and rights, now constitutes the basis on which general moral principles are anchored, such as 'one should not steal' or 'one should not kill'. Such principles can be seen either as a *means* or an *end*. The *end* is tied to the welfare of humans, the need to acquire moral personhood, and the needs of the relevant communal context in which human welfare can be achieved and moral personhood is acquired. With respect to the relevant ends, there could also be other substantive or sub-principles that may be characterized as *means*, such as, 'one ought not to curse' or 'one ought not to stab', in virtue of which the end is achieved. These substantive principles are lower in the hierarchy. The understanding of this characterization of morality is that the general principles and the sub-principles in a means-end scheme are moral only insofar as they are a means for enhancing the welfare of humans in the community. It is from this moral principle that a community may prescribe a particular action, and the circumstances in which such action will be acceptable. As indicated earlier, the circumstances and actions are informed by the epistemic state, i.e., the lived-experiences of the people, their evidence, their fundamental beliefs, and their general outlook on life, ontology, and cosmology.

The relevance of the epistemic state, with respect to justified beliefs that people are expected to bring to bear on morality, suggests the African traditional view of moral development is founded on the idea of fallibilistic epistemology. People realize that they are morally and epistemically fallible; as such, they consider their beliefs as tentative and justifiable only in relation to the available evidence. Some of the facts, evidence, and reasons that they bring to bear on their moral reasoning, decisions, and actions, they realize, are susceptible to error, and that such error can affect the adequacy of their moral reasoning and actions. As such, people accept moral reasons or moral principles and the moral duties or actions that they prescribe as tentative, in that the reasons and duties or actions are considered adequate only given the adequacy of their evidence and the moral consequences in the community. However, if they are confronted with better evidence or reasons that vitiate their prior thinking, they would be willing to change or modify their view and accept a new principle of action or a duty that is best supported by the prevailing evidence. It is obvious, as I shall argue, that Africans did critically examine their beliefs or principles and they did modify or change them as the need arose. Perhaps, this fallibilistic attitude toward beliefs and principles does not require any argument given the obvious changes that have taken place in African cultures. This view is practically supported by the changes that have taken place in Africa due to internal critical examination and external influence. A culture and people that cannot adapt to changes and new knowledge, information, or evidence cannot survive. The fact that many African cultures have survived and have made modifications in their beliefs and views should be an indication that they accepted or adopted fallibilism as an epistemic basis for their beliefs, principles, reasoning, and ways of life.

The idea of fallibilism also underscores the point that morality in African thought was not founded on supernaturalism. A person who approaches morality or moral reasoning from the perspective of supernaturalism would claim to have some divine perspectives of the rightness or wrongness of moral principles, which are deemed infallible and absolute.[64] Such perspectives will be inconsistent with the fallibilistic attitude or foundation of morality in African traditions. One plausible implication of this supernaturalistic moral perspective is the idea that people must be brainwashed to accept supernatural dictates. The idea of brainwashing removes rationality from moral reasoning and moral education by imparting ideas on people, such that by the very nature of the ideas as dogmatic doctrines and the process of imparting them, they cannot be rationally and critically examined. Because there are no rational basis for such moral principles, in that we cannot bring our fallible rational knowledge to bear on infallible and absolute divine dictates, people are just raised to dogmatically internalize and use them, or such principles and the duties they engender are imposed without question. The idea of brainwashing also implies that there are no rational grounds for moral disagreement, criticisms, moral enlightenment, moral growth or development. Although Africans regard some fundamental or general meta-moral principles as absolute, it is not because they are anchored in or are the dictates of some supernatural entities. The meta-principle indicating that it is morally good to do things that will lead to the fulfilment of human welfare is deemed to be absolute because it is anchored in natural facts that indicate or point to some obvious truth. However, this view does not imply that all natural facts are in themselves considered absolute; some facts may be based on human understanding, which could be fallible. Hence, some substantive moral principles in African traditions, which are characterized as means, are considered to be amenable to modifications given better evidence and understanding. Some moral principles are regarded 'absolute' only tentatively based on its relation to natural facts and human reason. A moral principle is deemed valid if, from a disinterested or dispassionate communal point of view, people can intuitively, reflectively, and rationally accept it as valid and applicable to human welfare in a relevant community.

In order to further appreciate the nature of morality and moral principles in African moral thought, and how, contrary to common views, morality in African traditions does not have supernatural foundations, it may also be pertinent to show the distinction and connections among moral rules, etiquette, taboos, social rules, and religious rules in African cultures, and the role that each plays in the communal ways of life. Lloyd's characterization of the distinction and relationship among these notions may be illuminating and instructive for the African view. He argues that these standards are like intersecting circles; the space common to them is where they are similar, but they also have their exclusive domains outside the common space.[65] From this general characterization, we can see that these notions are not necessarily mutually exclusive. But there are some spheres of life in which they have their exclusive domain. Moral rules in African cultures are perhaps not dramatically different from the way it is conceived in Western thought, in terms of how they are used by people to govern actions in order to achieve certain ends or purposes. When construed as an *end*, morality represents a set of rules, ideals, and principles that are universally, objectively, and rationally valid. They are principles that may be rationally and 'naturally' pursued by all human beings in specific situations. Moral principles *prescribe*, as *means*, a set of actions or attitudes that are other-regarding and geared towards some ends. But as means, moral principles are particular, in that they may vary with situations and cultures because different people may rationally develop different means in different situations to achieve similar sets of goals or ends.

The nature of morality, moral reasoning, or moral thought in African cultures may be viewed as having both universal or objective elements and relative or particularist elements. The moral principles that are conceived in terms of end are basically universal, in the sense that they are objectively valid, and they are principles that any person will rationally accept from a caring and other-regarding communal point of view. The ends in this case are human or humanistic ends, and they are ends that are generally valid for all humans in specific situations. The moral principles that are seen as ends are those that propose a set of ideals, goals, objectives, and aims that people, as humans, have to try to attain. However, the way people interpret these universal principles and how they decide to achieve the requisite humanistic ends, in terms of the necessary means to be used, will be contingent on the culture and context of their beliefs. These beliefs and context will determine what they consider to be the best and most efficacious means for achieving a particular end. For instance, the moral principles which prohibit stealing, doing harm, inflicting needless pain and suffering, lying with impunity to hurt others, and frivolous killing are universal as ends and ideals. However, these principles may appear relative in terms of the specific actions and conduct that a group of people subsumes under them or the means that the people use to achieve these ends. The kinds of moral principles that may be seen as means are those that propose particular actions or techniques or attitudes that people must adopt as necessary or useful for achieving certain moral ends, ideals or aims.

So, the ways that a group of people makes the appropriate justificatory connection between actions and principles may differ, depending on the circumstance. This makes moral reasoning contextual. For instance, if an African *justifiably believes* that verbal cursing in the sense of casting spells by incantations can actually have efficacy in order to cause harm, suffering, and death, then such action would be morally prohibited under the general and universal moral rule forbidding killing or causing death. This principle, considered in terms of *means* rather than *end*, within the context of the culture and belief system, is not fundamentally different from the rule which prohibits stabbing or shooting someone to death. Anyone who takes a simplistic look at the principle that prohibits verbal cursing outside the context of the culture, metaphysical assumptions about causation, and belief system will think that it is fundamentally different from the moral principle that one ought not to kill. However, the principles prohibiting stabbing and verbal cursing are only different as *means*, but are fundamentally similar in terms of the universal *end* of not killing. A Westerner who has a different conceptual scheme or metaphysical assumptions about causality may not be able to make sense of this moral principle about verbal cursing. Hence, such Westerner who does not believe in the efficacy of verbal cursing will not consider the act of cursing to be morally reprehensible, since he does not believe in the bad moral consequence of death, which an African believes could result from the act of cursing.

In this case, the Westerner will not consider it a moral duty not to curse verbally. But verbal cursing may be prohibited by the rule of common courtesy and decency. In other words, the way that a group of people may make a justificatory or rational connection between principles and actions will be based on their metaphysical assumptions and their epistemic state, in terms of what they justifiably believe. Different people can use different means to achieve the same end. So, a difference in the rules, which make references to *means* may not necessarily suggest a fundamental difference in morality if the rules about the *end* are substantially similar. In this respect, moral rules in traditional African cultures do function as epistemic, semantic, and normative criteria.[66] They constitute an epistemic criterion in the sense that they provide the methodology regarding a means-ends scheme for determining what constitutes a good or bad action or conduct. They also indicate a set of beliefs or conceptual scheme or categories of understanding, on the basis of which Africans reason about their actions and judgments. Moral rules are semantic, in that they specify the basis for meaning or what certain concepts or notions mean. They also specify what it means to say that, within the context of the people's language, culture, beliefs, and community, an action or conduct, in a means-ends scheme, is bad or good. Moral rules are normative in that they provide the standards for evaluating specific and particular behaviors in terms of goodness and badness. As normative standards, they *prescribe* actions and behaviors that are considered good for the purpose of maintaining the community, and they *proscribe* actions which are thus considered bad.

Many, if not all moral rules or principles, prescribe that the end to be achieved and the means by which it is achieved must consider the interests of the self or other persons or human welfare either by themselves alone or as a composite. As a result of this characteristic of morality, which demands that people must be sympathetic to other people's interests, moral principles thus have the utility of enhancing people's lives or human welfare by encouraging people to live with others in society or community. The notion of utility here is meant to suggest that it is considered reasonable that people should, in their moral reasoning, consider the probable consequences of their actions. Perhaps, if there were no human interests and needs that have to be met as ends, which in part have necessitated human communities where people can depend on others, the notion of morality would have been unnecessary and superfluous. Conversely, the absence of morality would lead to the decay and collapse of any human society. And the absence of society will mean that humans are uncultured, uncivilized, and unsocialized. The idea of an uncultured person is not the intuitive idea or usual moral conception of a person. For instance, in Aristotle's view, a moral person is a social animal. The intuition behind Aristotle's point is to indicate the distinction between a non-social animal, who cannot be socialized and cultured, and one who is cultured or has acquired or has the potential to acquire moral personhood or moral virtues. If one understands this intuition, one can appreciate the basis for the traditional African conception of a moral person and community, and why the notion of morality is fundamentally communalistic, naturalistic, and humanistic.

In spite of the general conceptual distinctions among morality, social rules, taboos, and religious rules, the substantive distinctions are difficult to make in African cultures. This is because, although the spheres of human endeavor in African cultures to which these concepts and rules apply and refer can be abstracted, they are in reality mutually reinforcing, coextensive, and connected. For instance, there is in reality no clear-cut distinction between social rules and religious rules, in that some of the core beliefs that people hold in society are, in part, shaped by their traditional religion, which is practiced by all in the community. Religion and its beliefs are an integral part of the people's general outlook on life. Moreover, because moral rules in African traditions are communal, they are also informed by the religious rules that are an integral part of people's lives. Hence, they are the basis for the social rules.[67] However, the basic difference that may exist among moral, social, and religious rules can be found in their sanctions. The violation of religious rules is sanctioned by the gods, ancestors, divinities, spirits or those who are believed to be their 'human representatives' on earth. The violation of moral rules is sanctioned by conscience or social approbation, which makes one feel a sense of guilt and shame. But the violation of a social rule is sanctioned by the community, which may result in social ostracism, doing community work, or the payment of fines. For instance, if you kill a stranger to safeguard yourself, the community, or another person, you may not be ostracized or socially punished, but instead, you could be socially applauded. However, this social response may not prevent you from the moral feeling of guilt that you killed somebody if you think that the situation could have been prevented.[68] Depending on the religion, you may or may not be punished by the gods or their representatives for the killing. Violating the dictates of the gods such as doing something that is sacrilegious on a sacred day may not attract social punishment, but you may, based your religious belief, seek redemption because you think you could be punished by the gods.

For instance, the moral rule: 'one should not lie' may be seen as a religious or moral rule; it may or may not be a social rule. It may be socially acceptable to lie in order to protect the community and yourself, although you may feel some guilt afterwards if your lie hurts somebody else, or if you think that lying could have been avoided. Greetings and being respectful to your elders, or showing courtesy to your peers and neighbors may be social etiquettes or social rules, but they are not religious rules. It is my view that greetings, being respectful, and showing courtesy may be viewed as moral principles in many African cultures. Greetings, respect, and show of courtesy are very important in many African cultures and traditions because they are seen as signs or indications of pleasantries, which are deemed important for enhancing human relationships, peace, and cohesion in a communal environment. It is also seen as a sign of moral respect for one who has acquired personhood. A refusal to greet a person may be seen as a moral lapse, a lack of recognition of a person, or in some cases, an insult. Such refusal may also be seen as an indication of a breakdown in personal relationships, which may usually call for intervention by neighbors or elders. Onwuanibe discussion of the moral under-pinnings for an Ibo conception of a person underscores this point: "The Ibo conception of the human person involves the notion of presence. High regard for the human person in terms of presence is displayed in everyday living in warm greetings. It is offensive not to be greeted."[69] He goes on to indicate that greetings and respect are not directed to the physical body: "Nobody greets a body but 'what' is manifested through the body."[70] He argues that what is manifested through the body is a complex self, personality, or personhood that includes the soul, spirit, and more importantly human values and dignity, which are the basis for moral person-hood. Wiredu argues that the idea of greeting people is a custom, which must be distinguished from morality: "the Akan rule of greeting . . . is a rule of custom rather than morality, strictly speaking."[71] I disagree with this distinction because custom is one of the necessary foundations for moral reasoning and contextual application of moral principles.[72]

There is a sharp contrast between how greetings are seen in Western thought and in African traditions, as a reflection of values and moral personhood. Greetings, show of respect, and courtesy, or lack thereof, are usually not placed in moral categories in Western thought. Perhaps, we can appreciate why greetings, respect, and show of courtesy are placed in a moral category in African traditions if we understand the role they place in enhancing communal ethos, human relationships, and welfare. In contrast to morality, social, and religious rules, taboos are special prohibitions or specifications of what people should avoid or what people are forbidden to do in specified circumstances. Taboos could be either religious, moral, or social or a composite of the three. They are designed, in part, to culturally train people to behave in a desirable way that would help them to attain spiritual, social and moral adulthood, and to maintain the moral and social equilibrium of the community. In general, social, religious, and moral rules could be either 'negative', in the sense of specifying what one should not do, or 'positive' in the sense of specifying what one must, should, or ought to do. But taboos are only 'negative'; they are prohibitions. For instance, it may be a social taboo to inter-marry from a particular group of people (for several reasons, such as lineage, caste, and 'social class'). It may also be a religious taboo to eat the meat of some animals that are considered sacred or unclean. It may be a social or moral taboo to spit on someone. In this sense, many of these rules (social, moral, religious, and taboos) are mutually reinforcing, in that they are all justifiably perceived as different ways of molding people's character and behaviors, for the purpose of achieving moral personhood and enhancing human welfare within the context of the community.

# Notes

1. H. Gene Blocker, *Ethics: An Introduction* (New York: Haven Publications, 1986), 7.

2. For the universalists' characterization of philosophy and Western philosophy, see Bodunrin, "The Question of African Philosophy," Wiredu, *Philosophy and An African Culture*, Hountondji, *African Philosophy: Myth and Reality*, Appiah, *Necessary Questions: An Introduction to Philosophy*, Appiah, *In My Father's House: Africa in the Philosophy of Culture*.

3. See among others the works of Menkiti, "Person and Community in African Traditional Thought," Ayoade, "Time in Yoruba Thought," Onwuanibe, "The Human Person and Immortality in IBO (African) Metaphysics," Gyekye, "Akan Concept of a Person," Gyekye, *An Essay on African Philosophical Thought--The Akan Conceptual Scheme*, Rev. Ed, J. O. Sodipo, "Notes on the Concept of Cause and Change in Yoruba Traditional Thought," *Second Order* 2, no 2, (1973): 12-20.

4. See Wiredu, *Cultural Universals and Particulars*, 61-77, in his efforts to distinguish between customs or cultural norms and morality. The stance of legal positivism is also another effort to distinguish between moral principles, religious rules, and legal rules.

5. Appiah, *Necessary Questions: An Introduction to Philosophy*, 200-210.

6. Appiah, *Necessary Questions: An Introduction to Philosophy*, 200.

7. For such characterization of the nature of moral thinking in African cultures and its relationship with or lack of with religion, see John Mbiti, *African Religions and Philosophy* (Oxford, England: Heinemann International, 1969), Gyekye, *An Essay on African Philosophical Thought—The Akan Conceptual Scheme*, Parker English and Nancy Steele Hamme, "Morality, Art, and African Philosophy: A Response to Wiredu," in *African Philosophy: Selected Readings*, ed., Albert G. Mosley (Englewood Cliffs, NJ: Prentice Hall, 1995).

8. Kai Nielsen,"Problems of Ethics," in *The Encyclopedia of Philosophy* Vols. 3 & 4, ed., Paul Edwards (New York: Macmillan Publishing, 1972),117.

9. This problem has been debated by the universalists and particularists in the form of the distinction between 'formal' and 'folk' philosophy—which people have categorized as ethnophilosophy—and its legitimacy as philosophy. I think a sufficient case has been made in the literature regarding the philosophical legitimacy of what people call ethnophilosophy.

10. Appiah, *Necessary Questions: An Introduction to Philosophy*, 207-210.

11. Wiredu, *Philosophy and An African Culture*, 15-17, 25-29.

12. Fortunes, *The Sorcerers of Dobu*.

13. Turnbull, *The Mountain People*.

14. This is one of the arguments that has been used to discount the existence of African philosophy; that is, Africa does not have individual professional philosophers (experts) who are comparable to individual professional philosophers in the West, such as, Plato, Aristotle, St. Thomas Aquinas, Descartes, Hume, Kant, and Wittgenstein, among others. See especially, Bodunrin, "The Question of African Philosophy."

15. See, among others, Robert Heinaman, "Aristotle and the Mind-Body Problem," *Phronesis* 35, no. 1 (1990): 83-102; Christopher Shields, "Soul and Body in Aristotle," *Oxford Studies in Ancient Philosophy* 6 (1988): 103-37; Herbert Granger, "Aristotle and the Concept of Supervenience," *Southern Journal of Philosophy* 31, no. 2 (1993): 161-178; Herbert Granger, "Aristotle and the Functionalist Debate," *Apeiron* 23, no. 1 (1990): 27-49.

16. By the way, this analytic way of doing philosophy is what the universalist regard as the paradigm way of way of doing philosophy. And to the extent that African philosophy may not have or use this analytical method, then it does not pass as philosophy in the paradigm Western sense.

17. William K. Frankena, *Ethics* (Englewood Cliffs, NJ: Prentice Hall, 1963), 4.

18. Frankena, *Ethics*, 4.

19. Frankena, *Ethics*, 4.

20. I cannot provide a full critique of this parochial approach and a defense of the inclusive approach here. For such critique, see Polycarp Ikuenobe, "The Parochial Universalist Conceptions of 'Philosophy' and 'African Philosophy'," *Philosophy East and West* 47, no. 2 (1997): 189-210.

21. Nielson, "Problems of Ethics," 117.

22. From the discussion of the metaphilosophical issues raised in the previous chapter, it is clear that the analytic method is not the only way of doing philosophy, and that there are other aspects of philosophy that are not fully and properly captured by analytic philosophy. I cannot provide a full critique of this parochial approach and a defense of the inclusive approach here; I have done this elsewhere: Ikuenobe, "The Parochial Universalist Conceptions of 'Philosophy' and 'African Philosophy'."

23. Achebe, *Things Fall Apart*, 10.

24. Onwuanibe, "The Human Person and Immortality in IBO Metaphysics," 184.

25. Nielson, "Problems of Ethics," 117.

26. I have done this in Ikuenobe, "The Parochial Universalist Conception of 'Philosophy' and 'African Philosophy'."

27. Hadot, *What is Ancient Philosophy?*

28. I make this point in detail in: Polycarp Ikuenobe, "Logical Positivism, Analytic Method, and Criticisms of Ethnophilosophy," *Metaphilosophy* 35, no. 4 (July 2004): 479-503.

29. See Polycarp Ikuenobe, "Moral Thought in African Cultures?: A Metaphilosophical Question," *African Philosophy* 12, no. 2 (1999): 105-123.

30. The point here that need to be stressed is that the attempt to analyze, reconstruct, and theorize about African thought systems is not being done from conjectures. These ideas are part of African people's intuitions, beliefs, and ways of life; so, the attempt here to analyze African moral thinking relies on these ideas in the same manner in which technical philosophers rely on their common sense beliefs and intuitions to argue for their views.

31. Blocker, *Ethics: An Introduction*, 12.

32. Frankena, *Ethics*, 5.

33. This idea is commonplace in the history of Western philosophy; that is, the philosophical ideas of individuals in the different periods of Western philosophy are shaped by their cultural, social, and historical circumstances.

34. Hord and Lee, *I Am Because We Are: Readings in Black Philosophy*, 8.

35. John Rawls, *A Theory of Justice*, 18-19.

36. Wiredu, *Cultural Universal and Particulars: An African Perspective*, 71.

37. Rawls, *A Theory of Justice*, 505.

38. Rawls, *A Theory of Justice*, 506.

39. Rawls, *A Theory of Justice*, 136-37.

40. Menkiti, "Person and Community in African Traditional Thought," 176.

41. See Nel Noddings, *Caring: A Feminine Approach to Ethics and Moral Education* (Los Angeles, CA: University of California Press, 1984); Marilyn Friedman. "Care and Context in Moral Reasoning," in *Women and Moral Theory*, eds., Eva Feder Kittay and Diana T. Meyers (Savage, MD: Rowman & Littlefield, 1987), 190-204; Carol Gilligan, "Moral Orientation and Moral Development," *In Women and Moral Theory*, eds., Eva Feder Kittay and Diana T. Meyers. 19-33.

42. Sandra Harding, "The Curious Coincidence of Feminine and African Moralities: Challenges for Feminist Theory," *In Women and Moral Theory*, eds., Eva Feder Kittay and Diana T. Meyers (Savage, MD: Rowman & Littlefield, 1987), 296-315.

43. For this view, see Lawrence Kohlberg, "Stages of Moral Development as a Basis of Moral Education," *In Moral Education: Interdisciplinary Approaches*, eds., C. Beck, B. Crittendon, and E. Sullivan (Toronto: University of Toronto Press, 1971), 23-92. Lawrence Kohlberg, *Essays on Moral Development: Vol. 1--The Philosophy of Moral Development* (New York: Harper & Row, 1981). Lawrence Kohlberg, *Essays on Moral Development: Vol. 2--The Philosophy of Moral Development* (New York: Harper & Row, 1984).

44. Lawrence Kohlberg, "From Is to Ought: How to Commit the Naturalistic Fallacy and Get Away with it in the Study of Moral Development," in *Cognitive Development and Epistemology*, ed., T. Mischel (New York: Academic Press, 1971), 151-231.

45. Lawrence Kohlberg, Charles Levine and Alexander Hewer, *Moral Stages: A Current Reformation and Response to Critics* (Basel: S. Karger, 1983), 20-21.

46. Kohlberg, Levine and Hewer, *Moral Stages: A Current Reformation and Response to Critics*, 137.

47. J. S. Mill. *Utilitarianism*, ed., Roger Crisp (New York: Oxford University Press, 1998).

48. Frankena, *Ethics*, 35.

49. Gyekye, *Tradition and Modernity: Philosophical Reflections on the African Experience*, 67.

50. Menkiti, "Person and Community in African Traditional Thought," 180.

51. Menkiti, "Person and Community in African Traditional Thought," 178.

52. Menkiti, "Person and Community in African Traditional Thought," 172.

53. Wiredu, *Cultural Universal and Particulars*, 65.

54. I will argue in a subsequent chapter that this kind of general moral outlook is necessary to rationally think about moral principles.

55. Kwasi Wiredu, "On Defining African Philosophy," In *African Philosophy*. ed. Tsenay Serequeberhan (New York: Paragon House. 1991), 92-121; Gyekye, *An Essay On African Philosophical Thought*, 129-138.

56. Kwasi Wiredu, "African Philosophical Tradition: A Case Study of the Akan," in *African-African Perspectives and Philosophical Traditions*, ed., John P. Pittman (New York: Routledge, 1996), 51.

57. Wiredu, *Cultural Universals and Particulars*, 393.

58. Gyekye, *An Essay On African Philosophical Thought*, 143.

59. See O. T. Oladipo, *An African Conception of Reality: A Philosophical Analysis*, Unpublished Doctoral Dissertation, University of Ibadan, Nigeria, 1988, 16.

60. For a distinction between rational and irrational forms of authoritarianism, see Polycarp Ikuenobe, "A Defense of Epistemic Authoritarianism in Traditional African Cultures," *Journal of Philosophical Research* 23 (1998): 417-440..

61. This view raises the question of naturalistic fallacy, which I cannot address here. However, Africans do not necessarily believe that the connection between natural facts and moral principles, values, beliefs, or judgment is a logical or necessary one. Some modern Western scholars have tried to explain the nature of that the connection between facts and value in terms of 'supervenience'. In other words, natural facts provide sufficient basis for moral principles or judgment but these facts do not necessarily imply them.

62. Gyekye, *An Essay On African Philosophical Thought: The Akan Conceptual Scheme*, 143

63. I cannot deal with the issue of whether or not authoritarianism precludes rationality here. I will do this in another chapter of this book. Also see Ikuenobe, "A Defense of Epistemic Authoritarianism in Traditional African Cultures."

64. Wiredu, *Cultural Universals and Particulars*, 398.

65. Dennis Lloyd, *The Idea of Law* (London: Penguin Books, 1981).

66. For a discussion of the distinction between the semantic and epistemic nature or adequacy of rules, see Jules Coleman, "Negative and Positive Positivism," *Journal of Legal Studies* 11 (January 1982): 139-164, and Charles Silver, "Negative Positivism and the Hard Facts of Life," *Monist* 68 (1985): 347-363.

67. This idea is the basis for people's view that the various aspects of people's lives in African culture are supernatural--that religious beliefs play a pervasive role in African people's live

68. Achebe, *Things Fall Apart*, illustrates this point in the character of Okonkwo who felt guilty by participating in the killing of Ikemefuna even though this act was socially and religiously sanctioned. Moreover, his friend, Obierika chastised him morally for participating in the killing.

69. Onwuanibe, "The Human Person and Immortality in Ibo Metaphysics," 185.

70. Onwuanibe, "The Human Person and Immortality in Ibo Metaphysics," 186.

71. Wiredu, *Cultural Universals and Particulars*, 66. Also see 21-33, and 61-76 for the distinction between 'custom' and 'morality'.

72. See Polycarp Ikuenobe, "Moral Epistemology, Relativism, African Cultures, and the Distinction Between Custom and Morality," *Journal of Philosophical Research* 27 (2002): 641-669.

# Chapter Four

# Oral Tradition, Narratives, and Moral Education

Some important features of the idea of communalism in African thought include the moral ideas of community, personhood, the symbiotic relationship between personhood and community, and the humanistic and communalistic nature of moral principles. Moral principles in Africa traditions are taught, internalized, and learned by people in a communal context, in the forms of negative and positive guides for their conduct and actions, so that they can acquire moral personhood. In other words, people are able to use moral principles to guide their conduct and acquire moral personhood by acting in a manner that is acceptable, and refraining from acting in a manner that is unacceptable. These moral principles and the communal duties they impose play a significant role in how we understand and account for the nature of community and how they help one to acquire moral personhood. There-fore, the interplay of moral principles, community, and the acquisition of moral personhood in traditional African cultures does explain how people acquire and justify their moral beliefs and principles as a basis for attaining personhood. So, another important element of the idea of communalism in African thought is the informal processes and methods of imparting knowledge, acquiring beliefs, inter-nalizing principles, and learning one's obligations and the general ways of life that provide the foundation for moral personhood. Thus, an account of moral education and moral epistemology, in terms of the methods by which people acquire moral knowledge, beliefs, obligations, and moral values in African cultures is pertinent for a proper understanding of communalism, the integration of a person into a community, and their mutual relationship.

The processes, methods, and context of moral education in African communi-ties involve the informal use of different forms of narratives, folklore, proverbs, and oral tradition. In African cultures, the community, traditions, and elders are the repositories of the moral knowledge, beliefs, and ways of life. The elder, a fully developed moral person, has an important role in the form of social and communal responsibilities, which include training and educating the youth and prodding others, in order to help them achieve moral personhood and elderhood. This duty requires the elder (the 'grown-up') to display his wealth of knowledge in his moral judgement by exhibiting robust moral sensitivity. An elder, by his very actions, is teaching and morally educating the youth by modeling his actions for them. In this sense, the elder becomes a mentor and role model. Children are supposed to imitate the actions of elders who are role models. This idea of imitation is an important process of learning and moral education. In which case, the actions of elders are seen as a kind of narrative or text that indicates an acceptable action. Children learn relevant moral principles by seeing and imitating the actions of elders. This seems to underscore the saying that, 'action speaks louder than words'. By paying attention to how elders behave and act, children are then able to *learn* the proper behavior or the line of moral action that is expected of them. It should be stressed that this process of modeling behavior is underscored by the moral conception of personhood or elderhood as a status that is earned and acquired in one's life by the process of acting in accordance with one's communal obligations and personal duty in the context of such social obligations.

The status of elders as the repositories of wisdom, knowledge, cultural beliefs, traditions, and wealth of experience is poignantly illustrated in the following proverb: what an elder can see while laying on his bed, a child would not be able to see even when he climbs to the top of a tree. We should bear in mind that the elder is not simply a person who is chronologically old. An elder displays his wealth of knowledge to children in words, proverbs, advice, and admonitions, by implicitly or explicitly providing the explanatory and evidential bases for moral principles, which specify and prescribe requisite moral duties. These evidential and motivating foundations are represented in the form of proverbs, anecdotes in real life experiences, or stories in the form of parables, folklore, folktale, myths, and narratives. Proverbs or folklore may also speak to abstract principles or concrete existential experiences from which children can draw moral knowledge or learn about the probable utility of particular actions in given circumstances. As a result, all the adults in the community, especially the elders, are saddled with the responsibility of educating children through various informal methods and processes of experiential learning so that they can grow up to be morally responsible adults. In traditional African cultures, there were no formal educational institutions, structures, and curriculum for imparting knowledge or beliefs or morally educating people. Perhaps, the community as a whole is the educational institution. Hence, people are educated about moral principles and their individual moral and social duties, regarding the accepted moral principles in a communal context through an informal process of day-to-day upbringing and living in the community.

## Community, Oral Tradition, and Informal Education

This point regarding the role of the community and elders in the informal moral education of a child is underscored by the saying: it is the moral responsibility of an elder to admonish and morally guide a child, but it is the moral responsibility of the child to heed the guidance and admonishment of the elder. Hence, it is the moral fault of the child who refuses to heed the guidance of the elder and it is the moral fault of the elder who refuses to guide and admonish a child. The moral guidance and admonishment by elders must be done in both words and deeds. This is another sense of the now popular African saying: it takes a whole community to raise a child. Another proverb that speaks to the communal nature of moral education in African culture also says that 'you cannot use the palm of one hand to *properly* cover the mouth of a pot'. There is a sense is which the pot is likened to the child, where covering its mouth amounts to protecting the child by filtering what goes into it. The metaphor of the pot is instructive because its wide mouth or opening represents the gullibility of the child and the tendency for the opening to let in various things. Hence, the pot needs some covering in the form of some filter to discriminate between the things that may go into the pot. In this sense, part of safeguarding the child or the covering of the pot's mouth is teaching him how to behave in his environment (community) in order to lead a meaningful life and achieve his life plans. This child is raised in a situation where he or she sees every person on a daily basis, accord respect to elders and accept a kind of moral deference and epistemic dependence. So, another feature of communalism in African traditions is the obligation for a child to morally depend on or defer to elders, adults, and traditions for moral guidance in moral choices and decisions.

This process of moral education involves children learning from elders in a hands-on manner what should be the prescribed mode of behavior. In this sense, the community as an informal educational structure represents a hierarchy of moral authority and teaching responsibilities, where those in the top hierarchy teach and reinforce for those in the lower hierarchy how they ought to behave in order to achieve harmony. In this hierarchy, children are at the lowest level and the elders who are not only the custodians of the traditions, but are people of wisdom (epistemically and morally) are at the top. The highest moral status in the community is being an elder or chief, or in some cases, king or queen.[1] It is pertinent to note that being a chief or king is not simply or solely a status of social or political leadership; it also represents a high moral status that children should strive to attain and emulate. The status of the elder, chief, or king in relation to the idea of moral hierarchy in African cultures is represented by the following proverb: If you wash your hands clean (that is, if you are morally clean), then you can *eat and dine* with elders and kings. It should be stressed that eating and dining here does not only refer to the literal sense of eating meals but also to a social communion based on social recognition. One must be morally clean and upright to be an elder and to partake in this moral and social communion. Another proverb says, if you want to be close to the king (or if you are close to the king) then you must be 'bright looking' (i.e., morally clean and upright). In other words, being morally upright or clean is a necessary condition for one to be 'close to a king'.

There is also the proverb, which say that when you are close to the king, his moral cleanliness will rub off on you. This implies that one will be morally upright if one tries to act like a king or to emulate him. So, the king, queen, and the elders of a community are the repositories of the morality, norms, and traditions of the community; in some respects, they personify the moral character of the community. Parents who are not yet recognized as elders and other adults are at the middle of the hierarchy. All these people have responsibilities in the community to morally educate children about the requisite moral principles and their moral obligation to themselves and the community in order to be fully and morally integrated into the community and earn the moral status of personhood. Children achieve the relevant moral status of personhood by learning from moral authorities the relevant obligations, and practicing what they have learned. Ancestors or gods also have a place, at least in principle, in this hierarchy of moral authority. They are, in a transcendental form, a moral part of the community. Thus, they may be placed on a level higher than elders, in that they are relied on or called upon by elders for moral guidance. Through such guidance, they are able to morally educate others, and in the process, are able to create moral harmony in the community. The idea of creating harmony and human well-being is the goal of morality, moral education, moral thought, and moral reasoning in a traditional African community. In this sense, the idea that everyone in a community has the social responsibility of morally educating, socializing, and acculturating children into the relevant moral principles, beliefs, values, and ways of life in order to achieve harmony is one important feature of communalism.

This very idea of educating, socializing, and acculturating children into the relevant communal moral principles, beliefs, values, and ways of life is the fundamental basis for the saying, 'it takes a village to raise a child', which is a core feature of the idea of communalism in African traditions. The informal moral educational processes, which involve the use of narratives, in the form of stories, proverb, parables, and folklore, as well as modeling of examples and acting as mentors, are bolstered by constant reinforcement of the relevant principles, values, and actions by all the members of the community, in the forms of prodding, ribbing, and chiding. In this sense, moral education in African cultures is an on-going process that goes beyond childhood to teenage years, young adulthood, and to married adults. People are always learning how they ought to behave by the informal processes of reinforcement. It is important to understand these informal processes and methods of moral education as well as their contents in the context of the metaphilosophical view that African philosophy is not just a set of abstract theories, but a practice and a lived-experience. The idea that the essential corpus of philosophy includes the knowledge, thought systems, beliefs, culture, tradition, and values in traditional Africa and the informal methods of imparting them may be what, in part, distinguishes traditional African philosophy from some of its modern or contemporary Western variants. Hence, an analysis of the narratives in African cultures may provide a way of retrieving or reconstructing the values, thought systems, philosophies (in the form of theories and practices), and history of the people.

It is pertinent to note that the method of oral history, which relies on oral traditions and narratives, is an acceptable method in historiography. It is therefore an essential feature of African historiography. The acceptance of this method came, in part, from the efforts of the Ibadan School of History.[2] Western scholars had argued that Africa did not have any history prior to its contacts with Europeans, because there were no written records and that there was no way to retrieve from oral tradition a legitimate history that was acceptable to European and Western scholars. Some scholars who were interested in African history, many of whom are considered to be members of the Ibadan School of History, had to argue strenuously that Africa had a history prior to colonialism. They substantiated their claims by not only arguing philosophically in favor of oral history, tradition, or narratives as a legitimate historiographic method, but also used it to reconstruct and retrieve significant parts of African history. According to E. J. Alagoa "Dike and Biobaku's books became the models for the new historiography. In an important departure from conventional historical canons of the day, they championed the use of oral tradition, which they used in their book to a limited extent together with British documents."[3] This point is pertinent for two reasons. First, the argument for the method of oral history is a philosophical argument for a unique African method of engaging in intellectual inquiry, including philosophy, which has been accepted as part of the canon of the discipline of history. Second, the criticisms that African historians faced with respect to the method of oral history and the non-existence of African history are similar to the arguments that have been used to question the existence of African philosophy and the legitimacy of ethnophilosophy as a philosophical enterprise. As such, the discipline of philosophy has something to learn from the discipline of history in accepting the method of oral tradition into its canon. Moreover, African philosophers also have a lesson to learn from their history counterparts about oral tradition and its legitimacy as a method for understanding African traditions, thoughts, and ideas.

One can appreciate this methodological point about oral tradition, if one understands that the relevant moral principles, beliefs, traditions, ideas, values, thought systems, and acceptable practices in African cultures that helped people to achieve harmony in their communities were taught and learned from parables, myths, proverbs, stories, folklore, and other forms of narratives. Some of these stories and folklore are told to children in the evenings after dinner. Some of these moral principles are usually indicated in and understood or made sense of via everyday maxims, proverbs, myths, and platitudes. These folklore and myths are a kind of explanatory posits to help people to understand and make sense of moral principles, responsibilities, and communal expectations. W. V. O. Quine's account of myths as cultural epistemological devices and explanatory posits will be illuminating here. In his view, myths, abstract entities, and posits are useful epistemological devices for making sense of our experiences and coping with reality. Hence, they are a useful method of understanding, learning, and educating people about their world and our place in it, in order to know how to relate to it morally. According to him, "abstract entities which are the substance of mathematics—ultimately classes and classes of classes and so on up—are another posit in the same spirit. Epistemologically, these are myths on the same footing with physical objects and gods, neither better nor worse except for differences in the degree to which they expedite our dealings with sense experiences."[4]

Quine indicates the cultural nature of myths and posits and the important role they play in different cultures in making meaning. Thus he argues that, "in point of epistemological footing the physical objects and the gods differ only in degree and not in kind. Both sorts of entities enter our conception only as cultural posits. The myth of physical objects are epistemologically superior to most in that it has proved more efficacious than others myths as a device for working a manageable structure into the flux of experience."[5] The essential point here is that we need physical objects and myths, as forms of conceptual, symbolic, and abstract representations, in order to make better sense of reality. Hence, in African tradition, the combination of myth, people's actions, and concrete experiences have proved to be a useful and an effective method or process of teaching, understanding, learning, and making sense of moral principles. This point about symbolic and abstract representation is further illustrated by the works of Parker English and Nancy Hamme. They indicate how art in African cultures, specifically Akan culture in Ghana, is used as an informal process of moral education.[6] Their conception of art in African cultures indicates that it is a kind of text or narrative: "It constitutes one of the ways in which the resources of the material environment are employed in the lives of people as social and communicative beings. The arts are also a collection of describable activities (responses to these activities) based on the proclivity to 'make special'."[7] They argue that art in this sense of a narrative or text plays a vital role not only in the process of moral education but also in the process of acculturation. Because morality is part of African culture—i.e., considering its communal nature—the process of acculturation is also a process of moral education.

N. K. Dzobo indicates that symbols and proverbs are the sources of information and knowledge in African cultures. He argues that "Africans have been using both visual and oral 'picture words' for a considerable time to express, transmit and store their thoughts, emotions, and attitudes. All over Africa, visual images and ordinary objects are used *symbolically* to communicate knowledge, feelings and values."[8] If we see art, symbols, folklore, myths, and proverbs as narratives and a part of oral tradition that is involved in the informal processes of moral education, then we can appreciate how they can be "used to facilitate or make palatable socially important behavior."[9] Art may also be seen as a form of documentation and "a residue of events whose purpose was to impose upon social individuals unforgettable patterns of essential knowledge and explanation."[10] If we understand African art in this broad sense, then it becomes a valuable source of knowledge or basis for understanding African thought, in terms of providing a window into African cultural and traditional beliefs, values, thought systems, especially with respect to morality.

English and Hamme illustrate the educational role of art by indicating its role in cultural practices and ceremonies, which represent the public process of expressing and transmitting the values, thoughts, principles, and beliefs of a culture. Such ceremonies are a part of the oral tradition of the people: this tradition represents a body of information (practices, values, history, skills, principles of action and organization, and beliefs) that are considered important to a group of people, by virtue of which the core identity and cultural legacy of the group or community are perpetuated and passed down from generation to generation. Art, according to English and Hamme, is essential in African cultures as a process and method of educating people because "it is used as an encoding and mnemonic instruments to make important information more easily and accurately assimilable. As a result, even in the absence of written texts, essential aspects of culture are not lost, ignored or dismissed. Instead, coded in nonliterate ways, they are integrated and expressed in socially shared symbols."[11] Some of the works of art in African cultures were also functional objects like robes, staffs, swords, drums, stools, jewelry, and hats, which had special cultural symbolism. As symbols, they represented either concrete or abstract ideas. Some of these artistic objects have symbolism that encapsulated certain values, norms, or principles on the basis of which certain behaviors were deemed acceptable or unacceptable. In their view, the form of education in African cultures involves some elements of indoctrination because it is a thoroughgoing, subtle, and robust process of encoding and imparting information and ideas.[12] However, it is, in my mind, an open issue whether this robust process is necessarily bad or good.

Based on what can be gleaned from practices, process, and proverbs or sayings that are passed down from generation to generation, we see that the African communal robust idea of moral education is effective and it serves the requisite communal needs. For instance, this idea or process of education indicates that the entire community is responsible for caring for, raising, educating, and the upbringing of a child. This involves a shared responsibility of parenting. Although it is not the sole responsibility of parents to raise and educate a child, this tradition does not suggest that the child is necessarily the ward of the community. The parents still have their parental rights and duties, except that the help of the whole community makes parenting an easier task in African cultures. Maybe the West has something to learn from this advantage. There is so much emphasis on rights in the West that people have become highly litigious as a way of defending those rights. There is no emphasis on the general obligation that adults besides parents have towards children, and as such, teachers are afraid of being sued when they discipline children. The idea of being sued and the fear of suits seem to come out of the over-emphasis on the rights of children and parents as opposed to the obligations towards children. In African cultures, where the emphasis is on obligation, it does not make sense to talk of parents raising their children alone since the parents are an integral part of the community.

From the communal nature of the society and morality, every moral teaching is reinforced by everybody in the community and the social institutions. Because everyone is saddled with the responsibility of caring for a child, the values that are imparted on the child are reinforced by the community. I do not mean to suggest that, simply because everyone is saddled with the responsibility of caring for children in the community, everyone actually do meet that responsibility. I am also not suggesting that the community in African traditions is a community of angels and upright citizens. In other words, because not everyone actually fulfils such responsibilities, it is not every old person or an adult that may indeed 'grow-up' to achieve elderhood or acquire moral personhood. However, the moral teaching is such that there are no mixed or contradictory messages from the neighbors and parents that may leave children puzzled about the correct action. Almost everyone seems to agree on the moral principles and the prescribed lines of action, in so far as these principles have their foundation in the community and its interests. The moral message or the voice of the community is consistent and persistent in people's actions and it is consistently reinforced by everyone in their everyday lives, where they have the duty to practice these principles by bringing them consistently to bear on their actions. It is through this kind of practice and reinforcement that people acquire moral virtues and develop moral conscience and their ability to feel shame when they do something that is morally reprehensible.

With constant reinforcements that derive from social interaction based on oral tradition and everyday discourse, the moral voice of the community is made clear and well articulated in order to help people to guide their conduct. Perhaps, the kind of community reinforcement that I am alluding to can be illuminated or illustrated by the following anecdote from Amitai Etzioni book, *The Spirit of Community*:

> I lived for a year on the Stanford University campus. Not far from the house I rented was a four-way stop sign. Each morning I observed a fairly heavy flow of traffic at the intersection. Still, the cars carefully waited their turns to move ahead, as they were expected to. The drivers rarely moved out of turn, and in those cases when they did, the offender often had out-of-state license plates. The main reason for the good conduct: practically everyone in the community knew who was behind the wheel. If someone rushed through, he or she could expect to be the subject of some *mild ribbing* at the faculty club, supermarket, or local movie theater (such as 'You must have been in an awful rush this morning'). This kind of *community prodding* usually suffices to reinforce the proper behavior that members of the community acquire early—in case, observing safe traffic patterns.[13]

The situation described above is very similar to what exists in traditional African cultures, in that everyone not only knew the other person, everyone had a responsibility to chide, rib, and prod other people if there was a moral slip. This is an important way of morally educating people and helping them to acquire the requisite moral virtues. When this is done in a community, there is usually no sense of the idea that one is not minding one's own business, because the issue of moral uprightness is everyone's business and it is for the good of everyone. It is everyone's business to make sure that people are morally trained regarding what is the accepted or acceptable rule of conduct. Any moral chiding or ribbing ought to engender some pangs from one's conscience, which would then put one a good moral path. It is reasonable to argue that this kind of community or attitude is usually lacking in bigger cities. But it need not be.

There is, usually, a natural sense of community in villages or smaller towns, but this natural sense of community can also be consciously created in big cities. The point of this book is to analyze the African idea of communalism as a theory that can be consciously applied to various situations, with the necessary efforts. People in big cities and other cultures can make concerted efforts to borrow and apply elements of this African idea of communalism since no theory can be applied wholesale to every situation. Some elements of this African communal idea that are being applied to big cities in the United States are the ideas of community's 'neighborhood watch' and 'community policing'. Concerted efforts must be made to change people's mind-set about extreme individualism and rights in order to embrace elements of the idea of communalism and a sense of obligation. People have to take the initiative of understanding the communal ethos and forming communal relationships with others. Usually, big cities encourage this kind of extreme individualism, where people mind their own business and do not engage in chiding, prodding, or ribbing other people for moral slips. We see the effect of this in big cities where people feel they do not have a responsibility to report a neighbor who is committing a crime or doing something that is unacceptable. There are more crimes or immoral acts in big cities because the individualistic ethos tells people that they do not have the social responsibility to others except to mind their own business. The idea of communal obligations is something that can be developed in big cities, but in order to do this, one must make a good case for the idea of communalism. The effort in this book is to make such a case by drawing on the African communal tradition.

## Communal Responsibility and Moral Education

Etzioni suggests that in a communitarian society, there is more emphasis on social and individual responsibility and duty than there is on rights and freedom; the emphasis on rights is the hallmark of an individualistic society. The emphasis on social responsibility, recognition of communal institutions, needs, or relationships, and the active engagement in communal life, is significant because these communal elements provide the basis for making meaning, articulating individual interests and rational life plan, and creating social identity. It is reasonable to understand how these communal conditions illuminate and provide the basis of the narrative methods and informal processes of moral education in communal African cultures. In other words, the methods and processes of moral education in African communal traditions may indicate some fundamental principles of moral education. In Helen Haste's view, these methods or processes underscore five principles of moral education that are associated with the requisite conditions, goals, and assumptions of a communal structure.[14] The reasonableness of these principles of moral education may provide a foundation and a plausible basis for defending the informal process and narrative methods of moral education in African cultures. These principles may be summarized as follows:

(1) One's ability to learn moral principles through the informal process and cultural practices of a community requires that the relevant values are entrenched in the community and institutionalized as a social practice. This means that these values are manifested in people's everyday's lives. They are also experienced in such a manner that they are presupposed to be the underlying factors for people's actions.

(2) Since people get their identity from the social interactions, relationships, and cultural practices in a community, it means that the stories, narratives, principles, and values in the community that indicate identity and give meaning to people's lives must represent commonly shared ideas and values. These shared ideas

and values are thus accepted as the basis for the way that people organize their lives, articulate their rational life plan, the interests of the community, and the justifications for why things are the way they are.

(3) People's social interactions and relationships allow them to be engaged in the affairs of the community, and such engagement gives them a sense of responsibility, belonging, and connection to other people. This sense of belonging or connectedness imposes the duty and responsibility to be caring in a way that will foster the equilibrium of the community. Such duty is expressed as explicit normative standards of behavior and they are accepted as the practical guide for actions and decisions.

(4) People are able to recognize that, as a community, there are explicit and implicit common or shared interests that everyone must try to achieve. These interests determine the processes and structures that give meaning to the community and people's lives. Understanding these interests in relation to one's own individual life creates the obligation to achieve and maintain the interests.

(5) People have to be independently aware of the interpretative processes of making meaning in the community. The awareness of these processes allows people to understand the norms of the community. Based on such awareness, people are able to reflect on these norms, in terms of how they evolve and function. Such reflection makes the cultural process and repertoires explicit; it also facilitates the efforts to generate new norms that could replace existing norms that people no longer find workable.

These principles are important, according to Haste, because they draw attention to the fact that morality and moral education are grounded in practice, experiences, and actions, not in abstract or disembodied principles. By reflecting on cultural practices, people are able to appreciate the value of the practices as a way to get at the principles that provide the foundation for people's actions and the interests of the community into which individuals should make their lives to correspond. By appreciating the overriding interests of the community as a basis for individuals' own interests—as the basis of communalism—people are able to appreciate the cultural interpretative processes of making meaning. These processes provide the basis for moving away from the absoluteness of the value of personal rational autonomy to the value of social responsibility, with respect to the community's interests on which individuals' interests depend. We can see how these principles are satisfied in African cultures, in that the community in traditional African cultures provides people with the experiential conditions or bases for making meaning of their actions and lives. These conditions reflect the processes of inculcating the principles and values that are institutionalized; they are also the basis for people's sense of identity, and the basis on which people engage in social interaction. This sense of identity leads people to take active part in the affairs of the community, and it is on the basis of such participation that they are aware of and are able to understand and appreciate the workings of the community and the justification for the relevant values and principles.

The idea of understanding the workings of a community, relevant moral principles, and their justification implies that children are supposed to learn how to reason on their own in order see the moral implications of actions, and the principles or values embedded in parables, myths, folklore or stories, and other forms of narrative. The essential point here is that children are not simply taught or indoctrinated to act in certain predetermined ways or to use certain principles without reasoning about them. They must be able to rationally see from stories or proverbs that the moral principles they are being taught do not apply wholesale to each and every situation that they may be confronted with. Hence, they must learn how to contextualize their behaviors in accordance with certain principles that are embedded in the stories that they are told. In other words, they must be able to use their reasoning and commonsense to decide how to apply a particular moral principle to a specific situation so that it could jibe with or lead to the expected moral end of enhancing the cohesiveness of the community. Thus, we must understand the fundamental principle that such cohesiveness is essential in order for every individual to be able to lead a meaningful life, which includes the ability to achieve and acquire full moral personhood. Understanding this idea and living it represent a fundamental moral essence of a person. Learning this moral lesson about the moral essence of a person is also an important aspect of moral education. People learn this by seeing, based on examples and real life experiences, the role and place of elders and chiefs in the community. Kevin McDonough underscores this point by indicating the importance of moral examples as a means of moral education, especially at the initial formative stages of helping children to acquire the requisite moral habits.[15] Learning the special recognition that is given to elders and the various benefits and perks that they get by virtue of their moral status seem to provide some practical incentives for children to aspire to this status. From experience, children understand the privilege, benefits, and respect that are accorded to elders and also their duties in the moral upbringing of children.

It is pertinent to say that as a child begins to mature into adolescence and early adulthood, he is not just expected to see certain kinds of behavior and simply copy or imitate them without any rational thought or justificatory basis. There is usually a concerted effort to educate people about the justificatory reasons for the communal ways of life and the basis for deference to and dependence on elders as moral and epistemic authorities. For instance, the proverb that 'it is the moral imperative or duty of the elder to morally admonish a child and it is the moral imperative of the child to heed the moral admonishment of the elder' has a rational basis, which is anchored in the moral structure of the community. The relevant moral duties of an elder and a child are not just provided as dogmas that must be accepted without a rational basis. The justification for moral dependence might be found in another proverb, which says that a defiant child who refuses to heed the moral admonishment of an elder is not only putting himself in danger but also the whole community. The idea of admonishing a child is justified on the basis of the individual child's interest because he stands the risk of not leading a meaningful life in order to achieve personhood, and by implication, his life plans and self-fulfilment. For the community, the actions of the individual may create problems for the community and prevent other people from leading meaningful lives. Thus, the status of the elder as a moral teacher and the status of the child as a moral student is justified in many different proverbs. The status of the elder as having the requisite wisdom and knowledge in order to be regarded as an expert in moral matters is captured by the proverb that, a young person may have more new clothes or items than an elder but the elder usually has more antiques and a greater variety of old clothes and rags. The idea is that there is hidden wisdom or value in antiques and a greater amount of practical functionality in having a variety of old clothes and rags that cannot be matched by many new items, property or clothes.

As an illustration of the wisdom of the elder, one proverb suggests that 'a young child cannot learn to how swim in the ocean if he is not helped by other adults; thus, without help, he would drown'. Life is considered to be a wide and deep ocean for which one needs guidance and help to navigate in order to avoid drowning. This view about life and one's ability to navigate it, Menkiti argues, requires education and incremental growth in knowledge, experience, and wisdom with respect to morality as well as other justified beliefs or principles of human action. As one grows in age and experience, one begins to learn how to act and acquire the moral excellencies that are considered necessary to navigate life in order to attain full personhood.[16] The incremental growth in knowledge and one's intellectual abilities alone (which is similar to Kohlberg's cognitive model of moral development) are usually not considered enough for one to be able to act morally or acquire the requisite moral virtues and character. For that, one would require a wealth of experience within which one may use and apply one's cognitive abilities. The idea is that cognitive facilities are formal structures; as such, their proper development must be supplemented by material knowledge and contents. This idea is expressed in the proverb that 'the mind of a child that has not seen many life experiences may not know what to do in many situations, hence he must depend on or defer to the elder who ought to know based on his life experiences'. This is the justification for requiring that a child should depend on and defer to the elder to educate him on the best line of action. In this regard, it is unacceptable for a child to be defiant by refusing to listen to or depend on elders.

The moral lesson that is taught as a remedy for a defiant child is expressed in the proverb that, 'the ear of the child who does not take instructions or the admonishment of elders ought to be cut along with the head before it causes trouble that cannot be avoided, leading to the destruction of the community'. There is also a proverb indicating that 'it is better to cut off a rotten finger that cannot be healed than to allow it to threaten the health of the whole body by allowing the rot or sore to spread to the whole body'. These proverbs indicate the strong mutual or organic relationship between the individual (illustrated with the finger or ear) and the community (illustrated with the body). This relationship indicates that the good or bad actions of individuals may also have good or bad implications for the community, and what is good or bad for the community may also be good or bad for individuals. All these proverbs that deal with the African idea of communalism with respect to the moral status of an elder as a teacher and his relationship with a child as a student are justified by the fact that the child needs guidance and moral education in order to grow and develop into a morally upright person—moral personhood. The community thinks that such growth and development are essential for an individual to be a contributing part of a community. Such growth would lead to the cohesiveness of the community in which children can grow. The moral growth of children involves the acquisition of certain moral attitudes, habits, or virtues, understanding and undertaking responsibilities, and learning or acquiring different virtues as well as learning to avoid different vices.

Some important virtues that children have to learn are, obedience, humility, respect, prudence, caring, and the ability to acknowledge fallibility and lack of adequate knowledge. These are considered to be important moral and educational virtues because without them, a child cannot be morally educated, he cannot learn moral principles or acquire other moral virtues, and he cannot acquire personhood. These virtues or attitudes make children amenable to the admonishments of elders and the acceptance of responsibilities. For instance, a child is told that he should not be too adventurous; he must listen to or heed the teachings of elders. This underscores the moral responsibilities of elder as moral teachers and children as learners. It is not always prudent or reasonable to allow a child to make his own mistakes and learn from them. Some mistakes are deemed too serious and far-reaching to allow a child to make and for him to learn from. Some mistakes may have devastating effects on a child's life or the community because of the organic nature of the relationship between individuals and the community. The community has a responsibility to raise and guide children in order to protect them from such mistakes. The role of a community or elders suggests some sense of paternalism. There are, however, situations where a child is allowed to make mistakes and learn from them. But it is also expected that a child should be able to learn from the past mistakes that other children have made in their bid to be morally defiant and autonomous. These mistakes are considered to be a constituent part of the broad experience or knowledge, which exists in the community and among elders that have to be taught to children as part of their moral education.

This idea of moral education is underscored by the proverb: if a child is burnt by fire, it is not only the child who learns not to go near fire next time, other children who saw the situation also learn from it. In some sense, other children who saw such experience can tell it as a narrative or story for other people to learn from. As such, it would be stupid for other children who witnessed the situation to be admonished not to go near the fire. Yet, there are situations where a child is told that he cannot be allowed to make such mistakes because, based on experience, the results of such mistakes are simply unacceptable. This idea of moral education based on experience, oral tradition, and narratives, also speaks to the idea of communal knowledge, beliefs, or inquiry, and socialized epistemology. The idea of communal knowledge implies that knowledge or justified belief is not individualistic and it is not based solely on an individual's rational judgment. It is based on collective and shared experiences and inter-subjective rationality. As a result of this epistemological assumption underlying the idea of moral education in African cultures, elders are justified in being paternalistic about some matters, to the extent of preventing one from using or relying solely on one's own individual will and rationality. This is one plausible justification for the idea of moral and epistemic dependence on or deference to elders in African thought systems.

## Using Folktale to Teach Moral Lessons

The following folktale illustrates this moral teaching or lesson and the virtue of listening and deferring to elders; it also indicates that it is bad for a child to be morally defiant. The story goes as follows: a small boy lived in small village. The father of this small boy had a very large farm in this village very close to the bank of a river. Beside the farm was also another farm. This other farm belongs to a wicked wizard. Nobody ever saw this wicked wizard during the day; he always does his farm work in the night. In this wizard's farm was a big mango tree. During the mango season, the tree always bears very good and beautiful fruits. This boy always wished he could have some of the beautiful mango fruit from the wicked wizard's farm. Another mango season arrived and the mango tree bore fruits that were very beautiful. This time, the mango fruits were very ripe and looked so attractive. One day the small boy asked his father whose farm it was that was beside theirs, and whether he could go to the farm to pick some of the very ripe and beautiful mangoes. His father warned him not to go because the farm belonged to a wicked wizard and that they could not trust the mangoes. There was the fear that the mangoes could possibly be poisoned by the wicked wizard. Moreover, the boy was told that he should never take somebody's property without the person's permission. Since no one ever saw the owner, the opportunity was not there to ask for his permission to pick some of the mango fruits. However, the boy was not convinced by what his father said to him.

So, one given day, the boy's father took ill and could not go to the farm. He told his son to go to the farm to pick some corn to bring home for lunch. This boy was very happy because he now has an opportunity to pick and eat some of those mangoes his father had warned him not to pick or eat. He went to the farm, and after picking the corn, he went to the wizard's farm to pick some mangoes. He picked about five that were very ripe and juicy. He put them in his bag and headed home. On his way home he began to eat the mangoes and they were indeed very sweet and juicy. After eating the mangoes, his stomach began to ache and swell. He became frightened. He started crying. He threw away the bag of corns he was carrying and ran home. Before he got home, his head, legs, and hands were all swollen. People could not recognize him. People were frightened and the people in the village summoned all the elders and medicine men to come and see what was happening to this small boy. They asked him what happened and he could not talk. Later, he was able to tell them that he picked and ate from the mango tree in the wicked wizard's farm. A medicine woman in the village gave him some antidotes and made some small incisions in his body to drain the fluid out of his body. He was eventually healed. The boy promised to always heed warnings and never to be greedy or defiant again. He also promised never to take someone else's property without the person's permission. If the boy had asked for permission from the owner and the owner granted it, and he is poisoned in the process, then the owner who gave the permission would be in trouble and would have been held responsible for poising the boy.

In this particular case, this boy was able to learn from his own mistakes. This experience is a story that other children have to learn a moral lesson from. Children are taught to realize that this boy was lucky to be able to learn from his own mistakes. Some other children who want to make a similar mistake by being defiant and unheeding to the admonition, warning, and teaching of elders may not be that lucky to be able to learn from their mistakes. Hence children must not refuse to heed the admonishment of elders, and the community cannot afford to leave it up to children to develop and grow on their own. The ideas of communal knowledge and the communal responsibility to share such knowledge and experiences via oral tradition provide the epistemic foundation for the communal mode of moral education and their conception of moral development. However, we must bear in mind that the decision whether or not a child should heed the admonishment of elders is, in many cases, left to the child who must use his own rationality and discretion to make his own decisions and choices. The idea of moral education in African cultures is founded on the mutual and reinforcing responsibilities that individuals and community have toward each other. It is pertinent to stress that the *formative* aspect of moral education is geared primarily toward young children but not fully developed adults. This is the stage of habituation, when children begin to form moral habits, which for Aristotle is the initial goal of moral education.[17] The idea of not subjecting adults to the formative aspect of moral education is supported by the proverb that you do not attempt to bend a dried fish; usually such an attempt is unsuccessful. Indeed such an attempt would culminate in breaking the fish. So, the idea is that you should try to bend the fish while it is still fresh. This means that one should morally educate a person while his moral character is still amenable to being molded. Any effort to morally educate or mold the character of an adult who is likened to a dried fish will culminate in breaking him; thus, nothing is gained in the process. Nonetheless, an adult who has not been morally formed properly is still held morally responsible for his vices, bad moral character or actions. Such a person still suffers moral and social approbation including lack of social recognition or respect, ostracism, and other forms of moral sanctions. In this sense, adults are always undergoing the *corrective* and *punitive* aspects of moral education. The *reinforcing* aspect of moral education for adults is manifested in the form mild ribbing, prodding, and chiding from others in the community.

The community teaches children that if they are morally defiant and refuse to heed the moral lessons of elders and parents, they will grow up to be adults with a number of vices, which could prevent them from acquiring personhood. The consequences of having such immoral character and lacking personhood would be undesirable for the individual and community. The story of the jealous mother is told in traditional African homes to speak to the consequences of the action of an immoral woman who had undesirable moral vices. This story is told to teach important moral lessons about the vices of jealousy, greed, and harming others. This story may have versions and variations depending on the culture, but let me paraphrase how it is told in the Edo culture of Southern Nigeria. A woman had a son and a slave, both of whom were of the same age. Her son was obviously treated better than the slave. This woman would usually prepare different meals and serve them in the respective plates of her son and the slave. As one would expect, her son's plate and food were better, and the slave's food or plate was not as good as her son's. As both the son and the slave were growing up, the slave was excelling in everything in the community and meeting his responsibilities and developing into a wholesome adult. The slave had more strength and energy and worked harder in the farm. The slave was developing along successfully while the son was having difficulties meeting his responsibilities. Whatever the slave touched with his hands turned out well, but it was not quite as good for the son. The slave now became the standard for measuring the son and the son was always compared and contrasted with the slave.

The mother of the boy became jealous and wanted to kill the slave. On a fateful day, she prepared a meal and dished it out into their respective plates. She decided to kill the slave by putting some poison in his food. As a cover-up, she decided to make the slave's share of the food more handsome and attractive. As a result of their status—son and slave—and the fact that they knew their respective plates, the son came in to get his meal when they arrived from the farm. He secretly peeked into the slave's plate of food that was covered, and found how attractive the slave's portion was compared to his own. He thought that his mother must have made a mistake; it could not happen that the slave's meal would be better than his. He was very conscious of his status as the son compared to that of the slave. He went to the mother to ask if she made a mistake. The mother told him categorically not to touch the slave's plate of food. He should eat the portion on his own plate. He was defiant; he refused to heed his mother's warnings. He could not fathom the fact that the slave's portion was better than his own. So, he decided to eat the slave's portion that had been poisoned by his mother. Immediately after eating the food, he became very sick. His mother became very apprehensive and asked him which portion of food he had eaten, and he replied that he had eaten the portion on the slave's plate that was more attractive and handsome. His mother was distraught. They did everything to try to save the boy but they could not. The boy later died from the poisoning. In this case, the son and his mother made mistakes by allowing their actions to be motivated by the vice of greed and jealousy. The son did not live to learn from his mistake but the mistake for his mother is irreversible. One only hopes that others will not make the same mistake and would learn from this woman's own.

There is a double moral message or lesson in this story that is told to educate children about what they morally ought or ought not to do. On the part of the mother, the story is supposed to teach children that they categorically must not, as a matter duty, do harm to any other person because, apart from being inherently bad, an attempt to harm others may inadvertently result in a harm to a loved one. The story also teaches children not to be jealous because jealousy is inherently bad. This lesson is made very poignant in the story by its consequences, in that it brought pain and sadness for the jealous mother. This is further supported by the proverb: you should not throw a stone into a market place or a gathering because it could be your mother who is eventually hit and hurt by the stone. This indicates the issue of unintended consequences. On the part of the son, the moral message is that you should not be greedy or jealous. The son was jealous that, for once, the slave had a larger and more attractive portion of the meal, despite the fact that he always had preferential treatment. He was greedy and was not satisfied with the portion that his mother had given him. Moreover, he defied the warnings of his mother. As a result of his greed and jealousy, he died. This is buttressed by another proverb: if you open your eyes too wide (being greedy), particles and debris will get in. Again, this story is not only to show what the moral obligation of people should be, but it also drives the point home by showing the possible unintended bad consequences of not adhering to one's moral obligation. The moral principles in this story are neither purely deontological nor purely consequentialist. Rather, they reflect, as I alluded to earlier, what may be called mixed deontology in the sense of considering both the justice and utility of principles regarding actions. People are taught their moral duties but the need to perform the duties is substantiated by the utility of the action, in terms of avoiding probable bad consequences for one-self, others, or community. Learning, knowing one's duties, and acting accordingly on a consistent basis seem to determine one's status in the moral hierarchy of the community.

In using folklore, proverbs, maxims, parables, stories, and narratives to teach and morally educate children, there is emphasis on the relevant moral principle, the associated moral actions, attitude, or habit regarding duty or virtue, and the un-pleasant and unintended outcomes of actions that may, in part, make the action morally reprehensible. The ability to see the possible and unintended bad outcome of action helps children to internalize a moral principle as indicating a categorical obligation. Moreover, the moral principle underlying a story in terms of what a child is supposed to learn, with respect to attitude, virtue, or action, is made robust by providing a context in the story to embellish the principle. McDonough under-scores the importance of using complex stories as a robust way of teaching moral principles by arguing that it encourages children to reflect about moral rules and context, and to appreciate the complexity of moral problems.[18] Many African moral stories emphasize bad outcomes in order to help children see what could possibly happen if they act in a way that is morally unacceptable. Some of the moral notions or principles that children must learn that are emphasized in these stories or folk-lore, such as, greed, disobedience, obstinacy, lying, dishonesty, and stealing, are negative. They indicate what people should avoid. Other principles are indicated in a positive form as categorical (perfect) or hypothetical (imperfect) duties, obliga-tions, and responsibilities.

Some of these principles and duties are highlighted in the following story. Once upon a time, there were three brothers. They left home to go for a walk and to play in the woods. On their way back, it was raining very heavily. They could not continue to walk in the rain, so, they decided to take shelter. They found a little hut by the side of the road. They decided to go into this hut to take shelter. They went to the hut, and in it, they found an old woman. She seemed to live alone. When she saw the three boys, she was moved pity and compassion. She let them in and showed them lots of love and kindness. Because they were drenched by the rain, she told them to remove their clothes so that they could dry out a little. More-over, the boys were also very cold. She made a fire to provide warmth for them and to dry their clothes. The boys sat around the fire to keep warm. Thinking that the boys may be hungry, she decided to prepare some yam porridge for them. The aroma of the yam porridge was so nice that the boys felt like having some.

When the food was cooked, the old woman offered the boys some of the meal. But because of shyness, they did not accept the food; they told the old woman that they were full. The old woman, sensing that they were shy, pressed and pressed the boys to have some of the yam porridge but they were adamant. They politely said no, thank you! So, the old woman had some of the yam porridge and kept the remaining portion in one of the corners of the hut. The aroma of the porridge was very tantalizing to the boys. The rain soon stopped and the three boys decided to head on their walk back home. They thanked the old woman for her kindness, put on their clothes, and went on their way. However, the aroma of the yam porridge and the thought of eating it did not leave the mind of the youngest boy. He wanted an opportunity to go back to the hut to have a portion of the food. After they had walked a few hundred yards, he decided to lie to his brothers saying he forgot his hat in the hut and wanted to go back to pick it up. The older brothers decided they would wait for him while he went back to pick up the hat.

The youngest boy went back to the hut and knocked on the door. Fortunately for the boy and his intention, the old woman was not in; she had just stepped out without locking the door. The boy went into the hut and ate very quickly a substantial portion of the yam porridge. He enjoyed it! After eating the food, he knew that the old woman would know that someone had eaten from the pot of porridge. So, he foolishly decided to add sand to the food so that the quantity of the food will remain the same. This boy went back to his brothers with the hat that he initially had with him before going back to the hut. When he got back to his older brothers, they continued on their journey back home. Before they walked about two hundred yards, they heard the voice of old woman shouting to get their attention. The old woman had come back home to find that somebody had entered her hut while she was out very briefly and had eaten out of her pot of porridge and filled it up with sand. She immediately suspected the three boys and ran after them to confront them. On hearing the voice of the old woman, the boys decided to stop to wait for her. Then the old woman confronted them saying that they were ungrateful children. She accused them of paying her back not by simply eating her porridge but by adding sand to the remaining portion. She was annoyed that this was her reward for giving them shelter, warmth, and even offering them food.

The two older boys were stunned and surprised to hear her talk that way and accuse them of this heinous deed. But the younger one knowing that he had done this was afraid and did not want to admit to doing such a thing. The other boys told the old woman that she must be mistaken and that they did not do such a thing. It occurred to them immediately that their younger brother had gone back to the hut to allegedly pick up his hat. So, they asked him if he did such a thing. But he denied doing that. The old woman did not believe them. She insisted that they would have to take a test to prove their innocence. The two older boys were willing to do this to clear their names. The old woman told them that they would have to walk a magic tight rope across a river. If they were innocent, then they would walk the rope without any problem. But, if they were guilty, they would not be able to walk the tight rope, but would, instead, fall into the deep river and die. The first boy walked the rope while singing the requisite song by appealing to the gods to let him walk the rope if he is innocent; otherwise, he should fall into the river and die. He walked the rope successfully; same with the second boy.

It then came to the turn of the third and youngest boy. He initially refused to take the big risk. But the old woman insisted that he must in order to prove his innocence like his older brothers had done. His brothers, who believed and thought he was innocent based on his denial, urged him to walk the tight rope. He sang the requisite song and walked the tight rope. At some point, he stopped, but the old woman told him to finish the song and the walk. This time, seeing how the boy was behaving, the two older brothers began to fear for him. They were now beginning to think that he was the one who actually ate the porridge and filled the pot with sand. The youngest boy then reluctantly sang on and walked the tight rope. When he got to the middle of the rope where the river was deepest, he began to fear from his guilty conscience. His legs shook and he fell to the river and died. This was the end of the greedy boy. And this consequence was the payment for his greed and dishonesty. This story teaches the important moral lesson regarding greed. However, it also accounts for the possibility of moral weakness, so that children can appreciate it and make efforts to remedy it. In other words, the boy compounded his problem of greed by lying about it. Indeed, one could be greedy as a result of one's moral weakness, and this boy had the opportunity to tell the truth and apologize, but he did not. He could have confessed by simply saying that he was tempted to eat the porridge and was stupid enough to try to cover it up by filling the pot with sand. However, if he was morally reasonable and sincere enough to admit his greed and thievery, perhaps he could have saved himself from his disastrous end.

This story also alludes to the belief that bad actions have a way of begetting bad actions; and good actions have a way of begetting good actions. Sometimes the substance of this belief is evinced by the pragmatic argument against lying. The idea is that one should not lie because if one tells one lie, one will need an interminable series of lies to sustain the first lie and the series of other lies. The idea is that it is practically and cognitively impossible to maintain an iterative series of lies. Lying is thus seen to have the logic of being iterative and endless. This idea of lying, and the difficulty associated with it, is sometimes expressed in the imagery of lying as a cobweb. This imagery is used to teach and illustrate the problem of lying and how one gets entangled in one's web of lies. This is a way of discouraging lying and teaching it as a moral principle. The moral lesson in the above story about the boy who ate the old woman's food and lied about it is, that if you do something that is morally bad due to moral weakness, you do not compound the problem by lying about it. This story is told to teach children in a very poignant way the bad consequences of greed, lying, and dishonesty. So, the message of this story is very clear and it is easy for children to understand. The intention is to make them see that is bad to do such things. Moreover, the odds are usually against you when you think that you can do morally bad things and get away with them. Apparently, the boy in this story had thought that he would not be caught and that he could get away with his action.

The substance of this story and the moral lesson it teaches must be placed within a broad system of beliefs. This system includes the metaphysical beliefs about magic and the existence of supernatural powers, among others. These beliefs are substantiated in the idea of the possibility and efficacy of using a means like the magical tight rope to find out who did a bad thing. Again, this story may not have the kind of efficacy in teaching a moral lesson if there is scepticism or disbelief that the magical tight rope is a fraud. The pertinent issue here is not whether the belief in such a magical tight rope is reasonable or whether such reasonableness is necessary for using the story to instill and teach the moral lesson that one should not be greedy, dishonest, or steal. Rather, the issue is whether believing in the efficacy of this kind of magical means or its effect, as a context, has the practical effect of teaching people to be morally upright. The significance of such beliefs has to do with their pragmatic role in moral education, moral actions, and the moral cohesiveness of the community. One can reasonably argue that it makes sense to hold these beliefs on pragmatic grounds. I do not think that truth is the only rational epistemic basis for accepting and holding on to a belief.[19]

What I have done thus far is to provide a description of the informal processes and methods that are employed in moral education in traditional African cultures and to indicate how these processes or methods help to achieve the main goal of moral education, i.e., moral development. However, the issue is whether there are philosophical arguments in support of these processes and methods as useful and heuristic modes or forms of moral education. The first argument or evidence, which may not be sufficient by itself, is experiential, and it may be regarded as anecdotal. However, these processes have a heuristic value, in that they raise critical issues that provide a motivation for exploring and critically examining, based on a comparative analysis, all the plausible processes and methods by which children could be more properly educated about morals. As Paul Vitz observes, providing arguments for the kind of informal processes described above—involving the use of narratives—would set one's stance at odds with Kohlberg's model, which has been dominant in the literature regarding the nature and processes of moral development that could be brought about by moral education. In Vitz's words, "the general approach offered in this article [the use of narratives and stories as a method of enhancing moral development and education] is in some important respects a critique of Kohlberg's model."[20] It is pertinent to say that the view I espouse with respect to the nature of moral education and development in traditional African cultures is not meant necessarily, to render Kohlberg's view suspect. The psychological evidence used by Vitz to argue for this informal model of moral education that is based on the use of narratives, does not necessarily indicate, in my view, that Kohlberg's model to which this informal narrative model is said to be opposed, is right or wrong, but Kohlberg's model is obviously not the only plausible model. In other words, the use of narratives may not necessarily be inconsistent with Kohlberg's view. But there is a marked difference, in that the sophisticated reasoning underlying the use of stories is absent at the lower developmental levels of Kohlberg's model. I am not sure whether Kohlberg's model necessarily precludes other models and modes of moral education and development, such as the use of stories and narratives. Or perhaps, it could plausibly be the case that the informal processes described above, which Vitz argues for, are complimentary to Kohlberg's model. That is, one's cognitive abilities could be enhanced by one's experiences, practice, and observations that are couched in terms of narratives. So, it is possible to have a synthesis or a blend of two different or more models. The use of stories, proverbs, and narratives, which Kohlberg seems to ignore could be added to his model to get a robust and adequate view of the methods of moral education and model of moral development. We see this kind of idea in the recent views of critical thinking, which indicates that being a critical thinker, i.e., developing the ability to think critically as a set of cognitive abilities, involves having a critical attitude and habit of the mind, and a disposition to use or employ this 'habit' in practice.[21] This habit must be cultivated via informal processes. This is consistent with Aristotle's view that moral education is, at an initial stage, a matter of habituation.[22] This point is relevant to moral education because it is not enough to have certain cognitive abilities that Kohlberg articulates in the various stages of moral development. It may be more important to have the disposition, habit, or attitude to actually use those abilities to inform everyday moral actions and decisions, so that one can in turn use these experiences as substantive context or material contents to inform, in a robust way, such cognitive abilities. The traditional African informal method of moral education ensures that the cognitive abilities are developed, but it also provides the context for encouraging and evincing the requisite habits or attitudes.

For instance, when stories are told to children in African cultures in order to teach a moral lesson, usually, the children are asked to analyze them by trying to infer and critically examine the moral principles embedded in the stories. This is to make sure that they have and develop the requisite cognitive abilities to understand the stories, and that they are able to draw inferences about the required moral principles and values from such stories. They also analyze the moral stories by understanding the implications and consequences of certain actions in the stories. They must decipher the bad and proper actions and their underlying principles, and the correct principles or actions that would help one to avoid or vitiate bad consequences. Such analyses help children to see the complexity and contextual nature of moral issues and problems. Appreciating such complexity also indicates to children that they cannot follow or obey moral rules in a simple-minded way that does not allow for reasoning and deliberation. So, beyond having the cognitive abilities to understand the requisite principles, proper actions, and consequences, the communal environment and informal methods provide the proper context for having the proper moral dispositions and displaying the relevant moral habits and attitudes. The communal environment and relationships, which specify the proper duties, actions, and social recognition, also provide the material contents, which seek to practically reinforce and imbue the relevant moral attitudes and habits. Hence, people are able to use narratives, folktale, and proverbs effectively to educate children and develop their cognitive abilities. It is on the basis of these abilities that children understand moral principles, articulate rational life plans, and make rational and moral decisions that are consistent with their life plans and communal interests. At the same time, the existential communal context, informal use of the method of narratives, and everyday experiences seek to evince and encourage the proper moral attitudes and habits that are necessary for one to acquire the proper virtues, act morally, and perform one's duties in order to achieve personhood.

## Justifying the Informal Processes of Moral Education

The anecdotal argument for the use of narratives as a communal mode of moral education derives from my experience and observations in Africa. There is a difference between the moral attitudes of children who are raised in big cosmopolitan cities where the communal traditions are waning and those raised in the semi-traditional African communities, in the villages where the communal traditions and customs still have powerful influence. By the way, these villages and their modes of moral interaction would mirror and reflect the kind of informal processes of moral education and reinforcement that I have described above. This is the kind of process that Etzioni alludes to in the anecdote about people's conduct in Stanford University's community, in which he indicates that a plausible explanation for people's good behavior involves the informal ribbing, prodding, and chiding. It is also pertinent to note that the big cities reflect the non-existence of communities or communal attitudes and principles, where the informal processes of moral education are not in place. In the big cities, you find people doing immoral things and getting away with such conduct because people can maintain a sense of anonymity and individualism. They seem to have lost the communal influence that produces shame and guilt for immoral acts. Because people do not know or socialize with each other, one may not be chided or ribbed by his neighbors for doing a bad thing. The advantage with communalism is that it helps people to develop communal and social interaction, which facilitates knowing and helping each other, as well as caring and having concern for each other. Such social and communal interaction, the need to help, and show caring and concern usually engender the moral attitudes of shame and guilt, which diminish immoral or criminal acts.

In big cities where there are no communal structures and the requisite moral attitudes, even when parents try to teach a child about the morally good thing to do, they usually do not have the communal support and reinforcement by the consistent ribbing and chiding. It becomes difficult for the children to acquire the proper virtues and to develop the right moral habits and attitudes. This anecdotal experience may indicate that the cognitive and formal models of moral education are inadequate in themselves to properly educate children about morals. My experience also shows that children raise in big cities, where they cannot develop the requisite communal moral attitudes of caring and concern, tend to be more selfish, individualistic, and less morally upright. There are many instances that I personally know of, where the parents of the children raised in big cities have been seriously chastised by their family folks in their home communities from which they hail for not morally raising their children in the proper manner. There is a sense in which the children raised in cities are cognitively 'smart' or developed, but are in some sense, morally inept with respect to their behavior because they have not developed the proper moral attitudes and habits of showing concern for others. One plausible explanation is that they did not have the proper communal environment and the informal context for developing the proper habits by constant reinforcement and modeling. Sometimes, they are actually able to use their intellectual sophistication and cognitive abilities to apply abstract moral principles to 'justify' or rationalize their morally bad actions. For instance, they may use such cognitive sophistication to abstractly justify stealing, lying, and other immoral behaviors from a purely selfish and individualistic perspective, without due consideration of the practical reality they are dealing with and the implications of their action in the relevant situation for others.

Perhaps, it is this kind of anecdote and experiential argument that Vitz alludes to when he says that moral education has been on the decline in the past decades, a decline, which he says, is a result of so many factors, and for which a panacea is now being sort.[23] He cites the social pathologies among the youth as a reflection of a decline in morality and the failings of moral education. According to statistics, there have been dramatic increases in the rate of different crimes such as homicide, robbery, car-jacking, rape, suicide, and violence in general, which may be an indication of moral decadence and lack of proper moral attitudes and habits, which require caring and concern for others and the respect for human welfare and the interest of others. There is also an increase in the use of drugs. The commercial dealings in these drugs have had a ravaging effect on inner cities. Many of these crimes or immoral acts can be reduced to a lack of the attitude of concern or caring for human welfare or the interests of other people. Moreover, some people have argued that there is less crime in smaller communities, and that people are more morally sensitive and caring toward other people's interest in these smaller communities where there is a greater sense of community than big cities. This sense of communities is conducive to and hence engenders the informal processes of moral education and reinforcement, which require people to acquire and display the proper moral attitudes and habits in their actions. In these communities, people know one another, they socially interact better with one another, they are able to engage one another in conversations and talk about common interests, and as such, they behave morally toward one another in order to preserve relationships. As a result, people are also able to engage in the informal moral chiding and ribbing that evince shame or guilt, and also engender or encourage the proper moral attitudes.

Social interactions, relationships, and community's involvement and participation result in having a dominant or common moral voice or ways of life, practices, attitudes, and habits, which articulate the interests of people that are translated into the interests of the community. The community, social interaction, and relationships create the social infrastructures that are necessary for engaging in the kind of informal moral education that I have described with respect to traditional African cultures. In order to avoid pervasive crimes and blatantly immoral or unacceptable behaviors, people are now advocating the idea of 'community policing'. In my view, the idea of community policing is precisely what communalism in African cultures and its model of moral education, social interaction, caring, moral reinforcement, and sanctions try to articulate. The idea of community policing indicates that everyone must keep an eye on each other and when they see a problem, it is a social and moral responsibility to take action and report to the authority. The police cannot be in every place at every time. We want people to work together to morally educate others and to police immoral or criminal acts. However, some people have argued that the decline in morality and a corresponding increase in crimes are the result of the changes in the contents or the principles of morality and not the methods or processes of moral education. It can reasonably be argued that the contents of morality in terms of *ends* as universal human ideals, welfare, and interests do not change as such relative to time, place, and culture. The *means* of achieving those ends are usually where people see differences or effect changes. One may also argue that the ways in which certain moral *ends* are inculcated, taught, and learned may affect or shape people's moral character and habits, which will also be manifested in how they behave.

In which case, the way people see moral ends and understand moral principles, based on the methods and processes of teaching and learning them, will determine or shape how they articulate or understand the relevant moral *means* that they chose, which we see in people's actions. The point here is that the communal context and the informal methods and processes by which children are morally educated in traditional African cultures shape the way in which they see the relevant moral ends and means that are manifested in actions. These processes, methods, and context do not simply teach the principles and values, but people also engage in the constant reinforcement of behaviors and they model relevant actions and conduct for people to imitate. As such, there may be a sense in which the contents or principles of morality for any particular person may be dependent on the methods and processes of teaching them. In other words, the contents of moral principles, which are indicated by what someone understands a moral rule to be, may largely be contingent on the methods or processes of teaching and learning the mora rule. For instance, what I understand the moral ideas or principles of not lying or stealing to be, may depend on whether or not someone simply indicated the principles to me and I learned it by rote. Or, it may depend on whether people gave me concrete examples of lying, modeled for me acts that constitute lying, taught me the bad consequences of lying, gave me abstract reasons why I should not lie, and whether I was allowed to act on a number of occasions so that in each situation people reinforced for me and helped me to identify the particular action and types of actions that constitute lying.

So, what I understand about lying or whether I properly understand it depends on whether all these different methods and processes were used to teach me what I should do and how I should act. The philosophical issue that is raised by the idea of moral education is largely the issue of the proper method or processes by which moral principles are inculcated. We have seen that one's ability to properly grasp the contents of a moral principle will depend on the robustness of the methods and processes by which such principle is taught and learned. I have indicated how the methods, context, and processes of moral education in traditional African cultures involving the use of narratives, stories, and proverbs are indeed very robust. They target one's cognitive abilities by helping one to acquire the proper skills and develop the relevant critical and analytical abilities. They also help one to develop the proper attitudes and habits. The relevant contents of morality are taught by explaining and learning the abstract principles, their abstract justifications, their practical justifications, their concrete implications in terms of consequences, the specification of the relevant duties that the principles imply, the modeling of behaviors to illustrate the principles, the use of examples, and the constant, persistent, and consistent reinforcement by everyone.

One heuristic value of the informal model of moral education in traditional African cultures is that it provides a motivation for further social science research and a basis for comparative analysis on two levels: the longitudinal/horizontal level and a cross-cultural/vertical level. On a horizontal/longitudinal level, we must analyze the factors or methods and processes of moral education that existed a few decades ago in various cultures that do not exist in the present day. Then we may try to find out how the missing factors in present day cosmopolitan cities, for instance, have over time resulted in the decline in morality and an increase in crime. On a vertical/cross-cultural level, we may proceed to analyze the processes or methods of moral education that existed and still exist in traditional African communities, which are lacking in Western cultures, in order to examine how they may have contributed to the moral equilibrium in African communities. Then we may be able to compare and contrast traditional African cultures and Western cultures in terms of their approach to moral education in order to determine whether the differences in the contexts of the methods and processes of moral education and the efficacy of these methods can account for the differences in moral sensitivity and the attitudes of caring and concern for others. My stance is that the robust factors in the communal context of traditional African cultures regarding their informal methods and processes of moral education are superior to the modern Western formal, individualistic, and cognitive view or model of moral education and development. In other words, the relevant factors in African communal cultures seem to have enhanced the efficacy of moral education, while their absence seems to have hindered the efficacy of moral education in modern Western cultures and in African cosmopolitan cities where people have adopted the Western ethos and individualistic attitudes.

I have described and alluded to certain important factors and elements in African communal traditions, which are necessary for a robust or effective moral education, the absence of which may hinder moral education. These elements are the informal processes of teaching, the constant and consistent reinforcement of moral values and principles in families and community by ribbing, chiding, and prodding, and having a situation where people can develop the proper attitudes, virtues, values, and habits, and learn by examples from mentors who model the proper actions. The reliance on formal systems of education in schools and churches, and the sole reliance on parents as those who should provide moral guidance for children are inadequate. And the people who are considered role models in the West, i.e., professional athletes, performers, and movie stars are usually not those you will want children to morally model their actions after. This is fairly different in traditional African cultures because elders who are role models are people who can morally educate children based on how they lead their lives and act. These elders are people who have direct contact with children and whose model actions and behaviors have direct impact on children in the community. Based on this African idea of role model, it is reasonable to argue that there is the need for a communal involvement in moral education. This requires people to articulate a shared moral voice or some commonly shared moral values that stress the responsibility of people to uphold certain values for themselves, the community, and others. The idea of articulating or having a shared moral voice and value with respect to humanistic ends is not to indicate where we disagree but where we commonly agree. There should be a moral core of principles or ends that form the basis of society and there could be other peripheral moral principles about means that people may disagree about.

The informal features of narratives as elements of moral education in traditional African cultures are plausible and effective because they are rooted in some fundamental theoretical and practical assumptions or conceptions about the nature of a person, community, humanistic goals, ends, and values. Moreover, these assumptions and conceptions are also based on strong philosophical, practical, and psychological arguments, some of which I have articulated or alluded to. Some of these assumptions or conceptions and their underlying arguments are also articulated by Helen Haste as follows:

(1) She indicates "that people are social beings who generate meaning through discourse and social interactions, and through cultural repertoires, stories and scripts transmitted by social practices and narratives."[24] The methods and processes of moral education in African cultures are effective, in my view, because they are sensitive to and consistent with this natural and social nature of human discourse.

(2) As social beings, there are desirable goals and ends that people consider to be values, which "foster an individual's sense of meaning, and a stable community."[25] In order to achieve these ends and maintain these values, people will need to "promote engagement with the community, and the transcendence of egoism and narrow instrumentalism."[26]

(3) An individual's sense of meaning is gained by being a member of a given community in which she can engage in social interactions, relationships, practices, discourse, and develop or acquire attitudes, habits, and virtues. Such engagement helps one to earn and develop values regarding how one must behave morally in the community in order to achieve one's rational life plans and self-fulfilment.

(4) An individual's sense of meaning is brought about by social interactions, relationships, and discourses in the cultural context of a community, which usually provides the basis for reflections and cognitive stimulation. Hence, one's cognitive development must involve contextual elements and substantive material contents.

(5) One's cognitive stimulation and development are contingent on an environment that allows one to use one's abilities to achieve one's life plans. And one's life plans are made possible by being a participating, contributing, and responsible member of a community. And one is able to develop and acquire the proper moral virtues, attitudes, and habits by being a responsible member of community.

The above assumptions and features of the informal methods and processes of moral education seem to be rooted in the assumptions and features of the idea of communalism in African traditions, and its conceptions of a person and community. These features and assumptions are also given credence by the arguments for the narrative method in social psychology. This narrative method is usually contrasted with the mechanistic approach. Some have argued in favor the narrative approach by indicating its value in helping us to unravel and understand the behaviors of people, especially in their social and cultural contexts. For instance, Theodore Sarbin has argued for the significance of using stories and narratives as a metaphor for understanding the behavior of people. He argues that the mechanistic approach in social psychology has a limited use, in that it ignores some aspects of human behavior that cannot be captured mechanistically or cognitively, but are best illuminated by personal narratives.[27] The underlying idea is that narratives give an account of people's lives in a very robust manner by including the contexts, intentions, interests, and broader relationships, in terms of how they give meaning to people's lives and how specific actions or behavioral patterns fit into that robust story of one's life. Thus, the narrative method, in Sarbin's view, allows a psychologist to capture and understand the historical, cultural, social, and familial contexts of people's actions in order to get an insight into how contexts and the factors underlying a person's life could provide an organizing principle for his behavior.

Sarbin argues that people usually understand their own lives in terms of narratives that offer the robust features and various elements of one's life. Hence, in his view, people write autobiographies and biographies, by virtue of which people's lives and behaviors are richly and robustly captured. As such, people see their behaviors and actions in a complex and wholesale manner, and not piecemeal. A wholesale understanding of one's life involves an account of a complex interplay of various factors, which only narratives can provide. In other words, people understand their lives as narratives that account for their behaviors and actions on the basis of their aims, intentions, interests, and context that provide the complex strings that tie together all their actions and behaviors. According to Sarbin, "Our plannings our rememberings, even our loving and hating, are guided by narrative plots."[28] The use of narrative is of a particular significance to moral education because people tend to make moral choices on the basis of their complex and robust understanding of their lives, and how they see the relevance of particular moral issues or principles in relation to their lives, in terms of their circumstances, ends, and interests. So, understanding the narrative of someone's life is to see his circumstances, motives, ends, and interests, and how he sees the connection between his moral choices and the context of his life. Providing this kind of narrative will give people a better understanding or teach them how to better make moral choices by considering the complex elements of context and interests. Teaching someone a moral principle as an abstract principle without providing some narrative and context for such principle, in terms of how a principle should apply to people's lives and actions, would not be adequate.

## Narratives and Practical Moral Reasoning

Paul C. Vitz argues that "a child's understanding of moral issues is an interpersonal, emotional, imagistic, and story-like phenomenon."[29] If this idea is true, then one can understand why the narrative informal model of moral education in traditional African cultures that I have described, which captures Vitz's view, is superior to the formal model. In particular, it is superior to Kohlberg's formal view of moral development, which sees morality or a child's understanding of moral issues as an abstract, cognitive, formal phenomenon. Hence, in Vitz's view, "Kohlberg's model fails to respond to much of the child's mental life."[30] In contrast to Kohlberg's approach, the informal narrative approach helps to provide a robust complex and concrete context for the abstract moral principles that are translated into people's lives by their actions and other people's responses to them in specific contexts. Hence, for Robinson and Hawpe, narratives are important for moral education and a child's understanding of moral principles, because relevant moral narratives are "context-based, concrete and testable through ordinary interpersonal checking."[31] Narratives remove moral issues and principles from an abstract cognitive level, instead, narratives present or explain moral principles in the contexts that make them concrete, practical, realistic, and understandable. As such, these principles can be tested by people in their ordinary lives and in their interpersonal relationships with others, in terms of other people's responses. One can appreciate this point in the communal context of traditional African cultures, where children can learn or understand moral principles and acquire moral virtues, habits, and attitudes by testing and checking the propriety of their moral ideas and actions through interpersonal relationship of social responsibilities and people's responses through social recognition, chiding, ribbing, prodding, and the acquisition of personhood.

In supporting the use of narratives as an important and effective method for moral education, and as a tool for moral development, Robinson and Hawpe argue as follows:

> First, where practical choice and action are concerned, stories are better guides than rules and maxims. Rules and maxims state significant generalizations about experience but stories illustrate and explain what those summaries mean. The oldest form of moral literature is the parable; the most common form of informal instruction is the anecdote. Both forms enable us to understand generalizations about the social order because they exemplify that order in a contextualized account. Second, stories can also be used as tests of the validity of maxims and rules of thumb. That is, stories can be used as arguments. Stories are natural mediators between the particular and the general in human experience. We should try to improve and refine this mode of thinking, not eschew it.[32]

This passage is particularly illuminating because it indicates that stories can be used as arguments and as a rational basis for reasoning about moral principles. This point seems to underscore an important element of the use of stories and folktale as a tool for moral education in African cultures. One important element of the use of stories is to provide a set of premises from which children can draw the relevant conclusions about the proper moral principle or moral actions. These stories are therefore used to stimulate children's reasoning and cognitive abilities. They help children to reason about moral principles and make rational decisions about their moral actions. This means that stories and informal methods are not necessarily used to indoctrinate or brainwash children about moral doctrines. The stories discussed above do not only provide moral conclusions in terms of principles, such as the idea that it is morally bad to be greedy, they also provide evidence to prove this by showing the implications of greed. The fact that a person is able to relate, realistically, to the context surrounding the implication of greed in the story means that he has substantive evidence to support the principle that one should not be greedy. He does not just accept the principle without proof, nor does he accept it on the basis of abstract reasoning alone. He has a better understanding of the principle because of the context, which helps him to apply it to his own life.

In Sarbin's view, the moral choices that an individual makes in any situation, are specifically informed by, or dependent on, her understanding of the relevance or significance of a particular moral issue to her understanding of her own life, and her existential condition as a narrative or story.[33] So, the significance of the use of narratives as a method of moral education is also given credence by the distinction between intellectual (abstract and logical) and practical modes of thinking, reasoning, or rationality, and the view that morality, moral reasoning or moral choice is fundamentally based on practical reasoning. These two modes of thinking have long been accepted in philosophy as two different bases for explaining and understanding people's decisions and actions. This distinction and the idea that moral reasoning is fundamentally based on practical reason date back to Aristotle. Practical reasoning involves a way of acting, which involves using a *means* in a specific context to achieve a desired *end*. Moral reasoning is said to be based on practical reason because it guides people in making practical decisions about actions. This is usually contrasted with pure or intellectual reason, which involves an abstract, logical, and theoretical method of making decision in order to determine coherence of beliefs or validity of reasoning. Kohlberg's abstract, logical, and cognitive ideas of moral development and morality seem to suggest that morality and moral reasoning are based solely on intellectual reason and not on practical reason. Although intellectual thinking is a way of determining the abstract truth of propositions, the idea of morality as a practical or action-guiding principle is not necessarily opposed to intellectual reason. In fact, practical reason can, in most cases, be informed by intellectual reason. One may use intellectual thinking to inform practical thinking in terms of determining whether a moral principle is logically true. For instance, if a principle is deemed to be objectively true and logically reasonable, then one may be justified and rationally motivated to use it as an action-guiding principle or a means for achieving an end.

Although the idea of 'practical reason' may be construed as a way or process of reasoning or thinking about one's actions or a method by which one decides to act in order to achieve an end, Richard Posner indicates that 'practical reason' does not have a standard meaning. But the literature shows that practical reason has been commonly construed in terms of rationality.[34] Practical reason, Posner argues,

> is most often used to denote the methods ('deliberation' and 'practical syllogism' are the key expressions here) that people use to make a practical or ethical choice, such as whether to go to the theater, or whether to lie to an acquaintance. Practical reason in this sense is action-oriented, in contrast to the methods of 'pure reason' by which we determine whether a proposition is true or false, an argument valid or invalid. Practical reason involves setting a goal—pleasure, good life, whatever—and choosing the means best suited to reaching it.[35]

Based on the above idea of practical reason, it has the following features: it is action guiding; it is a means-end scheme of deliberation with respect to the *choice* of the *best means* in terms of the strategy for achieving whatever *end* one wants to. Practical reason is not opposed to intellectual reason because it could be related to the abstract and logical adequacy of reasoning or the truth of a proposition, but only where such adequacy is relevant to choice and decision making. As such, the deliberation regarding such a decision or choice of a particular line of action is dependent on the epistemic state of the actor regarding the adequacy of end, the relevant alternatives, and the efficacy of the means of achieving an end. The force of 'practical' is sometimes not clear whenever one says he acted on the basis of 'practical reason'. John Finnis explains the force of 'practical' by contrasting it with the understanding of something being 'workable' as opposed to unworkable, and 'efficient' as opposed to inefficient.[36]

In analyzing the concept of 'practical reason', Finnis also argues that the idea of 'practical' must be understood in terms someone "with a view to decision and action."[37] This idea describes a particular point of view or attitude that an individual adopts with respect to a decision to act in a particular way. Thus, the idea of 'practical' may be said to have the following features in the notion of 'practical reason': (i) It describes the fact that someone has adopted a point of view or a certain attitude regarding a particular line of action. (ii) It makes some reference to the fact that someone has relativized her deliberation to a real or conceived situation which forms the context of the action. (iii) It also makes reference to the justified belief or knowledge that one has about the circumstances surrounding the action. (iv) It makes reference to the idea of efficiency, efficacy, and workability in a deliberation about a means for achieving an end and an adequate strategy. The important point about the features of practical reason, and distinction between intellectual and practical reason, has to do with the fact that moral reasoning is essentially a practical form of reasoning. It is a mode of reasoning that is often ignored by the formal model of moral education and development. This idea of moral education usually focuses on one's cognitive abilities, which seem to define intellectual reason. The dominance of Kohlberg's abstract, formal, and cognitive model of moral education and development seems to underscore this point.

So, my central point is that the idea of practical reasoning in morality is best enhanced by narratives, in that they are geared toward providing a robust context for understanding moral principles and their practical implications. The provision of such context and robust understanding of moral principles also tends to imbue the required moral attitudes, which are necessary for one to act morally by applying moral principles to concrete situations. This point is bolstered by Vitz's view that narratives "focus on people and on the causes of their actions: their intentions, goals, and subjective experience."[38] The goal of using narratives in moral education is to focus on the enhancement of a person's character, setting, experience, means, and ends, as opposed to abstract, theoretical, intellectual, and objective principles, which are more difficult to understand. The use of narratives for moral education in traditional African cultures gives credence to the two forms of thinking as the basis for organizing one's experience and action, in that the use of narratives seeks to enhance a child's abstract cognitive abilities and their practical abilities to use abstract principles in concrete reality. The distinction between intellectual and practical reasoning has been accepted in psychology as corresponding to the distinction between 'propositional' and 'narrative' thinking, which also seems to correspond to Endel Tulving's distinction between 'episodic memory' and 'semantic memory'[39] and the well-known distinction between the right and left hemispheres of the brain.

For instance, Jerome Bruner has argued that "There are two modes of cognitive functioning, two modes of thought, each providing distinctive ways of ordering experience, of constructing reality. The two (though complementary) are irreducible to one another. Efforts to reduce one mode to the other or to ignore one at the expense of the other inevitably fail to capture the rich diversity of thought."[40] Propositional thinking, which corresponds to intellectual mode of thinking, semantic memory, and the left hemisphere of the brain, consists of logical argumentation, abstract, theoretical, analytic, and formal reasoning, objective and universal truths. Narrative thinking, which corresponds to practical thinking, episodic memory, and the right hemisphere of the brain, consists of context dependent reasoning, spatial connections, image representations, and means-end thinking. In explaining this distinction, Vitz says that, "narrative thought presents concrete human and interpersonal situations in order to demonstrate their particular validity."[41] The essential point about these distinctions is that moral education must recognize and address both forms of thinking. The suggestion is that the communal context, informal processes, and narrative method of moral education in traditional African cultures recognize and address these two forms of thinking as a robust way to understand and think about moral principles. These distinctions and the idea morality in African cultures are also illuminated by Nel Noddings' distinction between informal (ordinary) and formal (intellectual and philosophical) conversations and their place in moral education.

According to Noddings, 'formal conversation' involves logical reasoning and judging the force of an argument, but 'ordinary conversation' involves the sharing of ideas and experiences between people who trust and care about each other.[42] The ordinary type of conversation that is illustrated by the above stories in African cultures is important for moral education because it has the feature, according to Nel Noddings, of creating a caring and loving relationship between the adult (teacher) and the child (student), who are involved in the conversation. The teacher is a role model who loves and cares for the child and the learning relationship is based on care and love. Moreover, the relationship demands that the adult or teacher must or try to be a reasonably good person in order to model her actions. The teacher must consider the effects of her actions on her students and she must respond to her students with concern and compassion. In ordinary conversation, according to Noddings, the partner in conversation, and the love and care for such a partner, are more important than the contents of the conversation. This is because there is a genuine interest and likeness for the other person with whom you are engaged in a conversation. For instance, the adult who is able to use this method to morally educate a child must be a mentor and must have the genuine interest in the moral development of the child. The child must respect the adult; the child must trust the adult and must see him as a morally good person who cares. The child sees the adult as a mentor or role model whose actions are examples that he is willing to emulate.

Noddings argues that, in ordinary conversations, "children learn all sorts of things—facts, the rules of polite conversation, manner and style, trust and confidence, how to listen, how to respond without hurting and host of other factors in human interaction."[43] One of the conditions that must exist for the effective use of ordinary conversation or narrative for moral education is, a community where people can socially interact freely. This kind of social interaction is underlined by people's ability to engage in different kinds of informal conversations and narrative discourses that are at the foundation of a community. The stories described above that are used as forms of moral education in traditional African cultures are effective because of the communal structures, which provide the basis for informal social relationships, interactions, and conversations, as well as a common set of values and experiences that everyone can draw from. In my view, the use of ordinary conversations or narratives as a method for moral education and the practical understanding of moral principles is based on and underlined by the Aristotelian commonplace idea that moral reasoning involves *practical reason*. It is based on the idea that moral principles have to be learned not solely for the purpose of determining and understanding their objective truth but also for the purpose of using them in particular contexts as practical and action-guiding principles. According to Kevin McDonough, "the aim of Aristotelian moral education is the person of practical wisdom, who evaluates each case with a sensitivity and perception designed to issue in a reasoned choice of action that is appropriate precisely for that situation."[44] Chaim Perelman has also argued that the kind of reasoning that people apply in their everyday lives is, fundamentally, practical reasoning or a narrative mode of thinking.[45] As such, we must appreciate the significance of narratives in terms of how they may be used to enhance people's practical moral reasoning, which is the basis for their decisions, actions, and behaviors.

The central point is that intellectual rationality is not the only mode of reasoning, especially with respect to morality. Moreover, we cannot fully reduce one mode of thinking to the other, and we cannot place absolute premium on one by ignoring the other. It is plausible that if the two modes of thinking (both intellectual and practical) are targeted and enhanced, then moral education is likely to be more effective. This is because practical modes of thinking can enhance intellectual modes of thinking and vice versa; thus, one may complement the other. The idea that the use of moral principles is based fundamentally on practical or narrative mode of thinking is not an attempt to overemphasize this kind of thinking to the detriment of intellectual reasoning. MacIntyre indicates that the use of concrete examples, illustrations, and experiences in narratives and stories for moral education gives credence to practical reasoning in a way that complements intellectual reasoning.[46] Because morality involves practical decisions in terms of how one should act in order to lead a meaningful life, it is reasonable to use narratives, analogies, realistic examples, and personal experiences for moral education, because narratives do not only illuminate the abstract and objective truth of moral principles, but also specify in a practical way how people should reason when applying acceptable moral principles to their everyday moral decisions and actions.

MacIntyre notes that Rawls, among other contemporary philosophers, has conceived of morality fundamentally as universal, general, and objectively true principles that are abstracted and sometimes removed from the personal contexts of human beings and their lives.[47] These universal principles then become the primary basis for forming the moral life of people, molding their character, and teaching virtues. This idea tends to reduce moral life and character to universal rational principles, which are prized because they are seen as capable of helping us to organize our lives consistently in accordance with a certain objectively valid principle that would be intellectually accepted as true by all rational people. MacIntyre indicates that morality cannot be derived or learned solely from abstract principles of rationality; they may also be derived or learned from one's everyday experiences and personal interactions with others. Based on human interactions and relationships, and what people think and experience about such interactions and relationships regarding the possible effect of their actions on others, people see themselves as having a duty. Such sense of duty is not derived from the truth of abstract moral principles Moreover, moral education is, primarily, not an attempt to teach people how to intellectually or logically articulate abstract moral principles, but how to adjust one's character and practically respond in one's actions and duty to substantive moral principles that are relevant to human lives and relationships An awareness of the proper moral principle of action is demonstrated in how a person acts. Learning how to act in accordance with socially accepted moral principles usually emerges from experiences, social interactions, and relationships. MacIntyre suggests that we have to train or educate people to acquire the right moral virtues, attitudes, habits, and character before they can properly or rationally understand how abstract moral principles should function authoritatively in the context of human relationships. The authority of moral rules has to be understood in terms of their inductive grounding in the personal lives and experiences of virtuous people who have effectively used them to guide their conduct.

Having described the nature of informal and narrative model of moral education and thinking in African cultures, and having provided a philosophical basis for its use, it may be pertinent to consider some of the epistemic conditions that must exist for this method to be effectively used. These conditions involve the idea of sharing evidence or beliefs, communal inquiry, and epistemic dependence on elders as the repositories of knowledge. We have to consider the communal situation described above and its epistemic features, so as to determine the propriety of the informal processes and methods of moral education in African cultures, in order to defend the idea that people did engage in moral education and that people were indeed morally educated. The point is to examine how well the informal educational processes in a communal structure are able to harness the social epistemological and psychological processes and the communal conditions that exist in African cultures for the purpose of attaining the requisite goals of morality, moral education, moral development, and the acquisition of moral personhood. However, Wiredu, among others, has charged that the conditions of communalism in African cultures involve moral and epistemic authoritarianism. Such authoritarianism implies, in his view, that moral principles are inculcated in a manner that involves indoctrination and that such indoctrination is necessarily bad.[48] We must therefore examine the extent to which communalism in African cultures involves authoritarianism before considering the issue of whether the processes and methods of teaching of morality involve rational education or indoctrination, and whether indoctrination is necessarily bad.

# Notes

1. There are some cultures where chieftaincy and kingship are hereditary, but an heir must exemplify or personify the requisite moral purity or integrity that is demanded by such status.

2. The Ibadan School History is used to refer to a group of Nigerian Historians who taught History at the University of Ibadan, Nigeria, in the 1950s. This School included people like Kenneth Dike, Saburi Biobaku, Ade Ajayi, E. A. Ayandele, A. E. Afigbo, Obaro Ikime, among others. In addition to these Nigerian historians, some expatriate historians, such as Michael Crowther, J. B. Webster, R. J. Garvin, Robert Smith, J. D. Omer-Cooper, joined in the efforts to use oral tradition to reconstruct a history of the African past. See Paul E. Lovejoy, "Nigeria: The Ibadan School of History and Its Critics," in *African Historiographies: What History for Which Africa*, eds., Bogumil Jewsiewicki and David Newbury (London: Sage Publications, 1986), 197-205.

3. E. J. Alagoa, "Nigerian Academic Historians," in *African Historiographies: What History for Which Africa*, eds., Bogumil Jewsiewicki and David Newbury (London: Sage Publications, 1986), 191.

4. W. V. O. Quine, "Two Dogmas of Empiricism," In *From A Logical Point of View* (New York: Harper & Row, Publishers, 1961), 45.

5. Quine, "Two Dogmas of Empiricism," 44.

6. Parker English and Nancy Hamme, "Using Art History and Philosophy to Compare a Traditional and a Contemporary Form of African Moral Thought," *Journal of Social Philosophy* 27, no. 2 (Fall 1996): 204-233.

7. English and Hamme, "Using Art History and Philosophy," 206.

8. Dzobo, "African Symbols and Proverbs as Source of Knowledge and Truth," 85.

9. English and Hamme, "Using Art History and Philosophy," 206.

10. English and Hamme, "Using Art History and Philosophy," 206.

11. English and Hamme, "Using Art History and Philosophy," 206.

12. I will argue in a subsequent chapter that what they refer to as indoctrination is a actually education, partly because of the difficulty in making the distinction between education and indoctrination as it relate to practice.

13. Amitai Etzioni, *The Spirit of Community: Rights, Responsibilities, and the Communitarian Agenda* (New York: Crown Publishers, Inc., 1993), 32-33 (emphases are mine).

14. Haste, "Communitarianism and the Social Construction of Morality," 53.

15. Kevin McDonough, "The Importance of Examples for Moral Education: An Aristotelian Perspective," *Studies in Philosophy and Education* 14, no. 1 (1995): 81-89.

16. Menkiti, "Person and Community in African Traditional Thought," 173.

17. McDonough,"The Importance of Examples for Moral Education," 82.

18. McDonough,"The Importance of Examples for Moral Education," 88-89.

19. I address this issue in Polycarp Ikuenobe, "Cognitive Relativism, African Philosophy, and the Phenomenon of Witchcraft," *Journal of Social Philosophy* 26, no. 3 ( 1995): 143-160, and Polycarp Ikuenobe, "In Search of Human Universality: Context and Justification in Cultural Philosophy," *Humanitas* 11, no. 2 (1998): 58-90.

20. Paul C. Vitz, "The Use of Stories in Moral Development: New Psychological Reasons for an Old Education Method," *American Psychologist* 45, no. 6 (June 1990): 709-710.

21.This view is espoused among others by J. E. McPeck, *Critical Thinking and Education*. (New York St. Martins Press, 1981); Robert H. Ennis, "A Conception of Critical Thinking," *Harvard Educational Review* 32 (1962): 83-111; and Harvey Siegel, *Educating Reason* (New York: Routledge, 1998).

22. McDonough, "The Importance of Examples for Moral Education," 82.

23. Vitz, "The Use of Stories in Moral Development," 709.

24. Haste, "Communitarianism and the Social Construction of Morality," 52.

25. Haste, "Communitarianism and the Social Construction of Morality," 52.

26. Haste, "Communitarianism and the Social Construction of Morality," 52.

27. Theodore R. Sarbin, "The Narrative as a Root Metaphor for Psychology," in *Narrative Psychology: The Storied Nature Human Conduct*, ed., T. R. Sarbin (New York: Praeger, 1986), 3-21.

28. Sarbin, "The Narrative as a Root Metaphor for Psychology," 11.

29. Vitz, "The Use of Stories in Moral Development," 711.

30. Vitz, "The Use of Stories in Moral Development," 711.

31. J.A. Robinson and L. Hawpe, "Narrative Thinking As A Heuristic Process," in *Narrative Psychology: The Storied Nature Human Conduct*, ed., T. R. Sarbin (New York: Praeger, 1986), 114.

32. Robinson and Hawpe, "Narrative Thinking As A Heuristic Process," 124.

33. Sabin, "The Narrative as a Root Metaphor for Psychology," p. 11.

34. This construal is rather commonplace in the literature on the issue of practical reason. This can be found in the works of Stephen Darwall, Bernard Williams, J. L. Mackie, Gilbert Harman, Kurt Baier, and Edward Bond on the issue.

35. Richard Posner, *The Problems of Jurisprudence* (Cambridge, MA: Harvard University Press, 1990), 71.

36. John Finnis, *Natural Law and Natural Rights* (Oxford: Clarendon Press, 1980), 12.

37. Finnis, *Natural Law and Natural Rights*, 12.

38. Vitz, "The Use of Stories in Moral Development," 710.

39. Endel Tulving, *Elements of Episodic Memory* (New York: Oxford University Press, 1983).

40. Jerome Bruner, *Actual Minds, Possible Worlds* (Cambridge MA: Harvard University Press, 1986), 11.

41. Vitz, "The Use of Stories in Moral Development," 710.

42. Nel Noddings, "Conversation as Moral Education," *Journal of Moral Education* 23, no. 2 (1994): 107-118.

43. Noddings, "Conversation as Moral Education," 117.

44. McDonough, "The Importance of Examples for Moral Education: An Aristotelian Perspective," 82.

45. Chaim Perelman, *The New Rhetoric and the Humanities* (Dordrecht, The Netherlands: Reidel, 1979).

46. Alasdair MacIntyre, *After Virtue* (Notre Dame, IN: Notre Dame University Press, 1981).

47. MacIntyre, *After Virtue*.

48. Wiredu, *Philosophy and An African Culture*.

# Chapter Five

# Communalism and Epistemic Authoritarianism

Wiredu argues that the communal structures of traditional African societies are characterized by a kind of moral and epistemic authoritarianism.[1] In his view, many of the beliefs in African cultures that provide the basis for moral values, principles, practices, and ways of life are accepted and held not on the basis of adequate evidence, but on the basis of the authoritarian dictates of tradition, and elders who are seen as repositories of knowledge. The groveling respect that is accorded to tradition and elders, may to some extent, imply the dogmatic and uncritical acceptance of their authorities, as well as their dictates and ideas. This unquestioning and uncritical attitude prevents people from raising critical questions and from engaging in rigorous inquiry about relevant beliefs. Kaphagawani also argues that this kind of authoritarianism is an essential but a negative aspect of African communalism.[2] He argues that elders in African communities were considered to be the authoritative source of all traditional beliefs and wisdom. Elders were accorded tremendous authority and power, and they had a status where their will and dictates are not questioned, but instead, are taken as representing the will of the community. This kind of epistemic authoritarianism, which is an essential feature of African communalism, also led to political authoritarianism of elders and tyranny. Such gerontocratic tyranny became a hegemonic ideology of oppression. Because of the status that was given to elders, they claimed to know what was good or right for the society. As such, their ideas were imposed on other people in the community. This authoritarian tendency, according to Kaphagawani, was inimical to the growth of individuality, in that it denied people the ability to critically reflect on and appraise the social system. As such, it also deprived people from making independent choices and from engaging in the active rational and cognitive participation in the affairs of the community.

Wiredu also echoes Kaphagawani's view that that kind of authoritarianism that is associated with communalism in African cultures limits the development of people's cognitive abilities and vitiates the autonomous use of reason by individuals. As such, people did not acquire and justify their beliefs based on the independent critical examination of the evidence. Wiredu indicates that authoritarianism is very pervasive in traditional African cultures, saying, "The very atmosphere we breathe in many areas of life in our society seems to be suffused with an authoritarian odour. . . ."[3] This authoritarian atmosphere prevented the independent, rigorous, and critical use of reason. The ability to use reason, will, and autonomy is considered a precondition for moral reasoning and moral education. Moral education involves the development of one's will, rational, and cognitive abilities, on the basis of which individuals are able to make rational, autonomous, and voluntary choices and decisions. According to Wiredu, "Any human arrangement is authoritarian if it entails any person being made to do or suffer something against his will, or if it leads to any person being hindered in the development of his own will."[4] He suggests that this definition may be too broad, but he insists that "authoritarianism is the *unjustified* overriding of an individual's will."[5] His criticism of authoritarianism in African cultures is based on the fact that he places a high premium on the importance of an individual's will to choose or make rational and autonomous decisions. As such, there is the need to provide a justification for any interference with such will. Wiredu suggests that there should be unimpeded development of an individual's will, and that such development, which is impeded by authoritarianism, involves the *manipulation* of one's will by others.

## Authoritarianism in African Cultures

Appiah seems to echo this point about authoritarianism in African thought system in terms of what he considers to be the irrational basis for beliefs. He argues that people in traditional African cultures justify their beliefs solely by reference to the fact that they are supported by the authority of tradition. In his view, "Justifying beliefs by saying they have the authority of tradition is one of the practices that demarcates traditional cultures from formal philosophy."[7] He contrasts thought systems in African traditions with the Western intellectual culture of formal philosophy by arguing that, even when authorities are cited in the Western intellectual tradition, they are not cited blindly, and they are not accepted simply because they have been regarded as authorities *per se.* He indicates that the adversarial style or method of inquiry in the Western intellectual culture is embedded in their conception and methods of education, and the processes of acquiring and justifying beliefs. This adversarial method implies that the view of an authority must be questioned in order to determine its appropriateness, and that it is the soundness of the evidence for the position which then confirms and sustains it as authoritative. The epistemic, political, and moral authoritarianism in African communal cultures, Wiredu and Appiah argue, discourages the attitudes and processes of critical inquiry, questioning, and curiosity, which are necessary to have a rational set of justified beliefs, values, and moral principles. As such, both Wiredu and Appiah doubt whether the use of reason is truly allowed to flourish in African traditions given its authoritarian tendencies.

Hence, Wiredu argues that "the disinclination to entertain questions about the reasons behind an established practice or institution is a sure mark of the authoritarian mentality."[7] Many African cultures had "the principle of unquestioning obedience to superiors, which often meant elders. Hardly any premium was placed on curiosity *in those of tender age*, or independence of thought in those of more considerable years."[8] Wiredu makes this point more poignant when he compares the custom in African cultures (Akan specifically, which specifies the respect for elders) with the attitudes of young people toward elders in America. He says that "American youth in a converse shift of environment would be likely to feel that traditional Akan society demands nothing short of groveling docility from the young in their relations with the old."[9] Wiredu argues that anyone who attempts to question the authority or adequacy of established beliefs, principles, and the procedures for doing things in many African cultures is met with a rebuff and told, "That is how it has always been done. I do not want any argument."[10] He argues that one ought to always use reason to decide between alternative beliefs and ways of doing things. These points seem to suggest, at least in part, that many of the beliefs that were substantial and significant to the traditional African people were beliefs or principles regarding how things should be done and achieved. In other words, many of these beliefs or knowledge or principles had practical relevance to the day-to-day lives of people. Many of these beliefs or principles were not held solely as abstract or theoretical, or conceptual ideas that could be questioned for the sake of theoretical inquiry.

However, even those ideas and beliefs that are abstract were viewed and approached from a concrete, practical, and an existential perspective. To a large extent, this may underscore an earlier metaphilosophical point that thought and philosophical systems were, for Africans, a practice and way of life. It is reasonable to argue that these principles and beliefs or their acceptance and justification were based on reason. Interestingly enough, Wiredu's appreciation of traditional African cultures and its structures, seems to implicitly provide a justification for what he characterizes as authoritarianism. As indicated in the previous chapter, the mastery of the extensive oral tradition and communal practical ways of life by children, shifted the burden of responsibility to elders as the repositories of such knowledge to impart it to children. For instance, Wiredu seems to appreciate the fundamental practical nature of beliefs and principles in African cultures. He alludes to this practical nature as a basis for justifying what he characterizes as the authoritarian attitudes in Akan culture. He indicates that: "In such societies, knowledge is likely to be, on the whole, more a possession of the old that of the young. Prestige and influence, will naturally go along with knowledge, more especially, *knowledge of a practical kind.*"[11] He indicates that there was a closeness in the relations between practical life and traditional philosophy, ideas, and thoughts.[12] This statement seems to indicate that Wiredu does appreciate why the adequate knowledge or justified belief in traditional African cultures is likely to be possessed by elders. Elders have the requisite experience and the opportunity of testing beliefs and principles over long periods of time. If this is true, then we can appreciate why respect and authority are accorded to elders in cultures as practical experiments in living.

This point can be underscored by Bernard Boxill's view that cultures are experiments in living or laboratories where people test and examine their cultural principles as different forms of hypotheses. According to him,

> People do not normally think of their own culture as an experiment in living. They do not suppose that their culture's mores and practices are hypotheses about how life should be lived and that in following these mores and practices they are behaving somewhat like scientists subjecting hypotheses to empirical tests. Normally they act as their culture dictates because they don't think about it, or because they believe that alternatives are wrong, or sometimes because they cannot conceive of alternatives. Still a culture is an experiment in living in the sense that things happen as a result of people following its mores and practices, and people do learn from how and why these things happen. This is why cultures change.[13]

If Boxill is correct about the nature of cultures, then we can appreciate why elders who are recognized in the community as reasonable people based on their actions, wealth of experience, knowledge of the tradition and culture, and their demonstration of such wisdom and knowledge, may be relied on as the source of knowledge and recognized as epistemic authorities. Boxill's point may indicate that elders had the opportunity of experimenting and testing out empirically many of their cultural principles or beliefs. It is reasonable to think that elders accept or continue to accept beliefs and use their cultural principles only because such principles have been proven, and they have the experience as evidence to prove this. Otherwise, if elders have any minimum rationality at all, they would modify or change their cultural principles that have not been effective. It appears that they will also make such modifications or changes only if they can understand and make practicable for their own needs, the alternative principles.

However, Wiredu's idea of authoritarianism seems to suggest that the value of an individual's will and autonomy is absolute and inalienable in every imaginable situation. Hence, he argues that, "a society would be seen as revoltingly authoritarian in as much as a person's will would usually be the result of manipulation by others."[14] The emphasis on 'manipulation' raises the issue of whether one can reasonably argue, as a philosophical claim that, in the context of the goals, processes, and features of communalism in traditional African cultures, the manipulation of an individual's will may be acceptable. So, the pertinent issue raised by this assumption underlying Wiredu's view of authoritarianism is whether the value of an individual's will or autonomy is absolute, such that it cannot be impeded in any circumstance. Or is it reasonable to argue that an individual's will or autonomy is valuable depending on a context and the nature of goods that an individual seeks to achieve with his choices? Moreover, the other issue is, what does it mean for an individual's will or autonomy to be *impeded*? Isn't an individual's will necessarily impeded by the obligations to obey laws or conform to the basic norms of a society, irrespective of the moral justification of such society? What constitutes an unjustified overriding of an individual's will? If, for instance, a child is being taught, educated, or brought up to act rationally or in accordance with some generally accepted and valid moral principles, and if the child sees the teaching of the elders and community as impeding his autonomy or the development of his will, then is such teaching necessarily bad based on the child's perspective?

In this case, let us suppose that the child wants to behave differently from the way that he is being taught or brought up, and the way he wants to behave is blatantly and obviously wrong and unacceptable. Usually, there are societal and communal strictures on how and in what directions an individual's will should develop. Hence, there are rules and laws, and legal and social sanctions on actions that derive from a bad will. Is it justified to impede the development of a child's will, if such development is justifiably deemed to be going in the wrong direction, which may prevent a child from attaining personhood and leading a meaningful and fulfilling life? Perhaps, we may also ask, what constitutes a meaningful life? Who determines this: Is it the individual *per se* or the society in which one lives or the individual in the context of the society in which one lives? These issues must be addressed in order to determine the adequacy of the criticisms of authoritarianism in traditional African communal cultures. Given what has been said so far in previous chapters, it is clear that in the African communalistic view, that an individual may determine what is a meaningful life, but only in the context of the community and the facilities, options, and goods that the community makes available. This point is not controversial; almost all moral and political theorists accept it. The epistemic implication is that an individual can determine what beliefs to accept and what principles to adopt only in the context of an epistemic community or an epistemic practice with its fundamental rules, meta-rules, shared or available evidence, and an inter-subjective justificatory basis.

Wiredu argues against epistemic and moral authoritarianism in African cultures on the following grounds: (i) it prevents questioning, inquiry, and the rigorous analysis of evidence or principles that could bring about growth and progress in knowledge; (ii) it perpetuates superstitious beliefs and dubious principles; (iii) it prevents the exercise of freewill and autonomy with respect to moral and epistemic moral choices and decision making; (iv) it prevents the use of reason in deliberation and consideration of relevant alternatives that are necessary for rational decision making; (v) it prevents creativity, ingenuity, and curiosity that are necessary for critical and rigorous inquiry. Thus, he suggests that:

> What is wanted is a certain kind of training in method, the kind of training that will produce minds eager and able to test claims and theories against observed facts and adjust beliefs to the evidence, minds capable of logical analysis and fully aware of the nature and value of exact measurement. Such training is not only likely to discourage superstition; it would also tend to undermine that authoritarianism.[15]

The point to note here is that Wiredu is suggesting that people in many African cultures, as a result of authoritarianism that is associated with communalism, are not trained to have eager minds by which they can test claims, principles, and theories against observed facts, adjust their beliefs and principles against the evidence they have, and do logical analysis. This criticism also suggests that what is characterized as moral education or training in African cultures may not be education as such, but indoctrination. However, it is my stance that one can *voluntarily* test claims, adjust beliefs to fit evidence, and do logical analysis within the context of a certain form of authoritarianism—and Wiredu seems to agree with this implicitly.

The main problem in Wiredu's characterization of authoritarianism is that he does not specify what would constitute an *unjustified* overriding of an individual's will nor does he provide an argument to indicate why it is absolutely necessary not impede individuals' will and autonomy. Perhaps, there are situations in which the overriding of an individual's will may be justified, and in my view, the structures of communalism in African cultures seem to appreciate this. With respect to the nature of the justification for overriding one's will, we may distinguish between the rational and irrational variants of authoritarianism within an epistemic community and practice. Authoritarianism is epistemically irrational, if and only if, a person, x, who is not epistemically superior to y, manipulates the will of y for reasons that are not epistemically valid, and these reasons are such that neither x nor y accepts them as warranted, or x subjectively accepts the reasons, but y does not. This definition (in its pejorative sense) is consistent with Wiredu's view of authoritarianism because it involves an *unjustified* overriding of an individual, y's will. Overriding y's will is unjustified because there are no epistemically or otherwise valid reasons for doing so. But authoritarianism may also be epistemically rational, if and only if, a person, x (an epistemic authority), who is 'epistemically superior' to another person, y, manipulates the will of y on the basis of a set of evidence that is inter-subjective ly justified, but which y does not consider justifiable because of his epistemic inferiority—an inferiority that he is not aware of. However, a person, x, is epistemically superior to y with respect to a belief w, just in case x is more knowledgeable or has a better understanding of w than y, and x has more relevant experience or evidence to prove the truth or reasonableness of w, to warrant w's acceptability.

It is pertinent to indicate that truth is not the only basis for accepting a belief. We accept many beliefs that are reasonable but whose truths we do not know or cannot prove. So, this rational variant is also consistent with Wiredu's definition of authoritarianism because, on one interpretation of *unjustified*, that is, from the perspective of the person (an epistemic inferior) whose will has been overridden, this act does not give primacy to the will of the individual and its development, hence it is unjustified from his perspective. This less pejorative type of authoritarianism, in my view, exists as a kind of paternalism in public policy where an official may use (in the context of the available information or 'tradition' in the community) an 'accepted' law or principle or belief, which an adult or reasonable person does not accept or understand, to intervene and restrict her actions against her own will. This kind of justifiable epistemic or moral or legal paternalism seems to reflect the kind of authoritarianism that Wiredu criticizes in some African cultures. We must place this rational type of authoritarianism in the context of an epistemic or moral community, which has a set of objectively acceptable epistemic and meta-epistemic principles that guide their epistemic inquiry and moral reasoning. The fact that these principles are objectively acceptable does not imply that they are in fact accepted and used as a guide to epistemic practice in all epistemic communities. One must, from an internal point of view, accept and use these principles or meta-principles in order to accept this view of authoritarianism. Some of the principles in African communal tradition include the dependence on epistemic authorities, the idea of engaging in communal inquiry and sharing evidence, and relying on the inter-subjective nature of such shared evidence as a basis for beliefs.[16]

The overriding of an individual's will or authoritarianism in this epistemic rational sense is, in some African cultures, based on some reasons, beliefs, and shared evidence that are *inter-subjective ly justified* in the community and social context. However, an individual from a different epistemic community with its different epistemic and meta-epistemic principles, or another person—from an 'external point of view'—may think that African beliefs are unjustified. A community, on this paternalistic, rational, authoritarian model, may decide for some inter-subjective ly justifiable epistemic reasons, that the harmful effects of 'light drugs' (marijuana in the USA, for instance) on society are such that they warrant the society to disallow their use. The society may disallow their use against the will of those who refuse to accept or are not aware of the reasons, but believe that the drugs are good for them and insist on using them. Does this involve the unjustified overriding of an individual's will? Not quite, in my view! Perhaps, it is easy for another person who does not appreciate the context and the contextual and pragmatic justification of this policy, to say that the overriding of the individual's will is unjustified. This person may not adequately appreciate the possible ramification for the society and the ramification for individuals, since individuals have to rely on the harmony of the society in order to lead meaningful lives. The hierarchical, contextual, and pragmatic nature of justification allows for a putatively unjustified overriding of one's will to be justified when such idea is subjected in an epistemic or moral context to a higher order of justification, that is, a meta-justification that incorporates the social context of acceptable principles and justified beliefs.

My stance is to provide an epistemic defense of authoritarianism in African cultures that is implied by the communal modes of, inquiry, moral thinking, and education. Such a defense is grounded in or involves an articulation of a plausible hierarchical, pragmatic, and contextual nature of justification. This view provides a basis and context, as a higher order of justification, to warrant a lower level of 'unjustified' overriding of an individual's will, with respect to an individual's rational justification of his own beliefs. The contextual and inter-subjective justification of beliefs in traditional African cultures is based on the experiences of the people in the context of their fundamental set of beliefs and meta-beliefs. Some of these beliefs and meta-beliefs have a foundational basis, in that they are generally accepted, intuitively obvious, and they have been positively confirmed or have not been disconfirmed. As such, it is on the basis of these foundational beliefs and meta-beliefs that people test and revise their other beliefs against the available evidence. This network of beliefs is accepted because of the pragmatic and heuristic values of the relevant beliefs, in that these beliefs allow the people to predict the future, and they have helped them to cope with their environment, and they still continue to help them to cope. This is why the accepted beliefs are entrenched in African communities and cultures. Because cultures may be characterized as experiments in living, elders have tested, analyzed, criticized, and revised these beliefs over time, and from their experiences, they have seen their validity, thus, these beliefs constitute part of the African tradition. This view implies that if the traditions or relevant beliefs warrant revision, they will be revised. This idea of justification and revision of beliefs is consistent with what Wiredu characterizes as the rational basis for accepting beliefs, which involves testing them against experiences.

However, the characterization and criticisms of authoritarianism in African cultures suggest that beliefs and traditions are usually not revised simply because they have hitherto been accepted as the tradition, and the elders have presented as unquestionable dictates. This view seems to unwittingly suggest that elders in African cultures are stupid and as a result, the cultures and traditions are extremely static because beliefs are never revised or modified. Wiredu's criticism of some African thought systems would be valid only if it is the case that beliefs are never modified or revised, or that the authoritarian tradition is underlined by the irrational variant of epistemic authoritarianism. Apparently, Wiredu does not seem to distinguish between these two variants of authoritarianism or qualify his notion of 'unjustified'. Rather, he construes epistemic authoritarianism to imply the irrational variant which would be unjustified *simpliciter*. In Wiredu's view, authoritarianism in African cultures does not allow people to use logical or scientific means to acquire and justify their beliefs, hence it is unjustified. Curiously enough, he suggests implicitly that this irrational construal of epistemic authoritarianism may not be fairly attributed to African cultures. Paradoxically, he argues that authoritarianism, which in my view cannot be the irrational variant, "is closely connected with one of the strongest points of our culture, namely, the great value it places on what we might call communal belonging."[17] If authoritarianism is a basis for communalism, and communalism is a strong point in many African cultures, then it is not likely that such strength could have been a function of or derived from an irrational form of authoritarianism.

Wiredu argues that, in communalistic African cultures, the communities or "societies were of a type in which the *elders* were *rightly considered* custodians of knowledge and wisdom [especially of the practical kind]."[18] It is pertinent to emphasize the reference to elders (plural), as opposed to an elder, to draw attention to the idea of shared authority, communal inquiry, and an approximate consensus among the elders that is based on persuasive reasons or inter-subjectively adequate and shared evidence. If this idea is reasonable, then it is not the case that we have in African cultures, what Kaphagawani describes as the tyranny or hegemony of elders. In order to have such tyranny, all or many of the elders will have to have eaten out of a conspiratorial dish that causes them to conspire and connive to irrationally accept a set of false and stupid or irrational beliefs, and will agree to impose them on the community. Wiredu underscores my point about the implausibility of such conspiracy and irrationality by arguing that under the conditions in African cultures "the respect accorded to age is not gratuitous."[19] And that those of them who were real thinkers were "not afraid to criticise, reject, modify, or add to traditional philosophical ideas."[20] This suggests that there were criticisms of beliefs and principles by elders, and that beliefs were not pushed down people's throats. And because the respect that is accorded to elders is not gratuitous, you will have to prove yourself as an elder in order for your criticisms, ideas, and suggestions to be accorded similar respect and taken seriously. This idea is reasonable because this is the tradition in science, which is considered the paradigm of rationality or rational inquiry by Wiredu. Not all scientific theories or criticisms are taken seriously; a theory or scientist must prove its mettle in order to be taken seriously.

## A Defense of Authoritarianism in African Cultures

Wiredu also argues that these "philosophers of old must have had some elaborate and persuasive reasons for their doctrines."[21] In my view, the philosophers of old were the elders who proved their mettle and were recognized for their knowledge and wisdom. They provided the necessary criticisms in traditional African societies that led to changes, modifications, and revisions of principles and beliefs. Obviously, these elders had elaborate reasons for their stances and they also saw the merits of the beliefs and principles that they did not criticize, hence they did not see the need to change, modify, or revise them. Therefore, it makes philosophical sense, from the perspective of African philosophy, to try to speculate and theorize from the available facts and structures in African traditions about the plausible reasons that these elders had for the belief systems or their reasoning. It is clear that parts of the reasons and reasoning were passed on as narratives by oral tradition. From the above comments by Wiredu, we cannot imagine that if the beliefs in African traditions were deemed unwarranted, that the elders would still have held on to them because of the authority of tradition. If these ideas and Wiredu's comments are true, it means that the African cultures that Wiredu refers to must have had or still have a rational method as a basis for their system of beliefs, and the people were justified in holding many of their beliefs in some sense, based on the rational method. However, I am not suggesting that because many African cultures have a rational method as a basis for their beliefs, that all their beliefs are true necessarily. It is a commonplace view in epistemology that the truth of a belief is not necessary for its reasonableness. Africans may be rational and still be fallible in their rational use of their methods. The rationality of a method or the rationality of a person does not necessarily imply that their accepted beliefs will be true.

Because of Wiredu's suggestion that African elders were rational and that they had rational methods or bases for their beliefs, it would appear that his criticism of epistemic authoritarianism, which implies irrationality, is unwarranted. In order for the criticisms to be plausible, he will have to equivocating on the notion of authoritarianism by shifting between the rational and irrational variants of authoritarianism, or at worst, he is inconsistent. Hence he arrives at the conclusion that African thought systems are not rigorous, analytic, and universally rational, simply because they were fundamentally dependent or based on irrational epistemic authoritarianism. If African thought systems were founded on a rational form of authoritarianism, and it allowed for criticism and revision of beliefs, then one can reasonably argue that the systems of thought must have been, to a significant extent, rigorous, analytic, and rational. In order to sustain this point, one will have to show how rational authoritarianism can allow for rigorous, analytic, critical, and rational thoughts and belief. To this end, it is curious to observe that Wiredu recognizes some important rational elements, features, or facts about African cultures. The first, as alluded to earlier, is that the authoritarianism he criticizes, is connected to communalism, which is one of the strongest points of the African culture. The communal organization of African societies involves their reliance on tradition, which provided the foundation for their stability and cohesion.

This communal structure also provided a justificatory or rational basis for accepting the views of elders as the source of warranted beliefs and knowledge. I would argue later that the acceptance of the views of elders is justifiably based on the notion of epistemic dependence and deference. Although Wiredu recognizes this strong point, he does not explore its epistemic component or foundation with respect to the social, contextual, and pragmatic nature of knowledge and justification, in relation to how people in African cultures justify their beliefs. The communal nature of African people with respect to their reliance on the authority of tradition and elders has an advantage, in terms of providing a context for determining what constitutes relevant alternatives or the available evidence, on the basis of which people ought to rationally accept or justify their beliefs. This point is important because one cannot rely on evidence that people in a community or context do not have as a basis for justifying, accepting, or discrediting beliefs. This is particularly important especially if such beliefs are relevant to how you make your decisions to act, perform your duties, and relate to others in the community.

The second point that Wiredu makes about the criticism of the authoritarian nature of African cultures is, that the charge of authoritarianism in African culture is a 'modern' charge, which derives from a different intellectual milieu. Because the traditional communities were organized as a community of shared beliefs and customs, people under this system did not feel any sense of authoritarianism or see it as a burden or something negative within the traditional milieu. He indicates that this authoritarian ethos and structures were pervasiveness in the communal everyday lives of people. In his words, "the very atmosphere we breathe in many areas of life in our society seems to be suffused with authoritarian odour."[22] As such, "our noses have been acclimatised to it through long conditioning [such that] we may possibly not find the odour offensive, or even remark on it in the first place."[23] However, the issue is whether we can say that because the people did not feel a sense of authoritarianism or feel its negative burden, or find its odor offensive, therefore there cannot be a legitimate charge of authoritarianism. Wiredu seems to suggest that such stance will not be legitimate even if one has to approach the issue of traditional African cultures with a certain measure of what he calls "practical relativism."[24] He indicates that there is authoritarianism in African cultures and it is bad whether or not Africans recognize it. He argues that the issue that faces the people in traditional African cultures is how to adapt their traditional ways to modern conditions so that the positive or good features can be preserved while eliminating the negative or bad ones. The need to do this is, in part, a motivation for this book. It is my view that the positive aspects of communalism or authoritarianism in African cultures have not been appreciated. In order to appreciate them, we must find some semblance of pragmatic and contextual rational criteria for what is acceptable or positive, which would help Africans to integrate the traditional and modern ways of life.

It is pertinent to note that Wiredu recognizes that, from an 'internal point of view' as opposed to an 'external point of view', people in African cultures did not think that their tradition and elders were authoritarian. This is because as epistemic practitioners, they justifiably accepted and used the epistemic principles and meta-principles in their epistemic communities. This is important because if elders thought that the communal structures and epistemic principles were bad, they would have criticized them. Wiredu indicates that elders usually engaged in the critical examination of African structures. And from a pragmatic contextual stance, these structures were reasonable and elders did not see them as bad. So, the authoritarian charge derives from an 'external point of view', which uses a different and questionable modern liberal standard of evaluation. So, the relevant issues to be addressed are as follows: (1) Why did people or elders not see the authoritarianism in African cultures as bad? (2) What was the rational basis on which it was accepted or found acceptable in African cultures? (3) How is this rational basis different from that of someone who adopts an externalist modern liberal perspective? (4) What is wrong with this externalist, modern, liberal perspective? People did not see the status of elders and tradition as the unjustifiable overriding of their own individual wills because they could rationally justify it on the grounds of epistemic dependence and deference. The principle of epistemic dependence says that, if one has good reasons to believe that others who are experts have good reasons for a belief, then one has good reasons for the belief that the expert believes. If this is plausible then the authoritarian charge and its negative connotation is illegitimate because the people had some epistemic justification for not believing that the dictates of elders and tradition had an authoritarian flavor. The people considered the tradition and elders as *reliable sources* and generators of reasonable beliefs. Hence, the authoritarianism of the elders and tradition is rational.

The circumstances that rationally led African people to reliably depend on traditions seem to be ignored by Wiredu's criticism of epistemic authoritarianism in African culture, even though his description of some traditional African societies gives credence to these circumstances. According to him,

> Traditional codes of conduct [and beliefs] evolved in the context of less complicated societies, in which extensive family and neighbourhood connections facilitated the development of a sense of communal fellowship and responsibility. The societies were a type in which the elders were *rightly considered* custodians of knowledge and wisdom. They were societies in which education was not formal but acquired through every aspect of a person's upbringing.[25]

These methods of acquiring and justifying beliefs in traditional African cultures were considered reliable because they tended to produce true or reasonable beliefs for the people most of the time in the pragmatic and social context of the communal living. The number of reasonable and significant beliefs that the methods produced for the people most of the time in their pragmatic and social context were higher in proportion to the unreasonable beliefs they produced. If this is what the people believed, then they were rational and justified to epistemically depend on the elders and tradition. Contrary to Wiredu's view, it is my view that the type of authoritarianism he identifies or characterizes in African cultures is not necessarily as negative as he thinks. From the above discussion and criticism, it appears Wiredu's conception of the nature of adequate rational justification involves an ideal sense of epistemic justification that is based on the objective truth of a belief. This idea of truth does not take into consideration the contextual basis for an epistemic practice and the actual availability of evidence. According to Harding: "Truth claims are a way of closing down discussion, of ending critical dialogue, of invoking authoritarian standards."[26] Whether one is rational in one's beliefs or not may, in part, depend on (i) the rationality and adequacy of the epistemic rules and methods that are used in the context of an epistemic practice, and (ii) the proper use or application of these rules and methods in arriving at a belief. In African cultures, the epistemic rules and methods, which require the reliance on elders as epistemic authorities are rational and adequate. Moreover, people who accepted beliefs by relying on elders were also rational in accepting their beliefs.

We can distinguish among three kinds of rational epistemic justification. These are: (i) the ideal rational justification, (ii) the inter-subjective rational justification, and (iii) the subjective or individual rational justification. One is *ideally rationally* justified in accepting a belief or in believing that a proposition is true, if and only if, the belief or proposition is, in fact, true; one has an adequate method or rules for getting the best evidence to prove its truth, and there is, in principle, *no defeater* to undermine such evidence. One is *inter-subjectively* rationally justified in accepting a belief or in believing that a proposition is true, if and only if, based on the acceptable beliefs, meta-beliefs, rules, and methods in a social or epistemic community, one has a set of prima facie good reasons, and available and acceptable evidence, and that there are no available or known defeaters in the community that would undermine the evidence. One is *subjectively rationally justified* in accepting a belief or in believing a proposition to be true, if and only if, given one's own reasoning alone and one's background beliefs, one has a set of prima facie good reasons or a set of evidence that is available and acceptable to one, and one does not individually know of any defeaters that may undermine one's evidence. The issue here is, which of the above is the most plausible understanding of the notion or idea of rational justification, and in what way is this justification consistent with the African idea of communalism and its feature of epistemic authoritarianism? In my view, the second type, i.e., inter-subjective rational justification, is the most plausible understanding of epistemic justification. It captures the ideas of group justification or inquiry, communal reasoning, the sharing of evidence, and my rational variant of epistemic authoritarianism that characterize the communalism in African cultures.[27]

The dominant idea of rationality involves the view that one must rely on one's own individual reasoning and rational justification. This involves the idea of someone being able to think for himself or the idea of preserving and adhering solely to one's own independent judgment.[28] This idea of rationality is assumed by Appiah and Wiredu in their critique of the authoritarian feature of communalism. This idea does not include or indicate the special standards that are necessary for a group of people to account for the reasoning and justification of the beliefs that they accepted as a group. The standards or reasons that are necessary for a group to accept a principle or belief may not depend solely on the contents and strength of the principle or belief, or an individual's own independent judgment. A group of people may justify a principle or belief based on the social advantage or practical or pragmatic role that the principle or belief may have for the group.[29] Such pragmatic role or social advantage for the group may not be relevant to an individual's own rational justification for such principle or belief. For instance, there may be a justification for a country to go to war, in terms of the pragmatic good for the country or the people as a group. This may involve the fact that the group or country is feared and respected. But such idea may not be a rational justification for why an individual soldier may need to go to war, given that he could be killed or injured, and the fact the respect for or fear of the group or country does not mean that an individual in the group or a citizen of the country is feared and respected. The standard idea of rationality, which assumes rational egoism, autonomy, or epistemic individualism, is inadequate for capturing the idea of 'group rationality' or 'what is rational for a group'. It is important to understand the idea of 'what is rational for a group' in order to appreciate the rational idea of epistemic authoritarianism and communalism.

From Wiredu's characterization of authoritarianism as the *unjustified* overriding of an individual's will and his criticism of the epistemic practice in African communalistic cultures, one might say that he understands rational justification in the ideal rational sense. If we consider the *primary importance and value* that Wiredu places on the individual's will and autonomy with respect to rational deliberation, and his view that justified belief or knowledge must derive from the universal, rational, scientific, and logical method of acquiring beliefs and determining truth, then with some qualifications, we may understand him as subscribing to the ideal sense justification. This view to which Appiah subscribes, suggests that an individual can arrive at the truth or knowledge based on adequate, ideal, universal, objective, or optimal reasons for believing a proposition to be true. Moreover, that such individual can arrive at knowledge or truth by using or relying solely on his own rationality and cognitive ability of testing, considering evidence, rigorous critical inquiry, and logical analysis, such that it will be impossible for a defeater for his justification to exist. Hence, in Appiah's characterization: "Rationality is best conceived as an ideal, both in the sense that it is something worth aiming for and in the sense that it is something we are incapable of realizing. It is an ideal that bears an important internal relation to that other great cognitive ideal, Truth."[30] The idea here is that the unjustified overriding of an individual's will would not only impede the cognitive abilities for engaging in such inquiry but would also discourage inquiry or independent reasoning and the use of the methods that could lead to the truth and generate the optimal reasons for accepting a belief. This implies that one may not depend on others' judgment, the 'accepted' set of beliefs in an epistemic community, and hitherto reliable processes for acquiring beliefs, without questioning them and making one's inquiries about their adequacy. To depend on or accept the beliefs of others without questioning, or not to allow for such questioning, even when there is no *obvious* cause for it, suggests an element of authoritarianism.

On my interpretation of the views of Appiah and Wiredu, and their criticism of authoritarianism in African cultures, it appears that the dependence on the authority of tradition and elders can never be justified based on the premium that is placed on the absolute value of an individual's will and cognitive autonomy. In other words, whenever one rationally depends on the authority of elders—in spite of whether or not there is a justification for it—such dependence involves the limitation of the development of the individual's will. Wiredu's idea is that an individual's will and cognitive autonomy is valuable because it implies the willingness and ability to always critically examine for oneself, the evidential basis for any belief that one must accept. As such, his argument against epistemic authoritarianism implies that one cannot rationally trust another person's expertise as a justificatory basis for accepting a belief, since one has not critically examined for oneself, the belief and its justificatory basis. In which case, one must always subject each and every belief that a person must accept to critical analysis and questioning, even when there is no plausible reason for it. So, the implication of Wiredu's view and criticism of authoritarianism is problematic. One may have the willingness and ability to engage in critical inquiry and analysis of a belief, but one may not find it reasonable in a particular context to engage in such critical inquiry, because there is no relevant basis to doubt the reasonableness of the belief. The essential point here is that many people in African cultures did not critically examine beliefs and principles because there were no pragmatic bases to do so. As Wiredu indicates, whenever there were reasons to do so, some elders were not afraid to criticize.

The views of Appiah and Wiredu as well as their criticism of authoritarianism raise questions regarding how one may critically examine beliefs and evidence as the basis for revising and modifying one's beliefs. Their views seem to imply that if one finds a belief in one's own set of beliefs for which a defeater has been found, or if such a belief suggests the unreliability of one's process of acquiring or arriving at belief, then one must rely solely on one's own judgment and one's rational, critical, and analytical ability to purge oneself of all beliefs in a single fell swoop. The plausible rationale for this may be that the faulty or suspicious belief that is identified in one's set of beliefs may be significant because it plays a 'linking' role in the chain of one's belief. For Wiredu and Appiah, authoritarianism is insidious because of its ability to contaminate other beliefs and to prevent one from being critical in order to be ideally justified. So, their views indicate that the idea of communalism is a set of beliefs, practices, and principles that implies epistemic authoritarianism or the uncritical dependence on elders as the basis for one's beliefs. These beliefs and practices are unreasonable in their view. Appiah sees "reasonableness as a matter of trying to develop habits of belief acquisition that make it likely that you will react to evidence and reflection in ways that have a tendency to produce truth."[31] So, Africans ought to realize that their epistemic principles are defective. They ought to realize also that their principles or methods for acquiring and justifying beliefs provide justificatory basis for beliefs that do not or cannot produce truth. As such, they ought to realize that in order to be justified about any belief in one's set of beliefs that is linked to or rationally derived from epistemic authoritarianism, one must seek to purge all the beliefs in one's set of beliefs by critically examining each and their authoritarian foundations. So, in order to be ideally justified in this sense, one has to be consistently justified along the infinite chains of beliefs, in that one has critically examined all the beliefs and made the judgment for oneself that one has good evidence for each belief and there could be no defeaters to render one's beliefs unjustifiable or false.

Wiredu and Appiah indicate that there are alternative scientific or modern Western philosophical methods and scientifically established beliefs that contradict African beliefs and the authoritarian method. And because these alternative Western beliefs and methods existed and Africans were not aware of them, therefore, they were not justified in their beliefs—at least, ideally in the sense of being internally related to truth. This ideal sense of justification implies that, in order for one to be justified, there could not possibly exist any information or evidence, which any other person could possess that could render one's beliefs unjustifiable. Appiah argues that we must avoid the implausible idea of strong cognitive relativism: the view that what is true about matters of fact may depend on an individual's conceptual scheme or a people's cultural beliefs.[32] The idea of ideal justification allows us to avoid this implausible view, which implies that two people could both have two incompatible true views or beliefs about matters of fact. However, the stricture of ideal justification is too strong in my view, hence a reasonable notion of epistemic justification should be contextually defined in relation to an epistemic community and the *available* set of evidence in their social context. Perhaps, Wiredu may argue that even when evidence and justification are contextualized to an epistemic community, this would not justify beliefs in African cultures because there may have been available but hidden evidence or counter-evidence, which individuals could have discovered if they were allowed to critically examine ideas for themselves. Wiredu may argue that it is in this sense that communalism and epistemic authoritarianism are insidious, in terms of the attitude and environment it creates. This point seems to ignore the fact that the authoritarianism that Wiredu criticizes is not irrational and it does not, as Wiredu admits, foreclose individuals' critical examination or imagination and creative thinking.

Epistemic authoritarianism is not as insidious or bad as Wiredu and Appiah suggests. Perhaps, the critics of epistemic authoritarianism in African cultures have simply overstated their case or criticism. The ideal sense of justification or rationality, which their criticism presupposes, is implausible. It is also clear that the subjective sense of justification is unreasonable because one can neither have one's own criterion of justification nor rely solely on one's own beliefs, rationality, and judgment to justify a belief. The idea of inter-subjective justification, which I think is a plausible account of epistemic and moral justification, is consistent with the *relationally absolute* (contextual, cultural, or social) nature of the notion of knowledge and justification. This idea of knowledge and justification, in Dretske's view, involves "an evidential state in which *all relevant alternatives* (to what is known) are eliminated. This makes knowledge an absolute concept but the restriction to relevant alternatives makes it . . . [relative or relational] and applicable to this epistemically bumpy world we live in."[33] This epistemically bumpy world indicates that things are not ideal and people are not perfect in their cognitive abilities. This relational account states that justification is dependent on evidence, whose appropriateness is considered only in relation to the social, pragmatic, and communal context of people, in terms of their justified beliefs or the evidence available to them.[34] Hence in Harman's view of justification, a person will be unjustified in holding a belief only if there exists contrary evidence (defeater) that it would be possible for a person to obtain for herself or is possessed by other people in the relevant social or epistemic group to which the person belongs.[35] This means that one cannot be justified in an ideal, complete, or absolute sense; one is only justified in a contextual absolute sense—in relation to the *available* set of evidence in a social or communal context.

The context in which one is justified usually specifies what is to count as 'relevant alternatives' or evidence, which must be ruled out as possible defeaters for one's evidence, in order for one to know. The epistemic community, which provides this social context also indicates the acceptable epistemic practices, principles, and meta-principles. According to Dretske's contextual account, the concepts of knowledge and justified belief are similar to the concept of 'empty' or 'flat', which is relationally absolute. He uses the following analogy to underscore this point: "For although nothing can be flat if it has *any* bumps or irregularities, what *counts* as a bump or irregularity depends on the type of surface being described. Something is empty . . . if it has nothing in it, but this does not mean that an abandoned warehouse is not really empty because it has light bulbs or molecules in it."[36] The contextual and social view of knowledge may illuminate the contextual and cultural view of moral principles, not in terms of the universal ends of these principles, but in terms of the *means* for achieving those *ends* or the interpretation of what those *ends* mean. For instance, the meaning and substantive or material contents of 'human or communal welfare' as a moral *end* depends on the social context that considers such end to be significant. The idea here is that the subject we are talking about or the end we have in mind and its context will determine what is to count as evidence or relevant alternative. An epistemic context of evidence is needed to circumscribe relevant alternatives because one cannot achieve ideal justification, in terms of having absolute standards for all cases of knowledge, rationality, or justified beliefs, and being able to satisfy such standards.

## Authoritarianism and Rational Justification

The absolute standard of ideal rationality or justification implies that one must know or determine in one's mind what is to count as a possible relevant alternative. In which case, to be justified in the ideal sense requires that we must evidentially exclude *all competing possibilities*. In order to exclude all the relevant competing possibilities, we would need to have an infinite set of beliefs by which we can determine whether or not any possibility would be relevant, or whether anything is even a possibility, since the beliefs that we already have function by helping us to restrict or determine what constitutes a range of relevant alternatives. Having absolute standards of justification without a context to delimit evidence, and trying to satisfy such standards in an ideal sense of justification, would therefore imply that one would need to have an infinite set of beliefs. One would need to possess all the possible beliefs in every conceivable circumstance in order to know and be ideally justified. Otherwise, a merely logically *possible* counter-evidence or idea, which may not be probable in a context, would count as a relevant alternative or counter example that would need to be discounted in order for one to be justified. But we do not and cannot, as a matter of fact, have an infinite set of beliefs that could help us restrict the range of relevant alternatives. Hence, it is reasonable for us to epistemically depend on others or experts whom we trust, in that we have good reasons to believe that they have good reasons to hold certain beliefs. But we must restrict such dependence to legitimate, trusted, proven authorities, and elders in an epistemic community whose views are substantiated by the available evidence that we may not be able to comprehend or ascertain.

Moreover, because of human fallibility and inferiority with respect to certain matters, we may not know whether or not we have the proper epistemic abilities and whether we are in the proper epistemic situation to make the proper judgment. Thus, it may be reasonable in some situations—not all—to depend on others or accept some imposed ideas by allowing our will to be overridden. We have seen that in African cultures, an individual's will is not overridden in every situation; people have autonomy and creative imagination to act or make decisions independently in some situations. In a situation where one may need to depend on others, in that one's will (as an epistemic inferior) is overridden by others (who are epistemic superiors), it is based on a justifiable epistemic principle. Hardwig indicates this epistemic principle as follows:

> Suppose that a person A has good reasons—evidence—for believing that p, but a second person B, does not. In *this* sense B has no (or insufficient) reasons to believe that *p*. However, suppose also that B has good reasons to believe that A has good reasons to believe p. Does B then, *ipso facto*, have good reasons to believe that *p*? If so, B's belief is epistemically grounded in an appeal to the authority of A and A's belief. And if we accept this, we will be able to explain how B's belief can be more than mere belief; how it can indeed, be rational belief; and how B can be rational in his belief that *p*.[37]

Wiredu's characterization of authoritarianism in African culture denies the sense of rationality that is embedded in epistemic communalism and epistemic dependence. But a proper understanding of the rational variant of epistemic authoritarianism in African culture would indicate that it is a variety of epistemic dependence or deference. These epistemic principles also have their moral variants.

If the idea of epistemic dependence is plausible, then it is sometimes irrational for someone to make or to insist on making epistemic judgement on his own, especially if he is epistemically inferior and does not have the requisite background beliefs. For instance, a person may not have the requisite or relevant information that would enable her to make the appropriate choice or decision regarding whether or not to depend on an authority. Suppose that a person rationally determines that because she does not have the appropriate evidence, she is, therefore, unable to make the appropriate choice regarding whether or not she should depend on an authority. However, she realizes that making a decision to depend on an authority is essential for her. But suppose after such realization and the rational determination that she is not in a rational position to make an informed decision, she does not decide voluntarily whether or not to depend on an authority; she simply makes no decision or sits on the fence. The pertinent issue in such a situation is, would it be reasonable to override her individual will such that it would necessarily result in her epistemic dependence on some legitimate authority or expert? It would be reasonable in the given circumstance, at least practically, to override the will of such individual. In which case, one cannot make a case for the absolute value of individual will and cognitive autonomy. If an epistemic inferior wants to make claims about epistemic autonomy in order to preserve the independence of his will, such that he is not willing or required to depend on an authority who is epistemically superior, then such an epistemic inferior is irrational. Hardwig argues along this line by indicating "that it is sometimes *irrational* to think for oneself—that *rationality* sometimes consists in deferring to epistemic authority and, consequently, in passively and uncritically accepting what we are given to believe. . . ."[38] The implication of epistemic dependence for the criticisms of epistemic authoritarianism in African cultures is that it is unreasonable to expect people to use their individual will *every time* to make every decision and it is irrational for them to even do so, especially if such a decision is contrary to the accepted views of epistemic authorities in the community and detrimental to the community.

It is reasonable, for instance, that a person can be said to have good reasons for accepting a belief if he has good reasons to believe that other people have good reasons to accept it. As a result, the person can also be said to have good reasons for accepting a belief that does not by itself constitute an evidence for the truth of the belief.[39] If this is reasonable, then it makes sense for an epistemic community to require, as an epistemic principle or practice, that in some justifiable situations, one's will be subjected to or overridden by the will of the epistemic authority. This principle or practice will constitute a justifiable or rational variant of epistemic authoritarianism, which is the communal practice in traditional African cultures. One of the intuitive or cognitive psychological basis for the principle of epistemic dependence has to do with the cognitive limitations that human beings have by their nature. There exist unlimited breadth and infinite amount of available information, knowledge, and evidence that an individual would need in order to be adequately justified and maximally rational based solely on his cognitive abilities. However, it is also true that no single individual alone can have and understand all the relevant information and evidence that one needs to meaningfully maintain cognitive autonomy. A single person is just simply incapable of fully comprehending, understanding, and evaluating independently all the relevant information that is necessary for him to adequately justify his beliefs, given that such adequate justification is necessary for him to be rational. Hence, we must have to rely or depend on others within a given epistemic community in order to determine what a person can justifiably claim to know.

The plausibility of epistemic communalism—the idea of communal inquiry, where there is epistemic division of labor and sharing of evidence—and epistemic dependence implies that it is not necessary for one to fully understand, adequately evaluate, and voluntarily accept the contents and adequacy of all the evidence that an epistemic authority may have in order to rely on him as a basis for justification. Some of the evidence may be too complex for us to understand and evaluate. Moreover, there are many complex beliefs that we usually accept or must accept in a given community in order to lead a meaningful life and relate properly to others. And also, because of the complexity of the justifications of our putatively simple beliefs, we have to accept (and justifiably so) infinite number of beliefs that will be necessary to justify a belief in an epistemic community. Such infinite number of beliefs will be more than anyone can actually or possible know, understand, evaluate, and justify individually on his own alone. There are some beliefs that other people have or reasonable accept, whose justificatory basis we cannot ascertain or understand. As such, we have to accept such beliefs on the basis of either epistemic trust or epistemic faith based on the reliability—in the past—of the 'expert' who provides this information or evidence. If this is the case, then we all necessarily have to acknowledge or accept some degree of epistemic inferiority with respect to some matters. Such acceptance would require us to necessarily subordinate our epistemic judgment or cognitive autonomy in allowing our will to be overridden, so that we can epistemically depend on others. Hardwig argues that if one were to attempt to pursue epistemic individuality and autonomy across the board, one could only succeed in holding a limited set of beliefs. And for the most part, these beliefs would be relatively uninformed, unreliable, crude, untested, and therefore irrational.[40]

Hardwig's point is underscored by Steve Fuller's argument that the social stricture on the idea of justification, which seems to give credence to communal inquiry and epistemic dependence, is motivated by the idea that we need to engage in robust inquiry that will help us to have a robust set of beliefs. In Steve Fuller's view, such robust inquiry is possible only if we engage in "a kind of optimal division of cognitive labor," which requires sharing cognitive responsibilities and relying on the help of other people's cognitive abilities.[41] So, the ideas of epistemic communalism and epistemic dependence are grounded on the idea of sharing cognitive and epistemic responsibilities. Given my analysis of communalism in African cultures, in terms of the community, personhood, and their symbiotic and organic relationship, the ideas of sharing cognitive and epistemic responsibilities as well as performing such responsibilities are a part of one's moral responsibility. This is because sharing and performing of epistemic responsibilities are aimed at general human welfare, of which the welfare of all individuals and that of the community are a part. In this case, individuals have a responsibility to share ideas, information, and evidence that could make the community better. For instance, if you know something, such as the cure for an illness, and you refuse to share it as part of your epistemic responsibility, then you have shirked your moral responsibility and you are deemed to have done something morally reprehensible. If one's father knows the art or craft of herbal healing, and as a child of that man, one refuses to learn the craft or art, then one is shirking one's epistemic and moral responsibilities. So, the practical and intellectual senses of rationality imply that we must share ideas and communally engage in inquiry. Hence, Hardwig argues that in order to be rational, one must avoid some sense of epistemic individuality and autonomy, and accept epistemic dependence on some expert (or his beliefs), because as a matter of fact one needs and must have more beliefs than one can fully understand and be informed about, in order to be adequately justified.

The general idea of rationality must involve the principles of cognitive division of labor and epistemic dependence. These principles, which imply the rational variant of epistemic authoritarianism may, in some situations, require the overriding of an individual's will. It appears Wiredu recognizes that there are situations in which it would be rational to prevent someone from relying solely on and using his own cognitive abilities or individual will. These circumstances would be those in which the cognitive ability or will of the individual is defective or limited, and it would be in the interest of the individual for such will to be overridden. Thus, he argues, "A mind too raw to grasp anything like relevant alternatives still needs to be led, at least, away from danger."[42] But he indicates that when an individual begins to understand relevant alternatives, no justification could exist for the deliberate restriction of his will. The central point is that even an adult's mind may be too raw about certain subject matter. Age *per se* does imply cognitive or rational sophistication. This point is fully appreciated in African thought. Hence, recognition is given to people who have proven themselves consistently by their actions. The rawness of a mind does not depend on age alone, it also depends on one's effort or willingness to know or inquire, one's imagination or curiosity, and the nature of the subject matter in question. For instance, the mind of an adult who is not a specialist or a medical doctor may be raw about a certain illness, its treatment, or cure. Such a person may not fully understand or be informed about all the evidence and information in order to make informed decision. But even when an individual understands the evidence and relevant alternatives, he cannot practically pursue absolute epistemic individualism and cognitive autonomy regarding all matters. He would require epistemic dependence on the views of 'experts' or other epistemic superiors in order to be able to recognize that some alternatives are 'real' or better, while others are not. To maintain epistemic individualism, cognitive autonomy, and doxastic voluntarism across the board regarding all matters, one must be able to have, understand, and evaluate a wide range of alternatives, and one must be able to make a reasonable choice on the basis of an *informed* evaluation of the alternatives. The information and cognitive abilities that are necessary for such reasoning one cannot have by oneself alone.

If one is to avoid the idea of epistemic dependence inherent in epistemic authoritarianism, then everyone must have and be able to evaluate an infinite number of beliefs as evidence and possible relevant alternatives or counter-evidence, which must be discounted. The views of Wiredu and Appiah seem to imply that human beings must have super human cognitive faculties and rational abilities that will allow them to immediately and consciously evaluate infinite amount of beliefs than their actual cognitive facilities could allow or accommodate. In other words, one will need to develop or have sophisticated cognitive and rational abilities that will enable one to evaluate by oneself alone the adequacy of all the evidence and rule out all the counter-evidence that will lead one to an acceptable belief. The idea of rationality, reasoning, or justification will require one to be consciously or immediately aware of all the beliefs on the basis of which one can evaluate, on one's own alone, the adequacy of the evidence, in order infinitely justify all the beliefs that one must accept. The underlying assumption about justification is that it is iterative in nature. So, if I use x to justify my belief y, then I need z to justify x, and w to justify z, and so on. Wiredu's view, which seeks to avoid epistemic dependence, because of its authoritarian implication, will therefore imply that one must be smart enough to reason, know, and make the best judgment on one's own alone at any given time about a belief. As such, any other belief that we have to or are asked to accept can be necessarily deemed to be either unjustified or justified given our prior set of beliefs. This will involve the immediate evaluation and occurrent recognition of the infinite justificatory links among these beliefs.

However, it is impossible for a person to have the kind of sophisticated cognitive abilities that will allow him to have an infinite number of beliefs in order to immediately evaluate and occurrently recognize the adequacy of an evidence on his own alone. Such a person will have to know all the *possible* beliefs that could justify or act as counter-evidence for his beliefs in order to be justified. But as humans, we cannot critically examine all our beliefs or seek to justify them on the basis of merely *possible* counter-evidence or ideas. We must have available to us a *real* counter-evidence in order to characterize it as a reasonable relevant alternative. With this in mind, one can understand why if any person brings up an idea that is merely possible, which is not seen in a practical sense as a relevant alternative, it would be dismissed by elders in African cultures. This kind of authoritarianism appears reasonable in my view. In other words, not all criticisms or possible ideas can be taken seriously. You cannot engage in the critical examination and questioning of beliefs simply for its own sake. There must be a legitimate basis for it. If a young person has an idea that is plausible, it is possible for him or her to bring up the idea informally to an elder. If an elder thinks it is reasonable, he may bring it before other elders to be considered. In my view, this evidentialist inter-subjective contextual account of justification, seems to lend credence to the epistemic authoritarianism in African cultures. In David Annis' view, the issue raised by the contextual model of knowledge or justified belief has to do with the extent to which a person's belief and its justifications are able to surmount certain objections that are available in the relevant epistemic community.[43]

Although the notion of epistemic justification is usually understood in terms of the rational and cognitive ability of an individual to willingly and independently deliberate and find acceptable reasons that any rational person would accept, it must also assume some fundamental standards or beliefs regarding what is rational. Epistemic justification in this sense seems to be contextual because it asserts a synthetic and contextual rational connection between one's beliefs and the available evidence. Feldman and Conee's evidentialist notion of epistemic justification would be instructive here. According to them, "Doxastic attitude D toward a proposition p is epistemically justified for S at t if and only if having D toward p fits the evidence S has at t."[44] This view of evidentialism, which attempts to state the necessary and sufficient conditions for epistemic justification, Feldman and Conee argue, is consistent with the notion that epistemic justification is not absolute; it is relational because it allows for degrees of strength based on the preponderance of evidence that one has in support of a belief at a given time in the relevant epistemic context of available evidence. It appears that Wiredu seems to accept a version of evidentialism as a plausible basis for epistemic dependence or deference. He argues that one's epistemic point of view is dependent on what the epistemological circumstances have determined. He defines one's epistemologically determined circumstances in terms of "such things as the nature of evidence available to the *most determined research*, the existing background of accepted knowledge and the degree of development of experimental and logical techniques."[45]

Wiredu construes the idea of available evidence in terms of the ideal or objective cognitive sense of justification, which is engendered by the most *determined research* and the logical and scientific experimental techniques that are based on universal cognitive rationality. In this sense, he argues that,

> it is as true in Africa as anywhere else that logical, mathematical, analytical, experimental procedures are essential in the quest for the knowledge of, and control over, nature and, therefore, in any endeavour to improve the condition of man. Our traditional culture was somewhat wanting in this respect and this is largely responsible for the weaknesses in traditional technology, warfare, architecture, medicine, etc.[46]

Wiredu seems to be suggesting from this passage that many African cultures are lacking in adequate and universally accepted rational and rigorous procedures of inquiry. In other words, because they lack the logical and experimental techniques for acquiring and justifying beliefs, their beliefs do not constitute rational or epistemic points of view that would provide a basis for talking about African philosophy. To emphasize the use of logical, mathematical, and experimental procedures in order to be justified is to ignore the contextual basis for knowledge and justification. But this contextual model of justification is similar to what we find in science, in that scientists have to rely on the beliefs or theories of others, which have been established in the relevant scientific community. These established theories also delimit the range of evidence or relevant alternatives and the possible counter-evidence.[47] When a belief is well-founded in an epistemic community such that the belief is able to delimit the range of relevant alternatives for that belief, and it is thus accepted as the 'tradition', it may exhibit some authoritarianism.[48]

As a matter of fact, any belief that has been well established in an epistemic community is usually, at an initial stage, resistant to any alternative beliefs or other beliefs that may broaden or help to question such beliefs. Doubt, inquiry, or questions about such belief are sometimes considered irrational or pointless. Because of human fallibility, we are usually not sure when questioning would be irrational or appropriate. As such, it is usually, as a matter of principle, appropriate to question in order to rule out the possibility that we may be wrong about what we know, hence extreme epistemic authoritarianism is, in principle, bad. However, we cannot, as a practical matter, deny the plausibility of a rational variant of epistemic authoritarianism because such denial could lead to iterative skepticism, in that it will lead to doubt and indefinite questioning of all the most fundamental and putatively obvious beliefs. Such skepticism is unreasonable and unnecessary because we must accept that some foundational beliefs are true and obvious, in order to justify any other belief or get any inquiry off the ground. For instance, we must believe that what our senses and reason present to us are believable or true. We need to believe these fundamental beliefs in order to inquire about other beliefs. Because we cannot be extremely skeptical about everything, we do not need to question every belief for the sake of questioning—i.e., even when there are no legitimate reasons to question. Hence, the mere possibility of defeaters will be irrelevant as to whether or not one is justified.[49] Wiredu might say that the problem with epistemic authoritarianism in African cultures is not that some beliefs are accepted as unquestionable or that people are not consistently skeptical about beliefs, but that the attitudes of questioning and independence are not encouraged.

## Authoritarianism and Voluntariness

For Wiredu, the main issue is that communalism does not allow people to voluntarily decide whether or not to question based on their own critical or considered judgement. The idea of not questioning is, in fact, imposed on people by the communal tradition, which gives absolute authority to elders. Wiredu may emphasize that his main criticism involves the imposition or involuntary or mindless dependence on the authority of elders and tradition as the sole basis for our beliefs. Such imposition or involuntary dependence vitiates an individual's autonomy or his independent will to use reason in the acquisition of beliefs, hence it is unjustified. He insists that a person must voluntarily, willingly, and independently rely on his own use of reason, to evaluate and make critical judgment about evidence, in order to accept or acquire a belief. In Wiredu's view, the person who seeks to override an individual's will or autonomy has the onus to justify his act of interference because of the primary and absolute value that is placed on an individual's will and its development. Hence, Wiredu's argument against epistemic authoritarianism in African cultures also hinges on the fact that it vitiates doxastic voluntarism. Doxastic voluntarism states that we must use our will, autonomy, freedom to voluntarily evaluate the evidence in order to make rational judgements regarding whether or not to believe, disbelieve, or suspend judgement. In other words, being able to voluntarily and freely engage in critical examination and evaluation of the evidence is necessary for rationality and epistemic justification. As Wiredu suggests, the people in African culture accept most of their beliefs not because they are warranted given the evidence, but because the elders and the tradition demand that people accept them without questioning.

This suggestion implies that elders do not care about the justificatory bases for beliefs. People are not voluntarily in control of their will and cognitive mechanisms with respect to the beliefs they accept, how they evaluate and acquire them, why they accept them, and how or why they make judgments about the adequacy of the beliefs. So, African people hold beliefs involuntarily. As a result of lack of cognitive autonomy and doxastic voluntarism, in the sense that African people cannot voluntarily evaluate, justify, and accept beliefs, they also cannot be ascribed epistemic responsibility or blame (with respect to unjustified beliefs) or praise (with respect to justified beliefs). We can appreciate this point when we consider its equivalence in moral discourse. A moral action is morally evaluated and a person is deemed responsible, praiseworthy or blameworthy only if the action is performed freely or voluntarily. The relevance of doxastic voluntarism to the absolute value that is place on an individual's will has to do with the view that the notions of epistemic justification and rationality are normative or value-based notions. They involve an evaluation of the rational epistemic responsibility of an individual in terms of how one uses one's cognitive processes, abilities, and will to arrive at or accept one's beliefs. So, an evaluation of one's belief as an internalist cognitive attitude state or doxastic attitude is, primarily, an evaluation of the cogency of the belief *per se*, and secondarily, an evaluation of the process by which that belief is acquired and hence justified. This evaluation involves a determination of whether or not one has acquired and justified one's beliefs 'properly', by using reliable information-gathering process, and whether or not this reliable process is exemplified in one's epistemic practices, such that one's beliefs have a high probability of being true.

If a belief is considered to be adequately or reliably acquired and justified, it would be accepted as warranted. So, one has an epistemic obligation to use one's cognitive abilities in a proper manner in order to adopt the *most reasonable* epistemic attitude of either believing, disbelieving, or suspending beliefs, given the evidence. This notion of epistemic obligation presupposes the possession of cognitive abilities, which one can voluntarily use to properly acquire and justify beliefs. The standards for epistemic evaluation should consider the normal limits of human cognitive abilities. Such abilities, which involve evaluating beliefs, discriminating between acceptable and unacceptable beliefs, and considering the grounds for their acceptability are, in Wiredu's view, an indication of rigorous inquiry, logical analysis, and rationality in a belief system. This kind of rigor and rationality are necessary to have and do philosophy. To the extent that many ideas, thoughts, and beliefs are not voluntarily acquired and justified in African cultures, they are not rational. Hence these ideas, which are characterized as ethnophilosophy do not constitute a philosophy. But we have seen that the communal nature of inquiry or contextual and relational idea of justification, which requires rational authoritarianism, does not involve the imposition or involuntary dependence on the authority of tradition or elders. People accept epistemic authoritarianism based on the reasons in the social context of evidence, communal inquiry, and the sharing of evidence.

The idea of a social context for knowledge, belief, and justification seems to be expressed in Wiredu's following point: "A fact about philosophy in a traditional society, particularly worthy of emphasis, is that it is alive in day-to-day existence. When philosophy becomes academic and highly technical it can easily lose this quality."[50] This problem was highlighted by Edmund Gettier in his seminal paper, in which he questioned the hitherto accepted logically necessary and sufficient conditions for knowledge.[51] He highlighted a problem with the nature of justification that came to be popularly known as 'Gettier's problem'. This problem indicates that we cannot specify logically necessary and sufficient conditions for one to be adequately justified. The voluminous literature that followed Gettier's paper highlighted how the attempt to find the logical or ideal conditions for knowledge and justification ignores the day-to-day lives of people and the limits of human cognitive abilities, which are the context and basis for human knowledge. Some argue that justification is contingent on a social context of adequate background beliefs, meta-beliefs, and the reliability of one's cognitive processes. This view has led to the attempt to articulate a contextual or defeasible account of knowledge. Thus, Ernest Sosa argues that we should depart from the traditional analysis of knowledge by placing justification of beliefs in the relative social context of available evidence in an epistemic community.[52] The attempt to recapture this social, practical, and 'human quality' in the processes of acquiring and justifying beliefs has led to new trends in epistemology.

These trends are, naturalized and socialized epistemology: they seek to understand the natural or cognitive and social human conditions, and how we can bring the understanding of these factors to bear on our analysis and view of knowledge and justification. One major point that Alvin Goldman makes about this in *Epistemology and Cognition* is that it is necessary and reasonable for human beings to seek epistemic standards or principles, which reflect the human social and cognitive conditions that can serve as *practical* guides for their belief formation.[53] In order to do this, one must consider the practical conditions of people and the practical implications of their beliefs and their belief forming processes. This consideration requires that we consider the limited cognitive capacities of people, hence we cannot expect people to be able to believe *all* the logical implications of their beliefs, which are infinite. We cannot expect people to believe all the logical implications of their beliefs because human beings cannot have an infinite number of beliefs. Thus, it appears rational, as a practical issue, for people in African cultures to epistemically depend on authorities, the accepted traditions, and the warranted views of elders who are reasonably considered to be 'experts' or epistemic superiors. Human cognitive and social conditions, in my view, seem to engender some reasonable sense of epistemic authoritarianism. This sense of epistemic authoritarianism has relevance for moral justification (moral epistemology), in terms of how people may justifiably bring their beliefs to bear on the justification of their moral principles and actions.

As alluded to earlier, Wiredu accepts that, knowledge, reasoning, justification, and beliefs have social and pragmatic dimensions. In every community including African cultures, there are fundamental beliefs and principles that people must practically adopt in order to be epistemic and moral 'practitioners' in that community. These beliefs and principles are accepted as fundamental and significant because they indicate the nature of beliefs that people accept, based on their experiences, which help them to explain, predict, and cope with their environment. In trying to understand, criticize, or analyze ideas, inquiry, and thought systems in traditional African cultures, one must be cognizant of their situation and the nature of the issues and problems that people were concerned about. These are practical issues or problems that have relevance for their everyday lives; these are beliefs that would help them to successfully deal with or interpret nature or reality, manage their environment, and make predictions. It is from this circumstance that they developed their ideas and beliefs. People in African cultures understand that practical relevance and efficacy are an important basis for accepting a belief. This understanding is also an important characteristic of the kind of reasoning, inquiry, beliefs, thought systems, and philosophy that exist in African traditions. Traditional African people were not interested in purely abstract knowledge, conceptual issues or ideas and theoretical inquiries or principles that did not have direct and immediate relevance to people's lives. The context in traditional Africa did not offer the luxury of engaging in purely theoretical inquiry about abstract knowledge, which may have *formal* significance in terms of logical truth. The communal environment of Africans and their subsistence living cannot be ignored as a justificatory condition and contextual basis for rationally understanding their beliefs, evidence, and reasoning.

The purely individualistic, abstract, and cognitive idea of rationality that is assumed by Wiredu and Appiah in their criticisms of African traditions suggests that one can independently determine for oneself alone, based on one's critical examination of all the evidence, whether one's independent or subjective judgment is true or consistent with the objective state of affairs. Such determination about truth or some kind of correspondence between one's belief or judgment and some objective state of affairs is what, in their view, makes one's subjective judgment to be the truth. This idea, which indicates that there must be a logical correspondence between elements of one's individual, subjective, independent judgment and some objective facts, is unsatisfactory. This idea does not give credence to the role that is played by other people in an epistemic community who, in the process communal inquiry and sharing of evidence, may have to confirm or corroborate one's independent judgment in order for it to be deemed adequate. This role is important because one can be wrong in evaluating the evidence and making a determination with respect to the adequate correlation between the subjective judgment and objective facts. This communal stricture is relevant to the idea of reasoning in African cultures as a part of how and what reasons or evidence people may bring to bear on the justification of their beliefs, moral principles, or actions. Hence, no one can reasonably insist on his epistemic autonomy or individualism across the board, because the highest court of appeal for rationality and epistemic justification lies outside the individual or his cognitive abilities. The highest court of appeal lies not solely in the facts but also how others in a community see the facts and whether there is some inter-subjective agreement regarding how others see the facts.

In this sense, it is reasonable to argue that the idea of truth in many African communal cultures and tradition involves, in part, some sense of communal approximate consensus or agreement. Such agreement need not necessarily be unanimous, in the sense of involving everyone in the community. Indeed, many African cultures recognize that some people, elders, or adults have a better judgment and they are duly recognized in the community as experts on certain issues. This is the rational basis for epistemic dependence. Although Wiredu disagrees with this communal idea of truth among the Akans, he indicates its plausibility if one tries to understand the literal meaning of *nokware*, which is translated as 'truthfulness'. According to Wiredu: "*Nokware*, then, means literally being of one mouth. Less literally, it means being of one voice. It is sometimes suggested that this oneness of voice refers to communal unanimity; so that the truth is that which is agreed to by the community."[54] Such communal agreement, in my view, is not simply an agreement among opinions, but an agreement that various individuals' beliefs about facts are in agreement among themselves, and that the different beliefs also correspond to the facts. So, one element of truth in African cultures is some sense of communal agreement regarding how they see, interpret, or understand the facts. But another element involves the idea that what one says or the communal agreement is, in fact, the case, in the sense of corresponding to the facts as they are. This means that there is some agreement between what one says and what is the case. But one cannot know that, what one says is the case, is truly the case—or that one is not deluded—unless and until that belief or statement is corroborated or confirmed by some others in the community.

It is obvious that rationality or justification involves the cognitive ability to evaluate in order to make the appropriate judgment about the adequacy of the connection between a doxastic attitude and the available evidence. This doxastic judgment involves whether one should accept or believe a principle or statement as true, disbelieve, or withhold judgment. This judgment or evaluation, Wiredu may argue, lies solely in terms of the cognitive idea of the ability of an individual to think for herself in making the requisite connection, evaluation, and judgment. With this as a backdrop, one can appreciate Wiredu's stance that communalism, the idea of truth as communal agreement, and epistemic authoritarianism in African cultures would vitiate the cognitive view of rationality and what it takes for a person to be intellectually responsible and rigorous in the acquisition and justification of beliefs in order to arrive at truth. Hence, authoritarianism is criticized as epistemically, morally, and politically reprehensible. The basis on which Appiah and Wiredu criticize communalism and epistemic authoritarianism in African cultures is also connected to one of the grounds on which the rational and philosophical status of some African thought systems, beliefs, or ideas (e.g., truth) has been questioned by those who adopt a universalist metaphilosophical approach to African philosophy.[55] The idea is that philosophy as a rational discipline is individualistic, rational, cognitive, rigorous, critical, and systematic. Philosophy involves the systematically written, well reasoned, and critical ideas or thoughts of individuals not groups. If the rational foundation of philosophy consists in the ability of individuals to willingly, autonomously, and independently engage in critical reasoning, and rigorous and systematic inquiry, then some communal and authoritarian accounts of African thoughts, beliefs, or ideas would be inconsistent with the cognitive sense of rationality. Hence, the rationality of these thought systems, beliefs, or ideas is deemed questionable.

## Authoritarianism and Epistemic Dependence

For instance, in questioning the communal idea of truth among the Akans, Wiredu seems to rely solely on the second cognitive element of truth as a basis for analyzing an individual's cognitive sense of truth.[56] He ignores or disagrees with the first communal element of truth because of his individualistic epistemic stance that an individual must determine what is true or justifiable for himself alone. He fails to appreciate the African inter-subjective communal sense of rationality and justification. It appears that Wiredu's disagreement with the communal idea of truth is also based on his cognitive idea of rationality, which is based on the ideas of epistemic individualism and doxastic voluntarism. Both of these ideas imply that an individual must, based on his voluntary and independent will, reason for himself alone to arrive at a true belief. Moreover, Wiredu also indicates that his view of the idea of truth as a cognitive notion is based on his formal training in analytic philosophy.[57] If this is true, it will be unreasonable and a violation of the principles of charity to expect that Africans who were not trained in this tradition will have such narrow individualistic and cognitive idea of truth that he wants want to see in African thought. One cannot interpret African ideas or thought outside of the context of their traditions. To do so is not give credence to the inter-subjective and communal idea of rationality on which many African ideas and thought systems are based.

In order to understand why the inter-subjective communal accounts of justification, rationality, and truth are plausible, let us consider the implications of the cognitive, individualistic, ideal, abstract account of justification or rationality. The notion of rationality that is embedded in this cognitive individualistic sense justification (considered in the context of Wiredu's criticism of epistemic authoritarianism) assumes epistemic individualism, absolute cognitive autonomy, and doxastic voluntarism, and also seeks to deny the plausibility of epistemic dependence and deference. The ideas of epistemic individualism and absolute autonomy seem to imply or indicate that the individual alone is *usually* in the *best* epistemic and rational state to make the *best judgment* regarding what she should believe given the available set of evidence. As such, it is important to allow one to be free to make such autonomous judgment. This means that one cannot depend on or defer one's own judgment to the judgment of others. Or even when one defers to others, one still has to make the final judgment. As already indicated, this view assumes that our rational and cognitive abilities or capacities are more sophisticated and

robust than they really are, in terms of the amount of beliefs that we can occurrently have and immediately evaluate. The problem is that, usually, people may not be
in the proper epistemic situation to make relevant judgments because they may not
have the evidence or they may lack the requisite robust and sophisticated cognitive
and rational abilities.

So, if the individualistic account of rationality is correct, it would contradict
the notion of epistemic dependence or deference. This idea implies that one may
rationally depend on or defer to another person or his judgment as a basis for
justifying some judgments regarding one's knowledge, justification, or rational
beliefs. Wiredu's stance with respect to his criticism of epistemic authoritarianism
suggests that, for y to epistemically depend on the authority of an epistemic superior, x, is for x to putatively override the will of y, which is unjustified, given the
absolute value and primacy of the individual's will and cognitive autonomy.
Hence, such dependence may involve some elements of authoritarianism. It is not
reasonable for any individual to have absolute cognitive autonomy or will. Although it may matter morally, it does not matter epistemically whether or not one
voluntarily agrees to cognitively depend or defer to others or whether the judgment
of an epistemic authority is imposed on epistemic inferiors. This is because, on the
one hand, if one does not have the proper epistemic abilities or one is not in the
proper epistemic state to make judgments regarding when one is knowledgeable
enough to make one's own judgment or to depend on others, then we cannot expect
such a person to determine when one should voluntarily defer to or depend on
others. On the other hand, it may not matter epistemically whether one voluntarily
agrees if the 'imposed' belief or principle is true or if it is the most reasonable in
the context.

Epistemology is concerned about the reasonableness or truth of a belief or
principle and the adequacy of the methods for arriving at them. If a belief is true
or reasonable and the method of epistemic paternalism or epistemic dependence is
adequate, then whether or not one voluntarily agrees is epistemically irrelevant.
Feldman and Conee have argued that the notion of justification is, fundamentally,
not an epistemic evaluation of the person who adopts a doxastic attitude but the
evaluation of the beliefs themselves. They argue that their evidentialist thesis of
epistemic justification is not a practical prescription for how one may properly
motivate the acquisition of justified beliefs; thus, it is not an account of the nature
of epistemic motivation. The evidentialist thesis does not seek to instruct someone
about what, precisely, one practically should believe. Evidentialism is an epistemic
thesis regarding how to determine the adequacy of a belief based on the available
evidence for its support. So, there is a plausible evidentialist basis for the idea
epistemic authoritarianism in African cultures. This idea is based on the principle
of epistemic dependence or deference, which indicates that one may rely on an
epistemic authority or expert to provide adequate evidence in support a belief. In

this case, the expertise of the epistemic authority is the available evidence in support of the belief. This principle also has a prescriptive and motivating or internalist element. In the communal societies of African traditions, the authority of tradition and the expert views of elders have been *generally* accepted on the basis of the available evidence.

The beliefs underlying African traditions have been well established and the reliance on elders is deemed to be a reliable process of producing reasonable beliefs. People in the community *rationally understand* and accept these evidential and reliability basis for the authority of tradition and elders. Their understanding and rational acceptance of the situation and principles provide a motivating and justificatory basis for them to voluntarily depend on the relevant authorities. This is, perhaps, the reason for Wiredu's indication that the respect that is accorded to elders in Africa is not gratuitous; it is well earned, and it is therefore, willingly and rationally accorded. So, if Wiredu's criticism of epistemic authoritarianism and communalism in African cultures is based solely on the *apparent* lack of freedom of the will, cognitive autonomy, and voluntariness in the acceptance of tradition and the view of elders, then it is epistemically innocuous because there are legitimate evidential bases for the principle of epistemic dependence or deference. If one's belief that is imposed is supported by the inter-subjectively and socially available evidence, then there is a reasonable epistemic basis that the belief is nonetheless justified for the person, irrespective of the voluntariness of the person's doxastic attitude. Thus, even if we accept that a rational variant of epistemic authoritarianism may, in some situations, vitiate doxastic voluntarism, it does not follow that the beliefs held as a result would be unjustified or irrationally held.

In Gilbert Harman's view, "What a belief is based on depends on how the belief came about; but a belief can be based on reasoning even if the belief is not the result of conscious reasoning."[58] So, vitiating doxastic voluntarism or impeding an individual's will does not imply that the resulting belief is unjustified. Feldman and Conee argue along the same lines by indicating that a belief may be involuntarily acquired, yet, it can be subject to the positive epistemic evaluation of being justified.[59] According to them:

> Suppose that a person *spontaneously and involuntarily* believes that the lights are on in the room, as a result of the familiar sort of completely convincing perceptual evidence. This belief is clearly justified, whether or not the person cannot voluntarily acquire, lose, or modify the cognitive processes that led to the belief.[60]

The fact that one has spontaneously and involuntarily acquired or accepted a belief does not necessarily imply that one is irrational or that the belief is unjustified for the person. Also, the fact that a belief has been imposed on me involuntarily, and the fact that I have not fought against the imposition or critically examined the belief, do not imply that the resulting belief cannot be rationally justified for me. For instance, suppose that a person has been *conditioned* by the authority of tradition and the teachings of elders in traditional African cultures to involuntarily believe that cassava and yams (some of the staple crops in West Africa) can only do well when planted during the period that has been *traditionally accepted*. But suppose also that the belief or practice is imposed on this person and he did not fight the imposition by critically examining the belief or practice. Many traditional Africans are subsistence farmers and they rely on this method or process of acquiring beliefs as the practical guide for their farming practices.

However, as a farmer in that culture and community, this person has neither bothered to question the reasons for planting during this period nor found a justification for the practice, such as the effect of weather on crops. He has never considered whether he could plant during other periods. However, his crops have always turned out well whenever he planted during the generally accepted period. He has not used his will to make a 'free' and rational choice in deciding to plant during a certain period. Based on the tradition in his culture, his experiences, and the accepted practices and beliefs, he does not have a basis for questioning this belief or practice. It is reasonable to assume that he may have a basis for questioning and experimenting whether crops will do well during other periods if his crops have done badly, two years in a row. If he experiments and he gets good results, I imagine that others will follow suit and the tradition may be modified. In this case, it is my view that this farmer's belief or practice is nonetheless justified, in that it has been positively confirmed and corroborated by experience. According to Wiredu, the farmer in the above example only shows an impeded will or an epistemically indoctrinated mind that does not allow for free choices in the strict sense. He claims that "an indoctrinated [or conditioned] mind can make 'free' choices, but only in a superficial sense."[61] These choices, in his view, are built into the indoctrination process and subject matter. Moreover, all the relevant alternatives are not available to the individual to choose from, so, the restricted alternatives available to him make his choice obvious and predetermined.

Wiredu's argument against the view indicated by the above example derives from his assumption that justification of beliefs should be cognitively autonomous and rationally ideal for an individual. As such, the indoctrinated person is not ideally justified because he is not cognitively autonomous, and did *not consider* all the possible relevant alternatives that exist, but are unknown to him. Suppose that it is also true that yams and cassava can do well at other periods, but as it were, the people in the community are *not aware* of this fact as a relevant alternative or a defeater to the justification for their belief that these crops can only do well during the accepted planting period. It is clear that they would have found this out if they had experimented. In this regard, I accept Wiredu's criticism that authoritarianism and communalism may, in theory or in principle, create the conditions that may not allow people to question or make inquiries or know the relevant alternative that these crops could have done well at other periods. But we must also accept that rational people cannot question or make inquiries or come up with a new hypothesis to be tested, if there are no anomalies to render an accepted theory, belief, or practice suspect. Hence, I do not accept that African beliefs were not justified in an inter-subjective rational sense, or that this condition created by tradition amounted to an *unjustified* overriding of the individual's will.

When Africans had the need to question their beliefs, they did. Apparently, they did not have the need to question their beliefs, especially the fundamental beliefs that gave the status of epistemic authority to their traditions and elders. They also did not question because of their epistemic rules, practices, and evidence in the community, which gave credence to their *understanding* of their communal, social, inter-subjective, and contextual nature of inquiry and justification. The determination of when one should question beliefs is circumstantial and contextual. It is in this spirit that Dretske argues,

> that knowledge depends not just on the evidential status of the knower vis-a-vis what is known, but on such factors as the general availability, and proximity, of (misleading) counter-evidence, on the sorts of things that are commonly taken for granted by others in the relevant community, on the interests and purposes of speaker (in claiming to know) and listeners (in being told that someone knows), and the importance or significance of what is known or someone knowing it.[62]

We need to draw attention to the fact that the significance of what one claims to know and the general availability of some counter-evidence (defeaters) are a part of the general context of knowledge and the justification of beliefs. If people in African cultures did not have counter-evidence to vitiate the justificatory basis and 'authoritarian' status of their tradition and elders, especially in relation to their understanding of the justification of their significant beliefs, then it cannot be claimed that the people's wills were unjustifiably overridden. If the people had good reasons, on the grounds of reliability, to believe that the beliefs of elders and the traditions were well-grounded, then they would be justified to hold the beliefs that they 'derived' from the elders and tradition. In fact, if this is true, it would be irrational for them not to accept the beliefs they derived from elders and tradition. With this kind of epistemic dependence on the grounds of reliability, it appears that what would putatively be regarded as unjustified in Wiredu's ideal sense may indeed be epistemically justified in an inter-subjective, social, and pragmatic sense.

It appears that the criticisms of epistemic authoritarianism in African communal tradition by Appiah and Wiredu are unfair, if this idea or practice is considered in the context of the traditional societies and their relevant epistemic community and communal principles. So, my defense of epistemic authoritarianism involves an attempt to indicate how social context, which is an important dimension of knowledge and beliefs, may justify the epistemic dependence on the authority of tradition and elders, who are considered experts and authorities. This idea in African cultures has a rational foundation that Appiah and Wiredu have not properly appreciated. However, considering that Wiredu's position is an attempt to consider the negative features in some African cultures in order to jettison them and retain the positive ones, I would agree that the idea of epistemic authoritarianism in African communal traditions deserves an examination and critical analysis. The essential point here is that when the basis for epistemic authoritarianism is examined in the social context of the African idea of communalism, it may be found to be rational. It is pertinent to note that an element of epistemic dependence that is associated with epistemic authoritarianism is accepted in science as a legitimate principle. For instance, a practitioner in science must accept certain theories, laws, and axioms without questions and without necessarily understanding or being fully aware of their proof, in order for his inquiry to get of the ground. Such acceptance involves epistemic dependence. If science is the paradigm of rationality, according Appiah and Wiredu, then if this principle is acceptable in science, then it is rational to accept it as the underlying rational principle of epistemic authoritarianism. This idea is underscored by the view that one cannot argue for epistemic individualism or cognitive autonomy across the board because one is not always in the best epistemic position to be the best judge of what is justifiable, and one cannot have an infinite set of beliefs to determine in every possible situation what would constitute all the relevant alternatives and evidence in order to rule out any possible defeater.

# Notes

1. Wiredu, *Philosophy and An African Culture*, 3.
2. Kaphagawani, "On African Communalism: A Philosophic Perspective."
3. Wiredu, *Philosophy and An African Culture*, 3.
4. Wiredu, *Philosophy and An African Culture*, 2.
5. Wiredu, *Philosophy and An African Culture*, 2.
6. Appiah, *Necessary Questions: An Introduction to Philosophy*, 202.
7. Wiredu, *Philosophy and An African Culture*, 4.
8. Wiredu, *Philosophy and An African Culture*, 4, (emphasis is mine).
9. Wiredu, *Philosophy and An African Culture*, 4

10. Wiredu, *Philosophy and An African Culture*, 4.

11. Wiredu, *Cultural Universals and Particulars*, 67-8. The emphasis is mine to draw attention again to the kind of belief or knowledge that is of paramount importance in African cultures.

12. Wiredu, *Philosophy and An African Culture*, 16.

13. Bernard Boxill, "Majoritarian Democracy and Cultural Minorities," in *Multiculturalism and American Democracy*, eds., Arthur M. Melzer, Jerry Weinberger, and M. Richard Zinman (Lawrence: Kansas University Press, 1998). 117.

14. Wiredu, *Philosophy and An African Culture*, 16.

15. Wiredu, *Philosophy and An African Culture*, 15-16.

16. Harding, *Is Science Multicultural?* She has criticized the idea of the universality of science or the universality, neutrality, and objectivity of the, methods, principles or meta-principles of inquiry and justification of beliefs. She argues that there are different epistemic communities or traditions with different epistemic principles or meta-principles. She indicates on pages 69-71 that the approach to inquiry or the principle of inquiry in Japan is communal and it involves the idea of communal inquiry.

17. Wiredu, *Philosophy and An African Culture*, 3.

18. Wiredu, *Philosophy and An African Culture*, 29. The emphases on 'rightly' and 'knowledge' are mine. It is my view that because he agrees that the people were *right* in considering their elders as the custodians of knowledge, using them as a basis for justification was *justified*. This suggests that the people accepted the principle of epistemic dependence which I shall address later. Moreover, Wiredu talks about knowledge and not just beliefs or opinions, which suggests that they considered their beliefs to be reasonably true on the basis of the evidence that they had. This view of knowledge I shall argue for later as being relatively or relationally absolute.

19. Wiredu, *Cultural Universals and Particulars*, 68.

20. Wiredu, *Philosophy and An African Culture*, 21.

21. Wiredu, *Philosophy and An African Culture*, 28.

22. Wiredu, *Philosophy and An African Culture*, 3.

23. Wiredu, *Philosophy and An African Culture*, 3.

24. Wiredu, *Philosophy and An African Culture*, 5.

25. Wiredu, *Philosophy and An African Culture*, 29 (emphasis is mine).

26. Harding, *Is Science Multicultural?* 145.

27. The distinction here is not necessarily that of degree in terms of which is better but that of kind. In other words, it is not that one form is necessarily better than the other. Rather, these could be different forms of rational justification that are reasonable in different contexts. For instance, the subjective rational form of justification would be appropriate in issues that are self-regarding.

28. Hardwig, "Epistemic Dependence," 340.

29. This idea is articulated by Frederick Schmitt, "The Justification of Group Beliefs," in *Socializing Epistemology: The Social Dimensions of Knowledge*, ed., Frederick Schmitt (Boston, MA: Rowman & Littlefied Publishers, 1994), 257-287.

30. Appiah, *In My Father's House: Africa in the Philosophy of Culture*, 116.

31. Appiah, *In My Father's House: Africa in the Philosophy of Culture*, 117.

32. Appiah, *Necessary Questions: An Introduction to Philosophy*, 203, 210-213.

33. Fred Dretske, "The Pragmatic Dimension of Knowledge," *Philosophical Studies* 40 (1981): 367.

34. For a similar social and contextual analysis of knowledge, see Gilbert Harman. *Thought* (Princeton, NJ: Princeton University Press, 1973); Alvin Goldman, "Discrimination and Perceptual Knowledge," *Journal of Philosophy* 73, no. 2 (1976); Keith Lehrer and Thomas Paxson, Jr., "Knowledge: Undefeated Justified True Belief," *Journal of Philosophy* 66, no. 8 (1969); Peter Klein, "A Proposed Definition of Knowledge Propositional Knowledge," *Journal of Philosophy* 68 (1971).

35. Gilbert Harman, *Thought*.

36. Dretske, "The Pragmatic Dimension of Knowledge," 366.

37. Hardwig, "Epistemic Dependence," 336-337.

38. Hardwig, "Epistemic Dependence," 343.

39. Hardwig, "Epistemic Dependence," 336.

40. Hardwig, "Epistemic Dependence," 340.

41. Steve Fuller, *Social Epistemology* (Bloomington, IN: Indiana University Press, 1988), 3.

42. Wiredu, *Philosophy and An African Culture*, 3.

43. David Annis, "A Contextual Theory of Epistemic Justification," *American Philosophical Quarterly* 15, no. 3 (1978): 213-219.

44. Fred Feldman and Earl Conee, "Evidentialism," *Philosophical Studies* 48 (1985): 15-34.

45. Wiredu, *Philosophy and An African Culture*, 66.

46. Wiredu, *Philosophy and An African Culture*, 12.

47. See Thomas Kuhn, *The Structure of Scientific Revolutions* (Chicago: University of Chicago Press, 1962).

48. There are examples of theories in science that were considered by many to be well established such that when there were counter-evidence or plausible alternative theories, these alternatives were not taken seriously as a basis for critically examining the established theory. For an example, when the Australian, Dr. Marshall discovered and suggested that H-pylori bacteria is the cause of peptic ulcer, people did not take him seriously. The medical and scientific community ridiculed, denigrated, and ostracized him for the idea because it was pretty much accepted within the scientific community that the established knowledge is that peptic ulcer is caused by stomach acid.

49. Dretske, "The Pragmatic Dimension of Knowledge," 376.

50. Wiredu, *Philosophy and An African Culture*, 16.

51. Edmund Gettier, "Is Justified True Belief Knowledge?"

52. Ernest Sosa, "How Do You Know?" *American Philosophical Quarterly* 11, no. 2 (1974): 113-122.

53. Alvin Goldman, *Epistemology and Cognition* (Cambridge, MA: Harvard University Press, 1986).

54. Wiredu, *Cultural Universal and Particulars*, 105.

55. See Appiah, *Necessary Questions: An Introduction to Philosophy*, Bodunrin, "The Question of African Philosophy," Wiredu, *Philosophy and An African Culture*, Wiredu, *Cultural Universals and Particulars: An African Perspective*, Hountondji, *African Philosophy: Myth and Reality*, among others.

56. Wiredu, *Cultural Universals and Particulars*, 106-108.

57. Kwasi Wiredu, "Truth and an African Language," in *African Philosophy: New and Traditional Perspectives*, ed., Lee M. Brown, 35.

58. Gilbert Harman, "Knowledge, Inference, and Explanation," *American Philosophical Quarterly* 5, no. 3 (July 1968), 164.

59. Feldman and Conee, "Evidentialism," 17.

60. Feldman and Conee, "Evidentialism," 17, (emphasis is mine).

61. Wiredu, *Philosophy and An African Culture*, 3.

62. Dretske, "The Pragmatic Dimension of Knowledge," 367.

# Chapter Six

## Moral Education, Rationality, and Indoctrination

Wiredu, Kaphagawani, and Appiah argue that communalism, which is an essential feature of African cultures, implies epistemic, moral, and political authoritarianism. As such, people accept various ideas and principles as well as justify their beliefs by relying solely on the unquestioned and unproven authority of elders and traditions, instead of relying on their own reasoning and judgment based on the evidence. This kind of authoritarianism, they argue, impedes individuals' will and their abilities to autonomously think for themselves and engage in rigorous inquiry by critically examining all evidence. Authoritarianism also impedes people's ability to be educated or their ability to learn, develop, and acquire the rational abilities that are necessary to engage in autonomous or independent critical reasoning and rigorous inquiry. Rationality, as indicated, is traditionally construed in philosophy as the ability of an individual to independently use reason and to think for himself by considering the evidence, in order to arrive at a belief or decision, make choices, and act on the basis of adequately justified beliefs. I have indicated that this idea of rationality, which is the basis for criticizing authoritarianism in African thought, is based on the implausible ideas of absolute cognitive autonomy, epistemic individualism, and doxastic voluntarism. I have argued that what we have in African cultures is a rational kind of authoritarianism that is justifiable on the grounds of epistemic dependence. The idea of epistemic dependence is reasonable, especially when we are dealing with beliefs that have practical relevance for the day-to-day lives of people and the functioning of a community. One can appreciate the plausibility of this rational kind of authoritarianism in terms of its role in moral education, the imparting of beliefs and values, and the acquisition of personhood.

## Authoritarianism and Indoctrination

Wiredu argues that the authoritarian methods or processes of imparting and acquiring knowledge are essential features of communalism in African traditions. These methods or processes, which involve indoctrination, seem to vitiate or impede one's rational abilities, cognitive autonomy, and the kind of independent critical thinking and inquiry necessary for one to be educated. As such, authoritarianism has some problematic implications, in that it raises questions about the rational adequacy of traditional methods of moral education. Wiredu argues that the methods and processes of education within African communal and authoritarian structures and practices seem to unjustifiably *manipulate* and *condition* people to accept beliefs without questions or proof, and without critically examining for themselves whether or not these beliefs are supported by adequate evidence. So, communalism and its authoritarian features imply that people are not rationally educated, but instead, are indoctrinated. In this sense, Wiredu distinguishes between education and indoctrination. In his view, "Education is the kind of training of the mind that enables people to make deliberate rational choices. Indoctrination, on the other hand, is the kind of molding of the mind which leads to built-in choices."[1] He argues that in African cultures, the community indicates that people should simply accept and use its principles without question, justification, or demand for reasons, and that they should think or make decisions or choices in a predetermined way.

In Wiredu's view, the African communal and authoritarian structures, processes, and methods of education prevent people from independently holding or accepting beliefs and making choices that are inconsistent with the accepted beliefs and dictates in the community. Holding or accepting beliefs and making choices independently that are inconsistent with accepted beliefs and dictates are seen as an affront on the community. Because one is taught and conditioned to hold the accepted communal or group beliefs, and because one is expected to behave in accordance with the beliefs and dictates or the enduring tradition of the community, there are no meaningful alternatives, and one has no choice in the matter regarding how one should act or what beliefs or principles one should accept. So, Wiredu's suggestion of moral indoctrination or brainwashing in African cultures raises issues about rational and voluntary moral agency, in terms of people's ability to make rational and voluntary choices and ascribe morally responsibility. It also raises questions regarding whether or not moral indoctrination may engender culturally induced ignorance to the extent of vitiating or mitigating individuals' responsibility. Wiredu argues that education in many traditional African cultures is "through the informal processes of day-to-day upbringing rather than through formal process."[2] Such informal processes, which involve subtle and gradual conditioning, depend on oral tradition rather than written records. This informal mode of education is also related to Africans' unsystematic and irrational modes of thought, ways of understanding, utilizing, and controlling nature, and how they interpret their experiences and the place of humans in the general scheme of things. These modes of thought, and ways of understanding and interpreting ideas lack rigor, are intuitive, uncritical, dogmatic, unanalytic, unsystematic, and unscientific.

Appiah echoes Wiredu's sentiments about the dearth of critical and rigorous reasoning by indicating that African traditional cultures seek to justify their beliefs solely by reference to the fact that they are supported by the authority of tradition or that they are dictated by elders.[3] This epistemic principle regarding how beliefs are justified and accepted is taught to people and people internalize it without questioning its adequacy. He contrasts this African epistemic practice or principle, which is overly *accommodative*, with the Western intellectual *adversarial* tradition, which is founded on the notion of an individual's autonomous rationality, independent critical inquiry, rigorous examination, and persistent questioning. He suggests that the idea that individuals must think through ideas for themselves in order to accept them on the basis of evidence have led to the adversarial and scientific style of inquiry, where ideas are subjected to critical examination and the most reasonable idea is accepted based on the available evidence. He argues that when the views of authorities are cited or references are made to traditions as the basis for a belief in Western tradition, they are not cited blindly and simply because they have been accepted as the tradition. Because of the adversarial style in this Western intellectual tradition, the view of an authority still has to be questioned in order to determine its adequacy, and it is the soundness of the evidence for the position that then confirms and sustains it as authoritative. This is the sense in which the views of authorities play a positive role as a basis for belief, reasoning, and the education of people in the Western adversarial systems of thought and their formal systems of education.

Communalism involves indoctrination and irrationality because, as indicated, the ideas and methods of having shared beliefs, ideas, and inquiry, and relying on elders and traditions are accommodative: they discourage curiosity, impede critical inquiry and the ability of individuals to think for themselves.[4] As such, a person cannot rationally act in creative and imaginative ways that are inconsistent with what is dictated by elders and the traditions of the community. Wiredu argues that although people have the spirit of critical inquiry, the communal, authoritarian, indoctrinating structures and context do not encourage it. For instance, he says although there are many proverbs that indicate the ways of life, thoughts, and belief system in Africa, "it is rare to come across ones which extol the virtues of originality and independence of thought."[5] For Wiredu, the goal of education is to enhance one's abilities to inquire, understand, analyze ideas or beliefs, evaluate and critically examine evidence and relevant alternatives, and make informed independent judgments, choices, and decisions about which ideas or beliefs one should accept. He suggests that the communal and authoritarian informal processes of raising or training children in African cultures involve molding or shaping or conditioning people to behave in a specified manner that does not allow for independent thinking and critical questioning. These processes or methods of education involve subtle manipulation and the provision of information with built-in or predetermined choices because there are no alternatives. Because the person being educated cannot see all the relevant alternative beliefs and evidence that would facilitate his ability to make rational and informed choices regarding whether or not to justifiably accept a belief, his rational and cognitive autonomy and abilities are impeded or vitiated, and his will is manipulated by the educator into accepting a predetermined belief or choice. As such, Wiredu argues that this informal communal and authoritarian processes and methods of inculcating and imparting ideas and beliefs are more or less process indoctrination.

Wiredu argues that the idea of using informal communal and authoritarian methods of inculcating beliefs or ideas cannot be characterized as rational processes of education. According to him, the kind of education that we want in Africa is training in methods of critical analysis. This kind of training or education will produce minds that are eager to critically examine, analyze, and able to test claims, ideas, beliefs or theories against observed facts, so that people can adjust their beliefs to match the available evidence. Such training in the methods of critical analysis will engender true and justified beliefs, diminish or eliminate dogmas and superstitions, and undermine Africa's authoritarian structures and practices.[6] As such, Wiredu suggests that indoctrination is logically different from and cannot be a component part of education, because education involves training someone to think for himself, while indoctrination involves inhibiting or preventing someone from thinking for himself. This logical distinction between education and indoctrination is underscored by John Wilson's point that: "If you *bring children up* to think for themselves, it is not intelligible to say, in general, that you have indoctrinated them: because 'indoctrination' is opposed to 'thinking for oneself'."[7] But it is not clear, in my view, whether education is opposed to indoctrination.

Let us consider what indoctrination involves in order to see, (1) the extent to which it is logically distinct from education, and (2) how it may or may not be a negative feature of African cultures or their communal and informal modes or processes of education. It is pertinent to note that indoctrination, like education, refers to a process, method, or act of inculcating or imparting ideas or beliefs. They both involve a tripartite relationship among a teacher, student, and the imparting of a subject matter. A teacher must be understood here in the very broad sense to include anyone who uses any means to impart knowledge. Education involves a process where the teacher imparts or inculcates the contents of a subject matter that would enhance the rationality and the development of the cognitive abilities of the student. In the case of indoctrination, the teacher imparts or inculcates a subject matter, a doctrine or dogma, that would hinder the rationality and the development of the cognitive abilities of the student. From this tripartite relationship, people have conceived of the idea or act of indoctrination to involve either or all of the following: (1) a doctrine or dogma, which is the content or subject matter of indoctrination; (2) the uncritical and dogmatic methods or processes of imparting, inculcating or imposing the subject matter; (3) the intention, goal, or aim of the teacher, which is to accept certain doctrines or dogmas or unproven or untrue ideas without question, reasoning, or evidence. Another view of indoctrination, which is coextensive with this tripartite view is that it involves an uncritical attitude and habit of the mind on the part of a student with respect to the acquisition and acceptance of the subject matter. This attitudinal sense of indoctrination may be expressed in terms of an outcome, which indicates that one has adopted an attitude or habit of the mind that is uncritical and irrational, in that one has not adequately considered the evidence and relevant alternatives. So, a mind that is indoctrinated in this attitudinal sense would be one that is trained not to think critically about issues, ideas, or beliefs, and their evidential bases.

Some people argue that whether or not indoctrination exists depends solely on the truth value of the contents of the subject matter. That is, one is indoctrinated only if the contents of a subject matter are false or unjustified. In other words, one cannot be indoctrinated about what is true irrespective of whether or not one accepts the truth of the subject matter for good reasons. So, according to this view, anyone who accepts a false or unjustified belief or idea, and refuses to see that there is no evidential basis for what he accepts is, indeed, indoctrinated about the subject that he thus accepts. For instance, T. F. Green argues that if a student ends up with non-evidential kinds of belief, he is in fact indoctrinated, irrespective of the fact that the teacher may not have intended to establish or make him accept the belief on a non-evidentiary basis.[8] In this sense, there is a conceptual connection between indoctrination and truth or justification, or the lack of and absence of truth or justification. John Wilson underscores this by arguing that the idea of indoctrination must be understood as deriving from the doctrinaire or dogmatic contents of instruction; that is, it involves presenting what is uncertain to a student as if it is certain.[9] This view is alluded to, in part, in the work Anthony Flew.[10] However, it is pertinent to say that Flew and Green do not hold the view that the content of indoctrination is exclusive of other features. Perhaps their views of indoctrination can be better seen as a conjunction or blend of content and intention.[11]

Flew argues that indoctrination involves the attempt to firmly implant an idea, belief, or conviction about the truth of a doctrine or set of doctrines that is in fact untrue, or at least, it is not yet known to be true or justified. For him, the intention of the teacher here, which involves the idea of *firmly implanting* in the mind of someone, is a very important aspect of indoctrination. This idea indicates that indoctrination may depend on the method of firmly implanting, or the outcome, which involves the idea that a doctrinaire subject matter has, in fact, been firmly implanted. Green also argues along the same line saying, "Indoctrination aims simply at establishing certain beliefs so that they will be held quite apart from their truth, their explanation, or their foundation in evidence."[12] Although Green is concerned about the aim that a teacher may have in imparting knowledge, it appears the aim would not matter if the beliefs are false or unjustified. The types of beliefs that are pertinent to Green's conception of indoctrination are, what he calls non-evidential beliefs, that is, beliefs that are held without regard to their justification or evidence or relevant alternatives. Because such beliefs do not have any evidential basis, they cannot be critically examined, revised, and modified on the basis of evidence. According to Green, "when, in teaching, we are concerned simply to lead another person to a correct answer, but are not correspondingly concerned that they arrive at that answer on the basis of good reasons, then we are indoctrinating; we are engaged in creating a non-evidential style of belief."[13] This evidential account of indoctrination appears to be the basis for Wiredu's and Appiah's criticisms of African cultures and beliefs, and the basis for Wiredu's suggestion that African cultures are indoctrinating. They argue that Africans do not care about the evidential basis for their beliefs. Such beliefs are simply accepted because they are dictated by tradition or elders.

In their view, the absence of evidential basis for the contents of these beliefs, as well as the context, processes, and methods of acquiring and imparting the beliefs, do not only indicate indoctrination but also the absence of education and rationality. Hence, Africans do not critically examine their beliefs in order to determine whether there is evidential basis for accepting them. However, some people hold the view that indoctrination involves, solely and exclusively, the intention or aim to implant unjustified beliefs, dogmas, or doctrines in the mind of someone. So, the key element or the single criterion for determining whether or not a person is indoctrinated is the intention or aim of the teacher, and whether such aim or intention is to make someone accept an unjustified belief. In other words, a person is indoctrinated only if the teacher actually intended to make a student accept and to continue to hold a view or belief or proposition independent of its evidence, truth or justification. This idea can be seen in the view of Snook, who indicates that the necessary and sufficient conditions for indoctrination may be stated as follows: "A person indoctrinates P (a proposition or a set of propositions) if he teaches with the intention that the pupil or pupils believe P, regardless of the evidence."[14] R. M. Hare also argues that the aim or intention of the teacher in imparting knowledge is the significant criterion for characterizing whether or not his student is being educated or indoctrinated.[15] However, it is pertinent to note that, although Snook suggests that the absence of evidence in the acceptance of belief is important for one to be indoctrinated, the significant feature is that a teacher actually intends or aims that the student accepts the belief irrespective of the evidence or the adequacy of its epistemic status.

In Wilson's view, the intention or aim of a teacher is an important element in the definition of indoctrination, and in distinguishing it from education. In other words, whether or not a person is indoctrinated or educated depends on whether it is the intention of a teacher to bring a child up to be able to think for himself.[16] The important point here about education, as opposed to indoctrination, is the *intention* that a student or pupil be brought up or taught to critically think for himself. Wiredu suggests that it is the intention of elders in African cultures to bring children up to accept traditions that have no rational basis and to refrain from questioning these traditions. The problematic issue with intention is that a teacher may have the right intention but may not use the proper processes or methods to create the proper environment that may enhance one's abilities to learn to critically think for oneself. However, in Wilson's view, whether or not a person is indoctrinated may also depend, in part, on the outcome, consequence, or result of teaching. In other words, even if it was not the intention or aim of the teacher to bring up a child to critically think for himself, if the actual outcome or result is the fact that the child is able to critically think for himself, then for Wilson, the child cannot be said to be indoctrinated. The teacher in this case cannot be said to have indoctrinated the child because, thinking for oneself, which is what defines the outcome of education, is inconsistent with indoctrination. Kaphagawani and Wiredu may argue that it is not only the intention or aim of elders and the communal structures in African cultures to use the informal processes and methods to indoctrinate people by inhibiting their ability to critically think for themselves, but it is also the outcome that people actually end up lacking the ability to critically think for themselves.

In this regard, Wiredu seems to indicate that the most important features of indoctrination have to do with the *epistemic* method of inquiry and processes of acquiring beliefs, and the *pedagogical* methods or processes of imparting knowledge. So, whether or not a person is indoctrinated will depend, for the most part, on *how* or *the way* the person is taught to internalize or acquire beliefs; that is, whether the methods of acquiring beliefs require that such beliefs be critically examined to ensure that they have a justificatory basis. For Wiredu, indoctrination depends on whether or not a student has learned or is trained in the epistemic methods of critical inquiry, logical analysis, and experimentation, regarding how he should engage in inquiry or accept beliefs. The essential epistemic and pedagogical questions regarding the negative characterization of indoctrination as a criticism of African communal traditions are, whether or not, and the extent to which the informal methods, processes, and the communal context of teaching children are able to enhance their rational and cognitive abilities to think for themselves and critically examine evidence. This question may be answered by determining whether the methods, processes, and context of teaching and learning result in a situation where a student is actually able to use methods that allow him to think for himself in order to critically examine the evidence.

If the pedagogical method by which a teacher imparts information to a student is such that it does not give him the epistemic method or allow or enhance his epistemic abilities to critically examine evidence or think for himself, then he has been *ipso facto* indoctrinated. Also, if a student is taught that the epistemic method for acquiring beliefs is such that those beliefs do not have to be questioned to find their evidential basis, then that student has also been indoctrinated. I have indicated that the epistemic principles and pedagogical methods in African traditions do not involve indoctrination in any of these ways because people are allowed and able to think for themselves and criticize beliefs. Given what I have described about the communal African tradition, its epistemic principles, and the informal or narrative processes of education, we see that there is a sense in which the pedagogical method of imparting knowledge and the epistemic method of inquiring, critically examining, or justifying beliefs are coextensive. The pedagogical method of teaching usually is a model for the student regarding the epistemic method of acquiring beliefs. As such, people argue that if you want to teach students how to think critically for themselves, you must use a pedagogical method that does not only allow for this ability but also enables them to see it, develop it, and demonstrate it. To some extent, a teacher must model this method and ability for students to imitate. This point is particularly essential to the African mode of education.

## Indoctrination, Education, and Critical Thinking

According to this view, indoctrination involves learning a method of acquiring beliefs such that the very method that one has learned and the way one has learned it actually inhibit or discourage one's ability to critically examine the evidence and think for oneself. We see that the lack of a critical method is one epistemic feature of indoctrination that Wiredu and Appiah criticize in African communal traditions. Sometimes, Wiredu suggests that it is not the epistemic method *per se* that he criticizes because elders—'real thinkers'—were able to criticize ideas and beliefs, and they were able to reason to find elaborate justificatory basis for their beliefs.[17] This suggestion indicates that he is criticizing the pedagogical method of teaching and imparting beliefs, which involves the informal processes that rely on oral tradition. This process does not enhance or allow people to develop their rational and cognitive abilities and the 'implicit epistemic critical methods' that exist in African cultures, based on his idea that there were real thinkers who were critical. Also implicit in Wiredu's view is the idea that education, which is contrasted with indoctrination, involve a critical attitude and habit of the mind that a student must display with respect to the acquisition and the continued acceptance of a belief. For Wiredu, people were indoctrinated, partly in the sense that they did not display critical attitudes. They did not display such attitude because the communal and authoritarian structures did not allow it. When one is educated, one must display an attitude that involves the method of critically examining evidence, testing claims, and accepting or revising beliefs on the basis of the available evidence.

In Wiredu's view, this kind of critical attitude is generally not seen in traditional African cultures, hence, the processes and methods of imparting knowledge and the resulting attitude that people display indicate indoctrination. His charge of indoctrination in African cultures and his criticism suggest that what is necessary to educate people is not just the contents or nature of subject matter, the pedagogical methods, or the intention of the teacher, but also the resulting attitude that people display regarding the proper critical and rigorous method for acquiring beliefs. In other words, the methodology that people actually adopt in acquiring beliefs may indicate whether or not they have a critical attitude or habit of the mind. So, if one is educated in the strict sense, then one learns to consistently use a certain critical methodology for acquiring beliefs. This means that one has internalized the methods and they show up as our attitudes, dispositions, or habits of the mind. The cognitive goal or outcome of education, therefore, is to learn, internalize, develop, and consistently use and display the attitude of critical examination. This liberal and cognitive idea of education involves enhancing independent rationality and cognitive autonomy or the ability of an individual to think for himself. This idea of education also seeks to focus on developing abstractly, the cognitive and logical abilities of an individual, in order to enhance one's rational ability to critically, independently, and autonomously think for oneself. This idea of rationality as the goal of education, which involves considering and evaluating all the evidence in order to arrive at the truth, comes from the liberal philosophical, political, moral tradition of Mill, Locke, Hume, Kant, and Rawls.[18]

The liberal and cognitive view of education is the foundation for Kohlberg's theory of moral education and moral development that has dominated the literature. This idea of moral education seeks to focus on developing abstractly, the cognitive and logical abilities of an individual, in order to enhance one's rational ability to critically, independently, and autonomously think and make moral choices for oneself. Kohlberg argues that the process of moral development can be described as the progressive movement from one intellectual or cognitive stage of awareness to another. This linear cognitive development, along which moral education—and perhaps, education in general—should be tailored, focus on an individual's autonomy and the development of one's abstract cognitive faculties. This view indicates that one's autonomy is enhanced or optimized by developing one's cognitive, logical, and rational abilities. As such, any process or method of education that omits or conceals a set of relevant alternatives will, *ipso facto* vitiate or diminish the possibility of autonomous rational choice and adequate decision making. The underlying argument, which is reflected in Wiredu's view and his criticism of African communal cultures, is that one cannot be educated in the strict sense of 'education' in a context or with a process or method that vitiates or diminish one's cognitive abilities to make rational independent choices and decisions. So, in Wiredu's view, indoctrination is one necessary implication of communalism and epistemic authoritarianism in African cultures, because the authoritarian, informal, and communal context and processes of education and training vitiate the voluntary, independent, and rational acceptance of beliefs based on the evidence. Given the charge of authoritarianism, we can appreciate the sense in which people may deny the possibility of moral education and why they may reasonably argue that African communal cultures only indoctrinates people about morality and other beliefs. However, it is obvious that the epistemological underpinnings for this individualistic and cognitive idea of education in contemporary Western tradition are fundamentally different from the epistemological underpinnings for the communalistic and informal methods or processes of education in African cultures.

I have argued that the view of rationality that emphasizes the ability of an individual to think solely and independently for herself, if taken as a thoroughgoing view of rationality, is implausible. Such a view seems not to fully appreciate the limits of an individual's rationality, in terms of *how far* it can take us and *how well* it can lead us, and the limits on one's cognitive abilities. As such, we cannot use such epistemological or cognitive assumption as a basis for articulating adequate methods and processes of moral education. Because of the limitations in our independent cognitive and rational abilities, it is rational for one to morally defer to or epistemically depend on others who are epistemic superiors in a community of rational people who are involved in communal inquiry and cognitive division of labor. So, the view of rationality, on which the cognitive idea of education is based, is problematic, in that it does not recognize that the limitations on an individual's independent rationality and cognitive abilities must be supplemented by depending on or deferring to others in a community. My robust view of moral education involves the development of the emotional, moral, cognitive, social, and spiritual aspects of personhood, and the ability to epistemically or morally defer to and depend on others. This view does, indeed, involve some elements of indoctrination. In other words, from the perspective of the person being indoctrinated or educated, indoctrination may involve the process or method of uncritical, unquestioned, and unjustified acceptance, internalization, or acquisition of some beliefs for which no proof or evidence is provided. This idea of indoctrination, which is necessary for one to develop into a wholesome person, is seen as necessarily bad by Wiredu, based on the individualistic cognitive idea of education, because it limits individual will and rational or cognitive abilities.

The thrust of my argument is that the process of indoctrination cannot be clearly distinguished from the robust idea, processes, and goals of education. Moreover, even if indoctrination can be legitimately distinguished from education, I indicate that indoctrination is not inherently bad. Whether or not it is bad depends on the extent of indoctrination, that is, the extreme nature of the processes or methods of indoctrination, and the extreme nature of the content or subject matter. Edmund Pincoffs seems to make this point by saying that: "The question, then, is not, When does education become indoctrination? as if indoctrination were necessarily a bad thing; but When does education become indefensible indoctrination? or When does education indefensibly become indoctrination?"[19] Pincoffs distinguishes between indoctrination and brainwashing, and he argues that education becomes an indefensible form of indoctrination only when it becomes brainwashing. Brainwashing is seen as necessarily bad because the subject matter and the process or method employed "makes it psychologically impossible for a person to deliberate to any purpose about certain matters."[20] This result may not occur with indoctrination; it may occur depending on the extreme nature of indoctrination.

It appears that the idea of indoctrination cannot be clearly distinguished from the robust idea of education because, some elements of indoctrination are, in reality and fact, a necessary part of or a precondition for education. This is especially so for young children, where education must also involve their acculturation or socialization into some accepted and well-established fundamental habits, values, attitudes, beliefs, principles, and practices. In this situation, a child has to internalize some fundamental values, principles, and attitudes that are necessary for him to be educated about any subject matter in a discipline. This may also occur for adults who are being assimilated into an epistemic culture. The process of educating people essentially involves, at least in part, their assimilation, socialization, and acculturation into a set of principles, beliefs, and practices. This process usually requires the use of informal methods, memorization, rote, imitation, subtle imposition, and consistent reinforcement by others. These methods are necessary for 'encoding' and imbuing into one's conceptual framework some of the general attitudes, values, meta-beliefs, and meta-principles that are necessary for further education about other substantive beliefs and principles. In other words, there cannot be education if there is no element of a moderate sense of indoctrination at an initial stage in the education process. In order to be able to learn and understand other principles and for any inquiry to get off the ground, one must learn, internalize, and assimilate some fundamental and foundational principles, beliefs, values, and meta-beliefs that one cannot or should not question at that initial stage of learning, and for which one may not have adequate justification.

According to Pincoffs, there is a moderate, defensible, and good form of indoctrination that is necessary for a robust sense and acceptable goal of education. I am arguing that this is the type of indoctrination that may reasonably be associated with African communalism and its informal methods of education. The extreme kind of indoctrination that is indefensible, in Pincoffs' view, is that which involves brainwashing.[21] So, the problem is, how can indoctrination be necessary for moral education, if indoctrination may vitiate or impede the rational autonomy that is supposed to be enhanced by education? My stance is that the indoctrination in African traditions is not brainwashing, and as such, it does not vitiate rational autonomy, hence it is a legitimate method at an initial stage in a robust process of education. The goal of moral education is to enhance one's ability to be a moral agent, which involves the ability to make rational, voluntary, and autonomous choices, and being free from external constraints. According to the African view, being a morally good person or acquiring moral personhood in the robust sense is something that can only be developed by the appropriate communal informal moral education, which includes the encoding of some habits, attitudes, moral points of view, and fundamental principles. This robust sense of moral education involves both the rational and non-rational acceptance and internalization of certain moral principles that one may use as a motivation and justification for action. The moral principles are, to a large extent, external to the individual. People may or may not internalize or accept them based on any obvious reasons. People have to learn to use them to justify, guide, and motivate their actions and conduct.

This idea of moral education implies that moral principles or one's understanding and use of such principles may be construed in either an internalist or externalist sense of justification. Construed in an externalist sense, the moral principles that one is rationally educated to accept may not *necessarily motivate* one to act. The idea is that motivation and the kind of things that can motive are internal to the person, not external. An external factor or justification cannot by itself motivate. However, we may construe moral principles in an internalist sense that we can morally educate people about such that they are a necessary part of individuals' attitude and inner motivation. As such, these moral principles are learned and seen by individuals as justifications that also motivate them to act. In other words, an effective form of moral education does not simply involve people learning and rationally accepting moral principles as external justifications for their actions, it also involves the idea of people internalizing moral principles as the inner motivations for their actions. The process of internalizing moral principles so that they can motivate must include or involve some moderate forms of indoctrination. Indoctrination is a way to make sure that moral principles provide both external and internal push for individuals to act in a specified range of ways. The African view of moral personhood and the communal and informal modes of moral education indicate that one cannot achieve moral goodness or moral personhood by relying solely and completely on one's rational individualistic abilities and cognitive autonomy. A morally good and wholesome person cannot completely divorce his actions and motivations from prodding or external push or constraints, hence a morally good person cannot rely solely on his own individual, inner, rational, and cognitive push. A moral person needs some external help to engender internal push. This is the reason for sanctions.

In African cultures, elders and the community play an important role by providing an external push to help motivate one's moral actions. Elders and community also play an important role in morally educating a person by imbuing in him the requisite inner principles, values, and facilities that provide the internal push or motivation for his moral actions. The constant and consistent ribbing, chiding and prodding by others in traditional African cultures and one's appreciation of such reinforcement, external constraints, push or motivation are important elements of or preconditions for moral autonomy and education. These preconditions do not only establish some external push and constraints, but they also provide the foundation for engendering the correct inner motivations and for internalization the external pushes and constraints as internal push that help people to act in morally acceptable ways. Thus, in order to be a morally good person, it is necessary to accept, in part, some moderate sense of moral 'indoctrination', which involves internalizing some doctrines, acquiring certain attitudes, and accepting certain principles without question or explicit justification, and using them to motivate and justify one's actions. The rational and cognitive idea of moral education provides a basis for one to understand a moral principle as an external justification, it does not provide a basis for helping internal motivations. This is because external justifications do not necessarily motivate.

The rational authoritarian and communal informal idea of moral education in African traditions, which is meant to provide external justification and internal motivation or push, is underscored by Wilson's view that adults have a moral mandate over children, in terms of giving them a robust sense of moral education so that they can develop wholesome character traits and personhood. Such mandate, according to Wilson, "includes the right to use *force* or *compulsion* on children, and the right to *condition* their behaviour to some extent. I am thinking here of such things as making a child go to bed, including feelings of fear and guilt about touching dangerous electrical equipment, and so forth. These methods are necessary partly in order to establish the preconditions for moral education."[22] One must understand force or compulsion here not in the extreme sense of violence but in a mild and constructive sense of rational imposition. This is consistent with the rational sense of authoritarianism. Such use of force may also be necessary for some adults. Without some preconditions regarding the context of rules, goals, principles, attitudes, relationships, and practices, one cannot engage in a meaningful moral education.

The preconditions for moral education seem to circumscribe and provide meaningful content to one's autonomy and ability to make choice. Hence the idea of moral autonomy in African cultures is not confused with metaphysical autonomy, which one may have outside of a community and relationships. In this sense, one can be indoctrinated and still be an autonomous, rational, and a voluntary moral agent. You may internalize moral principles by a process of indoctrination, but such process may not necessarily preclude your discretionary rational ability to use the principles to motivate, guide, and justify your actions and choices in a specific manner depending on the situation. All moral principles are *open-textured*. So, irrespective of how they are acquired, learned, or internalized, they can never determine particular actions or choices in every foreseeable circumstance. The individual still has to use his rational discretion and creative imagination to make choices and apply the principles to a given context in a justifiable and acceptable manner. Hence, the moderate process of indoctrination that is associated with the communal informal processes of moral education in African cultures does not involve brainwashing; it does not necessarily have built-in choices that preclude rationality, autonomy, and voluntariness.

## Moderate Indoctrination and Informal Education

This African idea implies a plausible basis for informal education that involves an initial moderate sense of indoctrination. If there is a plausible basis for informal education, then an adequate idea of moral education cannot be based solely and exclusively on the goal of enhancing an individual's cognitive and rational autonomy. Thus, this goal cannot be used as a basis for making the distinction between education and indoctrination. One also cannot use this goal as a plausible basis for criticizing indoctrination and arguing in favor of education. To appreciate this point, it is pertinent to recall the basis for the logical distinction between 'education' and 'indoctrination', the arguments in favor of education, and the arguments against indoctrination. The distinction between education and indoctrination is based on the view that indoctrination hinders rationality and the development of individuals' cognitive abilities, will, or autonomy, while education enhances them. The distinction and arguments seem to hinge on the dubious ideas of rationality, epistemic individualism, absolute cognitive autonomy, and the idea that one's ability to optimize one's cognitive abilities involves, solely, the individual's ability to independently think for himself.[23] The assumption underlying these ideas is that the ability of an individual to independently think for himself and to rely solely on his own judgment, is necessarily good. Thus, the idea of education, which is seen as the attempt to enhance this sense of rationality is considered to be necessarily good, while indoctrination, which is seen as hindering this sense of rationality is seen as necessarily bad. It is questionable whether the extreme individualistic, cognitively autonomous, and subjectivist notion of rationality is necessarily good. I have indicated in the previous chapter that there are problems with the epistemological underpinnings of this individualistic cognitive model of reasoning and education that can be overcome by the epistemological underpinnings of the communal informal models of reasoning and education.

A plausible distinction between education and indoctrination cannot be based on the dubious assumption about the absolute value of cognitive and personal autonomy. To assume the suspicious and questionable principle of epistemic individualism or cognitive autonomy as the basis for the distinction between indoctrination and education, is to beg the question that needs to be proved. Doyle summarizes Kaufman's suspicion about this distinction and the underlying view of education in the following passage:

> For Kaufman, the crucial question raised by Frankena's concept of education in whether personal autonomy should be given, in his words, the 'place of pride in our educational scheme of things'. Autonomy, he suggests, is the sort of general educational aim to which it is all too easy to pay lip-service, especially in liberal democratic societies. Yet in practice it is often not clear what is involved in becoming an autonomous person, how this can be achieved educationally, or even whether this is desirable from a moral, political, or social point of view. Nor is it clear that autonomy—even assuming that it is a desirable achievement for everyone—is relevant to judgments about all educational activities or all stages of education.[24]

As such, any argument in favor of education or against indoctrination that relies on this dubious assumption is also question-begging. Sometimes, this view of education presupposes without proof that an individual's absolute cognitive autonomy is necessarily good, and as such, it should be promoted or enhanced in all aspects of life. I have already argued that the individualistic or solipsistic idea of rationality is suspicious in so far as it implies (1) that epistemic dependence or deference is irrational, and (2) that epistemic individualism, cognitive autonomy, and doxastic voluntarism are absolutely valuable.

The primacy or absolute value that is placed on the kind of doxastic voluntarism and epistemic individualism and autonomy that is implied by the individualistic and autonomous view of rationality is unreasonable. Moreover, the view of education based on this idea, which involves the ability to enhance the independent rationality and cognitive autonomy of an individual, is parochial and narrow. Those who place absolute value on an individual's will, autonomy, and independent thinking, such as Wiredu, seem to argue that enhancing such will is the central, and perhaps, the only aim or ideal of education, especially moral education. I do not think that this is the only ideal or goal of education. Such ideal or goal may be appreciated in an extremely individualistic system of living. Such system of living is not desirable in every society. Any idea of education and rationality must be sensitive to the nature of humans and human societies. It is pertinent to note that these ideas of rationality and education are modern Western ideas that have become popular with the liberal defense of individualism and individual autonomy. It is also pertinent to indicate that the idea that autonomy is an absolute value is a cultural artifact that must be placed in the proper cultural context of modern Western liberal individualism.[25] I do not object to the view that enhancing rationality may be *one* aim of education. However, the priority of this aim must be placed in the social, practical, and human context of living and other societal and practical aims and goals. Perhaps, there are more practical and realistic aims of education and moral education, which should be considered.

Under the cognitive model of education, the individual is educated for the purpose of learning certain skills in order to develop his abstract cognitive abilities on the basis of which he independently acquires, accepts, and justifies his own values and beliefs. An individual's beliefs and cognitive abilities alone, it is assumed, will enable him to have and see a wide range of alternatives and options, on the basis on which he is able to use his will, rationality, cognitive abilities to choose autonomously between alternative lines of action. Recently, some have criticized the cognitive developmental model of education and they have sought better models of moral education that rely on the informal narrative methods and process.[26] These critics call into question not only the cognitive model of education but also its individualistic epistemological underpinnings. Some of these critics have emphasized the essential role of the community as well as the use of informal process or narratives in moral education and developing a robust emotional, moral, spiritual, social, and cognitive sense of personhood.[27] The efforts to emphasize the role of the community and the use of informal methods of education underscore the African idea of moral education and the saying, which is now popular in the West that, it takes a whole community to raise (morally educate) a child. These criticisms suggest that there is something to be said about the African mode of moral education and that it does not necessarily involve the kind of negative idea of indoctrination that Wiredu suggests. This African saying speaks to the critics' view that all the facilities of a community are to be employed for morally educating children in order for them to fully develop into a person.

The robust idea of moral education in African cultures has the goal of helping a person to develop a consistent moral character and a wholesome sense of personhood. This sense of personhood involves a person who has matured and is emotionally, spiritually, morally, socially, culturally, and cognitively well integrated and stable. One is able to acquire such personhood by being fully integrated in a community and by morally and epistemically relying or depending on and deferring to others. The reasonableness of the principle of epistemic dependence seems to indicate that enhancing and developing the extremely autonomous, independent, cognitive, and individualistic idea of rationality cannot be the sole or overriding goal of education. Sometimes, it may be irrational to independently think for oneself or make independent judgments, especially if one does not have the expertise and background information to do so. Rationality in that situation may involve epistemic dependence on or deference to others who are experts. These experts may also need to depend on other experts or work in conjunction with them to engage in communal inquiry and cognitive division of labor in order to arrive at the most plausible belief and the best decision, judgment, or choice. This is the kind of 'group rationality' and reasoning that goes on in medicine, hence an ordinary person who is not a physician cannot be said to be rational if he wants to (without epistemic dependence on physician) rely solely on his own independent judgment and choice regarding the best line of treatment. So, the assumption that, being able to think for oneself is necessarily good as an educational goal, is contentious and unproven. In my view, it is not necessarily good for a person to be 'brought up' to accept this as thoroughgoing principle and to adopt it across the board with respect to all his beliefs, decisions, and actions. Such upbringing will mean that this person is not able to distinguish between those situations where he can think for himself and those where, as a result of lack of knowledge and expertise, he is not able to or epistemically or rationally adequate to think for himself.

In John Wilson's effort to distinguish logically between education, which involves being able to think for oneself, and indoctrination, which does not involve being able to think for oneself, he argues that: "If you *bring children up* to think for themselves, it is not intelligible to say, in general, that you have indoctrinated them: because 'indoctrination' is opposed to 'thinking for oneself'."[28] This point is dubious because it is possible to 'to bring up a child' to be able to think for herself where such upbringing may involve an extreme form of indoctrination. Such upbringing may become an indoctrination if she is brought up to accept that 'thinking for oneself' is the only principle that she should accept as a basis for reasoning and making decisions. As a reminder, it is pertinent to note that my assumption here is that indoctrination is not necessarily bad. Whether it is bad will depend on the extent, processes, methods, context, and subject matter. So, bringing up a child to accept that the idea of thinking for oneself is the only principle of reasoning may become an extreme kind of indoctrination that is bad. It appears that Wilson does not recognize that you can bring a child up to think for himself in a way that indoctrinates him to uncritically believe that thinking for himself is always rational, necessary, and good for him in every conceivable situation. This upbringing will mean that he will fail to understand those situations where it is not rational for him to think for himself, such that he may need to depend on or defer to others. The way that someone is brought up to accept the principle or idea of being able to think for oneself would indicate whether or not he would refuse to accept the principle of epistemic deference or dependence as irrational.

Moreover, the idea of 'bringing up a child' is ambiguous; it is not clear, precisely, what it takes and what Wilson means by 'bring children up'. It may mean for Wiredu, "the education of children through informal processes of day-to-day upbringing rather than through formal institutions."[29] Wiredu has criticized these informal processes of education in African cultures as processes of indoctrination. Or it may also mean the formal process of education where one is brought up in a particular school of thought, discipline, practice, or methodology. It may also be understood in a robust sense of these two to include the various educational processes and aims of socialization, acculturation, moral education, as well as the cognitive, emotional, and psychological development of someone. So, the pertinent issues are: What are the processes or methods of 'bringing children up' with respect to the broad education goals and aims? Which processes or methods are legitimate? Do the processes and methods of education necessarily include or exclude indoctrination? The proper idea of 'bringing children up' ought to mean the robust and holistic idea of education, which includes all the different methods and processes that are necessary to help children develop rationally and cognitively, grow up to be emotionally stable, and mature into morally and socially responsible people who are and fully integrated into their society. In other words, the processes, methods, ideas, and subject matter involved in 'bringing up children' may involve teaching them to *recognize* all the relevant alternatives in order to *independently* make their own rational choices. The idea of 'bringing up children' may involve teaching them to *evaluate* all relevant alternatives in order to weigh the advantages or disadvantages of one over the other. This idea may also mean helping children to understand the advantages or reasonableness of a belief or an option to the exclusion of other beliefs and options. The idea of 'bringing up children' may mean gradually imbuing some ideas, ideals, values, beliefs, principles, attitudes, and habits into children without necessarily providing the justification for the ideas or beliefs.

In some regards, the idea of 'bringing up children' in a robust sense is coextensive with the broad idea or goal of education. This idea of 'bringing up children' cannot be understood to mean developing their cognitive or rational abilities, to the exclusion of being emotionally stable or being socially and morally responsible people. If 'bringing someone up' is used in the sense of gradually educating a person or making him to acquire various attitudes, habits, and behavioral traits that indicate the values of rationality, social relationships, moral responsibility, emotional stability, caring, empathy, creativity, and self-respect, then such upbringing in the robust sense of education would also imply that he has to be indoctrinated to believe and accept without question that these values are intrinsically good, since the intrinsic goodness of these values cannot be rationally proved. The notion of rationality, which means one's cognitive ability to independently think for oneself, implies that we must not to use the robust educational processes or methods of bringing up children that include indoctrination and other non-rational or affective means. All these various and robust educational means are necessary for ensuring that people care about, use, develop, and trust their rational processes and cognitive abilities. Moreover, these various educational means are also necessary for helping people to acquire other emotional, epistemic, social, and moral habits, virtues, and attitudes, which are necessary for someone to be a wholesome, educated, an adult human being, which is what it takes for someone to acquire personhood in African cultures.

In this sense of upbringing, there would be no distinction between education, socialization, acculturation, conditioning, and indoctrination because some conditioning, socialization, acculturation, or indoctrination (whether it is about the belief in the intrinsic value of rationality or otherwise) is necessary for one to be educated in the broad and robust sense of upbringing.[30] Depending on the method, process, context, and subject matter, the idea of 'bringing up a child' may suggest an element of *extreme indoctrination* which involves brainwashing or conditioning someone to have a habit of the mind, where one is not rationally and emotionally able to evaluate options and make choices. This sense of upbringing is opposed to the idea of teaching someone that she has the option of thinking for herself, if she deems it fit and she has the expertise and background knowledge and the option of depending on or deferring to others who may be more competent since she does not have the expertise or competence to think for herself. One of the criticisms against the conception of critical thinking as a kind of habit of the mind, attitude, or disposition to be critical, is that the relevant critical thinking skills or abilities may be taught in a way that involves extreme indoctrination, brainwashing, or conditioning. To avoid such process of extreme indoctrination and conditioning that will lead to fixed habits, it is necessary to be critical of the very habits themselves, their underlying principles and beliefs, and the methods of imparting or acquiring the habits. Depending on how critical thinking abilities are taught, the idea of critical thinking or being able to think for oneself may itself be held as a dogma. In which case, one may even refuse to be critical of the idea of thinking for oneself, which may not be rational in some situation where one lacks the expertise.

One may not critically examine the idea of critical thinking or thinking for oneself in order to discriminate between situations where one ought to be critical or think for oneself and those where one ought not to. One may actually end up making an irrational decision simply because one has been extremely indoctrinated about the idea of thinking for oneself. We can imagine a situation where bringing someone up to think for himself or insisting on thinking for oneself may not be necessarily good or rational. Suppose for instance, John has been brought up to think for himself and he thinks that there is some benefit in smoking—he enjoys it. He considers the evidence, some of which he does not have the expertise to understand, but he is not convinced that he would necessarily have cancer. His doctor tells him that he has a gene that increases his probability of getting cancer from smoking. He thinks for himself and decides to ignore the doctor's prescription that he must use some means to kick the nicotine habit. Based on his rational thinking and autonomy or his ability to think for himself, he decides that he would rather enjoy the years he has to live by smoking instead of being miserable for denying himself what he loves because he wants to live a long life, which is not guaranteed. This example may be controversial with respect to whether the decision to smoke involves the rational sense in which one should think for oneself. Perhaps, the controversial nature of this example may underscore the problems with the meaning of 'thinking for oneself' and whether it is necessarily rational and good to think for oneself.

It makes sense sometimes to say that someone who has been brought up or 'educated' to think for himself and has accepted the idea of thinking for oneself as the sole and thoroughgoing principle of action, has indeed been extremely indoctrinated. This narrow goal of education or idea of thinking for oneself does not acknowledge the contextual nature, goal, and the robust subject matter of education and the limits that such context, goal, and subject matter place on an individual's cognitive and rational autonomy. The unavoidable nature of indoctrination, and the view that it is not always necessary to think for oneself, imply that certain beliefs *may* be imposed, imbued, implanted, or internalized involuntarily. In which case, an individual does not necessarily have to rationally think about these beliefs for himself as a basis for accepting them. We learn or accept many ideas and beliefs, and are taught *how to do* many things for which rational justifications are never provided and cannot be provided. When we teach the same things to children, they are taught in the form of indoctrination: they are imbued in children and they learn by experience and imitation. In teaching these ideas to people, our intention or aim as educators is to make them accept, internalize, and adopt these ideas without questions or any justificatory basis. One such principle, doctrine, content, method, and attitude or habit of the mind is prudence, which requires us not question everything in life. If we question everything across the board, then we would become absolute skeptics. But we need to abandon the attitude of absolute skepticism in order to be educated. The idea of prudence may be called an ideology or doctrine that we acquire by indoctrination.

My point in the above example is that the view of rationality, which is couched in the ambiguous or vague idea of 'thinking for oneself' and based on epistemic individualism, cognitive autonomy, doxastic voluntarism, is problematic. This is because this view of rationality—no matter how it is understood—does not acknowledge prudence and the limitations of one's rationality, cognitive autonomy, and individualism, in that they may lead to a situation where one uses rationality for one's own detriment. The usual response to this point is that if one uses one's rational autonomy to make wrong choices, then one must accept the responsibility. The issue is not whether a person should be responsible for his actions but whether it makes sense to wait to hold someone responsible if the situation could have been avoided by utilizing the principles of epistemic deference, dependence, and paternalism. The heuristic or consequential value of deference or dependence is the motivation in African cultures for the kind of epistemic, moral, or social paternalism that is manifested in communalism, its rational authoritarianism, and the moderate indoctrinating mode of education. It is pertinent to place this issue of paternalism in the context of the moral attitude of caring and a community that seeks to maintain valuable social relationships. As a result of the relationships in a communal setting, what happens to one person may have lasting effects on others and the community. This is the reason why, according to the African communalism, anyone who lives in a society where he has familial and social relationships with others cannot overstate the value individualism, autonomy, and rights. The example of the smoker above may illustrate an irrational person who has been indoctrinated to belief that it is always rational to think for oneself. One can argue that if he had a robust kind of education that is manifested in communal African cultures, then he would have been brought up to know and decide that, in such situations, he must consider his social and moral relationships with others and the implication of continued smoking for such relationships. Such consideration requires and implies that he must depend on others and accept paternalistic intervention.

## Indoctrination and Goals of Education

According to Russell, the robust idea of what may be legitimately called 'education' has three aims or goals. It seeks (1) to provide opportunities for people to grow psychologically, moral, emotionally, and socially, and to remove any influences that could hamper such growth; (2) to socialize a person into certain cultural principles and practices with the hope of helping him to develop his capacities to the fullest; (3) to train people into useful members, good and active citizens of the community to which they belong.[31] In order to have a complete and robust view of education, we must consider the idea of imparting knowledge and beliefs as a process in the context of the aims for the individual and community. Some of the processes of education include the informal process of modeling a practice or principle, learning by rote or imitation, and reinforcement by constant and consistent prodding and chiding. Education may not, in all situations, have explicit and formal processes or methods, and education may also not have specific students or narrowly defined subject matter. This kind of education is informal. This informal process or idea of education is experiential and unorganized: students simply learn by examples and by watching other people, and practicing what they see other people do without critical deliberation or search for justifications. As such, there are no formal methods. The autonomous, individualistic, and abstract cognitive view of education, Alan Gerwirth argues, would preclude such informal modes or idea of education. He goes on to argue that much of the moral, social, and political education in different societies are informal.[32] This kind of informal education is a legitimate mode of education that is practiced in traditional Africa cultures. Efforts must be made to understand this informal form of education and its epistemic and rational underpinnings.

Wiredu agrees that these communal structures and principles are strong elements of African culture: "the great value it places on what we might call communal belonging."[33] This communal informal process of education is an essential way of inculcating and perpetuating the requisite value of communal belonging, which involves the integration of the individual into the community. This informal process of education and integration is so subtle that one is usually not conscious of it. According to Wiredu: "The integration of individuality into community in African traditional society is so thoroughgoing that, as is too rarely noted, the very concept of a person has a normative layer of meaning."[34] This process of integrating the individual into the community and its values involves the informal process of education and upbringing. This educational process is the process of making a person moral within the community. Such process usually does not require the kind of critical inquiry, examination of evidence, or the idea of thinking for oneself, which is required by the narrow idea of education. It is reasonable to insist that you cannot rationally challenge or critically examine the norms or principles of behavior in a society if you do not understand them by seeing how they operate in a given context. This idea may provide prudential reasons for indoctrinating children to accept norms and practices in a given community. So, if the informal processes of education in African cultures involve indoctrination, and these processes are necessary for the educational goals of the community, then indoctrination in the African communal context appears to be a necessary and an unavoidable element of education that meets the social and communal needs of integrating individuals into the community and making them moral persons.

Perhaps, one may argue that the social and practical reality of the nature of education has nothing do with the conceptual and normative idea of what education ought to be. Some may argue that the idea of distinguishing between education and indoctrination, and the views that education involves enhancing a person's ability to think for himself and critically examine evidence, and that this idea does not involve indoctrination, are not meant to address how education is indeed practiced, but to indicate normatively what it ought to be. In other words, philosophers usually do not concern themselves about what education *is* and how it is actually practiced, instead, they seek to give a normative account of what education ought to be. This normative account is then used to criticize or evaluate what education is and how it is actually practiced. Wiredu may argue that this is precisely what he is doing in his critique of the communal, authoritarian context and informal processes and methods of education in African cultures. However, it appears that this normative conception of education is implausible and impracticable because it is not sensitive to the social or practical context and educational processes and goals, which necessarily involve indoctrination. As such, Willis Moore argues that we may have to "frankly admit that learning necessarily begins with an authoritative and indoctrinative situation, and that for lack of time, native capacity or the requisite training to think everything out for oneself, learning for the rationally mature individual must continue to include an ingredient of the unreasoned, the merely accepted."[35] It is plausible that the human natural and social conditions may vitiate the possibility of attaining the ideal goal of education. Hence, there is the need to conceive of the normative idea and goal of education in a way that is sensitive to human natural and social conditions, in order to make it realistic, practicable, and achievable.

Thus, there is a need to naturalize the idea, goal, and practice of education and its cognates, pedagogy and epistemology, by putting them in the proper natural and social contexts of human beings. A motivation for this effort is to try to understand the natural, cognitive, and social constraints that are placed on humans in their efforts to be educated and to acquire knowledge, or their efforts to educate or impart knowledge. David Annis, among many others, has provided a plausible empirical and theoretical basis for the idea of naturalizing education, pedagogy, and epistemology.[36] Annis argues that there are differences in people's cognitive and epistemic skills, abilities, and practices, such as visual perception, which can be explained in terms of environmental, cultural, and psychological, and biological factors. Human beings develop certain cognitive skills and processes that are necessary for them to survive in and conquer their own environment. He cites the example of the Temne in Sierra Leone in West Africa and the Canadian Eskimos. The differences in their vegetation provided them with different visual stimulations such that they developed different perceptual skills which are thus required for them to survive: Eskimos as hunters and Temne as farmers. He argues that the epistemic and cognitive skills that these different people develop can be seen as different reliable means of drawing reliable inferences, which translate into epistemic habits, as well as reasoning patterns. The implication of a naturalized view of education, and in particular, moral education is that we must understand the African mode of education and inquiry in the context of their environment and how such environment shape their cognitive and rational abilities.

The negative characterizations and criticisms of African idea of education, beliefs, and thought systems appear to be scathing only because of a methodological flaw. These characterizations and criticisms fail to naturalize their analysis and understanding of these African phenomena, by ignoring the natural and social contexts of traditional African cultures. According to Annis, there are foundational basic beliefs which are necessary for one to know, believe, conceptualize, experience, develop, understand, make meaning and be educated. Some beliefs are basic only contextually while others may be basic biologically and universally.[37] What is epistemically basic in one context may not be basic in another context. As such, one has to accept without question some basic statements or beliefs in one context in order to be able to learn, be educated, socialized, and develop into a wholesome person in that context. In some cases, such contextual idea of education or socialization is necessary for one to survive and live a meaningful life. For instance, moral education in African cultures involves an attempt to teach children how to practically behave and organize their lives in order to survive and develop into moral personhood. Wiredu underscores this point by indicating that the methods of education and inquiry in African cultures must be viewed from the perspective of the "traditional mode of understanding, utilising and controlling external nature and of interpreting the place of man within it."[38] The goal of education is for people to understand these traditional modes of inquiry and to use them properly to lead a meaningful life.

The intent or goal of education and moral education in traditional African cultures is to teach people what is accepted and acceptable as the basic reasonable principles and beliefs for actions and conduct that would help them to organize their lives. Some basic principles may require indoctrination to imbue and implant in a person some foundations to build on. In building on these basic principles, one must sometimes rely on his independent thinking and creativity. Hence, how people will individually apply these basic principles to their everyday lives in different circumstances cannot be predetermined, indoctrinated or taught. No person is wise enough to know all the possible situations that one could be confronted with so as to 'indoctrinate' people and predetermine how they should act in each and every given situation. However, the attitude or habit of the mind that one must develop in order to use these basic principles cannot be rationally taught, in the strict or narrow sense of education, they must be indoctrinated, imbued, or implanted as doctrines. People acquire the requisite attitudes and habits of the mind by imitating, 'practicing' or using or applying the principles that they have learned and seeing how they play out in their everyday lives. This idea is consistent with Aristotle's view that one becomes a moral or virtuous person by constantly and 'habitually' performing (by practicing) moral acts. Hence, moral education must, at least initially, involve some elements of indoctrination, habituation, and acculturation. In this sense, becoming a moral and wholesome person cannot be taught solely by using formal methods of imparting explicit instructions in a formal system of education that seeks to develop an individual's ability to think for himself.

The habits necessary for acquiring personhood have to be cultivated in a community that practices and models some ideas of personhood. In order to do this, it must be informally taught and reinforced in different spheres of one's life. Gewirth makes this point by arguing that formal political, social, or moral education would not be successful if it did not have an antecedent foundation in some informal education or some form of indoctrination.[39] Moral education in African traditions cannot be characterized or criticized as involving an indefensible form of indoctrination, i.e., brainwashing. One may characterize or criticize such moral education solely as indoctrination only if one presupposes a logical distinction between education and indoctrination. Such distinction must assume a questionable and narrow view of education that precludes indoctrination, informal education, and the social practical aim of education. This narrow view of education is based on the questionable view that education seeks solely to enhance an individual's rational and cognitive autonomy. Hence one must understand education as a robust process of imparting and imbuing ideas in a person and cultivating certain attitudes and habits of the mind that are necessary to develop into a wholesome person. So, one way to understand this robust idea of education is, to place it in the broad context of a community and its social and political principles and practices.

To underscore this point, Gerwirth argues that we may contextually understand the idea or goal of education in the US by asking: "What should be the role of education in teaching young persons about the rights and responsibilities of citizenship in a constitutional democracy?"[40] He argues that we cannot overlook the important role that the informal processes of education may play in achieving the requisite goal in a particular context. According to Gewirth, "the most effective way for young people to become familiar with, accepting of, and even critically aware of the Bill of Rights and similar moral-political views is through their experience of living in a country where these rights are *firmly respected*."[41] The emphasis on 'firmly respected' here is to draw attention to the suggestion or idea that the relevant ideas are entrenched as a tradition. This process of socializing a person into a tradition involves imitation and learning informally by experience based on social interactions, which are engendered by living within the context of the relevant practices and principles. So, in order to understand the African idea, processes, and methods of education, we may ask what the role of education should be in teaching children their rights and responsibilities in communal society. If this is the proper question to ask about moral education in African traditions, then one may say that Wiredu's criticisms of African traditions, communalism, the informal methods and processes of education, and their authoritarian features miss the point. It appears that Wiredu has not adequately appreciated the important role that the informal type of moral, social, and political education plays with respect to the communal principles and values of African cultures.

Moreover, based on his critique of authoritarianism and his view that authoritarianism involves indoctrination, it appears that he does not sufficiently appreciate the robust idea of education and moral education in African thought. Perhaps, it is an appreciation of this informal mode of education that may have led many people in the US, for instance, to object to the formal idea of moral education in public schools. People expect that morality and other relevant values should be informally taught at home and in religious or social settings. Usually, the methods of teaching values at home and in society or religious communities are mostly informal and indoctrinating—only seldom are these methods formal. Moreover, we also have to appreciate that education usually takes place in the contexts of cultural, linguistic, moral, social, and political processes, practices, and accepted principles of actions. Such contexts usually have a necessary part to play in the educational process, methods, and aims. People are educated not as isolated individuals but as interacting members of a social group of people. This point is important for the African communalistic context and its informal methods and processes of education, because education must take place in the context of the language, the conceptual scheme, belief system, and principles of a community. To indicate or insist on the relevant cultural context of education does not necessarily involve or imply an extreme form of indoctrination or brainwashing, which is distinct from education.

So, the context, goal, processes, and the content or subject matter of education are relevant to how we understand education and how we actually educate people. The African idea of education indicates that it must be seen in terms of the broad and robust educational goals of socializing or acculturating people into a community of principles, ideas, inquiry, and practices, and imparting information or inculcating attitudes that have practical relevance their day-to-day lives. Many of the things we learn, on the basis of which we organize and practically lead our lives, are learned on an experiential basis by watching and imitating people, seeing results, and acting in accordance with what we have experienced or what has been firmly established as acceptable principles and practices. This type of learning is acquired informally in our everyday interactions with others. This kind of learning is also the basis for our upbringing and our robust sense of education. There are usually no formal processes or institutions and methods that are consciously used to impart these kinds of practical knowledge. The kind of informal moral, social, and practical education that Wiredu characterizes in Africa as indoctrination, Alan Gewirth argues, is a necessary feature of political, moral, and civil or 'legal' education.[42] He argues that we must understand the goal of education in terms of the need to meet social and community needs.

The African robust idea of education also indicates that it is problematic to see the idea of 'thinking for oneself' or cognitive autonomy as the overriding idea of rationality and the overriding goal of education, such that it must be seen as having intrinsic value or something that is worth pursuing for its own sake, to the necessary exclusion of any form of indoctrination. When, for instance, we are being taught how to use of language and concepts, we do not question linguistic rules, conventions, and practices. The process of learning language and concepts, which is the foundation of all forms of education, involves some elements of, but not the extreme sense of indoctrination. Language and concepts are necessary for one to be educated about any subject matter. Learning how to use language and concepts is a fundamental aspect of the robust sense of education, socialization, and acculturation. To learn a language and the use of concepts is to learn in some indoctrinating manner many of the cultural beliefs, values, and principles that are embedded in the language and concepts. We learn and use language without ever critically examining or thinking for ourselves whether the rules and conventions of language make sense or are justifiable. Moreover, using language and concepts also involves making epistemic, metaphysical, and ontological claims, in that many of the ontological claims that are embedded in concepts and language, provide the semantic basis for using them to make meaning.

To learn and use language is, to accept without question and without thinking for oneself, the ontological claims that the concepts in the language make. One may argue that the processes of learning and using language may, in some respect, inhibit rationality. This is because language provides us with a conceptual scheme or a way of making meaning, which may, in a sense, limit our reasoning. One can reason only within the context of a conceptual scheme or language. Apparently, the individualistic and autonomous view of education does not consider the social context of education and the role that education has to play for the social group to which an individual belongs. In order for a group to exist, it must have some fundamental principles that a person must to 'accept' or internalize in order to belong. So even if one is to criticize certain beliefs in an attempt to modify or revise them, one has to 'accept' certain fundamental principles initially without question. Sometimes, the criticism and the efforts to revise certain beliefs are done in the context of the fundamental principles of inquiry. If we view the idea of education very broadly as a process of acculturation or socialization and the process of acquiring wholesome and moral personhood, then in order to be integrated or socialized into an epistemic and moral community and practice, one must be initially indoctrinated to internalize certain epistemic and moral principles that define the epistemic and moral practice and community.

To be educated in or 'integrated' into the discipline of science or philosophy, for instance, is to be socialized into its practice and to internalize the principles of doing science or philosophy. Frankena alludes to this point by indicating that, although having rational autonomy is part of the aim of education, "the *means* of education must include introducing the pupil to the already existing 'literatures' of art, history, dancing, basketball, etc."[43] It would be difficult for a person to learn if he does not have the requisite foundation, which involves mastering and 'accepting' initially without question the prevailing views, beliefs, and principles of his predecessors that exist in the disciplinary tradition. This initial process of education, in the very broad sense, involves a process of indoctrination. According to H. Marron, "Education is a collective technique which a society employs to instruct its youth in the values and accomplishment of the civilization with which it exists."[44] This involves, in a very broad sense, training or indoctrinating people to have certain attitudes or habits of the mind, which may indicate the internalization of the requisite principles. In this sense, according to Bertrand Russell, "Education . . . may be defined as the formation, by means of instruction, of certain mental habits and a certain outlook on life and the world."[45] The initial acculturation and socialization into an educational practice is, for the most part, a process of indoctrinating people to internalize certain fundamental principles that define an epistemic community or practice. These principles are necessary for the educational processes to get off the ground and proceed in the community.

## Indoctrination and A Robust Sense of Education

The process of education requires, as the basis for our other beliefs, that people must sometimes have to rely on the views of some experts that they must accept without critical thought.[46] So, as alluded to earlier, the pertinent issue regarding the relevance of indoctrination to education is, when this process or aspect of education becomes an indefensible process of indoctrination. A clear-cut distinction between indoctrination and education will imply that indoctrination has no place in education. This point will be difficult to make, given a robust conception of education, its processes, methods, and aims or goals. This robust sense of education also underscores the problem with the distinction between education and indoctrination, and the circularity of the argument in favor of education, which is based on the absolute value that is placed on cognitive autonomy and epistemic individualism. The implausibility of this idea of education that is devoid of indoctrination is suggested by Bruce Suttle's point that, "educators must convey to the students the need to believe in the intrinsic value of human rationality."[47] He notes that the rational persuasion that is needed to convey this message is effective only if one accepts without question the value of rationality.

In other words, if a person does not already internalize or have a general rational attitude or a willingness to adopt a rational point of view, no rational argument would be effective in convincing him that he ought to be rational. Usually, one is indoctrinated to adopt a rational attitude, which then provides a necessary basis for education. Suttle goes on to argue that, "the assertion that human rationality has intrinsic value is similar to introducing a mathematical axiom—neither can be supported by more fundamental reasons and evidence."[48] However, the acceptance or assumption—without proof—of the intrinsic value of rationality is necessary for us to argue that people should be educated in order to be able to think for themselves. This seems to underscore why no arguments are usually offered to support the intrinsic value and worth of human rationality and autonomy; this is simply presupposed. Based on this presupposition, people construe education as the efforts to enhance autonomy and rationality, and educators proceed in their methods and pedagogy to ensure that students develop their cognitive abilities to independently use their rational faculties to think for themselves. The important point is that there is a sense in which people may have to be indoctrinated about the intrinsic value of rationality and autonomy or the plausibility of epistemic individualism in order to be educated.

Suttle argues that, "not only are educators actually not desirous of having the students question the assumed or posited intrinsic value of human rationality, but furthermore, it is actually impossible for the students to question the value of developing and using their rational capacities."[49] Since educators cannot prove to students that rationality or cognitive autonomy has intrinsic worth and value, the conclusion would be that "if educators desire students to believe that they ought to want to develop and utilize their rational capacities, then educators may very well have to indoctrinate the students in this belief."[50] Perhaps, the cognitive or rational idea of education, which is based on the goal of optimizing cognitive autonomy via critical thinking and independent reasoning, is indeed founded on the idea of indoctrinating students to believe that rationality or cognitive autonomy is intrinsically valuable. At least, the process of making people to care or to be passionate about rationality and rational processes cannot, and usually, is not in itself a rational process. Such process involves elements of unquestioning and blind acceptance of certain principles or attitudes. As such, in alluding to Charles Bailey's view about how children come to care and be passionate about rationality and rational processes, Suttle argues that the processes of molding attitudes and other non-rational affections that are necessary for caring about rationality in order to be rational, necessarily involve subtle forms of indoctrination.[51]

Besides the processes, goal, intent, outcome, and methods of imparting beliefs, some argue that another important basis for making the distinction between education and indoctrination is the nature of the subject matter. So, in order to be indoctrinated in this sense, the subject matter must be superstitious, ideological, dogmatic, and doctrinaire. The issue of what constitutes an ideology, dogma, superstition, or a doctrine is problematic because what is considered ideology may be contingent on one's assumptions, which may be questionable.[52] For instance, in the United States of America, some think that the contents of the Bill of Rights that guarantee various freedoms, may be said to be ideological dogmas or doctrines that many people accept without question. Many Americans are indoctrinated, especially as children in elementary school about the belief that they have absolute rights to freedom. They are also made to believe that freedom is an absolute value and that this value is the basis for patriotism and American citizenship. Many people, including politicians, accept these beliefs and proclaim them without critically examining their import. People claim, in a rather doctrinaire manner, that the US is a land of freedom and that everyone in the US is free. No matter the war the armed forces are fighting, people believe that the armed forces are fighting to protect their freedom. The dogmatic and doctrinaire nature of these beliefs about freedom and rights are made poignant by the rise of militias, who want to base their questionable views of their rights or the role of government on the provisions of the Bill of Rights. They believe that they have absolute rights to own guns and to overthrow the government by force, if they feel that the government is threatening their unreasonable beliefs or claims about their rights and freedoms. The essential point is that this kind of doctrinaire acceptance or indoctrination is partly essential for people to be educated about their rights and to be passionate about them, in order to sustain the social and political systems.

Some people also argue that the distinction between indoctrination and education make sense when we distinguish between the normative disciplines of morality, religion, and politics, which have dogmas, ideologies, and doctrines, and the disciplines of mathematics, science, and logic, which do not have dogmas or doctrines. The distinction between the subject matter of science (or mathematics or logic) and other kinds of beliefs is relevant to many of the criticisms of beliefs, thoughts, and ideas in African cultures. Wiredu and Appiah suggest that beliefs in African cultures are taught as dogmas and doctrines that are founded on religion, hence they lend themselves to group thought, superstitions, and indoctrination.[53] They also argue that many traditional African beliefs must be replaced with scientific beliefs that lend themselves to critical inquiry and the ability to think for oneself. They argue that Africans need to get rid of dogmatic and superstitious beliefs and the anachronistic practices that are conducive to these beliefs in order to develop and modernize. This argument and the critique of thought systems and education in African cultures assume that indoctrination cannot occur in such domains as science, logic, and mathematics, where the subject matter does not involve dogmatic beliefs. The idea is that the beliefs and statements in these disciplines can be objectively determined to be true.

The contrast between education and indoctrination, which is based on subject matter or contents, with respect to dogmas, ideologies, and doctrines, suggests that indoctrination is always avoidable in the processes of education in certain disciplines and subject matter such as mathematics, logic, and science, but are unavoidable in such disciplines as morality, politics, and religion. According to Atkinson, the fact that there are no clear criteria for truth regarding some moral issues may provide a reasonable basis for accepting some amount of moral indoctrination of children about certain moral principles.[54] For instance, if we cannot determine the truth of the statement: 'it is bad to curse', then we have to indoctrinate children to simply accept this statement as something they must use to guide their conduct. In order to have the proper moral upbringing, we have to accept certain principles without question as a basis for determining what is reasonable in certain contexts. If we have to question and consider the evidence for all our beliefs, such that if we do not have evidence for all of them, we will not believe them or use them as a basis for action, then life would be impossible and boring. It is pertinent to indicate that a moderate form of indoctrination is not only necessary in moral, social, and political education, but it is necessary for education in general in order to achieve the social aims of education and to be sensitive to social needs or goals, and the social context of knowledge, evidence, and justification.

A belief, which is the subject matter of education, is reasonable to hold, for instance, only if it is the case that when the socially and humanly available relevant alternatives, facts, and evidence are presented to a rational and sensible person, such a person would accept it. However, it must be borne in mind that what one considers to be *relevant alternatives*, facts, and evidence are circumscribed by a human, social, and cultural context and circumstance. In which case, it will be necessary for a rational person to make sure that his accepted beliefs are confirmed, corroborated, or not defeated by other people's beliefs in the social context.[55] It is the goal of education to enhance such social and communal rationality. Hence, Pincoffs argues that "Education . . . consists in instructing in such a way that the certainty with which a doctrine is taught is directly related to the publicly-acceptable evidence available for its support."[56] The goals and processes of education and the rationality of the beliefs, practices, and principles in traditional African cultures depended on their natural and social conditions.

This natural and social view of beliefs, knowledge, and education is underscored by Thomas Kuhn.[57] He recognizes that the social context and needs of science and science education require that science be seen, in part, as a practice that involves practitioners who rely on principles, traditions, rules, customs, and norms, training by mentors or experts, and the use of paradigms for solving relevant problems. The goals of science for Kuhn to which science education should be sensitive involve, (a) increasing and making progress in knowledge by engaging in critical inquiry, i.e., with respect to revolutionary science, and (b) helping to explain anomalies and solve puzzles or practical problems that confront human beings in their lives, i.e., with respect to normal science. Kuhn argues that education with respect to normal science involves being socialized, acculturated, and assimilated into a certain tradition based on an 'accepted' paradigm without critically questioning the paradigm. According to Kaufman,

> if Thomas Kuhn's views about the nature of normal science are correct, then there are long stretches of time during which it is desirable to discourage the overwhelming majority of budding scientists from cultivating a taste for autonomous inquiry. For, according to Kuhn, achievement in doing normal science depends, not primarily on creative departure, but on assimilation and application of what he calls 'the textbook tradition'. I do not claim that Kuhn is right: only that his arguments are sufficiently cogent that we cannot foreclose the possibility that a specialized zeal among scientists for probing first principles and presuppositions may, on the whole, be undesirable during specific periods of

time.[58]

The person who is 'educated' or socialized or indoctrinated in the 'the textbook tradition' of the practice of normal science accepts the paradigm without question, at least in some sense, because it has already been accepted and entrenched as an effective means of solving puzzles. Anyone who is educated in this practice simply learns how to use the paradigm or tradition to solve puzzles or practical problems.

If Kuhn's view about normal science is reasonable, then it is plausible that the criticisms of African traditions—as authoritarian, indoctrinating, and inhibiting of individuals' autonomy—based on the scientific model, are problematic. This is because critics like Bodunrin, Appiah, and Wiredu have over exaggerated the critical, rational, and autonomous nature of science and its relationship with philosophy. In my view, the plausible idea that is described by Kuhn's normal science education and practice captures the practice and education in African cultures, where children are initially socialized into the accepted cultural practices and norms. Later on, as they become older and have mastered the norms and practices, and have a wealth of experience, they can be more critical and autonomous in their thinking. This is the reason why, in Wiredu's view elders were not afraid to criticize African traditions. This is also one of the reasons that African cultures have undergone changes and modifications. Therefore, the kind of education or initial mild indoctrination into normal science, which characterizes many communal African traditions and the informal processes of education, does not necessarily prevent people from cultivating the attitude, habit, or taste for questioning or autonomous critical inquiry that underlies the rational conception of education and Kuhn's idea of extraordinary science.

Kuhn's account of 'normal' science education, which is also captured by many views of moral, social, and political education, gives credence to what Frankena calls the 'conservative view of education'. This conservative idea of education involves "the cultivation of dispositions *already* regarded as desirable by society [or at least by a group of practitioners or those in a discipline] by methods *already* regarded as satisfactory."[59] This conservative idea of education, which seems to capture what, in fact, practical educators do, is, in my view, a necessary element of a robust sense of education that seeks to enhance the wholesome growth and development of a person's social awareness, moral and aesthetic sensibilities, emotional well-being, character, and rational or cognitive abilities. This conservative view education indicates that it is necessary for a student to master and accept without question certain principles of science in order to acquire science education. The idea of conservative education is given credence by the distinction between *pure* and *applied* science. For instance, the practice of applied science may require an engineer to use a scientific theory or principle to design and built a bridge. He may accept such a theory, without being willing to critically examine whether the theory is formally valid or adequate, and whether there is a better theory. He may accept it because it is accepted by others in the profession and it is part of the practice, and for this person, the only justification for this principle is the fact that it serves his practical purposes in the social context and community of practitioners. One is, to some extent, indoctrinated to accept this as a principle in the community, as a part of the practice.

## Indoctrination, Education, and Practical Knowledge

The process by which an applied scientist may learn practices and principles in the discipline or community of practitioners may be described as a moderate process of indoctrination. However, the theoretical physicist may be able to prove and engage others in a debate with respect to whether or not a scientific principle or theory is formally valid, but this may not, as a practical matter, concern a civil engineer in so far as the bridge he designs and builds is functional and strong. It is not unlikely that an engineer may be cherished and appreciated more than the theoretical physicist: this may represent the social and practical reality and the goal of education in the world we live in. To some extent, there is a sense in which this kind of practical knowledge was also cherished and appreciated in traditional African cultures. Moreover, for many Africans, philosophy was a practice. Perhaps, a theoretician who wants to simply ask and examine theoretical questions may not be appreciated in traditional African cultures. This is a plausible reason why the critical examination of ideas and beliefs was not dominant. As Wiredu indicates, the kind of knowledge that was thought about, taught, and emphasized in African cultures was of a practical kind.[60] However, he argues that Africa must emphasize the disciplines of science, mathematics, and logic because they are not subject to indoctrination. As such, these disciplines are said to be helpful in enhancing people's rational abilities and cognitive development.

One may argue that the distinction between normative disciplines, where there are dogmas and doctrines, and non-normative disciplines, where there are absolute and objective truths ,is dubious. In every discipline or subject matter, there are core doctrines or dogmas that are fundamental, which one must accept or be indoctrinated about, and there are other peripheral beliefs that can be critically examined. As such, the effort to use this distinction as a basis for characterizing a subject matter that is amenable to either indoctrination or education is also dubious. In other words, it is not necessarily true that moral principles are always uncertain and without objective proof, nor is it necessarily true that mathematical statements or scientific beliefs are capable of being absolutely true. Some people have argued, for instance, that some moral principles or statements are synthetic *a priori*. That is, some moral principles are substantive statements about the world, yet their truths are capable of being known prior to or independent of experience. Some have argued that the moral statement: 'it is bad to kill babies for fun' is absolutely or objectively true, in that such truth is not a matter of personal or cultural preference. Many scientists also thought the idea that, peptic ulcer is caused by stomach acids was absolutely true until Dr. Marshall discovered that ulcer is caused by *H-pyroli* bacteria. The proposition that an atom is the smallest particle of an element was thought to be absolutely true until it was discovered that an atom can be split into parts. Many scientists would readily admit that beliefs, theories, or propositions that are said to be well established in science can be proven to be false. So, the principles of rationality and objectivity would seem to apply equally to the domains of morality and science. According to the principle of epistemic fallibilism, many of our beliefs must be held to be only conditionally true given the evidence. In order for children to be educated to develop their rational abilities in logic, mathematics, and science, so that they can examine evidence and think for themselves, they have to be indoctrinated about the idea that rationality and the rational methods or principles of inquiry and reasoning in logic, mathematics and science are intrinsically valuable. Moreover, they will have to be indoctrinated about the truth of certain axioms, posits, postulates, and the existence of theoretical entities. The fact that one must be indoctrinated about axioms, principles, and intrinsic value of rationality, that is, the ability to think for oneself, even within these disciplines, seems to indicate that indoctrination cannot be avoided in any discipline, even science, mathematics, and logic.

Without internalizing some basic concepts, beliefs, attitudes, and principles, a person being educated cannot develop the requisite rational abilities, the critical attitude, and habit of the mind that are necessary for approaching any subject matter. The relevant concepts, beliefs, principles, and attitudes become a part of their conceptual scheme and the foundation for reasoning any discipline. Snook seems to disagree with this point by arguing that the internalization of certain attitudes, the adoption of certain concepts and language, and the acceptance of certain doctrines, principles, formulae, axioms, and postulates that are necessary for education "may seem like indoctrination, but . . . [they] are not since they are unavoidable."[61] Pincoffs also argues that the kind of "moral training which forms character in early childhood in such a way that certain questions do not arise, is not necessarily moral indoctrination, but is in fact a necessary step in moral education."[62] The essential point here is that Snook and Pincoffs do not think that the ideas, principles, doctrines, and attitudes that we must accept or internalize without question involve indoctrination simply because they are practically unavoidable or necessary for the robust goal and purpose of education. The assumption is that simply because this indoctrinating kind of training does not involve extreme indoctrination such as brainwashing, it is not really indoctrination as such.

In my view, because the internalization of these fundamental principles, attitudes, and doctrines involve some elements of indoctrination—although not in the extreme sense—and, because they are unavoidable or necessary for education, it follows that indoctrination is a necessary aspect of education. However, indoctrination must be extreme to the extent of brainwashing in order to be bad. Indoctrination comes in degrees and some degrees of indoctrination are necessary for education, hence indoctrination is a necessary aspect or an essential element of education. Thus, one cannot plausibly make a logical distinction between indoctrination and education, but one can make a logical distinction between brainwashing and education. Therefore, the relevant issue is not whether there exists an element of indoctrination in the communal and informal model of education in traditional African cultures, but the extent or degree of indoctrination. The form of indoctrination that Wiredu criticizes in African cultures, in my view, is not the extreme form, and it is not different in degree or quality, from the unavoidable form of indoctrination that is necessary for a robust form of education that can engender a meaningful sense of autonomy, critical attitude, and rationality. Kaufman points out that in spite of Frankena's emphasis on cognitive autonomy as the goal of education, throughout his essay, he also "expresses the conviction that a student may properly be subjected to authoritative discipline by his elders. The elders generally know, better than a student himself, what best serves his interests in respect to autonomy."[63] In African cultures, elders have a responsibility to provide a robust education that involves the authoritative discipline that is necessary for a child to develop into adult personhood. A robust education in the African communal context, includes moral education, acculturation, everyday upbringing, and the practical development of the normative and wholesome sense of personhood. This sense of personhood, as a conceptual scheme, circumscribes, limits, or shapes one's beliefs, options, life plans, choices, and reasoning.

So, the social and communal goal of education and the practical nature of knowledge may have engendered the model of education that necessitated a moderate form of indoctrination. The fact that people are initially indoctrinated about some ideas does not vitiate their overall rational abilities. One can be indoctrinated about certain beliefs that form the foundation for one's knowledge but may not be indoctrinated about how one uses those beliefs to generate other beliefs. To underscore this point, consider that a scientist may use scientific methods in her scientific work but may not use them in some practical or other spheres of her lives; she may believe in God without seeking scientific proof for the existence of God. Some medical doctors believe in the ability of the mind to heal bodily ailments and the possibility of divine healing. These beliefs cannot be proven by the canons of scientific test and experimentation. So, one could be moderately indoctrinated about certain beliefs and not others. For instance, as practical or commonsense thinkers, people in African cultures may be indoctrinated about the principles of induction and the regularity of nature and they may internalize them based on experience. They use these principles in practical reasoning, and as the basis for organizing their lives, and for understanding their experiences. They accept these principles and use them based on the attitude or habit of the mind that they developed from indoctrination, everyday experiences, imitation, and informal upbringing. They cannot find any rational proof for these principle and the basis for their attitudes besides their own experiences. These experiences and habits by themselves presuppose the principles of induction and the regularity of nature. Their habit of mind or attitude suggests that they are indoctrinated.

Moreover, when a traditional African man leaves his house in the morning, he goes straight to the farm or garden with the plan of going to tend to his crops, without any thought that his farm may not be there. When he leaves his farm, he goes straight home without any thought that his house, wife, and children will not be there. This person or other people in the culture may not necessarily be indoctrinated about the other beliefs that the principles of induction and regularity of nature lead them to believe. They may critically examine whether the other beliefs they accept are necessarily supported by evidence or the principle of induction and regularity of nature that they already accept. One may be indoctrinated about a method such that the resulting attitude, disposition, or habit involves that ability to, in general, use that method consistently and in a wholesale manner regarding all beliefs. One may also be indoctrinated about a particular method for acquiring belief and one may use such method or display the relevant attitude in a discriminating manner, by applying it to some beliefs but not others. In which case, one is indoctrinated about a method for acquiring certain beliefs or subject matter but one may not use the same method that indicates indoctrination with respect to other beliefs or subject matter. For instance, I can decide to use the critical and rigorous method of examining evidence and the ability to think for myself when I am confronted with beliefs that involve abstract ideas or general principles, say, when I am doing philosophy. However, I may not engage this method when confronted with practical issues involving how I should act morally in a specific situation that requires me to show preferential treatment toward my son or on issues relating to religion, my ordinary dealings with people that I trust such as my friends, or in my dealings with some beliefs about mundane things and ideas that I think are self-evident.

According to Wiredu's criticism, the indoctrinating implication of the African idea of education and upbringing is that one's scope of reasoning is limited. But this implication is not different from the general implication of education. For instance, to be educated in science means adopting the conceptual scheme of science, which may, to a certain extent, circumscribe and limit one's reasoning only to empirical facts. In the same way, the conceptual scheme of religion may also, to a certain extent, limit or shape one's reasoning toward the transcendental or spiritual. Irrespective of how rigorous science claims to be, to be educated in science is, to some extent, to limit and shape our rationality to focus on the empirical world. Thus, if we assume that scientific and spiritual realms are contradictories or contraries, then accepting the principles of science implies discrediting the principles of spirituality. To the extent that even the rigorous method of science could, to a certain extent, limit our rationality to certain spheres of reasoning and inquiry, it does involve an element of indoctrination that is necessary for education in science. So, to be robustly educated in or about X is to limit one's sphere inquiry and the method of inquiry or reasoning to the realm of X, sometimes, to the exclusion of the realm of Y, because the realms of X and Y or the claims associated with each are either contraries or contradictories. To limit the sphere of inquiry is, to some extent, to limit one's rationality. To limit one's rationality to a sphere of inquiry is, in some sense, to indoctrinate one to exclude other spheres of inquiry from the realm of rationality. Scientists are indoctrinated not to take the realm of metaphysics seriously in their inquiries. To be indoctrinated in this sense of accepting ideas that limit one's sphere of inquiry involves acquiring certain attitudes and accepting doctrines or principles that may vitiate or limit rationality and cognitive autonomy.

The pertinent issues here is, whether if I hold a doctrine or falsehood or adopt a method or exhibit an attitude or habit of mind in one sphere of my life that involves indoctrination, but I do not exhibit the same attitude in other spheres of my life or with respect to other beliefs, am I necessarily indoctrinated? In other words, do I have to be indoctrinated across the board in all areas of my life in order for me to be regarded as indoctrinated? Must indoctrination be a thoroughgoing process in order for someone to be regarded strictly as indoctrinated? Can one be educated about some ideas and indoctrinated about others? Is it the case that education cannot coexist with indoctrination? Is it possible that our whole set of beliefs can be so strictly compartmentalized into rational and irrational beliefs? These questions are pertinent because they would need to be answered in order to evaluate the distinction between education and indoctrination and the criticisms of African cultures. These questions do illuminate Wiredu's criticism of African communal traditions. It is my view that people are not indoctrinated across the board but are indoctrinated about some matters as an unavoidable basis for education. The extent of indoctrination does not involve brainwashing, and as such, the mode of education is not necessarily bad. Wiredu suggests that people in African cultures were indoctrinated across the board in all their beliefs and that there was a thoroughgoing process and principle of indoctrination in the African communal traditions.

My answers to these questions also indicate that the distinction between indoctrination and education does not make sense in the communal African traditions to warrant the criticisms that their mode of education necessarily involves indoctrination. It is clear that one cannot criticize African communal cultures of indoctrinating people across the board on all ideas and beliefs. Moreover, an examination of

African communal living may reveal that the spheres of activities and beliefs to which education and indoctrination apply in African traditions intersect. From the discussion of the different views regarding the nature of indoctrination, those who make the distinction between indoctrination and education insist that each of the features of indoctrination (content, intention, method, and attitudes) or a conjunction of the features may be sufficient but not necessary for one to indicate that indoctrination is bad or that indoctrination does not involve education. But given the problems that I have identified with these features, they are not jointly or each sufficient to indicate that indoctrination is bad or that one is not educated. As such, it is not clear, precisely, what indoctrination means or involves, and since we do not know what it involves or means, it is difficult to indicate that it is necessarily bad simply because it has the feature of impeding the ability of an individual to think for himself. As such, we cannot use this feature to distinguish between indoctrination and education.

# Notes

1. Wiredu, *Philosophy and African Culture*, 2-3.

2. Wiredu, *Philosophy and African Culture*, 11.

3. Appiah, *Necessary Questions: An Introduction to Philosophy*, 202.

4. Appiah, *Necessary Questions: An Introduction to Philosophy*, 202-203, and *In My Father's House: Africa in the Philosophy of Culture*, 130-131.

5. Wiredu, *Philosophy and African Culture*, p. 4.

6. Wiredu, *Philosophy and African Culture*, 15-16.

7. John Wilson, "Indoctrination and Rationality," in *Concepts of Indoctrination*, ed., I. A. Snook (London: Routledge & Kegan Paul, 1972), 23 (emphasis is mine).

8. T. F. Green, *The Activities of Teaching* (New York: McGraw-Hill, 1971).

9. John Wilson, "Education and Indoctrination," in *Aims in Education: The Philosophical Approach*, ed., T. H. B. Hollins (Manchester: Manchester University Press, 1964), 24-46.

10. Anthony Flew, "What is Indoctrination?" *Studies in Philosophy and Education*, Vol. 4, No. 3 (1966): 281-306.

11. T. F. Green, "Indoctrination and Beliefs," in *Concepts of Indoctrination: Philosophical Essays*, ed., I. A. Snook, 25-46.

12. Green, "Indoctrination and Beliefs," 25.

13. Green, "Indoctrination and Beliefs," 37.

14. I. A. Snook, *Indoctrination and Education* (London: Routledge & Kegan Paul, 1972), 47.

15. R. M. Hare, "Adolescents into Adults," in *Aims in Education: The Philosophical Approach*, ed., in T. H. B. Hollins, 47-70.

16. Wilson, "Education and Indoctrination," 24-46.

17. Wiredu, *Philosophy and An African Culture*, 21.

18. For Kohlberg's theory see his "Stages of Moral Development as a Basis of Moral Education," in *Moral Education: Interdisciplinary Approaches*, eds., C. Beck, B. Crittendon, and E. Sullivan (Toronto: University of Toronto Press, 1971), *Essays on Moral Development: Vol. 1--The Philosophy of Moral Development* (New York: Harper & Row, 1981), and *Essays on Moral Development: Vol. 2--The Philosophy of Moral Development* (New York: Harper & Row, 1984).

19. Edmund L. Pincoffs, "On Avoiding Moral Indoctrination," in *Educational Judgments*, ed., James F. Doyle (London: Routledge & Kegan Paul, 1973), p. 62.

20. Pincoffs, "On Avoiding Moral Indoctrination," 62.

21. Pincoffs, "On Avoiding Moral Indoctrination," 61-65.

22. Wilson, "Indoctrination and Rationality," p. 17.

23. William Frankena, "The Concept of Education Today," in *Educational Judgments*, ed., James F. Doyle (London: Routledge & Kegan Paul, 1973), 19-32.

24. James F. Doyle, "Introduction," in *Educational Judgments*, ed., James F. Doyle, 5, in his summary of Anold S. Kaufman, "Comments on Frankena's 'The Concept of Education Today'," in *Educational Judgments*, 46-55.

25. The criticism that liberalism represents a cultural value or artifact that is presupposed as necessarily valid has been articulated by Bhikhu Parekh "Dilemmas of a Multicultural Theory of Citizenship," *Constellations* 4, no. 1 (1997): 54-62 and Rainer Forst, "Foundations of a Theory of Multicultural Justice," *Constellations* 4, no. 1 (1997): 63-71. The value of autonomy is plausible in the context of the modern European values of individualism, rationalism, liberalism, and the rejection of Catholic dogmas and authoritarianism.

26. See Vitz,"The Use of Stories in Moral Development: New Psychological Reasons for an Old Education Method," Noddings, "Conversation as Moral Education," Robinson and Hawpe, "Narrative Thinking As A Heuristic Process," Sarbin, "The Narrative as a Root Metaphor for Psychology,"

27. Haste, "Communitarianism and the Social Construction of Morality," 47-55.

28. Wilson, "Indoctrination and Rationality," 23 (emphasis is mine).

29. Wiredu, *Philosophy and an African Culture*, p. 11.

30. For this distinction, see I. A. Snook, *Indoctrination and Education*, 104-106. Snook argues that conditioning is concerned with behavior, indoctrination with beliefs, and education is concerned with the honorific process or manner of transmitting knowledge. However, there is a sense in which conditioning and indoctrination are processes of transmitting beliefs. Moreover, the conditioning of someone to behave in a particular way is based on some 'accepted' beliefs.

31. Bertrand Russell, *Education and the Social Order* (London: Allen & Unwin, 1967), 18.

32. Alan Gewirth, "Morality and Autonomy in Education," in *Educational Judgments*, ed., James F. Doyle (London: Routledge & Kegan Paul, 1973), 33-35.

33. Wiredu, *Philosophy and an African Culture*, 5.

34. Wiredu, *Cultural Universals and Particulars*, 71.

35. Willis Moore, "Indoctrination and Democratic Method," in *Concepts of Indoctrination: Philosophical Essays*, ed., I. A. Snook (London: Routledge & Kegan Paul, 1972), 97.

36. David Annis, "The Social and Cultural Component of Epistemic Justification--A Reply," *Philosophia* 12 (1982): 52-53.

37. Wiredu seems to appreciate some of these various human natural and social features that are universal and particular. See Kwasi Wiredu, *Cultural Universals and Particulars: An African Perspective*, chapters 3 & 4.

38. Wiredu, *Philosophy and An African Culture*, p. 11.

39. Gewirth, "Morality and Autonomy in Education," 37-38.

40. Gewirth, "Morality and Autonomy in Education," 36.

41. Gewirth, "Morality and Autonomy in Education," 38 (emphasis is mine).

42. Gewirth, "Morality and Autonomy in Education,"38.

43. Frankena, "The Concept of Education Today," 30.

44. Henri I. Marrou, *A History of Education in Antiquity*, translated by George Lamb (New York: The New American Library, 1964), xiii.

45. Bertrand Russell, *Mysticism and Logic* (London: Allen & Unwin, 1917), 37.

46. For a detailed discussion, see John Hardwig, "Evidence, Testimony, and the Problem of Individualism--A Response to Schmitt," *Social Epistemology* 2, no. 4 (1988): 309-321.

47. Bruce B. Suttle, "The Need for and Inevitability of Moral Indoctrination," *Educational Studies* 12, no. 2 (1981): 155.

48. Suttle, "The Need for and Inevitability of Moral Indoctrination," 155.

49. Suttle, "The Need for and Inevitability of Moral Indoctrination," 155.

50. Suttle, "The Need for and Inevitability of Moral Indoctrination," 155.

51. Suttle, "The Need for and Inevitability of Moral Indoctrination," 156, and the reference to Charles Bailey, "Morality, Reason and Feeling," *Journal of Moral Education* 9 (1980):121.

52. The three categories or cases that Snook discusses in "Indoctrination and Moral Responsibility," in *Concepts of Indoctrination: Philosophical Essays*, ed., I. A. Shook (London: Routledge & Kegan Paul, 1972), 152 & 158 indicate this, especially, when it is not clear what may be regarded as ideology, and what in certain situations are uncertain, untrue, and unjustified.

53. Wiredu, *Philosophy and an African Culture*, especially 1-25, 37-50; Appiah, *In My Father's House*, 107-136.

54. R. F. Atkinson, "Indoctrination and Moral Education," in *Concepts of Indoctrination: Philosophical Essays*, ed., I. A. Shook (London: Routledge & Kegan Paul, 1972), 55-66.

55. See Annis, "A Contextual Theory of Epistemic Justification," Dretske, "The Pragmatic Dimension of Knowledge," Harman, Thought, Goldman, "Discrimination and Perceptual Knowledge," Lehrer and Paxson, Jr., "Knowledge: Undefeated Justified True

Belief," and Klein, "A Proposed Definition of Knowledge Propositional Knowledge."

56. Pincoffs, "On Avoiding Moral Indoctrination," 72.

57. Kuhn, *The Structure of Scientific Revolutions*.

58. Anold S. Kaufman, "Comments on Frankena's 'The Concept of Education Today'," in *Educational Judgments*, ed., James Doyle (Routledge & Kegan Paul, 1973), 51.

59. Frankena, "The Concept of Education Today," 22-23.

60. Wiredu, *Cultural Universals and Particulars*, 68 He also indicates in *Philosophy and An African Culture*, 16, that there was close connection between philosophy and practical life or the day-to-day living of the African people.

61. Snook, "Indoctrination and Moral Responsibility," 152.

62. Pincoffs, "On Avoiding Moral Indoctrination," 72.

63. Kaufman, "Comments on Frankena's 'The Concept of Education Today'," 55.

# Chapter Seven

# Reflections on Communalism, Responsibility, and Liberal Criticisms

The major criticism of African communal traditions and its thought system is that it is authoritarian in various aspects of people's lives: in morality, political, and social, and in the acquisition or justification of beliefs. This kind of authoritarianism, it is argued, is bad because it involves irrationality, and it impedes individuals' rational and cognitive autonomy. Moreover, many of the beliefs and values that people hold are doctrines and dogmas that elders and tradition have dictated, and they are accepted without critical examination or proper evidence. The communal and authoritarian structures of African traditions and the dogmatic nature of their beliefs and doctrines make ideas readily suitable for indoctrination. Not only are most African beliefs doctrinaire and dogmatic in nature, but the communal context and authoritarian structures, in terms of the respect that is accorded to elders and traditions, also indicate that these beliefs cannot be questioned and critically examined. In other words, the dogmatic beliefs and communal context or structures and the informal methods and processes of inculcating and imparting knowledge or acquiring beliefs do not allow people to think for themselves, question beliefs, or critically examine evidence. People simply are indoctrinated via everyday upbringing into the communal modes of living, values, and beliefs, and they act in accordance with such principles and values that they have internalized. Usually, people do not have the ability or opportunity to consider reasonable alternatives, in order to make rational choices and autonomous decisions. As such, Africa does not have a philosophy. Moreover, a philosophical system of thought cannot be created out of dogmatic and doctrinaire ideas, authoritarian context and structures, and indoc-

257

trinating informal methods and processes. And because the communal context and authoritarian process seem to vitiate or impede individual rational autonomy, it is questionable whether people can be characterized as rational moral agents who are capable of making adequate moral choices. If it is reasonable to say that they are not rational moral agents in this sense, it also questionable whether they can be characterized as responsible moral agents.

## Communalism, Responsibility, and Moral Ignorance

A person is said to have acted morally only if she is rational and autonomous, in that she is able to act voluntarily based on her evaluation of the moral goodness or badness of the act. If her action is deemed to be morally bad, then she is considered blameworthy and held responsible. The notions of responsibility and blameworthiness presuppose that a person acted rationally by considering the reasons for her action, and that she acted voluntarily, in that she had options and made her own choices and decisions, and was not compelled by an external factor beyond her control. Wiredu's characterizations of the ideas of authoritarianism, communalism, and moral indoctrination that he criticizes in African cultures imply that people in such communities do not act rationally, voluntarily, and autonomously, and as such, they cannot be held responsible for their actions. In Wiredu's view, the features of authoritarianism in African cultures imply that, those people are made to do something against their will, the development of their will is impeded, their will is unjustifiable overridden by others, especially by elders, and people's wills are usually the result of manipulation by others.[1] For Wiredu, these features also indicate that people are indoctrinated because their minds are molded in such a way that there are built-in or predetermined choices.[2] Although it may appear is if an indoctrinated person is making free choices, the choices are really not free because they are superficial, in the sense that the choices are, in some sense, determined and built into the molding of the mind with respect to the contents of their beliefs and the methods or processes of imparting, inculcating, and internalizing them. In other words, African beliefs and moral principles or values, as well as the methods of inculcating them, imply that people are not given meaningful and relevant alternatives. In his view, no meaningful choices can be made in the absence of relevant alternatives.

To summarize, the implication of Wiredu's criticism of communalism, authoritarianism, and indoctrination in African cultures is that people cannot make rational choices because they have no alternatives and their wills are manipulated by others. In other words, based on authoritarianism and indoctrination, people's actions are based on external compulsion and the absence of choices. Hence, people cannot be held responsible for their moral actions, because they lack rational autonomy. In

Wiredu's view, people may be said to be morally ignorant about the rational moral choices that they independently, individually, and autonomously ought to make. Such ignorance is fundamentally induced by the cultural communal and authoritarian processes and structures, and the doctrinaire and dogmatic beliefs, which prevent people from seeing alternatives regarding right and wrong, and from making the proper choices about what is morally right. Wiredu's view implies the cultural view of the moral inability thesis: the idea that the culture in which one is raised may make one unable to know right from wrong in order to be able to make the proper choice between right and wrong. Based on the dogmatic contents of African beliefs or the communal, informal, authoritarian, and indoctrinating context, structures, methods of inculcating beliefs or values and processes of acculturation, Wiredu seems to be arguing that African people's cultures induce moral ignorance to the extent that they are prevented from knowing right from wrong. This idea of culturally induced moral ignorance is, as indicated, based on Wiredu's view that African cultures prevent one from seeing relevant moral alternatives, engaging in adequate reasoning, and making rational moral choices or decisions on the basis of one's own reasoning.

However, as a philosophical issue, two points or issues are pertinent here: (1) Is it reasonable to argue, philosophically, that a culture may induce moral ignorance to the extent of vitiating or mitigating responsibility? (2) Does the characterization or criticism of African communal culture imply that it may induce moral ignorance to vitiate rational moral agency and responsibility? Regarding the first issue, Michael Slote, Alan Donagan, and Susan Wolf seem to argue that it is plausible for a culture to induce moral ignorance and such ignorance may be said to vitiate or mitigate responsibility.[3] They argue that, in some sense, people may simply be unable to know right from wrong, and hence may not be held responsible, because of their cultural upbringing, which thus induces moral ignorance. For instance, Slote in his view, analyzes how the Greek culture culminated in the moral inability of slave owners to see the wrongness of slavery. Wolf also analyzes the various social circumstances that engendered people to own slaves in the 1850's, the Nazi regime of the 1930's, and some male chauvinists of our fathers' generation. Donagan argues along the same line by analyzing the Nazi 'culture' in which military officers were trained under Hitler. He argues that the Nazi culture was different from the culture of Sandhurst and West Point, such that anyone trained under Hitler may not be as morally culpable regarding their responsibility to noncombatants as Sandhurst and West Point graduates. Not that the soldiers trained under Hitler are not culpable at all, but that their culpability is mitigated by the authoritarian and indoctrinating nature of their training and the dogmatic and doctrinaire nature of the contents of the ideas imparted on soldiers. These views, Michele Moody-Adams, calls the inability thesis about cultural impediments or moral ignorance.[4]

She argues that the inability thesis is implausible, and that the existence of cultural impediments cannot vitiate or mitigate the standard attribution of responsibility because the very existence of a culture presupposes the ability of the people in that culture to be rational, to act responsibly, and to accept social rules by which their culture or its legacy is perpetuated. Moody-Adams argues that the inability thesis about cultural limitations or its ability to induce moral ignorance implies that a culture can constitute serious impediments to responsible agency, such that widespread moral ignorance may be attributed to such cultural limitations and not the moral defects of individuals. Thus, culturally induced moral blindness would provide exculpatory excuses for an agent, such that it becomes reasonable to withhold blame for the agent's action. This idea of cultural limitation appears to be one implication or suggestion in Wiredu's characterization and criticism of the authoritarianism and indoctrination in African communal cultures. If this implication is correct, then Wiredu is suggesting that the African moral universe or thought does not allow for people to be blamed or held responsible for their actions. The communal, authoritarian, informal, and indoctrinating contents and context of moral principles and practices do not provide the rational, voluntary, and autonomous basis for ascribing responsibility. But Moody-Adams' argument against this idea that is suggested by Wiredu's characterization indicates that the relationship between culture and human agency cannot vitiate the ascription of responsibility to human actions, thus, the existence of cultural limitations cannot exempt anyone from responsibility. Moody-Adams argues that the idea underlying the inability thesis derives from some misunderstanding of the relationship between agency and culture, a misunderstanding that is evident in the criticisms of African communal cultures.

Although Moody-Adams does not directly address Wiredu's point about African cultures, her criticism of the moral inability thesis is relevant to my analysis of communalism in African cultures and my criticisms of Wiredu's views and characterization of African cultures. Moody-Adams argues that "A culture may be thought of as the way of life of a given social group, that will be shaped by more or less intricate patterns of normative expectations about emotion, thought, and action. These patterned expectations will typically take the form of social rules that give distinctive shape to the group's practices."[5] In this sense, she accepts the anthropological view that people are, indeed, shaped or influenced by the culture in which they are raised, because they have to internalize the normative social patterns of behavior which then shape and provide a rational basis for their behavior. This anthropological view suggests that there is a sense in which, as a broad form of education, socialization or acculturation, people are partly, and perhaps unavoidably, indoctrinated in their cultural ways of life that then shape and provide the rational basis for their actions. However, the problematic issue is whether any cultural form of education can involve an extreme form of indoctrination or brainwashing to the extent of vitiating people's rational autonomy. In particular, whether the African communal culture is so authoritarian that it extremely indoctrinates or brainwashes people to the extent of inducing moral ignorance. We must approach these issues from both a descriptive empirical stance and a theoretical, analytical, or philosophical stance.

We may approach these issues from both of the two stances by empirically and conceptually describing and analyzing African communal culture in order to determine whether it has authoritarian and indoctrinating structures or features that vitiate rationality and autonomy. We will then determine the extent to which the conceptual description or analysis matches the descriptive empirical features and structures of communal cultures. We can also empirically examine whether the actual practical outcome or result of these structures or features, necessarily involves the existence of people who are morally ignorant, and to whom one cannot ascribe responsibility. This will mean that we have to find a causal link between the authoritarian and indoctrinating structures and the resulting outcome, in terms of identifying people who have culturally induced moral ignorance. Such a causal link must be based on a causal generalization, which will conceptually indicate that the relevant structures must necessarily lead to the requisite outcome or result. The implication is that if we can find in the same cultural structures and context a few people who are morally ignorant, and at the same time, we find a large number of others who are not morally ignorant, then we cannot attribute the moral ignorance solely to the structures and context. We will have to theoretically and philosophically find some extraneous factors or variables beyond the cultural structures and context that may have contributed to the few people's moral ignorance. Philosophers argue that the extra factors reside in an individual's rational autonomy and free will. The anthropological assumption is that cultural factors are *a given* or constant that will, in general, shape people's actions and choices. However, if we find an overwhelming number of people who are morally ignorant, then we have a prima facie basis to think that the culture may be responsible for the ignorance.

However, the extent and degree to which culture may shape people's actions and choices will also depend on the cultural structures and how well they allow individuals to rationally use or apply the data, information, and principles that are supplied by the culture. This rational use of principles may be vitiated only in situations where the communal cultural structures are very oppressive and brutally imposing, such that they brainwash and turn individuals into automatons. In my view, it very unlikely that a culture can or has been able to do this. The empirical or psychological support for this view is that two people who are raised in the same culture or household may turn out to have different character traits or personality, and they usually behave differently and make different choices given the same situation. I have indicated that people in African communal cultures are not brainwashed to think or behave exactly the same way. The communal context and moral principles provide general parameters or guidelines for circumscribing alternatives and evidence. In that sense, these principles only generally shape people's behaviors, choices, and actions, in terms of delimiting, circumscribing, and making meaningful and relevant, the various alternatives from which they can choose. Communal principles usually do not and cannot shape behaviors, choices, and actions in a specific manner toward a particular and determinate result. These principles also give room for individuality, discretion, individual creativity, ingenuity, independence, originality, and differences in the application of moral principles to different situations.

Some of the proverbs, stories, and narratives alluded to earlier that are used to teach moral values and develop moral character and personality indicate that people's actions are not mechanically determined by the communal cultural structures, beliefs, and values. Hence, Africans do not have any problems in ascribing blame and responsibility when people act immorally. This is the reason why people who refuse to act in the proper manner are not recognized as having acquired moral personhood. The African idea of a person is acquired based on one's choices, decision, and discretion. The social recognition of a person is a recognition of an individual's autonomy and independence in making choices and decisions. So, if the general anthropological stance, which indicates that human actions may be broadly or generally shaped by cultures must presuppose the extreme processes of indoctrination, brainwashing, imposition, and oppression, then it would have serious implications for the idea of blaming, praising, and holding one responsible for one's actions. Any culture, which includes, in a wholesale and thoroughgoing sense, the extreme processes of indoctrination or brainwashing, would be problematic; it cannot be called a human culture in which human beings can meaningfully lead their lives and survive. Such a society or culture will be akin to a mechanistic system. Moody-Adams argues that a defensible connection between culture and human agency should not imply that cultural limitations or culturally induced moral ignorance may vitiate or mitigate responsibility. For her, being human involves being cultured, which involves internalizing accepted cultural principles. For her, "being 'encultured' is a condition of the possibility of responsible agency."[6] So, to be cultured or socialized in a culture is not necessarily to be brainwashed or forced to accept certain beliefs or ideas. Acculturation involves being educated (including brainwashing) in the broad sense of using informal means and achieving the three broad aims or goals of education, which involves developing individuals' abilities to be the best citizens, in order to benefit themselves and their community.

The point to note here is the connection that Moody-Adams makes between the normative social rules that underlie cultures and responsible agency, which depends, for the most part, on the cultural context of education. According to Moody-Adams' analysis, culture involves a set of enduring principles or a social legacy. Such legacy, which is the hallmark of a culture and its ability to persist or modify its rules and practices, assumes or ensures that individuals in the culture are capable of rational, imaginative, creative, and responsible actions, and that they are not individuals who have been 'programmed' by the culture to act in a specific manner. Such rational or responsible agency cannot come, in Moody-Adams' view, from authoritarian, imposing, or oppressive structures that involve brainwashing or extreme indoctrination; it can only come from a robust context or processes of education. In her words, "cultures persist only because individual persons capable of responsible action persist."[7] They are capable of choosing actions or principles that are encouraged or discouraged as marks of the culture; their responsibility culminates in their choice and acceptance of social principles—a choice that perpetuates such cultural legacy. The idea is that if people are really brainwashed in their culture, they would not be able to differentiate and decide between those actions or practices that should be encouraged or discouraged in their culture. The idea of differentiating or deciding between practices or principles that may be accepted, encouraged, or discouraged in a culture involves adopting an internal point of view. The ability to adopt an 'internal point of view' toward social rules is central to the life of a cultural group of people. This point of view involves a positive attitude toward a set of rules by members of the group who accept the rules, use them to evaluate and guide their conduct, and expect others to do the same.

Moreover, people in a culture use their internal point of view to demand conformity with their rules and the criticism of the disobedience of those rules. Thus, they are able to engage in self-criticism from such internal perspective, regarding the shortcomings of the rules, with the aim of modifying or changing them. People are also initiated. acculturated, educated, and socialized into these cultural principles and practices from this internal perspective. So, according to Moody-Adams, if we can determine that people can adopt an internal point of view as a relevant aspect of their culture, then it would be difficult if not impossible to rationally defend a plausible case of the moral inability thesis that arises from culturally induced moral ignorance. This is because the idea of brainwashing people and imposing beliefs on them would prevent them from evaluating principles, engaging in self-criticism, seeing shortcomings, and deciding whether or not to accept, perpetuate, or modify their principles and practices. Moody-Adams argues that, by virtue of our fallible human nature, every person has the capacity in any given circumstance to do wrong or irrational things. As such, it is not only and necessarily monsters or sick people or perhaps those who are brainwashed that do irrational, wrong or evil things. Thus, she suggests the banality of wrongdoing. Such banality derives from affected ignorance, which "is essentially a matter of choosing not to be informed of what we can and should know."[8] Such choice, by the way, involves a deliberate and rational decision, although it may be shaped by cultural and contextual factors.

The idea of affected ignorance indicates the difficulty or the amount of effort that is required to admit one's fault or fallibility, and to critically examine problematic cultural principles. The idea of affected ignorance also acknowledges the difficulty of adhering to moral principles and the unwillingness of people to accept their moral fault. People in general may do bad things if they can benefit, if it is the easy way out, and if they think that will not be caught. The idea of affected ignorance also indicates the weakness of human will. A culture may provide parameters that are difficult to adhere to, but we have to make tremendous efforts to overcome human difficulties in order to use the parameters to do good or acceptable things. As such, Moody-Adams argues that the inability thesis cannot be established solely on the basis of what exponents regard as simple empirical facts regarding the connection between agency and culture. We can see that the cultural principles that a group of people accepts may, depending on how individuals understand and use them, provide rational basis for doing either bad or good things. She questions the extent to which we can be sure that widespread moral ignorance is due solely to cultural limitations and not personal limitations, or that such limitation derives from extreme indoctrination or brainwashing or external manipulation, which Wiredu argues, may vitiate rational free choices. She argues that the common sense view underlying the inability thesis, which derives from the idea that it is only fair that we judge people by the standards of their time, does make sense. This view presupposes that moral ignorance or the way people act or see things may be shaped by their cultural principles and time, in terms of the options it makes available to us. But it also does not indicate that we cannot make bad choices among the options based on individual human failings. This idea is supported by the anthropological view that people are, in general, influenced or shaped by their cultural principles or environment. So, deciding the specific factors that contribute to moral ignorance or a bad choice is hardly a simple empirical matter.

In Moody-Adams' view, to rely solely on the empirical fact of cultural structures, processes, or impediments as a basis for explaining people's actions, beliefs, and values, and to blame cultures in the case of widespread moral ignorance, is to ignore the ways in which cultural conventions are reshaped, modified, and revised. A culture is perpetuated because of people's ability to use independent judgment, discretion, and creativity to make modifications in their actions as well as in the normative expectations of social rules. A culture cannot be perpetuated or survive if everyone is pressured or brainwashed to engage in 'group thinking' and to behave in predetermined ways that are specified by the culture such that they cannot use their rational creativity or imagination to adapt to different situations. Any culture that does not allow people to use their rational capacities and discretion to make judgments is doomed—it cannot be called a culture. These points made by Moody-Adams, regarding the nature of cultures, underscore my defense of the conception of personhood in traditional African cultures that is shaped by the community, rational epistemic authoritarianism, and the informal modes of education. So, in spite of the communal structures, the moderate elements of indoctrination, and rational authoritarianism in African cultures, it is reasonable to say that people are not brainwashed or compelled to act in a predetermined manner. The communal context allows individuals to use their rationality and creativity in applying and adapting cultural principles to various situations in ways that cannot be predetermined by the culture.

## Liberal Critique of Communalism

One cannot adequately sustain the view that traditional Africans cannot or do not think independently, critically, and logically or act rationally and autonomously because they have cultural structures or processes of education, socialization, and acculturation that involve a particular view of authoritarianism and extreme indoctrination or brainwashing. One also cannot sustain the view that African communal structures impede or discourage rational and creative thinking. This is because, if this view is true, then people would not be capable of acting rationally and responsibly. And it is clear that people did act rationally, creatively, and responsibly. If they did not, then they would not be able to act in a way that would perpetuate some aspects of their culture as a legacy or tradition, since they must do so by rejecting some principles and accepting others as reasonable basis for their actions. In order for people to have an identifiable culture, they must have the rationality to recognize their own needs or interests and the factors that enhance such needs or interests. Such recognition implies that they must do away with factors that do not enhance their interests. They must be able to couch their cultural principles and practices in terms of the factors that enhance their human needs and interests. So, in order for people to perpetuate their cultural practices and principles as a legacy, they must be able to evaluate whether a principle is able to serve their pragmatic needs, and if it does not, they have to make changes. Moreover, people within a culture must be able to adapt to various uncontrollable human and natural changes, and such adaptation requires creativity, rational evaluation, and revision or modification of cultural principles and practices.

So, if brainwashing means that people cannot think critically in order to meet their needs and adapt to situations by making modifications, then brainwashing cannot be a necessary feature of a culture that is able to perpetuate its legacy and tradition, therefore, a culture cannot prevent critical thinking and modifications. Therefore, from a purely philosophical perspective, Wiredu's characterization and criticism of African cultures are conceptually or logically problematic. Because this idea of practical rationality and critical thinking are assumed as an inherent part of

human agency and human culture, people in every culture are always held accountable or answerable for their actions. This is the reason why it is practically possible
for cultures to change and modify. Hence, no culture is impervious to external
influence. Usually, external influences provide alternative standards with which
people examine their own cultures and make changes. To indicate that the ideas of
authoritarianism and extreme indoctrination or brainwashing are inherent aspects
of a culture is to imply that people may, indeed, be held responsible or answerable
if they fail to do what is expected of them, even though they do not have options
and choice, but to simply do what they did. Alternatively, they are not responsible
for their actions because the culture agrees that they cannot make choices or think
for themselves. Pincoffs argues that this problematic implication is the reason why
moral brainwashing is an indefensible form of moral indoctrination. That is, brainwashing makes someone to be held accountable for his action even though the
action in question is not the result or his own thinking.[9] It appears that a culture
needs to be able to hold people answerable for their actions in order for cultural
practices or principles to be perpetuated and amenable to modification.

Since extreme indoctrination or brainwashing would prevent the likelihood of
making changes in cultures and ascribing responsibility, people may realize, on the
basis of practical rationality that, it is culturally self-defeating for the achievement
of their interest to make the process brainwashing a part of a culture. This will
imply that we have to blame a culture and not people for people's actions. According to Moody-Adams, "what is wrong with blaming culture is that such blame
ignores the ways in which cultural conventions are modified, reshaped, and sometimes radically revised in individual action. No culture is perpetuated without some
modification of cultural patterns in the lives of individual agents. Because a culture
is a way of life shaped by normative expectations embodied in social rules, a culture simply could not be perpetuated in any other fashion."[10] It should also be noted
that cultural patterns are not modified in vacuum; they are done in the context of
the fundamental cultural background beliefs and meta-beliefs of the people. This
process involves the gradual and incremental revision and modifications of beliefs
and practices. This process of revision is consistent with all processes of inquiry.
For instance, the processes of making changes in scientific knowledge and in
philosophy are usually gradual and incremental; the processes in these disciplines
are, in Wiredu's view, the paradigms of rationality or rational inquiry. It would
appear that one of the sources of Wiredu's discontent with African cultures, which
led him to conclude that communal African cultures involve authoritarianism and
extreme indoctrination is, the slow rate in which Africa is developing, modernizing,
and adapting to the scientific ways of thinking.

Wiredu identifies this slow rate of change as the feature of anachronism in
African cultures.[11] He fails to realize this slow rate of change is not necessarily a
result of authoritarianism and extreme indoctrination but of prudence, a natural

tendency of inquiry and human rationality. Prudence involves the idea of being careful and making sure that one is not making changes in haste and against one's own interest. It will be irrational for Africans not to be prudent. As Wiredu indicates, there are many things about the African communal ways of life that people like, which may not jibe with the Western, modern, and scientific ways of life. So, the major problem is how to adapt scientific ways to the African ways of life. Africans cannot get rid of their ways of life in a single fell swoop and replace them wholesale with the scientific ways. We do not expect rational people to get rid of *all* their beliefs and principles or modify their cultural structures, institutions, norms, and expectations in a single fell swoop. It is unreasonable to expect a Cartesian methodological, holistic, skeptical, and radical model of rationality, which involves modifying and revising one's beliefs in a single fell-swoop. Moody-Adams accepts as reasonable, Otto Neurath's now popular model of rationality or method of modifying beliefs, which is couched in the metaphor of replacing parts of the raft one 'plank' at a time, piece by piece, while staying afloat.[12] One can say that African cultures are trying to replace the planks in their raft one piece at a time while trying to stay afloat. No one can deny that there are significant changes taking place from within African cultures, except that these changes are slow. If the traditional cultures were that authoritarian and people were so brainwashed, then no changes would have taken place from within the cultures.

The beliefs, principles, and practices of a culture are a complex web. So, the modifications that people make in a culture with respect to their beliefs are not totally divorced from the other fundamental principles of the culture, which may in some cases, create some impediments to other changes in beliefs. The modifications are still made in the context of and in accordance with the accepted fundamental principles or meta-epistemic principles. In other words, if changes are to be made in certain cultural beliefs, they have to be done so that the new beliefs are not inconsistent or incoherent with other fundamental beliefs or traditions. Every culture has meta-epistemic principles of inquiry that guide people in examining which changes to make and how, in general, such changes may be made. People may, at a rudimentary level or an initial stage of education, be moderately indoctrinated about some fundamental principles or beliefs in a way that precludes brainwashing. Such moderate indoctrination does not indicate in any specific or determinate way how these beliefs or principles are brought to bear on actions in different situations, and how these beliefs or principles may be modified. Some moderate degree of indoctrination is needed at some rudimentary level in order to be able to educated children about certain cultural beliefs or moral principles that are necessary to sustain the culture and perpetuate it as a legacy. This idea appears to be the point underlying Frankena's view that, although the goal of education is to enhance autonomy, a student would also need to internalize certain doctrines in order think for himself.

In African cultures, a child must, via indoctrination, learn from elders or experts certain cultural doctrines or principles. For instance, children must be indoctrinated about the values of life, community, relationships, and caring, in order to get a general sense of their own interests and needs. With this, they can begin to articulate their own rational life plans, and learn on an experiential basis what would best serve their interests or plans, and how they can best reason independently within the general framework of values and their own interest. In order for a child to adequately learn what will serve his needs and interests, even with respect to enhancing his autonomy, he has to participate in the social consciousness that is rooted in the traditions and fundamental values of the community. Usually, the elders are more familiar with, verse in, and have a better understanding of these values.[13] It is the responsibility of the elders to indoctrinate children about these fundamental values, but they are not indoctrinated on how these values are applied. In my view, this is the situation that we have in the traditional African culture where elders are deemed to be epistemically superior to the child, and hence, a child would have to rely on the wisdom of elders to learn the necessary moral lessons. This view of moral education in African cultures is different from the dominant view of morality and the idea of moral education in Western philosophy, which is based on the liberal, rational, and autonomous view of a person.

As earlier indicated, this view indicates that the goal of moral education is to train someone to be able to reason properly and logically, solely on his own, and to be able make moral decisions that are impartial and universally or objectively true. In other words, such ability must preclude any form of external imposition or influence, and other factors that could hinder such independent and rational autonomous choice. This view has been vigorously defended in many spheres and it has also been supported by some psychological theories of human moral development. In this regard, Kohlberg's theory has dominated the literature for the past few decades.[14] But Kohlberg's theory is based on the liberal ideas of Mill, Locke, and Kant. Kohlberg's view connects moral development with personal autonomy and abstract cognitive and rational abilities. In general, moral development according to Kohlberg's view, is characterized in terms of someone's progressive ability to formally reason about and verbally express abstract moral principles. Such moral reasoning, which indicates one's cognitive abilities, is for the most part, devoid of content. One's cognitive progress on this continuum involves replacing the reasoning about moral contents based on traditions, values, customs, authorities, and conventions, with independent reasoning based on formal and abstract principles. So, it appears that African communalistic views of a person, morality, and moral education are, on their face, opposed to this liberal, autonomous, cognitive, and rational view of a person, morality, moral education, and moral development. These liberal ideas have been used as the basis for criticizing African communalistic account of a person, morality, and moral education, in that the African view involves authoritarianism and indoctrination. Authoritarianism and indoctrination are considered to be bad because they vitiate autonomy and hinder individuals' rationality and cognitive development.

The implication or thrust of this criticism has to do with the idea that, because the situation created by communalism does not allow individuals to rationally engage in independent moral reasoning in determining and choosing how they should behave, it implies social determinism and totalitarianism, in the sense that one is compelled by external factors or other people to 'choose' certain actions, or that one is conditioned or predetermined to behave in a certain manner.[15] Such situations remove justification and motivation from the internalist rational independent realm of the individual. The idea of independent rationality seeks to ensure that one is objective and not impartial. Objectivity and impartiality are essential for making moral principles universally rational. Such universality, many Western moral philosophers argue, is a formal element of morality. Wiredu seems to agree with this idea in his efforts to distinguish between particular customs and universal moral principles.[16] To be compelled or conditioned to think in a particular culturally or customarily biased way is, for one's actions and choices to be predetermined or prejudiced by the society. Such a person is thus presented as a semblance of a robot who has been conditioned by his community to act in a particular way, such that he cannot reason and make decisions on his own. This implies that a person must necessarily act in the way that is dictated by the community; he cannot rationally consider other plausible alternatives as justifications for his actions. This may lead to the extreme kind of conformism and conventionalism. This suggests that there is pressure from the community on everyone to conform to a specific way of acting irrespective of whether or not the individual thinks that it is justifiable to act differently. This plausible criticism is consistent with the universalist and the dominant Western view that morality, which is the subject matter of moral philosophy, and perhaps, philosophy in general, should be grounded in individual rationality.

The notion of group thinking, group rationality, or collective thought in African cultures suggests the notion of a group mind.[17] Odera Oruka argues that reason is a universal human trait on which we should ground African thought systems. It will be a disservice to African thought system to deny it universal reason and dress it in some particularistic extra-rational traditionalisms.[18] Wiredu suggests that the supernatural, authoritarian, and indoctrinating account of morality, thought systems, and beliefs in communalistic African cultures indicates this kind of extra-rational traditionalism and particularism. Hence, a philosophy, which is the paradigm of rationality cannot be derived from or based on this traditional African culture or its particularistic, dogmatic, or irrational beliefs. This criticism that beliefs, principles, and thought systems in traditional African cultures lack rationality is coextensive with the criticism that African communalistic structures are restrictive of individual rational autonomy, which is the foundation for rights and freedom. The central point is that communalism in traditional African cultures emphasizes the good and interests of the community to the detriment of the rights and freedom of individuals. Communalism seeks to impose the public good or the group conception of the good on individuals, thus preventing individuals from articulating and pursuing their own conception of the good and their rational life plans. As such, the idea of communalism is seen as bad; it has a pejorative connotation, which suggests the totalitarianism of the community that is sometimes captured by the pejorative idea of communism.

The following response to Etzioni's idea of communitarian seems to summarize this criticism: "It is ironic indeed that at a time when the early American idea of individual rights as the highest purpose of government is reasserting itself all over the world—in the Soviet Union and elsewhere—Prof. Etzioni would choose to revive in this country the profoundly dangerous and statist notion that individual rights and the common good occupy distinct and oppositional spheres. If this is communitarianism, who needs it?"[19] The relevant point here is that many critics of communalism in African cultures have a similar sentiment that the liberal ideas of individual rights, autonomy, freedom, and rationality, which are the marks of modernity are not taking hold in African cultures fast enough. That is, communalism is an anachronistic idea that is best suited for a museum. I can imagine that some people with similar sentiments may shudder at may efforts to defend the idea of communalism in African cultures, when the whole world is modernizing in its adoption of individualism. In this sense, communalism and the authoritarian, indoctrinating, and irrational features that are associated with it are seen as anachronisms and as antithetical to modernity and development.[20] So, the major criticisms of communalism in African cultures have a liberal foundation or assumptions. Those who subscribe to liberal ideas argue that the value of autonomy implies that individuals must be left alone to make their own independent choices, articulate their own conception of the good, and pursue their self-interests in order to achieve their rational life plans and actualize their potentials. In general, liberalism assumes a minimalist view or conception of community as a non-organized group of people who come together freely only to pursue a few special common interests.

In this sense, the individual is seen as logically prior and morally superior to the community. The argument for this idea is that the community comes into existence and persists only because individuals have freely agreed to come together, based on some idea of a social contract, to achieve certain goals. Hence, the community or its good or interest cannot take precedence over those of the individuals that constitute the community. In some sense, the community has no interests or rights independent of those of individuals. The fact that liberalism sees a community as an unorganized or a semi-organized group of people implies that it is not supposed to have sufficient power or authority to wield control over people's lives and to impede their will, inhibit their autonomy, or restrict their rights and freedoms. It is pertinent to argue that this criticism is based not only on a misconception or an inadequate view of community, but also on a misconception of the nature of autonomy, rights, and freedoms. To argue that we can conceive of an individual's autonomy, rights, and freedom independently of the context of a person's social community and environment is to fail to adequately see human beings or persons in their proper natural environment. According to Will Kymlicka, liberals should be concerned about cultural and communal structures because they make it possible for individuals to maintain their autonomy, rights, and freedom, in order to achieve their rational life plans.[21] He argues that, "societal cultures are profoundly important to liberalism . . . because liberal values of freedom and equality must be defined and understood in relation to such societal cultures. Liberalism rests on the value of individual autonomy . . . but what enables this sort of autonomy is the fact that our societal culture make variable options available to us."[22]

Kymlicka argues that a community and cultural structures do not have intrinsic moral values. They have only instrumental values, in that "it's through having a rich and secure cultural structure that people can become aware, in a vivid way, of the options available to them, and intelligently examine their value."[23] He also indicates how cultural structures and its informal model and communal processes of moral education also help children to acquire self-respect, the sense that one's life plan is worth carrying out or pursuing. This sense of self-respect is essential or a precondition for one's rights, freedom, and autonomy. He argues that: "Without such cultural structure, children and adolescents lack adequate role-models, which lead to despondency and escapism."[24] In other words, without the informal mode of education, which requires imitating role models and learning by experience in a community involving cultural structures, values, and practices, into which children are acculturated about the relevant liberal values, they will not have any meaningful sense of the liberal values of rights or freedom. Kymlicka goes on to underscore this point by arguing that: "Cultures are valuable, not in and of themselves, but because it is only through having access to a societal culture that people have access to a range of meaningful options."[25] Properly understood, the liberal notions of autonomy, equality, freedom, and right are, indeed, contextual notions that make sense only in a community or cultural practice involving liberal values.

According to Kymlicka, "the liberal values of freedom and equality must be defined and understood in relation to such societal cultures."[26] These values only make sense in the context of a society where people interact and agree to respect such rights or freedom. These notions also make sense only in a society or community where there are social or natural human impediments to autonomy and freedom. Moreover, these notions are meaningful only in the context of pursuing certain interests and goals, which are options that a society provides and makes meaningful. In Kymlicka's view, "freedom . . . is the ability to explore and revise the ways of life which are made available by our societal culture."[27] In this sense, he argues that freedom does not exist in vacuum or in the absence of a society that makes options available. In order for this ability to be possible, there must be social responsibilities that we owe to each other and the community. Kwame Gyekye underscores this point by indicating that: "Individual rights, the exercise of which is meaningful only within the context of human society, must therefore be matched with social responsibilities."[28] In other words, it makes sense to say that one has freedom and right only because such right and freedom are capable of being infringed on by others by virtue of the fact that they interact with one another in limited time and social space. It is this limitation of space and the value of social interaction as a natural human trait that calls for social responsibilities. Such responsibilities, which indicate duties, are the jural correlatives of rights; they are necessary to make sense of rights.

Moreover, one can say that one has a right or freedom only because such a right is respected by other members of the community or in social context, as that sphere of life that other people should not intervene in. That is, other people owe us a duty to respect our rights. If such duty did not exist, there would be no rights. Also, if people lived isolated lives where they acted without any interactions with other people, the issue of right and freedom would not arise. As isolated or solipsistic individuals, we have infinite and unbounded rights and freedom. The idea of rights or freedom in such context is redundant and superfluous. So, the concepts of right and freedom, in their negative and positive senses, are logically connected to the concept of a community or society and cultural principles, values, and practices. In the negative sense, freedom makes sense only because a community or society of people exists to remove or prevent constraints that may not allow us to do whatever we want. In a positive sense, freedom makes sense only because there is a community of people that actually respects it by providing us the necessary environment or facilities that will help us achieve whatever we need to achieve. Etzioni alludes to this point about the logical necessity of a community when he argues that: "We suggest that *free individuals require a community*, which backs them up against encroachment by the state and sustains morality by drawing on the gentle prodding of kin, friends, neighbors, and other community members rather than building on government control or fear of authorities."[29] It appears that a proper understanding of communalism in African cultures will indicate that Africans have a contextual view of rights that is meaningful only in the context of a community. This is a better view than the extreme liberal view of individuals or rights.

As indicated earlier, this idea of community does not imply that Africans do not have a view of individuality or respect autonomy. The idea of individuality is very pervasive in African beliefs, thoughts, and value systems. However, there is a difference. The individuality in African thought is not an isolated, solipsistic, or abstract individual; this not an individual that is conceived of and abstracted from his natural, communal, and social conditions. The individual in the African view is a contextualized or naturalized communal individual, that is, an individual whose individuality makes sense only in his natural and social context or condition, which according to the African view, is his community. Gyekye underscores this point about a naturalized individual by saying that "Akan thought conceives of the human being as a social animal and society as a necessary [natural or logical] condition for human existence. This thought is expressed in the proverb: When a man descends from heaven, he descends into human society. But the person who descends into human society has [his own individual] desires, aims, interests, and will, and these have to be reconciled with those of others [in the community]."[30] While Africans recognize that individuals have natural rights, which derive from their natural individuality, interests, and desires, these rights and individuality would be abstract and meaningless except when they are contextualized, made substantive, given material contents, and made meaningful in the context of a community. Individuals cannot achieve the liberal values or goals of perfection and self-realization as isolated individuals.

Liberalism emphasizes the protection of individuals' rights and freedoms because such protection helps them to achieve the goals of self-perfection, self-governance, and self-realization. However, in African communal thought, such goals, which are contingent on peace, harmony, human well-being, human relationships, and mutual dependence, have to be achieved in a community or society. Hence, the Akan proverb indicates that: "The prosperity (well-being) of a man depends upon his fellow man."[31] This proverb also underscores my view that the idea of a community or the dependence of the individual on the community or fellow men, is not meant to obliterate or undermine or relegate individuality, but to help the individual to makes sense of his own individuality and to provide material contents and substance to an abstract or metaphysical individuality. Because the community does not or cannot obliterate the individual, we can understand how the rational authoritarian and moderate indoctrinating features of a communalism cannot necessarily vitiate an individual's will and rationality. Hence, an individual in African communal cultures and thought systems is blameworthy when he acts badly, and he is ascribed responsibility. Gyekye illustrates this point about individuality, autonomy, and rationality, and perhaps, responsibility in African thought with the proverb: "The clan is like a cluster of trees which, when seen from afar, appear huddled together, but which would be seen to stand *individually* when closely approached."[32] His analysis indicates that this proverb seeks to emphasize the reality of individual trees or the individuality of persons, and the idea that individuals have separate identities. However, the branches of these trees have to necessarily touch simply because of the environment and the fact that they exist as a cluster or forest.

## Individualism Within a Community

In other words, this analysis of the relationship between the individual and community in African thought indicates that "the individual is separately rooted and is not completely absorbed by the cluster."[33] As such, the individual has his rights, freedom, and autonomy within the cluster, but the individual cannot ignore the necessity and reality of the cluster, and the fact that its branches exist in the same space with those of other trees. In which case, the fact that the branches have to touch or that human beings have relationships and must interact with others within this cluster called a community will, in part, shape how individuals or trees will grow in order to survive within the cluster. This proverb or analysis, which suggests how we may understand communalism in African cultures, implies that the criticisms of communalism that suggest its undermining of individuality and autonomy, are specious. Moreover, the plausibility of this African view of communalism may also indicate that some of the assumptions of liberalism on the basis of which this African view of communalism is criticized may also be problematic. For instance, liberalism assumes that an individual's autonomy is itself an absolute value. This liberal idea means that autonomy need not be understood in the context of substantive choices, goods, interests, which are made available only in a community or society. Such idea of autonomy is also viewed in a negative and unbounded sense, which implies the absence of restraint in one's effort to be self-governing, self-authoring, and self-directing, or having the freedom to determine, choose, and will, whatever one wants or needs.

In spite of Gyekye's appreciation of the African view of individuality as contextualized, he fails to see that the African view of individual autonomy, which in part, defines one's individuality, is also contextualized to the choice of goods and interests that are made available within the communal structure or the cluster of trees. He disagrees with Raz's view that the value of autonomy must be contextualized to the choice and pursuit of the various human goods.[34] The good that one chooses for oneself makes sense only in the context of a community, which makes such good substantive, in terms of giving it some material contents. Gyekye thinks that the idea of autonomy is logically prior to any human good or interest, which one must use one's autonomy to conceive, articulate, choose, and pursue. He disagrees with Raz's view because, to contextualize the idea of autonomy to the choice and achievement of a good is to allow the good that is determined by a community to be morally prior to one's autonomy. Such contextualization of autonomy, Gyekye might argue, involves a communal obliteration of individuality and individual's autonomy. In my view, Raz's view of individual autonomy, which Gyekye criticizes is more reasonable and realistic, and it is consistent with the African communalistic and contextualized or naturalized view of autonomy. Raz's view of autonomy implies a positive view of freedom or right, which says freedom or right involves having the ability and facilities to choose, pursue, and achieve a particular good.

However, Gyekye's view implies a negative view of rights or freedom, which says that freedom involves the absence of any restraint in choosing, pursuing, and achieving an individual's own conception of the good. This good, in Gyekye's view, must be independent of a community's or other people's values and conception of the good. It is pertinent to note that many of the fundamental criticisms of communalism have their foundations in the idea that communal structures and ethos infringe on individuals' rights and freedoms, which are conceived of in a purely negative sense. Such negative view of freedom implies that the community is a restraint or an impediment to an individual's choice, pursuit, and achievement of an individual's conception of the good. As such, the criticisms of communalism in African cultures, and communitarianism in general, seem to ignore the positive sense or view of freedom, in terms of making available the options from which one can choose. This positive view of freedom requires the existence and influence of a community of people that makes an individual's options, interests, conception of the good, and rational life plan available, valuable, and substantive. So, the negative conception of freedom ignores the moral and logical necessity of a social community for a meaningful idea of rights and freedom. The moral necessity of a community derives, in part, from the fact that human beings have limited abilities and capacities: human beings cannot live in isolation, they depend on others and they require other people to make provisions to complement their lives materially, ethically, and intellectually, in order to fully achieve their rational life plans, perfection, and self-realization.

As such, the effort by some liberal theorists to pit the individual in a conflict against the community is wrong-headed. African thought system and its idea of communalism seem to recognize that there cannot be a conflict between the individual and the community because the individual needs and must recognize the necessity of and his dependence on the community. This is one of the ideas that moral education seeks to impart into children by the informal upbringing. This moral upbringing or moral education is necessary for the individual's self-realization, acquisition of person, and sustenance of the community. Therefore, the moral necessity of a community, according to African thought system and view of the community and morality, seems to vitiate the value of negative freedom or rights. This is because the very idea and necessity of living in a community where people have to interact socially within the ambit of some moral principles imply that there has to be some amount of restraint. Such restraint is not only moral, but it is also a good that must be built into a substantive conception of individual autonomy and freedom. At least, we need some nurturing in order to grow up properly, and adults need relationship with other people, friends, neighbors, family, and kin in order to flourish as people, achieve self-realization, self-fulfilment, and moral perfection.

Such human relationships necessarily demand social responsibilities, which are constraints on individual rights.

The negative sense of freedom suggests that there should be no restraints on individual freedom, autonomy and rights. Such view is unrealistic and wrong-headed as the African views of person, morality, and community indicate. So, the pertinent issue that is suggested by the African view of communalism, is not whether there should be any restraint on individuals' rights, freedom, and autonomy, but the amount of restraint that is necessary or justifiable for people to live meaningfully in a social community. According to John Rawls, there are justifiable restrictions on freedom that derive from the natural human limitations, accidents of human life, social and historical contingencies.[35] It is along this line that he argues that it is consistent with the principles of justice for one's freedom to be restricted if it is for the purpose of attaining a broader sense of freedom for all—in a community or society. In his words, "liberty can be restricted only for the sake of liberty [such that] a less extensive liberty must strengthen the total system of liberty shared by all."[36] Such restriction is necessary for a well-ordered society or acceptable community, which is morally necessary for people to achieve their rational life plans. It appears that the liberal idea of absolute individual autonomy, which for some, implies negative freedom and extreme individualism, is problematic. As such, it cannot be used as a basis for criticizing the African idea of communalism.

While liberalism emphasizes the protection of individuals' rights, freedom, and an individual's absolute autonomy to realize his rational life plan and conception of the good, there is no sufficient emphasis on social responsibilities. In others words, some liberal views do not realize that a certain degree of social responsibility is necessary to sustain the liberal ideas of autonomy, freedom, and equality. The social responsibilities that are emphasized by the African idea of communalism involve the community's efforts to circumscribe and make options available, in that these options make an individual's freedom or right to choose a mode of life substantive and meaningful. The community is able to do this by providing facilities and material contents, in virtue of which an individual may achieve his potentials and achieve his rational life plans. The atomistic and abstract view of an individual and the absolute value that is placed on his autonomy presupposes that individuals are rationally self-sufficient unto themselves such that they are solely able to choose for and by themselves what is the best form of life for them. This view seems to suggest that autonomy and the human ability, capacity, and freedom to make choices have absolute or intrinsic moral value and worth. The African communal view is that human autonomy and ability to make free choices are contingent on a context of options and the good of the material contents of these options. The liberal view also suggests that because freedom of choice or autonomy is an absolute human capacity and value, therefore, any choice made by the individual is a good choice per the person making the choice. In other words, every adult rational individual has the autonomy, ability or capacity, and hence the right or freedom to determine for himself what is morally good or bad with respect to how he should act or lead life in order to achieve his rational life plan and self-fulfilment or actualization.

Here, liberalism pays no attention to the issue of what constitutes an adequate rational life plan or what constitutes an acceptable self-fulfilment or self-actualization. Liberalism leaves the determination of this issue solely to the individual. According to Charles Taylor, "To say that we have a right to be free to choose our life-form must be to say that any choice is equally compatible with this principle of freedom and that no choices can be judged morally better or worse by this principle—although, of course, we might want to discriminate between them on the basis of other principles."[37] So, any other principle that we may use to evaluate and discriminate between one's choices cannot be logically prior to individual autonomy or the principle of freedom of choice. As such, whether or not the choice that one makes is judged socially to be morally bad or good is a secondary, or perhaps, an irrelevant issue. The primary and significant issue is that one has been able to make the free choice and has acted autonomously without any constraints. Again, no attention is paid to the social and communal human context that makes the alternatives or options available for me to choose from. The emphasis is on the individual and the subjective judgment or choices and the autonomous basis for such choices. According to Bruce Suttle, this emphasis involves a kind of subjectivism, which takes different forms of distorted existentialism and one's view of one's own existential conditions. This view, he says, "has the problem of equating 'acting autonomously' with 'doing what is morally justified'."[38] The problem with this kind of subjectivism is aptly indicated by Frankena's point that "To say that a developed moral agent must make up his own mind as to what is right . . . *is not* to say that we can make a course of action right by deciding on it."[39] To deny this important point by Frankena, is to somehow suggest that, the fact "that a developed rational man must make up his own mind as to what is true . . . is to say that he can make a statement true by believing it."[40]

The relevant point here is that, some of the criticisms of the idea of communalism in African cultures suggesting that it is bad because it necessarily involves authoritarianism and indoctrination about moral rules and principles, are problematic. This is partly because the criticisms assume an extreme, abstract, isolationist, individualistic, and subjectivist view of rationality, the good, freedom, rights, and autonomy. Moreover, these criticisms assume a problematic view about the epistemic, semantic, logical nature of moral rules. They presuppose that all moral rules are epistemically, logically, and semantic adequate and complete. In other words, one can articulate, teach, and internalize epistemically, logically, and semantically adequate and complete moral rules in a communal context such that these rules dictate precisely, and specify determinately, how exactly one should act in each and every situation, to the extent of limiting one's autonomy and rationality. So, by teaching and internalizing these semantically and epistemically *complete* and *adequate* moral rules, one does not have the autonomy, rationality, discretion, and imagination to determine how to act in each and every situation. The view suggests that some specific types of actions that are required by rules are rigidly built into the requisite rules that are taught by the community, such that they are seen as necessary limitations on an individual's autonomy, rationality, discretion, imagination, and creativity.

One may respond to the charge that communalism vitiates an individual's rationality, autonomy, discretion, and imagination to make moral decisions with respect to his actions in particular situations as follows: Moral rules in traditional African moral thought system(s), and perhaps any rule for that matter, cannot be and are usually not semantically and epistemically complete and adequate. In other words, moral rules—as epistemic and semantic criteria in traditional African cultures—do not, in terms of the method of determining how one should act and the meaning of the rule, specify all the circumstances and actions that can be subsumed under a particular rule. Moral rules are not closed-ended and they are not totally and completely all-embracing and inclusive. Hence, they do not foreclose the possibility or capacity of an individual in the communal system to engage in rational, independent, and creative moral reasoning and autonomous choices. Moral rules are open-textured and inherently incomplete: it is not possible that by the very meaning and nature of a moral rule, it will be all-inclusive and all-embracing, such that we are able to know by its specification, all the circumstances and actions that can subsumed under it and justified by it. The idea that moral rules are not semantically and epistemically complete or adequate is well appreciated in African thought; thus, the proverb: you do no make a rule or have a principle or specify conduct as if you know very early in the morning what the day will bring forth in the evening.

The idea here is that you must see, understand, and use a moral principle and teach it as if it is specified in the morning without knowing what the afternoon or evening will bring forth. So, given any circumstance and what the situation presents, the individual is expected to and must *reason* creatively and imaginatively to determine how, in relation to the rule, he must act given the circumstance. He must determine how, in the given circumstance, his action fits into the general rule, which purports to specify 'how *we* ought to behave' in the context of a community. He must be able to *figure out* within the context of the dictates of the community, how his duty should be brought to bear on his action in the circumstance.

However, it is pertinent to say that traditional African people realize that circumstances and beliefs do change. So, they usually allow for new knowledge or perspectives to be brought to bear on their moral principles and attitudes. In one's everyday life, one is usually confronted with some moral situations in which there are options and obvious choices, and other situations in which there are either no options or no clear choices among the options. If one is confronted with a situation that does not indicate an obvious choice or option or a clear line of action, one is allowed to use his imaginative and creative reasoning to make connections among the different levels of moral precepts in order to apply moral rules to a given situation so as to arrive at a plausible decision or action.

But one may be confronted with a circumstance for which there is a clear option or a prescribed line of action. In such situations, if one decides to appeal to one's own rationality and the ability to think for oneself, and in the process, one acts differently from the prescribed way, then if the action is morally bad, then one is morally responsible and blameworthy. But if in this circumstance, the action that is different from the prescribed way is, everything considered, deemed to be morally good, the situation is taken as a new circumstance that should illuminate or be brought to bear on the entrenched prescribed behaviors and principles. Obviously, such a person will not be blamed for acting in a way that is different from the prescribed line of action. The fact that Africans will withhold blame in that situation gives credence to the fact that discretion or imagination is allowed. The essential point here is that the authoritarianism in African cultures, as indicated earlier, is not irrational to the extent of saying that simply because one thought for oneself or used discretion and acted independently and differently from the prescribed dictates of elders or tradition, one has acted immorally. Moreover, the moderate indoctrination does not foreclose independent, creative, and imaginative forms of thinking. The moral principles and the type of moral reasoning that are taught in African communal traditions are not simply specific principles or reasoning regarding how one should behave in specific situations. The moral principles are usually general in nature and people are taught to reason creatively and to use their discretion in applying general principles to the specific situations that confront them in their daily lives.

Moreover, the use of narratives and modeling of behavior provide the rudimentary moral principles and the various creative ways that these principles could be applied differently to various situations. The lessons that are taught involve various plausible ways of understanding, explaining, and reasoning about what it is or means for an act to be moral in the various social, interpersonal, personal dimensions of life. People also learn how such understanding may be imaginatively translated into various ways of thinking and acting morally, and the various attitudes and habits that involve or underpin thinking and acting morally. A person who does not have a robust and imaginative understanding of what it means to be moral will not understand a moral precept, and will not have the moral sensibility and moral point of view to act morally on the basis of a moral precept. In alluding to Pincoffs' point, Bruce Suttle indicates that: "Without a general moral point of view, without a set of moral precepts and sensibilities, no moral argument in support of having a moral point of view could be judged convincing, let alone recognized as moral arguments."[41] In other words, if a person does not have the moral sensibilities, habits, or a general moral point of view that may be acquired by indoctrination, as well as an understanding of some moral precepts, such a person cannot be morally educated via any rational means. It may be difficult or impossible to correct moral deficiency in character, attitudes, and habits solely via an independent, rational, cognitive, and critical thinking approach to moral education. This approach involves offering rational moral reasons why a person should acquire a general moral point of view, basic moral habits, attitudes, and sensibilities that are necessary for one to be rationally educated and to be a rational moral agent. So, having a basic moral point of view, moral habits, sensibilities, and attitudes must derive from the group and the day-to-day informal, imitative, or indoctrinating processes of moral education and upbringing in a community.

Given the above situation, a plausible case can be made against the criticism that the communal nature of morality in traditional African cultures assumes the idea of a group mind and group rationality. This criticism indicates that the idea of group mind is inconsistent with the paradigm view of rationality that involves having the ability to independently think for oneself by critically examining the evidence. Also, this criticism indicates that this kind of group rationality or mind cannot square with the Western philosophical notion of morality, which is grounded in the notion of individual rationality, freedom, autonomy, and choice. A case can be made for a circumscribed or moderate idea of individual autonomy in African thought, which indicates an individual's ability to, in most cases, make independent choices. An obvious case can be made against any form of social or communal determinism that may vitiate rational autonomy and moral responsibility. The African idea of communalism appreciates the obvious demerits of social or communal determinism, hence it avoids it. Perhaps, it is more difficult to make a case for an absolute or unbounded or negative form of freedom or autonomy—the kind of autonomy or freedom that is not contextualized or relational to the choice of substantive goods, or circumscribed by some reasonable alternatives that are made available and meaningful by a community. We have seen that the communal views of morality, moral personhood, moral education, and moral reasoning in African thought do not vitiate individual autonomy. Rather, the traditional African view suggests and makes a case for a moderate, relational, positive sense of autonomy—the middle-ground kind of autonomy that avoids the extremes of absolute freedom and absolute determinism, i.e., a complete lack of freedom. It is commonly accepted that a human being cannot morally grow and develop by herself alone, hence the existence of a society or community is necessary as a middle-ground to help one to develop one's moral character.

Given the moral and logical necessity of a community, the African view suggests that a person's autonomy is circumscribed by and relational to a community and the set of goods, rational life plans, options, and interests that a community makes available to a person. It is from among these different options and rational life plans that the community makes available that a person can autonomously choose a particular plan, as a basis for developing as a rational moral agent and attaining moral personhood. As a moral agent, one is expected and able to rationally understand and make judgments about moral rules with respect to their substantive *means* and *ends* within the context of the available options. If a person has the appropriate evidence and experience, he can use his rational judgment and autonomy to make connections among moral principles, actions, and circumstances, and he can question the validity of moral principles in the community. To expect that one can, without the community, morally develop in isolation, on one's own alone, into an absolutely autonomous and rational person who can reason solely by herself, will be foolhardy. Even an adult moral agent may sometimes need to defer to, depend or rely on the guidance of experts or elders and the prodding, chiding, and ribbing of others in the community. The liberal notion of absolute autonomy, which cannot, without a person's consent, be mitigated, attenuated, or overridden by any other person's moral prescriptions and education, seems to assume that every individual, or perhaps all adults, are morally developed and fully rational to make moral choices for and by themselves solely without guidance from others or the community.

Moreover, this liberal view does not place any *qualitative strictures* on what it takes to be an adult. Sometimes, there is a reliance on the arbitrary criterion of chronological age or the number of years one have lived on earth. Age is arbitrary because it does necessarily imply the ability to make good and rational moral judgments. In the traditional African view, the normative idea of moral adulthood or personhood is not based solely on age. Age is respected but age alone does not confer moral and epistemic authority. In addition to age, authority or social recognition is based on the proven ability to meet one's responsibilities, wealth of experience, achievements, a track record of good judgment, and a consistent demonstration of knowledge and understanding of the tradition, customs, beliefs, values, and principles. Chinua Achebe underscores this point about the Ibos, when he said of Okonkwo: "Age was respected among his people, but achievement is revered."[42] Hence, Wiredu indicates that the high respect that is given to age in African cultures is not arbitrary or without a reasonable basis or justification.[43] An older person is accorded full respect and recognition only if he or she displays these qualitative features. As opposed to what the irrational form of authoritarianism implies, people do not respect elders or accept their dictates simply because of their arbitrary age or years. Not all elders are morally accomplished to warrant moral recognition. If the need for moral guidance, dependence, or deference is plausible, as the African view indicates, then the liberal view, which says that people must be given the unbounded opportunity to make individual free choices, whether right or wrong, is unreasonable. The liberal view is that people have the requisite rational ability and must be given the opportunity to make mistakes and learn from such mistakes. According to this view, this is the best way for people to morally develop. This liberal view, according to Taylor, is founded on the atomistic view of an individual who is severed or abstracted from the community and is denied of any responsibility to others in his community.[44]

## Communalism and the Case Against Liberalism

Social critics and commentators have argued that this liberal view has led people to be extremely egoistic and unwilling to accept responsibility, because they see responsibilities as social impositions by others or society, or constraints that seek to vitiate their autonomy and freedom. These people see their autonomy or freedom solely in a negative or absolute sense. This liberal view, some argue, has resulted in social malaise that has culminated in crime waves and other moral pathologies. If this is a reasonable diagnosis, then it appears that the liberal idea of morality or its foundation, i.e., autonomy, has an atomistic implication, underpinning, or connotation that is destructive of social cohesion. Yet, the intuitive notion of morality has a social connotation, in that it is supposed to engender social cohesion and enhance adequate human interactions for the purpose of achieving peace and harmony in society. Morality is a social and cultural necessity that presupposes a sense of community, relationships, interactions, and social responsibilities. That is, moral principles and practices are deeply social, and they are also deeply embedded in and made meaningful in the context of cultural and communal practices. The African idea of communalism appreciates this idea of morality, hence, its moral principles are founded on humanism. The formal elements or strictures of morality or the formal moral principles of universality, equality, and impartiality are simply meaningless skeletons. These skeletons have flesh, substantive contents, and are made meaningful, only in and by a social context or community that provide options and facilities for human good. The humanistic view of morality in African thought is concerned primarily about adding flesh and material contents to various formal moral principles or platitudes, such as the golden rule: Do unto others as will want them to do unto you. In the African view, it would seem meaningless to try to teach morality and moral principles by stepping out of a culture or community. I cannot know substantively how I will want to be treated or how to treat others the way I want to be treated outside a communal context.

Traditional African moral thoughts do not see absolute autonomy and abstract individual rationality as the foundation of moral reasoning or the substantive basis for developing one's moral character and personhood. The emphasis involves using the context of the community, its practices, and the reasonable options they provide as the material basis for circumscribing rationality and autonomy. It is therefore reasonable for people see personhood, moral character, and moral development as the rational product of moral education in this social, communal, and cultural context. With this context in mind, Africans see moral obligation in terms of the duty that people owe to themselves and others in the mutually beneficial relationships that exist in the community. Such obligation only makes sense in the context of the set of values that are shared by a community of people who accept some reasonable principles of social interaction and relationships. This idea is illuminated by Helen Haste's view that: "Certain values follow from locating the individual primarily in social space and community (an identity), a sense of obligation to the community (responsibilities) and the personal attributes needed for effective performance of those responsibilities."[45] So, it is reasonable to see moral education and the fostering of personal values, moral character, personhood, and social responsibilities as a form of interpersonal or social development of personal values. This social development of personal values involves knowing and understanding the community and its interests as a social group to which one belongs, and seeing the proper place of an individual's moral character or identity in that social group. The proper place of an individual is couched in terms of the mutuality and symbiotic relationship between the community and the individual: the individual or his interests cannot take precedence over the community and the community or its interests do not take precedence over the interests of individuals.

This African view of the non-conflicting moral relationship between individuals and the community implies that the ideas of absolute and uncircumscribed autonomy and abstract individualistic rationality are wrong-headed. In the African view, these ideas are wrong-headed because they seek to engender complete permissiveness, which may vitiate any form—even the defensible form— of indoctrination that would enable a child to learn without questioning some basic principles of actions. Such permissiveness will also vitiate any kind of authoritarianism— even the rational kind that allows for reasonable paternalism and the ability of someone to depend on or defer to an elder or expert who is more knowledgeable on an issue. According to Willis Moore, "complete permissiveness on the part of the adult with respect to the pre-rational child is both impossible and unwise."[46] Thus he argues that learning necessarily begins with an authoritarian and indoctrinating situation because a child necessarily has to learn by imitation without questioning what is being imitated. In these cases, there are usually no reasons provided for asking a child to imitate and learn the subject matter of imitation and from the 'object of imitation', i.e., the role model. In Moore's view: "The child naturally models his behavior and within limits, his consequent value reactions on that of others, chiefly of adults. Only by isolating him from other persons, especially from adults, could we keep him from learning in this way."[47] This process of imitation, which is for the most part, an informal indoctrinating process of education, is natural; it is essential and valuable for a child to learn form experts or elders some patterns of accepted behavior that have been tested and adopted by a community. This is the natural and intuitive motivation for accepting epistemic dependence and moral deference, to which absolute autonomy and abstract individualistic rationality are opposed.

To argue for the kind of permissiveness that is implied by complete or absolute autonomy and abstract individualistic rationality is, to imply, on the one hand, that, without the broad sense of moral education that includes mild or moderate indoctrination, socialization or acculturation, every person or adults can and would always be in the best epistemic and rational moral position to see all the evidence and relevant alternatives. This absolute idea of autonomy also implies, on the other hand, that all persons or adults either are, or must be, rational egoists, in that they can and would necessarily choose what is best for them irrespective of their narrow epistemic situation. According to Charles Taylor,

> The kind of freedom valued by the protagonists of the primacy of rights, and indeed by many others of us as well, is a freedom by which men are capable of conceiving alternatives and arriving at a definition of what they really want, as well as discerning what commands their adherence of their allegiance. This kind of freedom is unavailable to one whose sympathies and horizons are so narrow that he can conceive only one way of life, for whom indeed the very notion of a way of life which is *his* as against everyone's has no sense. Nor is it available to one who is riveted by fear of the unknown to one familiar life-form, or who has been so formed in suspicion and hate of outsiders that he can never put himself in their place.[48]

The relevant point here is that the kind of narrow-mindedness that is engendered by complete or absolute autonomy and abstract individualistic rationality is inadequate for making meaningful moral decisions. The assumption about the acuity or adequacy of independent human rational capabilities and abilities, which is the basis for justifying the principle of absolute autonomy, the primacy of rights, and negative sense of freedom, is problematic. The traditional African moral thought system seems to appreciate the problem with this assumption in terms of the narrow-mindedness that it may engender.

The liberal assumptions about individuality and autonomy, and the narrow-minded implication, ignore the limits of individual human rationality and cognitive abilities; they fail to acknowledge the existence of ignorance that may be induced by our special individual cognitive and social circumstances. They also ignore the possibility of weakness of the will, which could prevent us from choosing what is *apparently* the best alternative or what is in our long-term interest. In some cases, it may be necessary for another person to override the will of a morally weak person. In other cases, the chiding, ribbing, and prodding by others may compel someone whose will is weak to act properly. These points may indicate why the assumption about the absolute value of an individual's autonomy and rationality is wrong. If the assumption is true that people need absolute autonomy and individualistic rationality in order to achieve their potential, rational life plans, and self-realization, then we would not, as rational adults need, for instance, to go to a doctor to give us prescriptions for drugs. Perhaps, the government will not require appropriate license for a doctor to issue prescriptions, we will not need a proper prescription in order to buy prescription drugs, and it will not be necessary to designate certain drugs as 'prescription drugs'. As rational adults, we would know or be able to know the best prescription drugs among all the options, and we will have absolute autonomy to buy and take any drug we want. Moreover, we would not have plausible *prima facie* justifications for any government to make paternalistic laws that may, for instance, require the use of crash helmets, seat belts, and prevent the use of illicit drugs.

The pertinent point here for me is not to defend paternalism *per se* but simply to indicate that the seeming or *prima facie* plausibility of paternalism may render specious or suspect the assumption about the intrinsic value of complete autonomy and abstract individualistic rationality. However, the main point with the example of the medical doctor, although it may seem overstated, is to show that as a result of the limited human epistemic condition, we cannot and are not always or in *every circumstance*, in the best epistemic or rational position to know and choose what is best for us. This point is substantiated in our everyday actions when we ask other people, friends, spouse, parents, children, neighbor what they think about the decision we are about to make. Other people usually provide us with ideas, facts, and insights, which we did not rationally think about or could not know, yet, they are very helpful with respect to our final decision. Sometimes, the mere status of the person who provides an idea may, without any other reasons, compel us to accept the idea as the basis for our action or decision. We, sometimes, are as ignorant about the proper drugs for some illnesses as we are in knowing the best line of action in some situations, if we do not have moral guidance and education from others and the community. The fact that people take illicit drugs and smoke cigarettes prior to addiction or engage in actions that they know are risky to their own lives, *even when they know there is conclusive evidence* that such behavior is not good for them, is a plausible evidence that people are not always in the best rational and epistemic position to choose what is good for them, and they may not be able to act along such lines for their own best interest.

I do appreciate the fact that weakness of the will or self-deception could play a significant role in those kinds of circumstances where we do not choose or do what is best for us. The crux of my point is that the underlying basis for placing intrinsic or absolute value on individual rationality and autonomy seems to ignore the fact about weakness of the will and self-deception. One of the goals of the communal moral structures and moral education in African cultures is to attempt to *mitigate* against factors that may engender weakness of the will, self-deception, ignorance, and human epistemic and moral fallibility, by employing all the agencies, structures, and facilities of the community to educate people to acquire and develop the requisite moral habits, attitudes, character, and a general moral point of view. Etzioni acknowledges that, although the ultimate factor in one's moral conduct is one's own conscience, one's conscience is neither an innate element nor does it necessarily enforce itself. We need the community to mold our conscience along the lines of an acceptable moral point of view and to compel, enforce, or direct our conscience to the right action via moral sanctions prodding, poking, ribbing, and chiding. The communal moral point of view that molds and enforces our conscience is logically prior to our rationality on the basis of which we make moral choices and decisions. In other words, what we deem to be morally rational is contingent on our moral point of view or conscience, which is molded by our community. Because our conscience is, somehow, prior to rationality, the initial process and rudimentary sense of molding it may, for the most part, involve indoctrination. An individual's acquisition of a general moral point of view, which shapes and molds his conscience, cannot take place abstractly in isolation. Such acquisition involves a social process by which we imitate others, internalize, and learn what is acceptable in a social community in order to rationally bring such idea to bear on our moral reasoning, actions, and decisions.

The processes of initiating, socializing, and acculturating someone into a moral order or point of view and of inculcating moral habits and attitudes have indoctrinating and communal underpinnings. These processes involve and require the ability to see and understand the moral significance of one's action in terms of one's relationships and actual dealings with others in a concrete communal or social context. This is the process of inculcating in someone an attitude, habit of the mind, and a disposition to act and make choices in such a way that considers other people. So, to a large extent, traditional African thought appreciates that, without a communal underpinning for moral education, via informal processes of initiating, acculturating, and moderately indoctrinating one into some moral order, moral education will fail. In other words, moral education that is founded on a rational and abstract cognitive model or approach will not succeed in the relevant African context. The choice and adequacy of the method or processes of moral education are not determined by formal validity but by the practical relevance, utility, and the ability to achieve the requisite outcome, result, and goals. It may be fruitless to try use rational means to convince someone who does not have a general moral point of view, moral sensibilities, habits, and attitudes, to act on principles whose justifications are grounded in an intuitive general moral outlook. The communalistic and informal approach to moral education in African traditions offers a good basis for encoding into one's conceptual scheme a general moral point of view. This point of view now provides the foundational basis, in virtue of which one can be rationally morally 'educated', so that one can rationally and cognitively understand them, in order to be able to creatively and imaginatively apply relevant moral principles to different situations in an acceptable manner.

# Notes

1. Wiredu, *Philosophy and An African Culture*, 2.

2. Wiredu, *Philosophy and An African Culture*, 3.

3. See Michael Slote, "Is Virtue Possible?" *Analysis* 42 (1982): 70-76, reprinted in *The Virtues*, ed. R. Kruschwitz and R. Roberts, (Belmont, CA: Wadsworth, 1987), 100-105, Alan Donagan, *The Theory of Morality* (Chicago: University of Chicago Press, 1977), Susan Wolf, "Sanity and the Metaphysics of Responsibility," in *Responsibility, Character and the Emotions*, ed., F. Schoeman (Cambridge: Cambridge University Press, 1987), 46- 62.

4. Michele M. Moody-Adams, "Culture, Responsibility, and Affected Ignorance," *Ethics* 104 (January 1994): 291-309.

5. Moody-Adams, "Culture, Responsibility, and Affected Ignorance," 294-95

6. Moody-Adams, "Culture, Responsibility, and Affected Ignorance," 304.

7. Moody-Adams, "Culture, Responsibility, and Affected Ignorance," 292-293.

8. Moody-Adams, "Culture, Responsibility, and Affected Ignorance," 301.

9. Pincoffs, "On Avoiding Moral Indoctrination," 69.

10. Moody-Adams, "Culture, Responsibility, and Affected Ignorance," 306.

11. Wiredu, *Philosophy and An African Culture*, 1-2.

12. Moody-Adams, "On the Old Saw that Character Is Destiny," in Owen Flanagan and Amelie O. Rorty, eds., *Identity, Character, and Morality* (Cambridge, MA: MIT Press, 1990), pp.127-129. A similar point is made by Paul Feyerabend with respect to the scientific method (which is regarded as the paradigm of rationality) in terms of how modifications are or ought to be made in a system of beliefs. He argues that such system consists of a 'core' and a 'periphery', and that scientists make constant modifications only in the periphery and not in the core.

13. Frankena, "The Concept of Education Today," 19-32.

14. For Kohlberg's theory see his "Stages of Moral Development as a Basis of Moral Education," *Essays on Moral Development: Vol. 1--The Philosophy of Moral Development*, and *Essays on Moral Development: Vol. 2--The Philosophy of Moral Development*.

15. For the criticisms against authoritarianism that is engendered by communitarianism in African cultures, see Wiredu, *Philosophy and An African Culture*. I have defended authoritarianism in African cultures and responded to Wiredu's criticisms in chapter 5 of this

book and "A Defense of Epistemic Authoritarianism in Traditional African Cultures."

16. Wiredu, *Cultural Universals and Particulars*, 61-77.

17. See Bodunrin, "The Question of African Philosophy."

18. Odera Oruka, "African Philosophy," in Guttorm Floistad, ed., *Contemporary Philosophy: A New Survey, Vol. 5: African Philosophy* (Dordrecht: Martinus Nijhorff, 1987), p. 66.

19. Cited in Amitai Etzioni, *The Spirit of Community*, 47.

20. Wiredu, *Philosophy and An African Culture*, 1-2.

21. Will Kymlicka, *Liberalism, Community, and Culture* (Oxford: Clarendon Press, 1989), 162-181, and Will Kymlicka, *Multicultural Citizenship: A Liberal Theory of Minority Rights,* (Oxford: Clarendon Press, 1995), 75-106.

22. Kymlicka, *Politics in the Vernacular*, 53-54.

23. Kymlicka, *Liberalism, Community, and Culture*, 165.

24. Kymlicka, *Liberalism, Community, and Culture*, 165-166.

25. Kymlicka, *Multicultural Citizenship*, 83.

26. Kymlicka, *Politics in the Vernacular*, 53

27. Kymlicka, *Politics in the Vernacular*, 53

28. Gyekye, *Tradition and Modernity*, 65.

29. Etzioni, *The Spirit of Community*, 15.

30. Gyekye, *An Essay on African Philosophical Thought*, 146.

31. Gyekye, *An Essay on African Philosophical Thought*, 155.

32. Gyekye, *An Essay on African Philosophical Thought*, 158.

33. Gyekye, *An Essay on African Philosophical Thought*, 159.

34. Gyekye, *Tradition and Modernity*, 54-57.

35. Rawls, *A Theory of Justice*, 113-118.

36. Rawls, *A Theory of Justice*, 250.

37. Charles Taylor, "Atomism," in *Communitarianism and Individualism*, eds., Shlomo Avineri and Avner de Shalit (New York: Oxford University Press, 1992), 34.

38. Suttle, "The Need for and Inevitability of Moral Indoctrination," 159.

39. William Frankena, "Towards a Philosophy of Education," *Harvard Educational Review* 28 (November, 1958), 309 (emphasis is mine).

40. Frankena, "Towards a Philosophy of Education," 309.

41. Suttle, "The Need for and Inevitability of Moral Indoctrination," 156.

42. Achebe, *Things Fall Apart*, 12.

43. Wiredu, *Cultural Universals and Particulars*, 68.

44. Charles Taylor, "Cross Purposes: The Liberal-Communitarian Debate," in *Liberalism and the Moral life*, ed., N. Rosenblum (Cambridge, MA: Harvard University Press, 1989), 159-182.

45. Haste, "Communitarianism and the Social Construction of Morality," 51.

46. Moore, "Indoctrination and Democratic Method," 96.

47. Moore, "Indoctrination and Democratic Method," 96.

48. Taylor, "Atomism," 43.

# Conclusion

Some essential features of the idea of communalism in African thought include the normative conception of personhood and the dependence of moral personhood on the community. This dependence implies that one acquires personhood by being integrated into the community and being morally educated and socially responsible about the communal ways of life and values. The normative idea of personhood emphasizes the primacy of social responsibility as a precondition for an individual's right, freedom, and autonomy. The processes of moral education, which emphasize responsibility, involve the informal use of narratives for learning requisite communal values, beliefs, principles, habits, attitudes, ways of life, and responsibilities that normatively define personhood. These communal values include caring about other people and relationships, and acting in ways that contribute to human well-being and communal peace and harmony. African communal values are fundamentally humanistic, and they are founded on a naturalistic view of ontology, where human beings, community, ancestors, deities, and spirits are in natural harmony. The values and social responsibilities that define personhood in a community engender social recognition and respect for the epistemic and moral authority that elders have, in that they are seen as the repositories of wisdom, knowledge, and traditions. This implies another feature of communalism, which involves a rational type of authoritarianism, that is, the dependence and deference to the authority of elders. Knowledge in this communal tradition is based on communal inquiry, which requires people share evidence and ideas by relying on oral tradition. Thus, individuals do not have the epistemic responsibility of relying solely and exclusively on their own cognitive and rational abilities, which require them to think for themselves by critically examining the evidence as a basis for making independent judgment.

Moreover, the idea of communalism in African thought is founded on the view

291

that there is no logical distinction between thought and practice. The idea of communalism as a philosophical theme is, fundamentally, a practice and a way of life; it is a practical methodology of inquiry, organizing society, acting, and living. As such, it is also, fundamentally, a moral notion. The African communal conceptions of morality, moral reasoning, and moral thought are founded on the idea that they are practical, humanistic, naturalistic, hierarchical, and rationally authoritarian. African moral notions and practices are encoded in and thus derived from oral tradition, narratives, arts, folklore, proverbs, practices, beliefs, and ways of life. In a broad sense, African moral ideas are, on comparative grounds, different form the dominant Western philosophical views of morality. Although the Western view is not monolithic, the dominant theme in the modern era has been the liberal view, on the basis of which, the African view is criticized. I have indicated that some of these criticisms are specious, and those that are not specious may not be as devastating as some people think, if the traditional views of morality are properly analyzed and understood in their relevant contexts. Perhaps, one important lesson to be learned from a proper understanding of the African communal view of morality is that the apparent conflict between individualism and communalism is a pseudo problem. The African view indicates that there is no meaningful or significant tension between the interest of individuals and the interest of community. A proper understanding of the notions of the individual and the community will indicate that one is dependent on the other, and that the effort to logically and abstractly conceive of one to the exclusion of the other is fundamentally wrong-headed.[1] The position that is indicated by the African view, which is anchored in their view of the individual, community, and their relationship, seems to be captured by Gyekye's idea of moderate communitarianism, which tries to balance individual and communal interests.

In Gyekye's view, there is a practical and functional mutual dependence between the individual and the community that equally recognizes both, in that one is not emphasized to the detriment of the other. This practical dependence requires finding equilibrium or harmony and negotiating a balance between the interests of individuals and those of the community. He indicates that, "it is moderate communitarianism that, in the final analysis, adequately reflects the claims of both individuality and community, both of which need to be recognized morally and functionally."[2] This moderate communitarian view is not simply an abstract or theoretical account of the individual, community, and their relationship, but a practical and existential account of how these ideas are applied to everyday lives, lived as a way of life, and experienced. This view underscores the point that African thought seeks to approach the notions of morality, the individual, and the community from a practical and an existential perspective, given the African metaphilosophical stance that 'philosophy' is a practice, mode of living, and a way of life. In this regard, the African philosophical stance and thought regarding morality, the individual, community, and the connection between them have some heuristic practical and theoretical values that other traditions can learn from. Sometimes, the call for Africa to modernize is a call to embrace the modern Western liberal, individualistic, and scientific culture, among other things, such as capitalism, democracy, industrialization, and technology. Usually, Western philosophical views or ways of life are used to criticize and denigrate African philosophical views or ways of life. Sometimes, these Western ideas are used as a basis for suggesting that Africans do not have any significant ideas and beliefs, or if they have any, they cannot offer anything substantive to the West or other traditions, and that these traditions have nothing to learn from African ideas.

Given some of the advantages or heuristic values of communalism in African cultures and what many people have suggested as the moral decadence and permissiveness in the industrialized, liberal, urbanized, and individualistic cultures of the West, it is questionable how much Africa should modernize.[3] According to Wiredu, "industrialization seems to be proving deleterious to that system of communal caring and solidarity which was a strong point of traditional communalism, and one of the greatest problems facing us in Africa is how to reap the benefits of industrialization without incurring the more unlovable of its apparent fallouts, such as the ethic of austere individualism."[4] So, the question is not whether Africa should modernize or industrialize but 'how much' and 'how' Africa should modernize and industrialize. The issue of 'how' and 'how much' have to do with how to adapt the Western modern ways of life to the African communal situation. In my view, this question of 'how much' and 'how' Africa should modernize must be illuminated and informed by the enterprise of African philosophy, which should seek to analyze, critically examine, reconstruct, and systematize, many traditional African ideas, beliefs, principles, and practices that should provide the context and foundation for Africa's modernization and industrialization. My analysis and defense of communalism and morality in African traditions may illuminate what is good or valuable about traditional African ideas that we may want to keep in the process of modernizing. In other words, we should use the African communal ways of life and moral views to circumscribe and inform our modes of modernization and industrialization, and perhaps, nation-building and democratization. In order to modernize and adapt modernization to these communal ways of life, communalism must be properly understood, examined, and analyzed—such analysis is precisely what I have tried to do. But the issue is, what does communalism have to offer?

Indeed, Wiredu has suggested that: "The philosophical thought of a traditional (i.e., preliterate and nonindustrialized) society may hold some lessons of moral significance for a more industrialized society."[5] One advantage and heuristic value of communalism is that it specifies the obligation of everyone to participate in the social affairs of the community. This includes the responsibility of knowing your neighbors, keeping an eye on them, and prodding, chiding, poking them to behave properly. This creates the moral pressure to be morally transparent, 'clean', and upright. Moreover, the African approach to morality and moral education, which is community-based, makes daily living, raising children, and parenting easier tasks than in the modern, liberal, and individualistic culture of the West. Communal moral sensibilities engender caring, sympathy, and offer of help from neighbors. Perhaps, an anecdotal example of the contrast in certain practices in the West and African may illustrate this point. In most African cultures, when one has a problem, one is not likely to hide it or try to deal with it solely by oneself. Usually, you tell family, friends, and neighbors, and everyone will come to your aid and offer help. The maxim is, when you have a problem, you tell everyone because you never know who can help or solve it. When your love one dies, the community grieves with you. When you have a baby, people come to visit, bring you food, and help you to take care of the baby so that the parents, especially the mother, can rest.

Moreover, when one is sick, the whole community comes to one's help or aid. The problem of an individual becomes other people's or the community's problem, and usually, the community's problem becomes the problem of every individual. When people come to your aid or offer help, you do not feel the enormity of a problem in terms of its real weight because people are helping you to bear the burden in order to share in the weight of the problem. This is underscored by the proverb: when many people carry a heavy load, the weight is less on each individual. The communal structures in African cultures help to reduce the stress of dealing with many life problems by oneself alone, and they also provide strictures of social responsibilities, relationships, and expectations by constant and consistent reinforcement, chiding, ribbing or prodding. This is a sharp contract from the practice or attitude in the West. Some people may actually be offended if you come to visit when they have a baby or lose a loved one. I was actually told by someone (a friend) in the US that I was rude when I visited him because he lost a loved one. He indicated that I was rude because I refused to give him the opportunity to grieve by himself. To a large extent, grieving is seen in the Western individualistic mode of thinking as an individual and private thing. Rather, grieving in African cultures is a communal thing. These examples that reflect the attitudes of extreme individualism and privacy are very pervasive in various aspects of life in Western cultures.

The situation I describe about the West is hardly the case in most African cultures. Coping with different situations and various aspects of life and parenting could be difficult and stressful. The communal way of life, and the social responsibility it engenders, indicates that family, friends, and neighbors have to help one to cope with difficult and stressful aspects of one's life. My experience in the United States, though anecdotal, indicates a very different Western way of life. Because of its extreme individualism and privacy, when one has a problem, one keeps it to oneself. That is, when a person has a problem in modern Western societies, the tendency is to deal with it alone. Very often, this problem becomes overwhelming and debilitating. When this happens, some commit suicide, some pay to go to professional counselors, and some find quick fixes such as using hard drugs and alcohol to momentarily suppress the pain of the problem. Perhaps, the high rates of drug addiction and alcoholism in the United States may attest this, or perhaps, these rates are the consequences or symptoms of one's extreme freedom and autonomy to choose to do what one wishes. These social problems are directly or remotely related to the extreme autonomy and individualism, which are the foundation of modern Western liberal conceptions of a person and morality. The moral attitudes and social responsibilities that are engendered by communalism and its view of morality can be viewed positively, in the sense that it allows people to help one another in difficult situations.

Communalism in African traditions and its view of morality and moral education brought about cohesion in many African communities because of the practice of caring and the consistency between actions and principles; this moral principle was devoid of mixed and contradictory messages. The moral sensibilities and points of view were similar or they were based on a moral consensus. Moral precepts were reinforced by everyone via mild ribbing, chiding, prodding, or strong sanctions and condemnations. Everyone in the community looked out for all kids or everyone else. Any adult in the community could discipline any kid. Kids would dare not say that you could not discipline them because you were not their parents. When I was growing up in Africa, all adults had a social responsibility to watch out for and correct a child who was doing a wrong thing. This was, however, feasible because there was a common moral sensibility and a consensus on acceptable principles of morality and how they should be imparted. This responsibility by every adult to show caring, watch out for, and correct children tended to put pressure on children not to misbehave, because they knew that there was always somebody to correct them when they acted wrongly. This made parenting easier. What happens in many modern Western societies is that, because of the individualistic and autonomous view of morality, people are afraid to correct other children because one is not sure of what children were 'taught' by their parents— in terms of what the parents teach their children verbally and what the children observe their parents do. Sometimes, when the correction is at variance with what the children are taught, they are confused with respect to the proper mode of behaving. Parents often make things worst because most parents usually object to other people correcting their children with respect to what is morally correct.

These discussions indicate the differences between the role of adults in African communal cultures and what is perceived to be the exclusive role of parents in Western cultures. The differences seem to explain why some speakers at the 1996 Republican Convention in San Diego snipped at Hilary Clinton's reference to the African idea that it takes a village or community to raise a child. These speakers claimed that it does not take a village or community to raise a child, instead, it takes a family, a traditional nuclear family of mother and father to raise a child. The issue of what constitutes a family is problematic in America, given (1) numerous divorces and remarriages, which create mixed or step families, and (2) gay couples who are adopting or having children. Given the ways of life in many Western industrialized and urban societies, children are not being morally educated. Such moral education does not take place in schools, and because of work, parents hardly can spend enough time with their children to teach or model for them the proper moral conduct, and many people do not fully participate in or utilize religious settings to morally educate kids. The issue is, since only parents can teach children their moral values in the West, when can they realistically have the time to do this? Some children are virtually raised by babysitters and daycare providers. Given the individualistic culture of the West, most parents also object to the idea of babysitters and daycare providers teaching their children moral norms or values because they cannot be sure of the kind of things that they would be taught by these providers, in that they may not approve of their moral point of views on a number of issues. This is partly because the moral principles that people accept are not anchored in some substantive fundamental principles, such as communalism, that all can relate to.

The fundamental communal moral principle in African cultures involves the idea of enhancing the interests and needs of the community for the sake of human well-being and individuals' interest. This humanistic goal becomes the principles that give rise to other moral principles, conduct, and way of life. The informal and moderately indoctrinating modes of moral education, socialization, and acculturation seems to make sure that these principles are imbued in people and are internalized by all. The communal and humanistic moral principles or ways of life provide the foundation for many practices, attitudes, the conception of family, and the social responsibilities of family members. For instance, the notion of an extended family that constitutes the basis for clans, kinship, and community in African traditions does not seem to make sense in the West. People in the African communal setting are always willing to help in various forms to relieve the stresses of life and parenting. This includes moral education, discipline, acting as mentors, providing care and so on. You get help from friends, neighbors, and extended family members at no cost. The communal system is not capitalistic, and it is therefore, not as materialistically inclined in the economic sense as compared to what we have in the West. There is a general attitude of caring and the willingness to help. This attitude of caring usually engenders the attitude of reciprocity because of the social responsibilities that are engendered by communalism. In African traditions, for instance, one cannot imagine a friend, neighbor, relative, mother or grandmother babysitting for you and demanding that you pay for the services. This is part of their social or moral responsibilities.

This practice is very much acceptable in the Western culture, although however, not everyone in the Western may necessarily demand pay for such services. The significant difference is that this practice is acceptable in the West while it is not acceptable in African communal cultures. The essential point is that individualism and capitalism in the West, with respect to the need to accumulate wealth for oneself, has exacerbated the problem of people not having time to help others and the need to demand pay when such help is rendered. For instance, one cannot imagine that your son or relative could live in your home and pay rent. It is a moral and social responsibility on the part of others (relatives, friends, and neighbors) in a community to provide one with shelter. Expecting and accepting rent from a relative or friend may be considered an abomination, but this is acceptable in the West, or perhaps, it is the norm. Moreover, it is very common or it is perhaps the norm that immediately people have reached the age of eighteen, they are expected to leave their parent's home. Or if they live in their parent's home, they ought to pay rent and contribute to the up keep of the house. In the African communal tradition, there is no arbitrary age that determines whether or not one has reached adulthood, which then indicates that one must be independent. The African communal tradition recognizes that it may take some people more time to achieve adulthood and independence. As such, the community, friends, relatives, and neighbors are willing to offer help up to a reasonable time that a person is expected to be able to stand on his own.

Although there is the advantage of having the buffer of a community and an extended family, there are also strings and responsibilities attached to that advantage, which some people may see as a disadvantage. From a liberal individualistic perspective, some people may object to the communal social responsibilities to the community and others because such responsibilities are seen as external impositions that limit one's freedom and autonomy. Some argue that such responsibilities prevent people from pursuing their own individual rational life plans and achieving self-realization. In this regard, some people have argued that the general poverty in Africa is due to the enormous social responsibilities that people have to their extended family and community. Anyone who is wealthy feels an enormous pressure to share his wealth with members of the extended family and such help is indeed expected and demanded as a social responsibility. The argument is that the enormous responsibilities to members of the extended family make your resources so thin that you are not able be to accumulate sufficient capital for investment, in order to establish or grow a business. Some also argue that the social responsibilities to one's kin, family, friends, and community are the source of corruption and nepotism in many African countries.[6] In other words, any person in government or leadership position feels a sense of social responsibility to his community and kin such that he may employ or appoint them to positions that they may not be qualified for or for which there are other better qualified candidates.

A government official or political leader may also feel a need to give contracts to friends, relatives, and kinfolks. He may locate industries in his home district or give it preference in the allocation of resources, irrespective of other countervailing economic and social reasons or factors. While there may be some truth to these claims about the source of corruption, I do think that the issue is more complicated. One cannot provide such a simple and mono-causal explanation to this complicated problem. There are other explanations or combination of factors that may explain corruption and nepotism in Africa. These factors include personal moral failing, selfishness, greed, the need to adopt the Western capitalist, materialistic, and individualistic ways of life, among others. P. P. Ekeh argues that this problem may also be explained, in part, by the phenomenon of 'two publics' that emerged out of colonialism and the different anomalous social structures it created.[7] In Ekeh's view, the communal ethos and values are in play in the primordial public one's dealings with one's community. But these values are not in play in the civic public, where leaders engage in corrupt practices. In my view, if people adopted the communal moral ethos as a thoroughgoing principle of action both in the civic and primordial publics, there would likely be no corruption and nepotism, or it will be reduced to a minimum. Such corrupt actions would be frowned at and there will be communal chiding and ribbing for such actions.

This is the more reason why Africans should go back to their communal roots and values in order to use them as the normative foundation for modernizing and adapting to the modern social structures and their ways of life. This is the reason why we must analyze, reconstruct, and defend communalism in order to make it understandable so that we can utilize it to address African problems. I strongly agree with Ekeh's point that the destruction of the communal social structures and ethos by colonialism has created a situation where people do not think that their actions as government officials are subject to the normative strictures of communal moral ethos. Thus, I do not particularly see a significant problem with the demands of social responsibilities. If current African leaders adhered to their communal values, which demand social responsibilities, they will likely not engage in corrupt actions. In my view, these social responsibilities are the price that one may have to pay for the advantages that one gets from enjoying the help of neighbors, friends, family, and community. Such responsibilities are a reasonable price to pay for the promotion of human well-being, living in peace, safety, or harmony, and the communal buffer that one gets when one is confronted with difficult times. In the United States for instance, the buffer of social security imposes the social responsibility for many people to contribute to it. Such contribution is a reasonable price to pay for the buffer it provides for old people and their loved ones who would have had to bear the burden alone. This is consistent with the African idea of communalism, which is indicated by the proverb: if many people carry a heavy load, each individual does not feel the burden of its weight.

In accordance with this spirit of communalism, I am not sure, personally, whether I would want to be rich and comfortable while I see my relations, friends, and neighbors in abject poverty. I am not sure that I will be comfortable if I show that I am unwilling to help them or share some of my wealth with them. This communal moral attitude is underscored by the proverb or saying that, if one person is rich in a family or community and one does not feel a sense of responsibility to other people, kin, and family, then one is, in reality, very poor. This proverb suggests that one is only rich if one is able to use one's wealth to help family, friends, and community in order to make them rich. One is only wealthy if other people around him are comfortable. I have a personal experience, which may indicate a bias. But this experience which may appear to be a bias also underscores my point about the justification for my position on communalism. My father died when I was very young and my mom had to raise nine children. I was able to go to school to be in the position that I am in today because of the contributions from the community in which my mom lived, and the help from relatives, friends, and neighbors. With this upbringing and a realization of how I came to be who I am, I also have a social and moral responsibility to help others.

This idea of responsibility is a fundamental communal moral point of view or attitude of mutuality that is pervasive in African traditions. This experience also underscores how communalism and its values, as a philosophical theme, are a practice or a learned or lived experience that cannot be adequately taught abstractly as a theory. Many similar stories abound among Africans. I am not sure I would have the person I am today if my mom and her nine children lived in an individualistic society. Perhaps, it would have been more difficult to have turned out as I did. This kind moral attitude that is imbued in people, which they internalize, live, and experience, is the foundation for the idea of communalism in African traditions. This kind of attitude is something that one must acquire on the basis of indoctrination, imitation, experience, and rational understanding. With the example of my own experience, I would say that I was initially indoctrinated into the communal ethos or values, and I imitated other people who behaved this way, but now, I have rational understanding of it based on my own experience and existential situation. I also have the philosophical skills to critically reflect on the idea, analyze it, and to justify or defend it. This indicates that an initial moderate indoctrination about an idea does not necessarily foreclose rational ability to critically reflect on it, understand, and justify it.

One cannot avoid the initial process of indoctrination as a basis for imbuing the idea or value in people. This is because the communal moral attitudes of caring, social responsibilities, and helping others are very pervasive in African traditions. Many of the institutions and practices in African traditions are influenced and shaped by this attitude or principle. As such, many of the institutions that are considered personal and private in the West are considered social in African cultures because of their communal underpinnings. For instance, the institution of marriage is, for the most part, a social institution in African cultures. Marriage is not simply a conjugal or companionate union between two consenting adults. Usually, marriage is a conjugal union of two families or clans or communities, as the case may be. Marriage has implications of the community. A woman is married into a family and clan; she is not just the wife of her husband. She is married into the complex relationships and dynamics of the family in which she has to participate, and to which she has social responsibilities. Being a wife or husband in a marriage involves complex relationships, dynamics, and responsibilities that go beyond their spouses and their relationship. As a result, it is not usual for two people to elope and claim to be *truly* married without the necessary ceremonies to initiate both the man and woman into these complex relationships and dynamics.

The various ceremonies associated with marriage and the complex relationships associated with the institution do place moral responsibilities on the couple regarding how they should live their lives in the public realm (community) and how they should live that part of their private life that has relevance for the public or community. One such responsibility is the raising of children beyond one's own. As already indicated, it does not take only a nuclear family to raise children; it takes a community or clan in the form of an extended family. As a result of this communal set up and the responsibilities it imposes, one learns or realizes that one cannot wake up one day and simply decide one wants to have a child when one is not married. One also has this in mind if one wants to engage in premarital sex. According to Nkiru Nzegwu,

> In some West Africa societies, the Igbo included, socialization and marriage provide an entry into fatherhood, a clear recognition that parenting is a social act to be exercised only by those who have formally and publicly declared [in the context of community] their readiness to perform the role. It is for this reason that in Onitsha (Nigeria) paternity claims are not entertained on the flimsy ground that one is the biological instrument of conception.[8]

This analysis is not meant to imply that anomalous situations do not occur, where teenagers may have premarital sex or have a child out of wedlock, but the fact is that it is not acceptable, and as such one would have to face the consequences of not getting the appropriate rights and recognition that are needed for one to live 'comfortably' in the community. In the same manner, a person cannot wake up one day to argue that he or she wants to divorce his wife or her husband. He or she has to think of what it would take to engage the whole family, clan, or community in the decision and processes of divorce, because since marriage is a social institution involving social rituals and initiation, divorce is also a communal issue.

For instance, because my marriage to my wife is also a marriage to her family, community, kin, and clan and vice versa, we do have certain social and moral responsibilities to both of our families, which have to be taken seriously as the basic underpinning for our marriage. We cannot relinquish those responsibilities in a blink of an eye, on a whim, or at will. Usually, because of the important role of the families, there is also a rapport that a couple develops with both families that make it difficult for both spouses to give up on a marriage very easily. However, from a Western individualistic perspective, marriage is a personal and private issues. Thus, if I consider myself to be married to only my wife, the decision to divorce her would be our decision or perhaps mine or hers. Such a decision would be much easier for both of us or me or her individually. However, it would be more difficult if other people (family and community) are involved in it. This is precisely what happens in the communal African tradition where the institution of marriage and the principles that underpin it have communal foundation and strictures. However, one may argue that the African communal system has its problems in terms of the tremendous pressure and responsibilities it places on people. For instance, the social pressure on people who want to get married is enormous. They have to get the approval of family members such that if such is not given, a person may have to forgo the woman or man he or she loves—if one assumes that love is both necessary and sufficient for marriage. This pressure also means that a couple may have to remain in a marriage even when there are irreconcilable differences between them.

The communal practices and ethos of marriage make it extremely difficult for divorce. It provides limits and parameters for one's autonomy or freedom of choice to get in and out of marriage. Because communalism does not allow one the choice to get out of a marriage on a whim, some argue and criticize it for impeding autonomy, will, freedom, and choice. These are the kinds of criticisms of communalism that people might provide from an extreme liberal individualistic perspective. This argument, like its ancestors that I have previously criticized, has only reincarnated in a different shade. While there is some apparent merit to this stance, I am not convinced about it because it is grounded in an absolute sense of autonomy, which seems to overstate the power of individual rationality or the need for individual freedom. In a more substantive and functional sense, and as a matter of practice, the communal system does not allow one to give up on marriage too easily but it does not totally prevent divorces. Marital problems usually call for and necessitate counseling and intervention by elders and family members. As a communal issue, the people who have to intervene and counsel the couple have a stake and social responsibility in ensuring the success of the relationship. This is different from the Western practice of counseling where a professional counselor does not have a stake except his or her fees; he or she does not have a social responsibility toward the relationship. There are no enduring and mutually acceptable moral principles that the counselor can use as a moral basis for reference, in terms of the needs, demands, and expectations of each person in the marriage.

In the African communal system, there are proven and justifiable enduring substantive principles that counselors or elders may use as a basis for reference regarding what is expected of a husband and wife on the basis of which both can evaluate and modify their behaviors for the success of the marriage. There are traditional communal ways of resolving issues and conflicts that a couple may have in their relationship, and they have models and mentors that they may use as a point of reference or standard. This communal set up, with the associated social responsibilities and expectations, has the implication or consequence of controlling—not necessarily preventing—premarital sex, teenage pregnancy, and having children out of wedlock. In an extreme individualistic society where absolute value is placed on autonomy, an arbitrary age—usually eighteen— is the sole basis for determining adulthood, and there are no social responsibilities, ethos, or initiation processes for controlling sexual behavior, pregnancy, parenting, and marriage. One may underscore why the moral and social issues of sexual behavior (premarital sex), pregnancy (teenage pregnancy), having children out of wedlock, parenting, and marriage are important for communalism, by indicating how they may affect social conditions and equilibrium in the community. These behaviors are important because they may conduce or lead to the disintegration of the traditional families and communities, which in the history of humans, have provided the foundation of morality, moral upbringing, and social associations. These are important issues and concerns that members of the Republican party have couched in terms of family values. Some people have argued that the destruction of the family structure based, on these moral and social anomalies and pathologies, is the reason for many of the current social problems that exist in America.

In my view, these problems are, in part, related to some liberal moral values involving extreme individualism, autonomy, negative freedom. The primacy of rights associated with liberalism tends to vitiate or de-emphasize social responsibilities or sees social responsibilities as social constraints on freedom and autonomy. However, some people who subscribe to a social constructionist view of morality may argue that what is going on in many Western countries is the transformation or modification of the standard notions of family, community, and morality. In other words, these notions and practices are being socially reconstructed. And given the fact that cultures and social institutions are not static, what we are noticing is simply a social or cultural dynamism or transformation. As such, we have to change our attitudes to accept these changes and modifications in our social institutions as an outgrowth of the human social conditions and construction. There is a sense in which my analysis of the communal structures in African cultures indicates that clans and communities founded on communalism are relatively, socially stable internally, compared to the present day communities in Africa. In other words, the social problems of present day African communities may seem to lend credence to this social constructionist argument. Some people may argue that the traditional African communal structures are dying away as a result of the dynamism of cultures and the influence of Western culture. As such, many African cultures are undergoing significant transformations and modifications that have been brought about partly by colonialism and globalism. This point may be true for the most part. However, the essential point is that in our understanding of communalism, we must be cognizant of its advantages so that we may use it as normative basis for making transformations and modification in African social structures. Again, this is consistent with the idea of keeping what is good about African cultures, while making changes to what is bad, in the process modernization.

Some people may argue that my analysis of communalism in Africa cultures and my identification of its advantages involves a romanticization of African past. For instance, Bodunrin argues that the African past that some people want to romanticize was not glorious and it may not be worth reconstructing. He underscores this by saying "Certainly not everything about our past was glorious. Anyone who has watched *Roots* (even if he has not read the book), and however melodramatic the movie version might have been, does not need to be told that. The interminable land disputes between communities, sometimes within the same village, show that the communalism we talk about was between members of very close groups. A way of life which made it possible for our ancestors to be subjugated by a handful of Europeans cannot be described as totally glorious."[9] Although I cannot respond satisfactorily to this criticism, it is pertinent to say that *the whole* of African past may not be that glorious but this does not mean that there were no glorious *parts* of African past. In the same vein, although African communalism has its problems, this does not mean that it does not have its advantages. More importantly, it is not clear how much Bodunrin fully appreciates the nature of communalism in African cultures as I have analyzed it, and its different features, underpinnings, and ramifications. The issue here is, whether we should focus solely on the negative by ignoring the positive or try to provide a balanced view of African traditional structures, such as communalism. While I want to accentuate the positives about African communalism, I do not want to ignore the negatives. It is unreasonable to focus solely on the negatives, which is precisely what many people have done in criticizing African cultures or communalism, and in denying the existence of an African philosophy that is based on African traditions and its communal culture.

Critics who use the Western liberal values and scientific method to criticize African beliefs, ideas, values, and traditions adopt a similar stance of accentuating only the negatives in Africa. Usually, these critics present the positives of the Western liberal values and the scientific method without highlighting the negatives. One may reverse Bodunrin's argument that African value system or communal tradition is not glorious because it enabled our ancestors to be subjugated by a handful of Europeans. One may argue that European values and tradition cannot be considered glorious if such values enabled them to rob, plunder, enslave, subjugate, and cheat our ancestors. Some of the immoral values that allowed Europeans to do these include individualism, selfishness, greed, and capitalistic exploitation, which engendered cheating, lying, deception, lack of caring and sympathy. These were some of the immoral basis on which Europeans colonized, exploited, plundered Africa and enslaved Africans. History has indicated that many Europeans cheated, lied to African chiefs, and deceived them into signing treaties and agreements. The concerns of these Europeans were solely their own gains and interests. Many African chiefs were trusting and caring, thinking that these attitudes were the reasonable ways or means of doing business with Europeans. These trusts were betrayed. In some cases where the chiefs wanted to negotiate fair terms, Europeans used force and violence to get what they wanted. Interestingly enough, some of these immoral values and methods or traditions that allowed Europeans to do these evil things to Africans are what Africans are now being asked to accept wholesale without critical examination or efforts to modify them or smoothen their rough immoral edges by infusing them with some elements of communal morality and ethos.

Many of the conflicts, wars, squabbles, and social problems in traditional Africa were mostly inter-communal problems, i.e., problems between or among communities. This issue is not unique to Africa. These are human problems. There were similar problems between nations and states all over the world. Human beings have not yet devised good structures or means for resolving such problems between or among nations. The United Nations that was supposed to do this has not been successful or effective for various reasons. Most African communities had some internal problems but they devised means for dealing with them, hence the communities were mostly stable, internally. However, many of the current problems in modern African states are problems of nation building that have arisen from the tension and conflict between traditional African ways of doing things and the new social and political structures that emerged from Africa's interaction with Europeans as a result of colonialism, imperialism, neo-colonialism, and globalism. Many people have not made the efforts to understand and analyze the anomalies that were created by colonialism as a result of the 'unholy alliance' between European and African values and traditions. For instance, colonialism created a witch's brew by putting together into one state, a mixture of different ethnic groups that did not quite get along in traditional African society, but coexisted on the basis of mutual fear or respect. The artificial creation, imposition of states, and the forced cohabitation of incongruous peoples have lead to conflicts in values among different ethnic groups. This problem has been highlighted in various forms, some of which are, lack of national integration, massive corruption, incessant coups, civil wars, genocides, and the efforts by some ethnic groups to gain power and dominate the others by imposing their values and will. These are the sources of the problems between the Hutu and Tutsis in Rwanda, in the Darfur region of Sudan, and between the Muslims and Christians in Nigeria, where the Muslims are trying to impose Sharia law on Christians and other non-Muslims.

These problems have arisen partly because there are no authentic dominant values or workable social and political structures, such as communalism, which may be acceptable to all ethnic groups, and to which a modern African state structure can be firmly engrafted. The traditional communal values and ethos have been contaminated or adulterated by the extreme Western liberal and individualistic values. In order to understand and fully appreciate these problems, we must see that what we have in modern African states are enigmatic and anomalous hybrid social structures and values that emerged out of colonialism. Colonialism represents an epochal event in Africa that has created enduring social structures and a system of values and norms, powerful, influential, and pervasive enough to determine people's actions, reasoning, and ways of life.[10] The pertinent point that people have not fully appreciated is the enduring nature of the relics of the epochal event of colonialism, in terms of the social structures and values it created. Ekeh argues that colonialism must be understood and analyzed in terms of "the relationships between the colonizers and the colonized, between the elements of European culture and of indigenous culture."[11] It should be understood and seen as "a *social movement* of epochal dimensions whose enduring significance, beyond the life-span of the colonial situation, lies in the *social formations* of supra-individual entities and constructs. These supra-individual formations developed from the volcano-sized social changes provoked into existence by the confrontations, contradictions, and incompatibilities in the colonial situation."[12] As a social movement, colonialism created many social structures that are enduring, and are still very active today many years after it apparently disappeared.

The unhealthy mix between the incompatible extreme individualistic European values and the communalistic African values or ethos has created an enigmatic and anomalous hybrid culture that is still pervasive today. This hybrid culture has created a normative vacuum, in that people do not understand what its incoherent norms and values truly mean, the responsibilities they impose, and how they ought to be applied to substantive political and social problems. This is the reason why I think—as topic for another project and further research—an analysis of communalism as a moral foundation for political structures in African traditions will be fruitful. In other words, the idea of communalism as an authentic African norm could provide the foundation for anchoring a uniquely adapted form of democracy and democratization in modern African states.

Bearing in mind the issue of finding an authentic African normative basis for the social, political, and economic structures in modern African states, we can appreciate why Ekeh has questioned the conceptual adequacy of the notions of 'decolonization', 'independence', and 'neo-colonialism' in Africa. He argues that:

"As a social movement, the impact of colonialism cannot be terminated abruptly in one day or one year . . . colonialism therefore implies that the social formations . . . could be traced to issues and problems that span the colonial situation into post-Independence social structures in Africa."[13] One such problem involves finding an adequate and workable normative basis for modern African states in order to address the problems of cultural or ethnic differences and conflicts, and national integration. Many Africans have not adequately appreciated these problems, which have been highlighted by how political and government officials see their responsibilities, the expectations of citizens, and how citizens view the actions and policies of these officials. There is usually no moral indignation from citizens when officials are corrupt. Instead, kinfolks or home communities expect government officials to be corrupt in appointments and the allocation resources so that they will be favored. In my view, these moral attitudes are, in part, a result of colonialism and not African communalism. Since there is no clear moral guidance, officials cannot clearly see or understand their obligations or the expectations of citizens in the context of the enigmatic and anomalous hybrid mixture of the communal ethos and the extreme individualistic ethos of Europe.

Many African leaders, politicians, and government officials have difficulty understanding this hybrid mixture or its moral ethos. They also do not understand how the idea of a modern African state that is conceived and exported from Europe to Africa ought to operate or be operated by them in the African context. We should recollect that many modern African states are artificial creations that emerged from 1884-85 Berlin Conference for the scramble and partition of Africa. According to Ekeh: "It is important to note that the European organizational pieces that came to us [including the modern state] were virtually disembodied of their moral contents, of their substratum of implicating ethics. And yet the imported models were never engrafted onto any existing indigenous morality."[14] In the traditional African communal structures, people clearly understood their obligations and they knew what they ought to do. The enigmatic hybrid colonial mixture of African and European social structures has, in part, resulted in nepotism, massive corruption, bad governments, and the inability of African leaders to articulate adequate ethos and good public policies that can resolve ethnic conflicts and other problems in order to achieve national integration. In this respect, I will acknowledge that a person like me who is trained in the West and has imbibed or internalized some Western cultures and values could be part of this African problem. People of my type tend to have a kind of 'colonial mentality', that is, the idea of wholesale internalization of the colonial European ethos and values, and then seeing everything and criticizing African ideas or ways of life solely from a colonial Western or European perspective that is not critically examined.

Usually, people of my kind go back home to the traditional African system to question the ways of doing things and to castigate the traditional ideas and structures as backward and crude, without seeing or making efforts to understand and see the advantages of the system. We also do not make efforts to understand the anomalous situation that has been created by colonialism in order to find ways to address the problems. We mostly engage in the kind of destructive criticism of Africa that has not been very helpful. Many of us do not provide constructive ways to understand our problems, the problematic situation from which the problems arose, and creative ways to solve them. Some of us may argue that we should not blame colonialism for everything and we should accept that our leaders are simply inept, bad, and immoral. But we also fail to understand that the leaders and the structures within which they are leading are anomalous and enigmatic, and that we do not fully understand this hybrid culture. This is the kind attitude or sentiment that is displayed by many critics of African traditions, African philosophy, and those who argue that a genuine African philosophy, political theory, or political system cannot be reconstructed or culled out of African traditions and communalism. The effort in this book is to buck this trend. The effort here is to provide a normative basis on which a genuine African political system may be built. Such a system will be more in tune with the African way of life that we understand, live, and experience.

Sometimes, because African people have a communal way of life that they understand, live, and experience, and because they are uncomfortable with the 'foreign', enigmatic, and anomalous hybrid social structures of colonialism in Africa, they act out or engage is some resistance. Such resistance seems to culminate in the different forms, shapes, kinds, manifestations, and magnitudes of social upheavals that we find in Africa. The macabre debacle in Rwuanda and Burundi between the Tutsis and Hutu was perhaps one such manifestation. These two incongruous groups were forcibly put together in artificial states. Moreover, they seem to have had traditional ways of solving their troubles and living together amicably either on the basis of mutual respect or fear. But with colonialism, their traditional ways of doing things were undercut. Because of the existence of states that are artificially created and imported into Africa by Europeans, one group wanted to use the European state structure to acquire and wield power through the government in order to dominate the other group. The resistance was, in part, the source of the conflict and the eventual result was the debacle. Perhaps, another example of this can be found in Kwame Anthony Appiah's book, *In My Father's House*.[15] In the Epilogue of this book, Appiah describes a situation in which there is tension between the European patrilineal system or values and the traditional Asante matrilineal system and values. Kwame Appiah's father married an English woman, and based on Asante's culture, which is matrilineal, Kwame Appiah did not have a lineage with his father's folks. According to his mother's (English) culture, which is patrilineal, he did not have any lineage with his mother's kin. Kwame Appiah has been brought up and educated in Europe, precisely, England, and in the process, imbibed and internalized European values and views of family and lineage, and the relevant practices. These European values shaped Appiah's outlook in terms of how things ought to be done.

From Kwame Appiah's account in the Epilogue of his book, he made efforts to undercut and denigrate the Asante traditional matrilineal system by trying to claim that he has a lineage with his father's kin. But the Asante tradition and people will not allow him to have his way or impose his European values on them. This created a conflict that seemed to have frustrated or infuriated him. This situation, and especially the way he describes it in his book, presents some African cultures, precisely the Asante culture of Ghana, as problematic, backward, and inherently full of intrigues. This is because he failed to accept the Asante culture or he wanted to impose the European culture on his father's kin and traditions as a way of modernizing and civilizing the backward people. Hence, when *some people* talk about the modernization of African cultures, I am suspicious of their intent and agenda. When Appiah could not impose his accepted European cultural values on his father's kin, he criticized the culture and saw it as backward and problematic. For someone who does not understand the situation, the impression one will take away is that African cultures are inherently problematic in brewing social problems. Thanks to Nkiru Nzegwu, who has done a good job of clarifying the source of the problem that Appiah describes in an African culture. Nzegwu suggests that the problem is that of imperialism and the attempt not only to view African principles from a Eurocentric perspective, but also to see these principles and traditions solely in pejorative terms.[16] He could not make any claims of lineage in his mother's kin, but he thought he had legitimate claims of lineage in his father's kin. Because his father's culture did not allow him to make such claims, which was legitimate from an English perspective, he saw it as bad.

Excluding the colonial and imperialistic factors, which are the major sources of social problems in Africa, for the most part, communities in African cultures are relatively stable and are peaceful *internally*, because of the communal principles and structures, which shaped the dynamics of family and the different ways of life. I have tried not to paint a picture of an absolutely rosy traditional African communal society. The main point here is to give credence to the point made by Wiredu that there are advantages in traditional African communal cultures that modern Western thought and societies can learn from in terms of how they address many of their social problems. The irony of this is that African people are actually moving away from their traditional ways of life and are imbibing or internalizing the Western view or ways of life. Africans seem to have been culturally influenced, socialized or indoctrinated to think and accept the view that whatever is Western is good and better than what is African. In this respect, the African traditional communal views of a person, morality, moral reasoning, and moral education may provide a basis to contrast contemporary analytic philosophical notion of liberal morality, which is founded solely on an individual's rational autonomy. The contemporary view of the moral person, moral education, and moral reasoning has had a major influence on how people *now* see their moral duties and obligation toward others, authority, and community. Thus, many scholars and social critics have argued that the modern individualistic view of morality that is founded on the absolute value of autonomy has led to certain malaise in Western society. I have tried to show how this individualistic view, when contrasted with the traditional communal African view, may not be the most plausible way of conceiving of morality, personhood, moral reasoning, and moral education. In this sense, African thought and its communal principles have heuristic practical and theoretical values, in that they provide an alternative that we may use to critically examine the dominant Western liberal views.

# Notes

1. Wiredu, *Cultural Universals and Particulars*, 72. Wiredu argues that the distinction, relationship, or tension between individualism and communalism is a matter of degree, in that one cannot logically preclude the other.

2. Gyekye, *Tradition and Modernity*, 61.

3. Wiredu, *Philosophy and An African Culture*, 21-22. Here, Wiredu extolls the virtues of African communalism and the vices of Western model of modernization, which involves capitalism, and urbanization, and industrialization that have the tendencies to create big cities and its moral decadence.

4. Wiredu, *Cultural Universals and Particulars*, 72.

5. Wiredu, "On Defining African Philosophy," 98.

6. See, for instance, Wiredu's point in *Philosophy and An African Culture*, 23.

7. Ekeh, "Colonialism and the Two Publics in Africa," 91-112, and *Colonialism and Social Structure*.

8. For a detailed analysis, see Nzegwu, "Question of Identity and Inheritance," 186.

9. Bodunrin, "The Question of African Philosophy," 7.

10. Ekeh, *Colonialism and Social Structure*, 4.

11. Ekeh, *Colonialism and Social Structure*, 4.

12. Ekeh, *Colonialism and Social Structure*, 5.

13. Ekeh, *Colonialism and Social Structure*, 5.

14. Ekeh, *Colonialism and Social Structure*, 17.

15. Appiah, *In My Father's House: Africa in the Philosophy of Culture*.

16. See Nzegwu, "Questions of Identity and Inheritance," 175-201.

# Bibliography

Achebe, Chinua. *Things Fall Apart*. New York: Fawcett Crest, 1993.

Appiah, Kwame Anthony. *Necessary Questions: An Introduction to Philosophy*. Englewood Cliffs, NJ: Prentice Hall, 1989.

————. *In My Father's House: Africa in the Philosophy of Culture*. New York: Oxford University Press, 1992.

Alagoa, E. J. "Nigerian Academic Historians." Pp. 189-196 in *African Historiographies: What History for Which Africa*, edited by Bogumil Jewsiewicki and David Newbury. London: Sage Publications, 1986.

Annis, David. "A Contextual Theory of Epistemic Justification." *American Philosophical Quarterly* 15, no. 3 (1978): 213-219.

————. "The Social and Cultural Component of Epistemic Justification—A Reply." *Philosophia* 12 (1982): 51-55.

Atkinson, R. F. "Indoctrination and Moral Education." Pp. 55-66 in *Concepts of Indoctrination: Philosophical Essays*, edited by I. A. Snook. London: Routledge & Kegan Paul, 1972.

Ayoade, J. A. A. "Time in Yoruba Thought." Pp. 93-111 in *African Philosophy: An Introduction*, edited by Richard A. Wright. New York: University Press of America, 1984.

Bailey, Charles. "Morality, Reason and Feeling." *Journal of Moral Education* 9, (1980): 114-121.

Bernal, Martin. *Black Athena: The Afroasiatic Roots of Classical Civilization Vols. I and II*. New Brunswick, NJ: Rutgers University Press, 1988.

Blocker, H. Gene. *Ethics: An Introduction*. New York: Haven Publications, 1986.

Bodunrin, P. O. "The Question of African Philosophy." *Philosophy* 56 (1981): 61-79. Reprinted, pp. 1-23 in *African Philosophy: An Introduction*, edited by Richard A. Wright. New York: University Press of America, 1984.

Boxill, Bernard. "Majoritarian Democracy and Cultural Minorities." Pp. 112-119 in *Multiculturalism and American Democracy*, edited by Arthur M. Melzer, Jerry Weinberger, and M. Richard Zinman. Lawrence: Kansas University Press, 1998.

Brown, Lee M., ed. *African Philosophy: New and Traditional Perspectives.* New York: Oxford University Press, 2004.

Bruner, Jerome. *Actual Minds, Possible Worlds.* Cambridge, MA: Harvard University Press, 1986.

Busa, Ananyo. "Communitarianism and Individualism in African Thought." *International Studies in Philosophy* 30, no. 4 (1998): 1-10.

Coetzee, P. H. and A. P. J. Roux, eds. *The African Philosophy Reader.* London: Routledge, 1998.

Coleman, Jules. "Negative and Positive Positivism." *Journal of Legal Studies* 11 (January 1982): 139-164.

Diop, Cheik Anta. *The African Origin of Civilization.* New York: Lawrence and Company, 1974.

———. *The Cultural Unity of Black Africa: The Domains of Patriarchy and of Matriarchy in Classical Antiquity.* Introduction by John Henrik Clarke. Afterword by James G. Spady. Chicago: Third World Press, 1978.

Dixon, Vernon. "World-views and Research Methodology." Pp. 51-80 in *African Philosophy: Assumptions and Paradigms for Research on Black Persons,* edited by L. M. King, Vernon Dixon, and W. W. Nobles. Los Angeles: Fanon Center Publication, 1976.

Donagan, Alan. *The Theory of Morality.* Chicago: University of Chicago Press, 1977.

Doyle, James F. ed. *Educational Judgments.* London: Routledge & Kegan Paul, 1973.

Dretske, Fred. "The Pragmatic Dimension of Knowledge." *Philosophical Studies* 40 (1981): 363-378.

Dzobo, N. K. "African Symbols and Proverbs as Source of Knowledge and Truth." Pp. 85-99 in *Person and Community: Ghanaian Philosophical Studies I,* edited by Kwasi Wiredu and Kwame Gyekye. Washington, D.C.: Council for Research in Values and Philosophy, 1992.

Ekeh, Peter P. *Social Exchange Theory: The Two Traditions.* Cambridge, MA: Harvard University Press, 1974.

———. "Colonialism and Social Structure." *An Inaugural Lecture.* University of Ibadan, 1983.

English, Parker. "Nigerian Ethnophilosophy, Unitary Experience, and Economic Development." *Journal of Social Philosophy* 22, no.1 (1991): 102-124.

English, Parker. and Nancy Steele Hamme. "Morality, Art, and African Philosophy: A Response to Wiredu." Pp. 407-420 in *African Philosophy: Selected Readings,* edited by Albert G. Mosley. Englewood Cliffs, NJ: Prentice Hall, 1995.

———. "Using Art History and Philosophy to Compare a Traditional and a Contemporary Form of African Moral Thought." *Journal of Social Philosophy* 27, no. 2 (Fall 1996): 204-233.

———. "Spiritualism and Authoritarianism in an African Moral System." *Philosophical Forum* 28, no. 4/29 no. 1 (Summer/Fall 1997): 320-350.

Ennis, Robert H. "A Conception of Critical Thinking." *Harvard Educational Review* 32 (1962): 83-111.

Etzioni, Amitai. *The Spirit of Community: Rights, Responsibilities, and the Communitarian*

*Agenda*. New York: Crown Publishers, Inc., 1993.

Evans-Pritchard, E. E. *Theories of Primitive Religion*. Oxford: Clarendon Press, 1965.

Eze, Emmanuel. *Race and Enlightenment*. London: Blackwell Publishers, Ltd., 1997.

Feldman, Fred and Earl Conee. "Evidentialism." *Philosophical Studies*. 48 (1985): 15-34.

Finnis, John. *Natural Law and Natural Rights*. Oxford: Clarendon Press, 1980.

Flew, Anthony. "What is Indoctrination?" *Studies in Philosophy and Education* 4, no. 3 (1966): 281-306.

Floistad, Guttorm. ed. *Contemporary Philosophy: A New Survey, Vol. 5: African Philosophy*. Dordrecht: Martinus Nijhorff, 1987.

Forst, Rainer "Foundations of a Theory of Multicultural Justice." *Constellations* 4, no. 1 (1997): 63-71.

Fortunes, R. S. *The Sorcerers of Dobu*. London: Routledge & Kegan Paul, 1963.

Frankena, William K. *Ethics*. Englewood Cliffs, NJ: Prentice Hall, 1963.

———. "The Concept of Education Today." Pp. 19-32 in *Educational Judgments*, edited by James F. Doyle. London: Routledge & Kegan Paul, 1973.

———. "Towards a Philosophy of Education." *Harvard Educational Review* 28 (November 1958): 298-311.

Friedman, Marilyn. "Care and Context in Moral Reasoning." Pp. 190-204 in *Women and Moral Theory*, edited by Eva Feder Kittay and Diana T. Meyers. Savage, MD: Rowman & Littlefield, 1987.

Fuller, Steve. *Social Epistemology*. Bloomington, Indiana University Press, 1988.

Gbadegesin, Segun. "*Eniyan*: The Yoruba Concept of A Person." Pp. 171-199 in *The African Philosophy Reader*, edited by P. H. Coetzee and A. P. J. Roux. London: Routledge, 1998.

———. "An Outline of a Theory of Destiny." Pp. 51-68 in *African Philosophy: New and Traditional Perspectives*, edited by Lee M. Brown. New York: Oxford University Press, 2004.

Geertz, Clifford. "On the Nature of Anthropological Understanding." *American Scientist* 63 (1975): 47-53.

Gettier, Edmund. "Is Justified True Belief Knowledge?" *Analysis* 23 (1963): 121-123.

Gewirth, Alan. "Morality and Autonomy in Education," Pp. 33-45 in *Educational Judgments*, edited by James F. Doyle. London: Routledge & Kegan Paul, 1973.

Gilligan, Carol. "Moral Orientation and Moral Development." Pp. 19-33 in *Women and Moral Theory*, edited by Eva Feder Kittay and Diana T. Meyers. Savage, MD: Rowman & Littlefield, 1987.

Goldman, Alvin. "Discrimination and Perceptual Knowledge." *Journal of Philosophy* 73, no. 2 (1976): 771-791.

———. *Epistemology and Cognition*. Cambridge, MA: Harvard University Press, 1986.

Granger, Herbert. "Aristotle and the Concept of Supervenience." *Southern Journal of Philosophy* 31, no. 2 (1993): 161-178.

———. "Aristotle and the Functionalist Debate." *Apeiron* 23, no. 1 (1990): 27-49.

Green, T. F. *The Activities of Teaching*. New York: McGraw-Hill, 1971.

———. "Indoctrination and Beliefs." Pp. 25-46 in *Concepts of Indoctrination*, edited by I. A. Snook. London: Routledge & Kegan Paul, 1972.

Gyekye, Kwame "The Akan Concept of a Person." *International Philosophical Quarterly*

18 (1978): 277-287. Reprinted, Pp. 199-212 in *African Philosophy: An Introduction*, edited by Richard A. Wright. New York: University Press of America, 1984.

———. *An Essay On African Philosophical Thought: The Akan Conceptual Scheme*, rev. ed. Philadelphia: Temple University Press, 1995.

———. *Tradition and Modernity: Philosophical Reflections on the African Experience*. New York: Oxford University Press, 1997.

———. "Person and Community in Akan Thought." Pp. 101-121 in *Person and Community: Ghanaian Philosophical Studies 1*, edited by Kwame Gyekye and Kwasi Wiredu. Washington D.C.: Council for Research in Values and Philosophy, 1992.

Gyekye, Kwame and Kwasi Wiredu, eds. *Person and Community: Ghanaian Philosophical Studies 1*. Washington D.C.: Council for Research in Values and Philosophy, 1992.

Hadot, Pierre. *What is Ancient Philosophy?* Translated by Michael Chase. Harvard University Press, 2002.

Harding, Sandra. *Is Science Multicultural?: Postcolonialism, Feminisms, and Epistemologies*. Bloomington, IN: Indiana University Press, 1998.

———. "The Curious Coincidence of Feminine and African Moralities: Challenges for Feminist Theory." Pp. 296-315 in *Women and Moral Theory*, edited by Eva Feder Kittay and Diana T. Meyers. Savage, MD: Rowman & Littlefield, 1987.

Hardwig, John. "Epistemic Dependence." *Journal of Philosophy* 82, no. 7 (1985):335-349.

———. "Evidence, Testimony, and the Problem of Individualism—A Response to Schmitt," *Social Epistemology* 2, no., 4 (1988): 309-321.

Hare, R. M. "Adolescents into Adults." Pp. 47-70 in *Aims in Education: The Philosophical Approach*, edited by T. H. B. Hollins. Manchester: Manchester University Press, 1964.

Harman, Gilbert. *Thought*. Princeton, NJ: Princeton University Press, 1973.

———. "Knowledge, Inference, and Explanation." *American Philosophical Quarterly* 5, no. 3 (July 1968):164-173.

Haste, Helen. "Communitarianism and the Social Construction of Morality." *Journal of Moral Education*. 25, no. 1 (1996): 47-55.

Hegel, Georg. *The Philosophy of History*. Translated by J. Sibree. New York: Dover, 1956.

Heinaman, Robert. "Aristotle and the Mind-Body Problem." *Phronesis* 35, no. 1 (1990): 83-102.

Hernstein, Richard J. and Charles Murray. *The Bell Curve: Intelligence and Class Structure in American Life*. New York: The Free Press, 1994.

Hord, Fred Lee (Mzee Lasana Okpara), and Jonathan Scott Lee, eds. *I Am Because We Are: Readings in Black Philosophy*. Amherst, MA: University of Massachusetts Press, 1995.

Hountondji, Paulin. *African Philosophy: Myth and Reality*. Bloomington: Indiana University Press, 1983.

Ikuenobe, Polycarp. "The Parochial Universalist Conceptions of 'Philosophy' and 'African Philosophy'." *Philosophy East and West* 47, no. 2 (1997): 189-210.

———. "A Defense of Epistemic Authoritarianism in Traditional African Cultures." *Journal of Philosophical Research* 23 (1998): 417-440.

———. "Moral Epistemology, Relativism, African Cultures, and the Distinction Between Custom and Morality." *Journal of Philosophical Research*. 27 (2002): 641-669.

———. "Logical Positivism, Analytic Method, and Criticisms of Ethnophilosophy." *Metaphilosophy* 35, no. 4 (July 2004): 479-503.

. "Cognitive Relativism, African Philosophy, and the Phenomenon of Witchcraft." *Journal of Social Philosophy* 26, no. 3 ( 1995): 143-160.

. "In Search of Human Universality: Context and Justification in Cultural Philosophy." *Humanitas* 11, no. 2 (1998): 58-90.

. "Moral Thought in African Cultures?: A Metaphilosophical Question." *African Philosophy* 12, no. 2 (1999): 105-123.

. "Cognitive Relativism Without Incommensurability, Truth, and Particularism." *International Studies in Philosophy* 33, no. 2 (2001): 31-57.

Jackson, Gerald G. "The African Genesis of the Black Perspective in Helping." Pp. 314-331 in *Black Psychology* 2*nd* *Ed,* edited by R. L Jones. New York: Harper & Row, 1980.

Jackson, Michael and Ivan Karp, eds. *Personhood and Agency: The Experience of Self and Others in African Cultures.* Washington, D.C., Smithsonian Institution Press, 1990.

James, George. *Stolen Legacy.* Newport News, VA: United Brothers Communications Systems, 1989.

Jewsiewicki, Bogumil and David Newbury, eds. *African Historiographies: What History for Which Africa.* London: Sage Publications, 1986.

Kant, Immanuel. *Critique of Judgment.* Translated by J. H. Bernard. New York: Hafner, 1951.

Kaphagawani, Didier. "On African Communalism: A Philosophic Perspective," *A paper presented at the First International Regional Conference in Philosophy.* May 23-27, 1988, Mombassa, Kenya.

. "Some African Concepts of Person: A Critique." Pp. 66-82 in *African Philosophy as Cultural Inquiry,* edited by Ivan Karp and D. A. Masolo. Bloomington, IN: Indiana University Press, 2000.

Karp, Ivan and D. A. Masolo, eds. *African Philosophy as Cultural Inquiry.* Bloomington, IN: Indiana University Press, 2000.

Kaufman, Anold S. "Comments on Frankena's 'The Concept of Education Today'." Pp. 46-55 in *Educational Judgments,* edited by James F. Doyle. London: Routledge & Kegan Paul, 1973.

Keita, Lacinay. "The African Philosophical Tradition." Pp. 57-76 in *African Philosophy: An Introduction,* edited by Richard A. Wright. New York: University Press of America, 1984.

Klein, Peter. "A Proposed Definition of Knowledge Propositional Knowledge." *Journal of Philosophy* 68 (1971): 471-482.

Kohlberg, Lawrence. "Stages of Moral Development as a Basis of Moral Education." Pp. 23-92 in *Moral Education: Interdisciplinary Approaches,* edited by C. Beck, B. Crittendon, and E. Sullivan. Toronto: University of Toronto Press, 1971.

. *Essays on Moral Development: Vol. 1—The Philosophy of Moral Development.* New York: Harper & Row, 1981.

. *Essays on Moral Development: Vol. 2—The Philosophy of Moral Development.* New York: Harper & Row, 1984.

. "From Is to Ought: How to Commit the Naturalistic Fallacy and Get Away with it in the Study of Moral Development." Pp. 151-231 in *Cognitive Development and Epistemology,* edited by T. Mischel. New York: Academic Press, 1971.

Kohlberg, Lawrence, Charles Levine, and Alexander Hewer. *Moral Stages: A Current*

*Reformation and Response to Critics.* Basel: S. Karger, 1983.

Kuhn, Thomas. *The Structure of Scientific Revolutions.* Chicago: University of Chicago Press, 1962.

Kymlicka, Will. *Liberalism, Community, and Culture.* Oxford: Clarendon Press, 1989.

———. *Multicultural Citizenship: A Liberal Theory of Minority Rights.* Oxford: Clarendon Press, 1995.

———. *Politics in the Vernacular: Nationalism, Multiculturalism, and Citizenship.* Oxford: Oxford University Press, 2001.

Lehrer, Keith and Thomas Paxson, Jr. "Knowledge: Undefeated Justified True Belief." *Journal of Philosophy* 66 (1969): 225-237.

Levy-Bruhl, L. *How Natives Think.* London: Allen & Unwin, 1926.

Lloyd, Dennis. *The Idea of Law.* London: Penguin Books, 1981.

Lovejoy, Paul E. "Nigeria: The Ibadan School of History and Its Critics." Pp. 197-205 in *African Historiographies: What History for Which Africa,* edited by Bogumil Jewsiewicki and David Newbury. London: Sage Publications, 1986.

MacIntyre, Alasdair. *After Virtue.* Notre Dame, IN: Notre Dame University Press, 1981.

Mackinnon, Barbara. ed. *American Philosophy: A Historical Anthology.* Albany, NY: State University of New York Press, 1985.

Marrou, Henri I. *A History of Education in Antiquity.* Translated by George Lamb. New York: The New American Library, 1964.

Masolo, D. A. "The Concept of the Person in Lou Modes of Thought." Pp. 84-106 in *African Philosophy: New and Traditional Perspectives,* edited by Lee M. Brown. New York: Oxford University Press, 2004.

———. *African Philosophy in Search of Identity.* Bloomington, IN: Indiana University Press, 1994.

Mbiti, John. *African Religions and Philosophy.* Oxford, England: Heinemann International, 1969.

McDonough, Kevin. "The Importance of Examples for Moral Education: An Aristotelian Perspective." *Studies in Philosophy and Education* 14, no. 1 (1995): 81-89.

McPeck, J. E. *Critical Thinking and Education.* New York St. Martins Press, 1981.

Menkiti, Ifeanyi. "Person and Community in African Traditional Thought." Pp. 171-181 in *African Philosophy: An Introduction,* edited by Richard A. Wright. New York: University Press of America, 1984.

———. "Physical and Metaphysical Understanding: Nature, Agency, and Causation in African Traditional Thought." Pp. 107-135 in *African Philosophy: New and Traditional Perspectives,* edited by Lee M. Brown. New York: Oxford University Press, 2004.

Mill, J. S. *Utilitarianism,* edited by Roger Crisp. New York: Oxford University Press, 1998.

Moody-Adams, Michele M. "Culture, Responsibility, and Affected Ignorance." *Ethics* 104 (January 1994): 291-309.

———. "On the Old Saw that Character Is Destiny." Pp. 111-131 in *Identity, Character, and Morality,* edited by Owen Flanagan and Amelie O. Rorty. Cambridge, MA: MIT Press, 1990.

Moore, Willis. "Indoctrination and Democratic Method." Pp. 93-100 in *Concepts of Indoctrination: Philosophical Essays,* edited by I. A. Snook. London: Routledge & Kegan

Paul, 1972.

Mosley, Albert, ed. *African Philosophy: Selected Readings.* Englewood Cliffs, NJ: Prentice Hall, 1995.

Nielson, Kai."Problems of Ethics." Pp. 117-134 in *The Encyclopedia of Philosophy* Vols. 3 & 4, edited by Paul Edwards. New York: Macmillan Publishing, 1972.

Noddings, Nel. *Caring. A Feminine Approach to Ethics and Moral Education.* Los Angeles, CA: University of California Press, 1984.

———. "Conversation as Moral Education." *Journal of Moral Education* 23, no. 2 (1994): 107-118.

Nzegwu, Nkiru. "Questions of Identity and Inheritance: A Critical Review of Kwame Anthony Appiah's *In My Father's House.*" *Hypatia* 11, no. 1 (Winter 1996): 175-201.

Nyerere, Julius K. *"Ujaama*—The Basis of African Socialism" in *Freedom and Unity.* New York: Oxford University Press, 1968.

Ofiemu, Odia. "Africa's Many Mansions." *West Africa* July 20-26 (1992): 1231-32.

Ogbonnaya, A. Okechuckwu. "Person as Community: An African Understanding of the Person as an Intrapsychic Community." *Journal of Black Psychology* 20, no. 1 (February 1994): 74-87.

Oladipo, O. T. *An African Conception of Reality: A Philosophical Analysis.* Unpublished Doctoral Dissertation. University of Ibadan, Nigeria, 1988.

Onwuanibe, Richard C. "The Human Person and Immortality in IBO (African) Metaphysics." Pp. 183-197 in *African Philosophy: An Introduction,* edited by Richard A. Wright. New York: University Press of America, 1984.

Onyewuenyi, Innocent C. "Traditional African Aesthetics: A Philosophical Perspective." Pp. 421-427 in *African Philosophy: Selected Readings,* edited by Albert Mosley. Englewood Cliffs, NJ: Prentice Hall, 1995.

Oruka, Odera. "African Philosophy," Pp. 57-69, in *Contemporary Philosophy: A New Survey, Vol. 5: African Philosophy,* edited by Guttorm Floistad. Dordrecht: Martinus Nijhorff, 1987.

Oruka, H. Odera and D. A. Masolo, eds. *Philosophy and Culture.* Nairobi: Bookwise Limited, 1983.

Parekh, Bhikhu."Dilemmas of a Multicultural Theory of Citizenship." *Constellations* 4, no. 1 (1997): 54-62

p'Bitek, Okot. "On Culture, Man, and Freedom." Pp. 105-119 in *Philosophy and Culture,* edited by H. Odera Oruka and D. A. Masolo. Nairobi: Bookwise Limited, 1983.

Perelman, Chaim. *The New Rhetoric and the Humanities.* Dordrecht, The Netherlands: Reidel, 1979.

Pincoffs, Edmund L. "On Avoiding Moral Indoctrination." Pp. 59-73 in *Educational Judgments,* edited by James F. Doyle. London: Routledge & Kegan Paul, 1973.

Posner, Richard. *The Problems of Jurisprudence.* Cambridge, MA: Harvard University Press, 1990.

Presbey, Gail M. "Maasai Concepts of Personhood: The Roles of Recognition, Community, and Individuality." *International Studies in Philosophy* 34, no. 2 (2002): 57-82.

Quine, W. V. O. "Two Dogmas of Empiricism." In *From A Logical Point of View.* New York: Harper & Row, Publishers, 1961.

Rawls, John. *A Theory of Justice.* Cambridge, MA: Harvard University Press, 1971.

Raz, Joseph. *The Morality of Freedom*. Oxford University Press, 1986.

Rescher, Nicholas. *Philosophical Reasoning: A Study in the Methodology of Philosophizing.* Oxford: Blackwell Publishers, Ltd., 2001.

Riley, Patrick. "A Possible Explanation of Rousseau's General Will." Pp. 167-189 in *The Social Contract Theorists: Critical Essays on Hobbes, Locke, and Rousseau*, edited by Christopher W. Morris. Lanham, MD: Rowman & Littlefield Publishers Inc., 1999.

Robinson, J.A. and L. Hawpe. "Narrative Thinking As A Heuristic Process." Pp. 108-132 in *Narrative Psychology: The Storied Nature Human Conduct*, edited by T. R. Sarbin. New York: Praeger, 1986.

Russell, Bertrand. *A History of Western Philosophy*. London: George Allen and Unwin, 1975.

———. *Education and the Social Order*. London: Allen & Unwin, 1967.

———. *Mysticism and Logic*. London: Allen & Unwin, 1917.

Sarbin, Theodore R.. "The Narrative as a Root Metaphor for Psychology." Pp. 3-21 in *Narrative Psychology: The Storied Nature Human Conduct*, edited by T. R. Sarbin. New York: Praeger, 1986.

Schmitt, Frederick. "The Justification of Group Beliefs." Pp. 257-287 in *Socializing Epistemology: The Social Dimensions of Knowledge*, edited by Frederick Schmitt. Boston, MA: Rowman & Littlefied Publishers, 1994.

Senghor, Leopold Sedar. "Negritude: A Humanism of the Twentieth Century." Pp. 45-54 in *I Am Because We Are: Readings in Black Philosophy*, edited by Fred Lee Hord and Jonathan Scott Lee. Amherst, MA: University of Massachusetts Press, 1995.

Shields, Christopher. "Soul and Body in Aristotle." *Oxford Studies in Ancient Philosophy* 6 (1988): 103-37.

Siegel, Harvey. *Educating Reason*. New York: Routledge, 1998.

Silver, Charles. "Negative Positivism and the Hard Facts of Life." *Monist* 68 (1985): 347-363.

Slote, Michael. "Is Virtue Possible?" *Analysis* 42 (1982):70-76, reprinted Pp. 100-105 in *The Virtues*, edited by R. Kruschwitz and R. Roberts. Belmont, CA: Wadsworth, 1987.

Smith, John E. *Spirit of American philosophy*. Albany, NY: SUNY Press, 1983.

Snook, I. A. *Indoctrination and Education*. London: Routledge & Kegan Paul, 1972.

———, ed. *Concepts of Indoctrination: Philosophical Essays*. London: Routledge & Kegan Paul, 1972.

———. "Indoctrination and Moral Responsibility." Pp. 152-165 in *Concepts of Indoctrination: Philosophical Essays*, edited by I. A. Shook. London: Routledge & Kegan Paul, 1972.

Sodipo, J. O. "Notes on the Concept of Cause and Change in Yoruba Traditional Thought." *Second Order* 2, no 2, (1973): 12-20.

Sosa, Ernest. "How Do You Know?" *American Philosophical Quarterly* 11, no. 2 (1974): 113-122.

Suttle, Bruce B. "The Need for and Inevitability of Moral Indoctrination," *Educational Studies* 12, no. 2 (1981): 151-161.

Taiwo, Olufemi. "Appropriating Africa: An Essay on new African Schools." *Issue: A Journal of Opinion* 23, no. 1 (1995): 39-45.

Taylor, Charles. *The Ethics of Authenticity*. Cambridge, MA: Harvard University Press,

1991.

————. "Atomism." Pp. 29-50 in *Communitarianism and Individualism*, edited by Shlomo Avineri and Avner de Shalit. New York: Oxford University Press, 1992.

————. "Cross Purposes: The Liberal-Communitarian Debate." Pp. 160-182 in *Liberalism and the Moral life*, edited by Nancy Rosenblum. Cambridge, MA: Harvard University Press, 1989.

Tempels, Placid. "Bantu Philosophy." Pp. 62-86 in *African Philosophy: Selected Readings*, edited by Albert Mosley. Englewood Cliffs, NJ: Prentice Hall, 1995.

Tulving, Endel. *Elements of Episodic Memory*. New York: Oxford University Press, 1983.

Turnbull, Colin. *The Mountain People*. New York: Simon & Schuster, 1972.

Verhoef, Heidi and Claudin Michel. "Studying Morality Within the African Context: A Model of Moral Analysis and Construction." *Journal of Moral Education* 26, no. 4 (1997): 389-407.

Vitz, Paul C. "The Use of Stories in Moral Development: New Psychological Reasons for an Old Education Method." *American Psychologist* 45, no. 6 (June 1990): 709-710.

Wilson, Bryan R. ed. *Rationality*. London: Basil Blackwell, 1970.

Wilson, John "Indoctrination and Rationality." Pp.17-24 in *Concepts of Indoctrination: Philosophical Essays*, edited by I. A. Snook. London: Routledge & Kegan Paul, 1972.

————. "Education and Indoctrination." Pp. 24-46 in *Aims in Education: The Philosophical Approach*, edited by T. H. B. Hollins. Manchester: Manchester University Press, 1964.

Wiredu, Kwasi. *Philosophy and An African Culture*. London: Cambridge University Press, 1980.

————. *Cultural Universals and Particulars: An African Perspective*. Indianapolis, IN: Indiana University Press, 1996.

————. "On Defining African Philosophy." Pp. 92-121 in *African Philosophy*, edited by Tsenay Serequeberhan. New York: Paragon House, 1991.

————. "African Philosophical Tradition: A Case Study of the Akan." Pp. 35-62 in *African-African Perspectives and Philosophical Traditions*, edited by John P. Pittman. New York: Routledge, 1996.

————. "Truth and an African Language." Pp. 35-50 in *African Philosophy: New and Traditional Perspectives*, edited by Lee M. Brown. New York: Oxford University Press, 2004.

Wolf, Susan. "Sanity and the Metaphysics of Responsibility." Pp. 46-62 in *Responsibility, Character and the Emotions*, edited by F. Schoeman. Cambridge: Cambridge University Press, 1987.

Wright, Richard A. ed. *African Philosophy: An Introduction*. New York: University Press of America, 1984.

# Index

ability to feel shame, guilt: as a feature of moral personhood, 112, 128, 142. *See also* moral personhood

ability to think for oneself: as a feature of liberal individualism, rationality, 244, 248, 279. *See also* liberal individualism, rationality

absolute autonomy: as a feature of liberal individualism, 205, 276, 281, 282, 284, 285

accommodative feature of, or attitude in, African philosophy and thought, 17, 217. *See also* African philosophy: features of

acculturation, 72, 73, 97, 141, 225, 232-241, 249, 259-265, 284, 296. *See also* brainwashing, conditioning, indoctrination, moral education, moral upbringing, social interaction, socialization

Achebe, Chinua: on personhood, 71-72, 102, 128, 281, 311

activism, 36-39, 41, 73, 104. *See also* nationalism, particularism

adulthood, 69, 129, 139, 146, 281, 297, 302. *See also* elderhood, elders

adults: role in communalism, 61-62, 69, 136-142, 147-151, 203, 220, 225-227, 275, 281, 283-285, 295, 300, 314

adversarial method: feature of Western philosophy, 27, 177

affected ignorance, 259-266, 316. *See* moral ignorance

African art as narrative, 96, 102, 140-141, 196, 241, 312

African cosmology, 53, 123

African cultures, thought, beliefs, traditions, practices: features of, 17, 33. *See also* accommodative feature of, anachronism, authoritarianism, dogma, dogmatism, oral tradition, primitive, supernaturalism, uncivilized

African historiography, 139, 316

African philosophy: a basis for critique of, 35-39, 41, 42. *See also* cultural hegemony, racism, Western philosophy: features of

African philosophy: features of, as accommodative, dogmatic, irrational, lack of critical analysis, lack of rigor, oral tradition, pre-scientific, unanalytic, uncritical, unsystematic, 17, 24-29, 31-38, 43, 96, 97, 101, 105-107, 139, 201, 217, 312, 314

# *About the Author*

Polycarp Ikuenobe is an Associate Professor in the Department of Philosophy at Kent State University, Kent, Ohio. He obtained his Ph.D. from Wayne State University, Detroit, Michigan, in 1993, an M.A from University of Ibadan, Nigeria, in 1983, and a B.A. from the University of Ibadan, in 1981. He was born in Nigeria. Before coming to the United States in 1987 to pursue graduate studies, he taught at the then Bendel State University (now Ambrose Alli University) at Ekpoma, Nigeria, from 1993-1987. His first job after the completion of his Ph.D. was at Alverno College, Milwaukee, Wisconsin. He taught at Alverno for four years before moving to Kent State University.

His research and teaching interests have focused on African and African American Philosophy, Philosophy of Law, Social and Political Philosophy, Ethics, Metaphilosophy, Informal Logic, and Critical Thinking. He has published widely in all these areas, in such journals as, *Metaphilosophy, Journal of Social Philosophy, Journal of Value Inquiry, International Studies in Philosophy, Public Affair Quarterly, African Philosophy, Vera Lex, Argumentation, Educational Philosophy and Theory, Studies in Philosophy and Education, Journal for the Theory of Social Behaviour, Philosophy East and West, Journal of Philosophical Research,* among others. He has also edited six volumes of textbook of readings in the series, *Symposia: Readings in Philosophy* with Pearson Custom Publishing.